CROSSING BORDERS

Dorothee Schneider

Crossing Borders

Migration and Citizenship in the
Twentieth-Century United States

HARVARD UNIVERSITY PRESS

Cambridge, Massachusetts, and London, England   2011

Library of Congress Cataloging-in-Publication Data

Schneider, Dorothee, 1952–
    Crossing borders : migration and citizenship in the twentieth-century United States /
Dorothee Schneider.
        p.   cm.
    Includes bibliographical references and index.
    ISBN 978-0-674-04756-3 (alk. paper)
    1. United States—Emigration and immigration—History.   2. United States—
Emigration and immigration—Government policy.   3. Immigrants—United States—
History.   4. Citizenship—United States.   I. Title.
    JV6450.S345 2011
    304.8'7300904—dc22   2010037211

For Jack and Ben

Contents

Acknowledgments

I wish to thank many friends, colleagues, and family members for their support during the years it took to prepare this book.

At the very beginning Michèle Lamont and Daniel Segal supported me in my exploration of contemporary immigration policies in the context of U.S. history. When it came to finding the archival sources for this project, the help and insights of Marian L. Smith, Senior Historian of the U.S. Citizenship and Immigration Services, proved crucial. Marian rescued the historic policy files of the Immigration and Naturalization Service when their future was uncertain, and she has made these materials accessible to an entire generation of historians. Her knowledge has furthered our understanding of this complex agency immeasurably. Without her dedicated and exemplary service as a public historian there would be much less to my history.

Over the years I have had the great pleasure of making friends and working with many immigration historians and social scientists whose work goes beyond borders in the truest sense. For their support, critical reading, and help with sources, I wish to thank Elliott Barkan, Irene Bloemraad, Tobias Brinkmann, Roger Daniels, Tom Dublin, Nora Faires, Donna Gabaccia, Nancy Green, the late Christiane Harzig, Dirk Hoerder, and Mae Ngai.

While I was researching and writing this book, a number of fellowships and guest professorships allowed me time away from my regular teaching duties to focus on research and writing. During the spring of 2000, I had the privilege of spending a semester at Princeton

University's Davis Center for Historical Studies under the director-ship of Anthony Grafton. I thank the staff and colleagues of the Center as well as the librarians at Princeton University's Seely G. Mudd Manuscript library for making my stay productive and enjoy-able. A short-term residency at the École des Hautes Études en Sci-ences Sociales at its Centre de Recherches Historiques in 2003 pro-vided me with a stimulating and very productive period in which to write and discuss my work with students and colleagues from around the world. My time in Germany during the academic year 2006–2007 was another opportunity to write and reflect with students and scholars outside the United States on the transnational dimensions of my work. I thank librarian Gesine Bottomley and the staff at the Wissenschaftskolleg Berlin for their hospitality and help in locating research materials as well as Sophia Manns and Hartmut Keil of the University of Leipzig, who welcomed me as a Fulbright Professor at Leipzig in the spring of 2007.

The University of Illinois has been my home as a scholar and teacher for many years. The Campus Research Board of the univer-sity awarded me a grant to visit archives at the Immigration History Research Center at the University of Minnesota. The Migration Studies Group at the University of Illinois provided intellectual stim-ulation and support during years of research and writing. I wish es-pecially to thank James Barrett, Gillian Stevens, David Roediger, and Doug Kibbee for exploring different topics in contemporary and historical research on immigration as part of our lunchtime meet-ings over the years. While working on this project, I also taught a series of research seminars on immigration to groups of extraordi-narily talented undergraduates at the university's Campus Honors Program. I thank Bruce Michelson, the director, for keeping this program the preserve of true liberal arts learning and exploration. Finally, the University of Illinois Library and its extraordinary staff have greatly supported my work. I especially wish to thank Mary Stewart, the history librarian, and Jo Kibbee, the head of reference, for their help and their steadfastness in maintaining the university's magnificent collection of materials on immigration.

Kathleen McDermott at Harvard University Press encouraged me early on to write this book as a story of people first. Her steady support saw me through the many years of writing. In the final stages of this project, Mary Siegel of Alexander Street Press provided access to a digital collection of immigrant materials not accessible through a library. Melody Negron and Vickie West were meticulous and responsive production editors.

Finally, I wish to thank my family, near and far, for their unwavering support. My father, whose own life as a scholar and teacher spanned most of the twentieth century, did not live to see the publication of this manuscript, but my mother, herself a participant in and observer of migrations and border crossings, has remained an important conversation partner throughout this project. My husband, Harry Liebersohn, encouraged and prodded me from the beginning to think big and tell the whole story. Our conversation about history has now been ongoing for many years, and his ideas and insights have enriched me in countless ways. I have dedicated this book to our sons, Jack and Ben, who have lived with this project for most of their lives. They grew into citizens of the world while I was reading and writing about borders and the people who cross them.

CROSSING BORDERS

Introduction

Crossing Borders and Nation Building

Like all works of history, this book emerged within a number of different contexts—political, scholarly, and personal. The politics of immigration and citizenship have supplied a background for historians of immigration for over a decade now, and a political controversy over immigrant rights contributed in important ways to my original motivation to start this project. Congress launched a debate in the spring of 1996 about Immigration Reform resulting in a number of laws passed in the same year. The discussion, which I have analyzed in detail elsewhere, highlighted profoundly divergent views on immigration, immigrants, and citizenship.[1] The laws that passed as a result of this debate, the Illegal Immigration Reform and Personal Responsibility Act and the Personal Responsibility and Work Opportunity Act of 1996 limited immigrants' access to a variety of social support systems and financed an elaborate program of border security, focusing on fences, walls, patrols, and other aspects of the physical border. Both the debate and the resulting laws were, at their core, attempts to redefine the American welfare state and to recast the nation's borders in social and legal terms. Immigrants, or at least certain immigrants, were to lose their rights to participate in the welfare state—to lose what T. H. Marshall calls parts of their social citizenship. At the same time, the nation's physical and legal borders were to be fortified against unwanted immigrants: the poor, the undocumented, and the criminal. But, as so often in the past, the politics of immigration and immigration reform proved more complicated than the law outlined. In the long run, the legislation of the mid-1990s limited the access of legal immigrants to social services, diminished the flexibility of the Immigration and Naturalization Service (INS) in immigration admissions, and increased border fortifications considerably. The laws did not redefine citizenship, although limiting the social citizenship rights of noncitizens led to increased naturalization among recent immigrants.[2]

The immigration policy debate of the 1990s cast a spotlight on how much ideas about immigrants, citizenship, and national belonging had shifted over the past one hundred years, but politicians and the media showed little understanding of these historical changes. The imagery of the congressional debates in 1996 reflected the well-established bipolar view of immigration as both a problem and an asset to the nation. On one side, debaters described immigrants as passive, powerless, and tossed about by the forces of history. On the other side, immigrant advocates portrayed immigrants as determined and strong individuals who were firmly in charge of their destiny. Depending on one's perspective, the role of government was supposed to be active and strong (in protecting helpless immigrants) or modest (because most immigrants could fend for themselves). But when it came to the details of the legislation, when advocacy groups, the courts, and the immigrants themselves raised their voices, the scenario became more complicated. In the late twentieth century, immigration policy no longer depended, as in the past, on national priorities of the labor market or hegemonic ideas of moral worth and racial fitness. Citizenship was not defined primarily as access to the voting booth or a display of patriotism. The connection between immigration and naturalization often seemed more tenuous in the late twentieth century than it had a hundred years ago. As a result of the many conflicting and complex forces at play, formulating a cohesive immigration and naturalization policy seemed to be beyond the ability of Congress in the late twentieth century.

My book represents an attempt to explain how our understanding of immigration and citizenship has changed over the past hundred years in ways that have deeply influenced immigration and naturalization policy. I approach this project from both sides: the side of government policy and administration, and the side of immigrants and their individual and collective experiences. Laws and administrative practices always emerge from the interplay of lawmakers and those at whom the laws are directed, even if, as in the case of immigrants, they are not citizens of the country that governs their lives. Laws dealing with immigration and naturalization have given shape to the nation's political identity. The delineation of borders, both physical and legal, has defined the citizenry of the United States in a structured, fundamental way. Immigrants in turn have interpreted and used the laws and practices to fit their lives and build their communities. They have made choices within the spaces provided by the law and have chosen alternatives outside of it. Sometimes they secure a path for themselves via direct negotiations with the authorities; at other times, they more indirectly adopt or refuse certain provisions.

The zone of negotiation has usually been situated at the multiple border crossings that govern the lives of immigrants. Some are physical; others, equally real, are legal and cultural: the departure from home, the arrival at the border of the United States, the admission into the country, the possible removal from the country through deportation, the social and cultural assimilation after arrival, and the naturalization process to become a U.S. citizen. At each of these transition points, immigrants encounter the power of the state in various forms, sometimes directly, sometimes only indirectly. At each crossing, the law and the lives of immigrants are tested and often changed as a result of the encounters and negotiations. In this process, immigrants are both self-directed agents of their own fate and objects of law and restriction. Although the path for immigrants often has not been straightforward, crossing the many borders has always been a part of the immigrants' passage. Each border crossed has represented a necessary transition to continue the journey, and each has been a place of potential crisis.

As I turned from contemporary politics to the scholarship on immigration, I found that few immigration historians had focused outright on the theme of border crossings. The scholarship of legal historians and political scientists, and most of all the writings on citizenship and civil rights instead oriented my work in its early stages. In a number of foundational studies by Michael Walzer, Rogers Smith, T. Alexander Aleinikoff, and others, the emergence of immigrant rights from the nineteenth century to the post–World War I era have been studied in the context of growing citizenship rights for immigrants during the same period.[3] The central theme of these scholars is the great expansion of citizenship and citizens' rights from the nineteenth to the late twentieth century as well as the growth in the ranks of fully enfranchised citizens in the United States. Within this scholarly project, most have focused on the struggles over slavery, women's rights, or the rights of Native Americans; the story of immigrants, especially European immigrants, sometimes has gotten lost, though a few historians who have written about the 1930s and 1940s took up the theme of citizenship and developed it in the context of European immigrant communities of the interwar era.[4] In path-breaking studies, some scholars have taken up the general themes of citizenship and immigrant rights as they applied to distinct groups of non-European immigrants, especially Mexican and Chinese.[5] Other important works have highlighted the experience of women, refugees, and illegal immigrants, demonstrating how the history of these border crossers proved central to our understanding of migration and immigrants in the twentieth century. By focusing on the relationship between American law and immigration history, these scholars' writings provided me with crucial building blocks for my own project.[6]

While I began this project as an inquiry into the historical roots of policy-making in regard to citizenship and immigration in the United States, I wanted to avoid the exclusive national focus of many such studies. An inadvertent American exceptionalism has characterized much of the new and critical legal analysis of immigration policy. To understand the development of immigration and naturalization policy in a transnational context, recent scholarship has helped me understand the perspective of migrants in a global context. Migrants, particularly in Europe and East Asia, had to engage with multiple states and innumerably different nationality rules in their search for work and livelihood. From the work of the new global migration historians the story of population movement and citizenship emerges as a truly transnational historical phenomenon.[7]

During the past forty years, social historians have developed a nuanced picture of countless immigrant communities in the United States and beyond, which shows a history of both struggle and independence, agency and subjugation. The many studies of specific immigrant groups, regions, and time periods lightened my load in writing this book and enabled me to address specific questions about immigrant encounters with the government. For the most part, however, social historians did not focus on immigrants' relation to the state in their studies. Rather, the question of assimilation and cultural self-definition usually took center stage, in contrast to my investigation of the immigrant–state dynamic.[8]

The scholarship of historians and social scientists who focus on migration usually emphasizes the fluidity and the global reach of the immigrant experience, in contrast to the—by necessity—nationally defined approach of scholars more focused on legal and political constraints. The emphasis on immigrants and their movements also allows us to see the multidirectional aspect of modern migration, including immigration to the United States. Too often, the story of immigration is seen in teleological terms: immigrants made the decision to leave home with the goal to come to the United States and settle here. Settlement is followed by assimilation and naturalization as a U.S. citizen. The departure from their birthplace is thus supposed to mark the beginning and the oath of allegiance to the U.S. constitution to mark the end of a trajectory. Although this story is deeply embedded in the discourse over immigration, it served a political purpose and often did not reflect most immigrants' experiences. In the real life of immigrants, decisions over migration were made under varying circumstances and with shifting goals. Immigrants might return or stay, their assimilation might occur quickly or imperceptibly, and their decision to become U.S. citizens might come at some point early or late—or, in about half of all cases, never. Swearing the oath of citizenship represented one stage in a continuous journey that had begun with the decision to leave home and continued with goals that might change over future border crossings.

I have decided to limit my analysis to the twentieth century, emphasizing the first decades, because that is when contemporary borders and border crossings were organized in ways that have endured to this day. In the nineteenth century, crossing the borders of one's home country to come to the United States was often difficult for legal and technical reasons. Those who wanted to leave their European homelands encountered laws that restricted the movement of citizens. Movement out of China was entirely prohibited, and leaving Japan was also restricted. Indeed, for most nineteenth century emigrants, the problems of exit were larger than the hurdles at the point of entry into the United States. On the American side, neither borders nor immigration were tightly regulated by the United States during most of the nineteenth century. The absence of a guiding law and a federal border administration turned immigration into a process governed by international commercial interests, regional powers, and local customs.

Even crossing the legal and administrative border into American citizenship, a process clearly defined and guided by federal law, was de facto in the hands of local courts and governed by local traditions and politics. Only gradually, toward the end of the nineteenth century, would the federal government strengthen its hand in immigration admission and in naturalization practice. The passage of the Naturalization Act of 1906 set the stage for a centralized federal control of all border crossings, marking the end of regional and local contexts in which immigrants negotiated their entry and residence in the United States. This book will focus on the period after 1906, and the process that unfolded in which all borders and border crossings came under increasingly stringent and bureaucratized federal control.

The five chapters of this book trace the border crossings of twentieth-century immigrants in the order in which they most frequently occurred: departure, arrival, deportation, assimilation, and naturalization. The story also follows a chronological order: the earlier parts of the immigrants' journey will take place mostly in the first decades of the twentieth century, while Americanization and naturalization will focus on the period between the World Wars and beyond. In chapter 1 we will trace the decisions and routes taken by emigrants as they left their home countries in Europe and Asia to come to the United States in the nineteenth and early decades of the twentieth century. For the most part, emigrants encountered the authority of their home state when they tried to leave, but as the twentieth century dawned, the long arm of the U.S. government also made itself felt as emigrants planned their exit, especially from Asia. The cooperation and collusion between European states and the United States, mediated through commercial transportation agencies, also helped fortify European borders. The quota laws of the 1920s marked an end point in this respect: from then on, the U.S. government handed out the required visas in consulates abroad, in the immigrants' home country, far away from the physical border of the United States.

Much of the history of immigration and the border has traditionally focused on the actual arrival of immigrants at the physical border of the United States, at Ellis Island or at Angel Island in San Francisco Bay, for example. At the port of arrival, immigrants met American officials face to face, often for the first time. This is where they had to answer questions, justify their claim to enter under existing law, and convince American officials of their suitability as legitimate immigrants. Chapter 2 will explore these encounters on a variety of levels. Written law codified controls, but impromptu judgments by the immigration inspectors also played a role in this meeting. Immigration officials encountered the strategies of immigrants who used their knowledge of American law and custom to provide their own interpretation of what the United States expected of them. Experts, facilitators, friends, relatives, and lawyers on the immigrants' side, and courts of justice, medical experts, and local officials on the government's side were mobilized. It was where the visible and invisible lines of race and gender were also drawn and sometimes redrawn by law and negotiation. The importance of the personal encounter between immigrants and representatives of the federal government (and individual state governments) overshadowed all other border crossing experiences for immigrants until 1924. With the passage that year of the quota law, most Europeans and all Asians needed to qualify for a quota spot and visa while still abroad—limiting the importance of the port of entrance for the rest of the twentieth century.

Not all immigrants who succeeded in their negotiations and were admitted remained in the United States. In many cases, early twentieth-century migrants returned to Europe after a few years, as they had planned to do from the beginning. The story of the return migration has been told elsewhere and is not be part of this study, because remigration was not regulated nor tracked by officials in North America for much of the twentieth century.[9] However, another group of twentieth-century immigrants calls for our attention: thousands of individuals who were deported after having lived in the United States. This forced border crossing in reverse reveals an unappealing underside of American ideas about worthy immigrants and deserving future citizens. Deportation was rarely used in the nineteenth century, but it increased in importance as an enforcement tool with the advent of mass immigration and after the quota law of 1924. Chapter 3 will trace the history of deportation and focus on how immigrants tried to negotiate their way around deportations, sometimes on their own, often with the help of support groups that also promoted political and legal change to affect the immigrants' problems.

Toward the end of the book, we will take up two border crossings that involved not physical migration but cultural, social, and legal borders. Americanization and naturalization were processes that were voluntary and sometimes nearly invisible to outsiders. Immigrants could live in the United States for many years, even decades, without becoming U.S. citizens and without becoming overtly Americanized. The history of "Americanization" as a state-supported, official program directed at immigrants before, during, and after World War I will be juxtaposed with the individually negotiated Americanization that actually took place for most immigrants in the 1920s and 1930s. To a large degree, immigrants had and used the power to reject elements of official Americanization and to figure out and shape their own border crossing into America as a social and cultural landscape in the mid-twentieth century.

Americanization was a psychologically transformative border crossing, but naturalization, the acquisition of U.S. citizenship by a person not born in the United States, was the most legally transformative process that any immigrant could undergo. Citizenship gave an immigrant the right to stay in the United States indefinitely and protected her or him from expulsion from U.S. territory. Becoming a U.S. citizen ended the second-class legal status of immigrants. Unlike Americanization, which was a lifelong process interwoven with an immigrant's daily life, naturalization was a formal, rather short process with definite preconditions and a point of completion.

Both immigrants and Americans understood the finality of the naturalization process; as a result, the debate over who had the right to acquire U.S. citizenship was fundamentally contested during many decades of the twentieth century. The demand for stricter screening procedures and exclusions from naturalization remained an important undercurrent of racist and exclusionary policy-making throughout the twentieth century and beyond. At the same time, welcoming immigrants as new citizens became a staple of pro-immigrant and liberal movements from World War I on. An immigrant's decision to become a citizen was voluntary, although the process of naturalization itself was not negotiable. On the other hand, immigrants could withhold their citizenship, decline to become naturalized, and thus diminish the legitimacy of the nation as a place that welcomed and integrated newcomers successfully. In this field of tension between welcome and refusal, between withholding and adoption, naturalization represented a psychological as well as a legal border crossing for some immigrants, and became border that was never crossed for others.

In the many stories and journeys told in this book, what will emerge is not what many politicians wanted us to believe in the late twentieth century: that all migrants who come to the United States try to stay permanently, that successful immigration means Americanization, and that successful immigrants become U.S. citizens in the end. Instead, this book shows how immigration is in many ways an open-ended process. Immigrants cross many borders, often not in the order intended by law and politics, and with uncertain results. In the course of the many negotiations that do take place on their journey across borders, immigrants encounter a government and its representatives in many forms. Both sides negotiate with varying degrees of flexibility. In the end, most immigrants will conclude their journey successfully, though on terms that are solely their own.

CHAPTER 1

Leaving Home

For immigrants, leave-taking from home is often re-membered as a defining, traumatic moment, the beginning of a long journey into an uncertain future. In the reminiscences of the migrants or observers, the drama of departure from home cast dramatic shadows and the light of finality and decisiveness on an infinite, ill-defined future journey. This reality of exit was only one perspective on a usually drawn-out process of leaving, both in the nineteenth and the twentieth century. Leaving home was the first in a series of border crossings with an uncertain outcome.

The character of departure changed from the first third of the nineteenth century to the era of World War II for immigrants to the United States. In general, nineteenth-century departures were dom-inated by concerns about the safety of the passage and the logistics of travel. Depending on the part of the world the emigrants left, official permits and regulations of home countries posed a significant hurdle and formed an administrative border crossing that had to be negoti-ated by prospective immigrants to North America.

Exit was least regulated and supervised by governments in the Americas: migrants from Mexico, Canada, and the Caribbean islands could leave their homes largely unhindered so long as they could find and pay for transportation. For these emigrants, the experience of border crossing likely started at the U.S. border station, not before. For Europeans, however, leaving home was far more complicated and usually involved contacts with government representatives. By the late nineteenth century, many European states delegated de facto border control to transportation companies and their agents; the importance of exit controls declined in many countries, but significant exceptions remained. Free movement of populations would become an important principle for many Europeans by the early twentieth century, but in reality the presence of the state in regulating emigration remained quite strong.

Such commercialization of exit control also occurred in Japan and China, with governments remaining all but invisible (in China) or in the background (in Japan). Thus, negotiating one's exit with transportation companies, travel agents, and other facilitators grew to be the most important part of leave-taking for immigrants from Europe and Asia between the 1890s and the 1930s.

The U.S. government and its representatives remained for the most part invisible for European and East Asian emigrants at their point of departure. It was only gradually, first in East Asia, then in Europe, that the U.S. government became a direct force in regulating exit for future immigrants from Europe. By the 1920s, this had changed: the U.S. government, in combination with commercial facilitators and transport companies, became the primary negotiation partner for emigrants as they sought to leave their homes and cross the first border.

Leaving Europe in the Nineteenth Century

Since the establishment of the first British and Spanish colonies on the North American continent, voluntary emigration to North America from Europe had been steady but limited in numbers in the seventeenth and eighteenth centuries. In general, the difficulties and risks, the cost of the voyage, and the prohibitions against leaving the home country limited the emigration of individual Europeans before the nineteenth century. The collapse of the Napoleonic empire and the end of continental European wars after 1815 made movement within and beyond Europe easier. Economic distress was also a factor; grain prices in much of Europe collapsed as trade barriers began to crumble. A quickly growing population had few employment opportunities outside agriculture, so emigration, despite its risks, costs, and uncertainties became a more tempting alternative for Europe's peasants, for younger sons whose inheritance rights were limited, and for craftsmen whose working opportunities were diminishing. As a result, an unprecedented number of Europeans departed for North America immediately after the end of the Napoleonic wars. About 15,000 Irish men and women (most of them Protestants) left from 1816 to 1818 for North America. German authorities talked about an immigration "fever" and watched over 20,000 depart in the years 1816 to 1817.[1]

The organizational, financial, and administrative difficulties remained formidable for the pioneers of nineteenth-century migration. The governments of most central and western European countries were unprepared for the sudden pressures and changes that came with their citizens' outmigration. Conservative powers such as the Prussian and the Austro-Hungarian monarchies sought to assert their commitment to the old monarchical order and wanted to strictly control the movement of their populations. Other countries, especially France and Great Britain, adopted a more liberal view, which saw migration as part of a market mechanism that allowed "surplus" populations to leave in search for better opportunities elsewhere. Freeing populations to move and at times encouraging outmigration became part of the state policy in western Europe.

For prospective emigrants, these different sets of expectations meant that for some emigrants getting permission to leave home from the government authorities could be administratively simple or even unnecessary; for others, it could be fraught with problems. British citizens needed no permission to leave, and costly passports were not required to embark for North America. A rarely enforced prohibition against the emigration of British artisans ended in 1826. In fact, Britain developed a limited system of assisted emigration in the 1820s, in which villages and towns subsidized and organized the overseas migration of their poor villagers. The British government itself paid the overseas passage for a limited number of people to Canada in the 1820s, but attempts to further such schemes were controversial and were not extended. Individual landlords and parishes in England and Ireland continued to sponsor outmigration through cash subsidies in the first half of the nineteenth century. Overseas export of surplus populations was the acknowledged solution to lack of employment prospects and rural poverty.[2]

In continental Europe, a passport and exit visa (granted by local authorities) were usually required. These documents would certify that the government had no objection to the person leaving permanently. The difficulty of gaining such a permit varied depending on the country and the status of the persons who wanted to leave. French citizens had a right to a passport and could only be denied the exit visa under special circumstances. Emigration from France was therefore tolerated, though it met with disapproval from the authorities. Until the 1840s, French authorities were mostly concerned with policing transit migrants through France; regulating the entry and transit of German, Swiss, and Dutch citizens was their primary concern.[3]

Germany presented a more complicated landscape of emigration in the nineteenth century. The earliest centers of emigration, the southwestern German principalities, put few effective hurdles in the way of those who wanted to leave. Some even assisted poor villagers in their emigration, leading to complaints by groups in the United States. On paper at least, the requirements were strictest in Prussia, the largest of the German states and an important player in emigration policy from the beginning. Prussia required the proper exit permits not just from its own citizens but also from those who traveled through its territory—and almost all emigrants who left from German ports had to move across Prussia. Prussia would issue neither visas nor passports to men who had not done their military service, who might be politically suspicious, or who were unwilling or unable to pay the *Nachsteuer* (an emigrant tax).[4]

There were ways around the German hurdles. Emigrants could leave "temporarily," because only permanent emigrants were assessed emigration taxes and needed emigration visas. Young men of draft age could leave without announcing their intentions, moving across the Rhine into France from the German southwest, and hoping to evade the French police on their way to embarkation in Le Havre. Government emigration restrictions had the effect of shifting most migrants to nearby urban centers, and it also contributed to the growth of undocumented migration across borders and the Atlantic.[5]

The combination of politics, permits, and logistics made emigration difficult for Europeans in the early and mid-nineteenth century.[6] The length of the journey to the port of embarkation was the first stage that could pose a test of the strength of an emigrant's end resolve. For example on May 17, 1839, Johann Pritzlaff left his home in Silesia as part of a group of fellow "Old Lutherans" who had the intention of settling in the Midwest. After a ten-day voyage to Hamburg, his little band had to wait one month for fellow believers to catch up with them because the Prussian authorities did not grant them exit passports. From Hamburg, the group traveled for three and a half days to Newcastle, from there by train to Carlisle, and then again by boat to Liverpool. The sea voyage from Liverpool to New York lasted from July 11 to September 6.[7]

Thirty years later, after the arrival of transatlantic passenger steamships, an immigrant named Olof Olson described a somewhat speedier but still circuitous route of departure. The Olson family and fifty-five other villagers from Dalarna (Sweden) loaded their possessions and their young children into covered wagons and then walked the 175 miles to Arvika, the closest railroad station in Western Sweden. In Arvika, they sold their horses and wagons. A train then took the group to Oslo, which was about 100 miles away. From there, a boat took the emigrants to Litt in Scotland (a rough, three-day voyage). From there, another four-hour train ride was necessary to take the Swedish emigrants to Glasgow. The Olsons and other members of their group had been traveling under difficult conditions for at least two weeks before they reached their port of embarkation for overseas. The crossing itself to New York took less time, two weeks, in the summer of 1869.[8]

Before steamships became the rule in the 1860s, even arriving at the port of the scheduled departure merely marked the beginning of another period of waiting. Carl Berthold from the central German province of Hessen-Waldeck had to wait in Bremerhaven for more than a week for his ship to arrive in 1852. "Our ship called the Liverpohl is said to be lying in front of the canal and because of unfavorable winds, cannot come here, so we may lay here for several more days before we can get away. This emigrating is just terrible," he wrote to his siblings.[9]

En route and at the port, emigrants had to negotiate both with government authorities, and more directly with businesses involved in
emigrant transport and care. Private and public interests intersected
and sometimes collided here; emigration businesses became powerful sources of revenue and influence in port cities, whose local governments were reluctant to interfere. To be sure, the deplorable and
unsanitary conditions under which departing emigrants had to live
and fend for themselves in departure cities drew the attention of governments. The situation in Le Havre, for example, required the intervention of German consuls a number of times in the 1840s; finally, in
the early 1850s, the Prussian government forbade its citizens to emigrate via that port, a measure that propelled the French government
to pass its first set of passenger laws.[10] Conditions in British ports
were no better: Liverpool and Southampton, even more than Le
Havre, competed for emigrants on the basis of price. Lack of services
and open competition of ship lines kept prices low there, so even emigrants from continental Europe booked passage from there well into
the late nineteenth century, despite efforts to rein in the worst
abuses.[11] In Germany, the shippers of Hamburg and Bremen dominated their respective cities' municipal governments, but the Prussian authorities and the governments of other German states nevertheless sought increased regulation and oversight of passenger traffic.[12]
Ultimately, the interests of the Prussian government and the merchants
in the port cities were reconciled through a system of licensing and
supervising the transportation agencies and emigration agents in many
provinces, especially Prussia. These regulations were more comprehensive in Germany than anywhere else in the late nineteenth and
early twentieth century, and they provided quasi monopolies for the
shippers and more predictable conditions for travelers. The system of
privately run and government supervised travel functioned well for
emigrants who left via Germany, and for their governments, which
profited from licensing fees paid by ship lines and their agents without giving up control of the exit process.

The sea crossing made emigrants confront the finality of their exit.
The ocean in all its vastness and unpredictability and the small and
cramped ships that confined emigrants to steerage compartments
symbolized the dangers of an unknowable future. The journey was

most frightening for those for whom seafaring was unfamiliar, though nearly everyone commented on it during the first half of the nineteenth century.[13] The sea passage also acted as a great equalizer. Even the rare emigrant who traveled as a cabin passenger would get seasick. Most passengers shared cramped quarters and dismal food. The best-laid plans, solicitous agents who had looked out for the passengers on land, well-organized groups—all mattered little in steerage, where men, women, children, and the elderly shared cramped decks, got seasick together, and suffered from lack of fresh air and fresh water.[14] If the wind did not turn the right way, sea voyages could last seven weeks or more. Anna Maria Klinger, a servant who emigrated from southern Germany in 1848, reported that she and other German emigrants had to wait for seven weeks in Plymouth until they could board for departure. Her voyage then lasted 105 days, one of the longest transatlantic trips for emigrants recorded in the nineteenth century.[15]

Journeys could be stormy from beginning to end; they were rarely calm for the entire way. Even emigrants familiar with the sea could be frightened and miserable. The Dutch emigrant Jacob Harms Drunnick wrote back to his family describing his seven-week Atlantic crossing in the summer of 1848: "almost all of us were seasick . . . I was seasick nearly the whole time and spent most of the trip in bed." Comfort was provided by a Protestant pastor who traveled on the boat with fellow Dutch emigrants. "He held prayer services every morning and evening. He read selections from the bible and we sang psalms, on Wednesdays he taught children catechism."[16] Angela Heck and her family from the Catholic Rhineland remembered that during the stormy crossing: "We . . . prayed 17 rosaries before we stopped. All those who did not know how to pray had to learn. We all called on the saints in heaven and God, the Holy Mother of God, Saint Nicklas."[17]

Leaving Europe became easier as transportation networks improved (and ticket costs plummeted) during the last third of the twentieth century. By the 1880s, railroad lines reached into almost every corner of northern, central, and western Europe, and few emigrants even in southern and eastern Europe had to walk for days to reach the closest railroad stop, as Olof Olson had done in the late 1860s.

Overseas passage became faster, safer, and more predictable with the introduction of steamships in the 1850s and 1860s. A series of Federal laws called the Passenger Acts of 1847 and 1855 passed by the U.S. government provided for minimal standards of accommodation and provisions on ships bound for North America. By 1870, as steamships plied the North Atlantic in large numbers every day, prices for the passage to North America had dropped enough so that the vast majority of immigrants could afford steamer passage. This shortened travel time from an unpredictable number of weeks to twelve to fifteen days from continental Europe to New York. Transition times at the port of embarkation and at the port of arrival were also shortened, sometimes through organization, sometimes by rebuilding piers and railroad terminals so that railroad passengers could walk directly onto ships from their trains.[18] Compared with the dramatic and often traumatic journeys of earlier emigrants, the passages of later emigrants became shorter and more predictable. By the late nineteenth century, transportation technology, the availability of travel and migration services, and benign deregulation by governments made it possible for millions of Europeans to emigrate overseas.

With relatively little to stand in their way, Europeans seized the opportunity to leave in unprecedented numbers by the 1880s; emigration soared in the second half of the 1880s and after. Much of that exit stream went to North America, especially to the United States. Over 788,000 immigrants were admitted at U.S. ports in 1882, and even during the economically depressed 1890s, migration into the United States averaged over 360,000 people a year in the official statistics.

From an American perspective in the late nineteenth century, the freed exit from Europe was seen as a mixed blessing. Before then, American opinion had been in favor of free exit for Europeans. There was widespread sentiment that, like Americans, Europeans should have freedom of movement to the United States, if they chose. But with the arrival of large numbers of poor people from England and Ireland in the 1840s, the mood shifted. Only free people should be allowed to become immigrants, some argued, while those bound by contracts, oppressed by their home countries, or "assisted" (i.e., financed) out of public funds to facilitate their emigration to North America should not be admitted to the United States. Over the second half of the nineteenth century, the immigration of "paupers," unfree workers whose passage was prepaid by government or other groups, or contract workers whose were obliged to worked for certain employers for fixed sums in return for passage money became illegal. But while such measures, notably the 1885 Foran Act (the so-called contract labor law) and a variety of anti-Chinese restrictions, reshaped immigrant admissions, for Europeans such restrictions had only a limited effect until the 1890s. Until then, the U.S. government had neither the administrative means nor the political will to impose a border crossing regime for European emigrants.[19]

Leaving Asia, 1860–1930

The "exit revolution," as Aristide Zolberg has called the falling of restrictions on migration from Europe, also took place in Asia.[20] As Adam McKeown has pointed out, by the second half of the nineteenth century, Asian migrants were considered ipso facto unfree, or at least not free in the European or North American sense. The access of unfree immigrants to the United States could therefore be limited without violating the principles of free movement among free individuals, which Americans continued to support. Exit restrictions by the U.S. government shaped the migration flow from Asia from the mid-nineteenth century on.

Chinese emigrants had been the first to make the passage to North America in greater numbers, beginning in the 1850s. For them, leaving was complicated by some of the same factors as for Europeans during the first sixty years of the nineteenth century: the Chinese government traditionally forbade its citizens to leave for overseas permanently, although merchants could travel and temporary absence was tolerated. There were also cultural inhibitions about leaving the territory of one's ancestors permanently, though moving away temporarily to help the family at home was culturally accepted and widespread.[21] By the 1860s, China had a century-old tradition of regional migration within Asia. Chinese emigrants had established chains of migration to far-flung destinations such as Hawaii,

Australia, South America, Cuba, and California, though closer destinations in Southeast Asia such as Malaysia, Singapore, and the Philippine Islands received many migrants as well. Chinese who left for the United States in the second half of the nineteenth century therefore saw themselves as part of a history of labor migration in search of better work opportunities.[22]

The inconvenience and expense of emigrating to North America, as opposed to Southeast Asia or even Hawaii, limited the number of emigrants from China to North America in the nineteenth century. It took more commitment of time and financial resources to cross the Pacific all the way to the U.S. mainland. But the higher wages and stable employment opportunities (compared with Southeast Asia, for example) continued to attract a growing share of Chinese men to North America. Nearly 50,000 Chinese were estimated to have arrived in California during the first half of the 1850s alone.[23]

Almost all nineteenth-century Chinese emigrants came from the Pearl River Delta. The area was at the center of a large trading network that brought ships from abroad as well as from the Chinese interior, tying together laborers, peasants, craftsmen, and traders. Hong Kong and Macau became official territories of European powers. Foreign merchants and, over time, official representatives of foreign governments were also present in Canton (Guangzhou), and all three cities attracted a network of Chinese merchants and their associations, who played the role of facilitators between Asia and North America.[24]

As Chinese emigrants prepared to leave in the 1860s and later, their exit was marked not just by pressures to raise money for the trip and arrange for travel and work in advance, but also by the need to negotiate with the U.S. government, which began to enforce a growing array of exclusionary laws, beginning in 1862. The anti-coolie law, passed that year by U.S. Congress, prohibited U.S. participation in the "coolie trade" (the term was not defined in the law) and allowed Chinese laborers to emigrate to North America if they had a certificate issued by a U.S. consular official in China to show that they were free laborers and were emigrating voluntarily. This first piece of legislation was followed by the Page Law, passed by Congress in 1875: it expanded the anti-coolie provisions of the 1862 measure (by increasing the penalties) and covered all Asian emigrants. It also specified that "the importation into the United States of women for the purposes of prostitution is hereby forbidden." Female emigrants from Japan or China henceforth had to satisfy the U.S. consul at their port of departure that they were not prostitutes (certificates were issued to that effect). European women did not have to produce such certificates, though they might be subject to special scrutiny when they arrived in the United States.[25]

From the 1860s on, these laws to limit "unfree" immigration from Asia were a significant part of the border that had to be crossed before Chinese (and later, Japanese) emigrants could leave home. But their impact was small compared with the much more comprehensive Chinese Exclusion Act, passed by Congress in 1882. This law, one of the most severe immigration restrictions the United States has ever enacted, categorically forbade the emigration of Chinese workers to the United States. Legal migration to the United States was only available to a very narrow segment of Chinese: merchants, their close family, students, and the children of bona fide U.S. citizens. For a few decades, returning migrants could also reenter the U.S. provided they had the required American documents. Because Americans were almost entirely responsible for enforcement, U.S. authorities had to build a bureaucracy of control in the countries of emigration, at the physical border to the United States, and also within the United States. The Chinese Exclusion Act presaged the building of legal borders for all migrants to the United States during the twentieth century.

For emigrants from China, the passage of the Chinese Exclusion Act led to a whole new set of deliberations over exit strategies. Prospective emigrants and their families needed first to decide if the difficult, lengthy, and risky process of trying to gain admission to the United States was worth the investment in time and money, compared with easier but less lucrative migration to Southeast Asia. Another possibility was to sail for Mexico or Canada and cross the U.S. border illegally from there. For those willing to risk rejection upon arrival in the United States, an alternative was to claim merchant status and enter with a so-called section six certificate as a recognized treaty merchant. Chinese emigration facilitators provided help in getting such a certificate from the U.S. consulate by showing that an applicant had money in the bank, a history of participation in businesses in China, and possibly shareholder or partner status in a merchant enterprise established in the United States. If necessary, emigration facilitators put together the (often fictitious) merchant companies, and helped emigrants with bank accounts and letters of reference from established merchants in China and the United States. In China, U.S. consulates often had limited means to verify such information, and—like the emigrants themselves—relied on their established facilitators. Good preparation and coaching was an expensive but viable way to get around the Exclusion Act.[26]

Establishing oneself as the child of a U.S. citizen offered the best chances for Chinese applicants to gain permanent admission to the United States. This was straightforward for those who could actually trace their family histories in the United States back to the 1870s or earlier. William Fok Yee remembered that his grandfather had emigrated to Washington State in the 1860s, become a U.S. citizen, and succeeded in bringing his son to the American West in the 1890s as a U.S. citizen as well. For the Chinese-born Yee, claiming U.S. citizenship in the third generation was possible because of his well-maintained record of family migration.[27]

Few families could claim such a well-documented record of family migration, and it remained difficult to convince both the American consul in China and the steamship companies that the family records were solid enough to made admission at the U.S. border likely.[28] The destruction of records in the San Francisco earthquake of 1906 and sparse record-keeping in the American West in the nineteenth century made the claims of Chinese-born children to U.S. citizen status feasible. A Mr. Tom, interviewed by historian Him Mark Lai, remembered that his exit was possible because he was claimed as the "paper" (fictive) son of another man, who in turn had been recognized by the U.S. government as an American citizen of Chinese descent. "All the papers then were false and cost $100 per year of age," he remembered later.[29] Tung Pok Chin remembered how his father, himself a paper son, arranged for a set of fictitious papers for him: "in a manner befitting a spy novel, I obtained it from an 'agent' in my village." Families whose different generations wanted to leave together for the first time had to invent more complicated strategies. "My father . . . used a student paper, since he studied at church. He paid $1,500 to a fellow villager who had reported he had four sons in order to buy entry papers for me. I came over with one of the 'brothers,'" remembered another Chinese emigrant who came in 1913.[30] Some Chinese emigrants chose multiple legal identities in different phases of their lives, each requiring the services (and payment) of emigrant facilitators. The emigrants themselves were also challenged by these complicated arrangements. "For months before leaving," Tung Pok Chin remembered, "I studied these facts: my paper name, my paper father's name, my paper mother's name, my age, their ages, my place of birth, their occupations and so on."[31]

Very few Chinese could hope to raise their own money for the expensive preparations for exit and the lengthy passage overseas in the nineteenth and early twentieth centuries. Even relatives and extended family usually did not have the resources to allow the pioneers to borrow money informally from kin. Instead, would-be emigrants had to turn to Chinese merchants or facilitators, who would advance them the fare under a kind of indenture system called the credit-ticket system. Early on, merchant groups would finance a voyage for hundreds of men at a time by chartering a boat and provisioning the emigrants and crew. The majority of Chinese migrants to California and Hawaii left China under such arrangements from the 1850s on.[32]

As exit to the United States became more complicated in the late nineteenth century, the well-developed network of emigration facilitators charged more and developed more complicated pricing and repayment schemes. Tung Pok Chin, for example, had to pay $100 for each year of age of the paper son's identity (in his case, $2,000 for a 20-year-old's identity). He was given credit by the agent and his organization with the obligation to repay them over time after his arrival in the United States.[33] The agents had representatives within the Chinese American *tongs* in North America, which in turn would enforce the contracts and repayment schedules. Emigration societies also helped with the trip and lodging to and at the port of departure (usually Hong Kong). S. Low remembered how he had to stay at a boarding house owned by the Sze Yup organization before departure from Hong Kong in the 1920s until his papers had cleared with the U.S. consulate. Such stays could be quite lengthy, so the support of organized sponsors was crucial while emigrants secured papers, underwent physical examinations, and outfitted themselves for the long journey.[34]

Passage for Chinese emigrants from East Asia was arduous in the mid-nineteenth century, more so than for Europeans during the same period. Sailboats across the Pacific took a long time—over two months on average, some taking over three. Scheduled steamships dedicated to passenger traffic were only introduced in 1867 by the Pacific Steamship Mail Company. Later, steamships usually took over three weeks to make the trip. Before the steamship era, there were no dedicated passenger ships for Chinese emigrants. Improvised accommodations aboard freighters had to be "home" for the emigrants.[35] Especially in the early years when the boats were chartered and provisioned entirely by Chinese merchant associations, food and water were often insufficient. In 1854, a few ships arrived in San Francisco Bay with so many passengers dead and ill that an inquiry was launched and the captains of the vessels were charged with breaking the law: the Passenger Acts of 1847 and 1855 limited the number of passengers per boat and also prescribed minimal food and water rations. But as the number of Chinese arrivals soared during the 1850s, concern about hygienic conditions aboard ship declined.[36] It was of little concern to the American authorities that Chinese emigrants risked their lives in order to have a chance to enter "Gold Mountain."

Conditions improved with the arrival of steamship passenger traffic. By the early twentieth century, ships were outfitted for passengers, although unlike the steamers that came from Europe at the same time, they still offered relatively primitive, dormitory-type steerage accommodation in the form of wooden platforms in one large room. They bore little resemblance to the much more comfortable steamers that plied the North Atlantic. The ships were usually owned by British, Japanese, or sometimes U.S. companies.[37]

For Europeans, the passage marked physically their symbolic border crossing into a new continent and unknown life, but for Chinese emigrants, passage to North America marked a double uncertainty:

the uncertainty of safe arrival and the uncertainty of admission. For most, admission was in the hands of officials on the other side whose objective was to send them back. A new identity—in fact, a new life—had to be fashioned and memorized during the passage in order to have hope for admission as an American citizen, a merchant, or a returnee. Thus, Chinese emigrants left behind more than their known homes and families when they tried to cross the physical border. Unlike Europeans, they exchanged their old identities for newly constructed ones even before they arrived in the United States in the hope of negotiating the border crossing under the new parameters mandated by American law.

Emigration from Japan was shaped by similar forces as Chinese and European emigration: economic change at home, labor needs, and a restrictionist movement in the United States. But in contrast to China and the European countries in the late nineteenth century, the government of Japan used emigration to remedy systematic shortcomings in its own economic and financial structure. After it had officially permitted emigration of its citizens as laborers in 1887, the imperial government took measures to control and supervise emigration, and used emigration as a way to finance and shape the restructuring of the rural economy and society. The Japanese government was also sensitive to the position of migrants in the political and economic landscape of the countries of destination. Comprehensive emigration protection laws were passed in the 1890s, and their reach went beyond the physical borders of Japan into the United States, governing all Japanese who worked abroad.

For the Japanese emigrants themselves, negotiating the border crossing from home therefore involved first of all negotiating with their own government for permission to leave and travel to North America. Between 1894 and 1908, 130,000 Japanese gained this permission and left for the United States and the Hawaiian Islands, most of them as contract laborers bound for Hawaii.[38] Until 1907, the U.S. government enforced few restrictions against Japanese immigration, and thus the Americans were not a direct factor in planning exit from Japan. Nevertheless, exit from Japan was costly (permits and passage cost at least $100) and needed to be arranged with the help of either the government labor contracting office itself (until 1894) or with an officially licensed emigration agency. The agency examined the applicant's background, helped with the passport application, and then arranged the passage to Hawaii or North America. Laborers usually entered a contract to work for a certain employer in Hawaii under prenegotiated conditions and for fixed wages. While this limited the options for individual migrants, it also made a successful passage more likely. Emigration agencies were not identical with shipping lines. They merely bought the tickets for their passengers from the lines (mostly Japanese before 1900, mostly American thereafter). After the annexation of Hawaii made the immigration of contract laborers to the islands illegal (as it was in the rest of the United States), emigration agencies continued to provide extensive services but did not issue a labor contract. Their fees merely covered the passage and "help with departure."[39]

Japanese emigration agencies were closely supervised by the Japanese government. When contract laborers were barred from entering Hawaii, emigration agencies lost some of their hold over emigrants in Japan. From then on, what Eiichiro Azuma has called "entrepreneurial laborers" predominated among Japanese emigrants: rural male laborers who left without families to find work on their own in the mainland United States.

By the first decade of the twentieth century, a decade and a half of Japanese emigration had begun to create emigration chains that reshaped rural society, especially in southwestern Japan. Historians have observed that for a time emigration proved so massive in certain regions of Japan that the class of landless tenant farmers declined and the control of wealthy landowners diminished with it. As in Europe, some parts of the Japanese countryside emptied out, while in their place smaller though prosperous "emigration villages" sprang up as entire regions benefited from remittances of emigrant workers, allowing small businesses to prosper. Thus, the emigrants' departure created opportunities for those who were left behind.[40]

As the emigration of independent Japanese rural laborers to the U.S. mainland increased quickly after 1900, it ran into a growing anti-Japanese movement in California. The Japanese government, worried about its status as an emerging regional power, its relationship to the United States, and the control of the emigration process at home, reacted swiftly: it stopped issuing exit permits to laborers to the U.S. mainland in 1902. Would-be emigrants had to apply for exit passports as merchants, businessmen, or even "industrialists." A relatively elaborate control apparatus in Japan was then designed to supervise the legitimacy of merchants and other nonlaborers before they were issued passports to travel to the United States. Hawaii remained within reach of workers until 1908. In a final step to maintain both control over the remaining migrants and a semblance of partner status with the United States, the imperial government and the Roosevelt Administration negotiated the so-called Gentlemen's Agreement of 1907–1908. This memorandum put a permanent halt to Japanese rural labor emigration to the United States. Only returning migrants and the wives of those already in the United States were exempted. Students and merchants could also continue to leave.[41] In contrast to the Chinese Exclusion Act, the Gentlemen's Agreement retained a superficial mutuality: "It was, of course, much better that the Japanese interdict emigration of their own people than that we offend that nation's pride by preventing their entrance, although it was made clear that we would pass an exclusion law if they did not take prompt and effective action," as Secretary of Commerce and Labor Oscar Strauss observed.[42]

Thus, American attempts to control the exit of potentially undesirable immigrants were not only successful in the case of Japan, but the way exit was handled by the Japanese government almost entirely freed the Americans from direct involvement. Japanese emigration policy worked in tandem with anti-Asian immigration restriction on the American side in a successful, though delicate and uneasy, relationship. The Gentlemen's Agreement did not end the exodus from Japan, but it did redirect the official movement of laborers from Japan to South America. It also increased the flow of Japanese migrants to the United States via Mexico and Canada.[43] The United States and Hawaii remained an open destination only for Japanese women who left Japan as "picture brides." Until the late 1920s, these women, who married their husbands in absentia and only knew them from their photographs, continued to arrive in Hawaii and the mainland United States in considerable numbers until the late 1920s. For them, planning to leave Japan for overseas migra-

tion was never an individual decision, but the result of family negotiations and a marriage contract. Planning a marriage to an overseas
laborer required elaborate preparations before a woman could leave
home. Families of potential brides needed to engage the services
of a matchmaker; the matchmaker would then have to find a match
among laborers overseas that was agreeable to both the wife's and the
future husband's families. Usually, the husband would be a much
older man with years of life in the United States behind him but
without the funds to finance a trip back to find a wife. Only after the
agreement between the families and the consent of the future partners could a marriage ceremony could be held. At that point, the
women and their agents could arrange for their passage to the United
States. Approval from the U.S. government was not necessary before
leaving (before World War I), but picture brides faced considerable
uncertainty in making their claim for admission on the other side.
Like Chinese men, Japanese women had to assume a new identity,
as women married to strangers, before they could even hope to enter
the United States legally.[44]

As emigrants from Asia prepared to leave their homes for the
United States in the late nineteenth and early twentieth centuries,
they confronted a difficult set of logistical problems, rules and ex-
penses that made this first part of the journey the most complicated
and riskiest. Beginning in the 1880s, emigration was permissible
under such limited circumstances that emigrants from Asia often
had to rebuild their biographies to fit the U.S. immigration restrictions for Asians. Chinese workers had to become businessmen, U.S.
citizens, or students. Women had to come as brides or wives of merchants. Many constructed entirely new families, family histories,
and identities, all in the hope to fitting through the eye of the needle
that was Chinese and Asian immigration. Thus, American identities
and ideas of legitimacy determined Chinese lives long before the migrants ever saw the Gold Mountain from afar, before they encountered an American official in person, and before they began the
physical journey across the Pacific Ocean.

Americans and the New Emigration from Europe

While the exit doors for Chinese and Japanese were closing during the last quarter of the nineteenth century, emigration from Europe grew, facilitated by improved and cheaper transportation and at least indirect support from many European governments. By the early twentieth century, the European exodus reached new heights. In 1907, over three quarters of a million emigrants departed from four emigration ports alone: Naples, Bremen, Liverpool, and Hamburg. Europe seemed to have turned into a giant sieve, whose population was pouring overseas in search of better lives; the flood appeared to have caught up millions, many of whom had no definite plans but only a vague desire to come to the United States. In reality, however, the movement was neither indiscriminate nor unidirectional. Over 8.8 million passengers left Europe between 1899 and 1909 to cross the Atlantic for the United States in steerage class, reported the U.S. Immigration Commission. An additional 1.2 million Europeans left their homes to emigrate to Canada in the first two decades of the twentieth century. South and Central America were also important destinations. A third of all Italian emigrants left Italy for South America during the first decade of the twentieth century. Significant numbers of Spaniards also left for Argentina, Brazil, and other South American countries during this time period.[45]

European ports of departure were also increasingly crowded with return migrants. About half of all Italians who arrived in the United States returned to Italy, sometimes temporarily, sometimes permanently. Greeks and southern Slavs were also numerous among the returnees, as were Poles. By the early twentieth century, emigration had become a strategy linked to a planned return for many Europeans. Emigration and return migration in the early twentieth century occurred especially in the more underdeveloped regions of Europe: Italy and eastern and southeastern Europe.[46] As Germany, France, England, Belgium, the Netherlands, and Scandinavia industrialized during the early twentieth century, large flows of emigrants still left from the port cities of these countries; however, for the most part, they were transit migrants who made use of the efficient, long-established transportation networks of northern and western Europe.[47]

To Americans, the increase in European emigration was not a surprise, but as emigrants turned into U.S. immigrants or temporary migrants, the new migration was also not altogether welcome. Beginning in the 1890s and increasingly in the first decade of the twentieth century, a restrictionist movement directed against southern and eastern Europeans, anti-Semitism, and a push for legal exclusion of certain classes of immigrants all gained force.[48] But in contrast to the case of Asian immigration in which American officials moved unilaterally to exclude all newcomers from China and Japan, when it came to Europeans, American officials hesitated to make such a move; instead, they introduced laws or administrative practices that, in effect, moved American border controls to Europe. A law passed in 1897 increased the burden on commercial ship lines to strengthen their own inspection system for embarking emigrants in Europe. Ship lines had to pay a fine of $100 for every passenger found inadmissible at the port of entry according to U.S. law (due to illness or physical frailty, for being "likely public charges," or because of a suspected violation of the contract labor law) if these conditions had existed prior to departure. This provision, though unevenly enforced, put almost the entire process of emigration control in Europe firmly in the hands of commercial interests, with little direct influence or interference from the U.S. government.[49]

Thus, emigration control was outsourced. While this was an economical alternative to the more expensive model of direct government control of exit, which prevailed for Chinese and later Japanese emigrants, it also had its flaws. Transportation companies were interested in high-volume migration and had little incentive to limit emigration. For a nation that was interested in shaping its own society by selecting immigrants, delegating this selection to commercial enterprises abroad was fraught with potential conflict.

To negotiate the selection of immigrants more effectively was one of the key items of the Progressive agenda at the turn of the century, and the federal government set about tackling it with the movement's typical zeal. The first step the administration took was a systematic investigation of the migration flows and the causes for emigration from Europe. During the early twentieth century, both immigration officials and congressional delegations studied the structure of migration in considerable detail through multiple trips and in-depth investigations. In the late nineteenth century, the problem had been studied from afar and had been guided by problematic assumptions. American observers believed, for example, that some types of immigration were "natural," while others were "artificial" and "induced." Only the so-called natural immigration was thought to be beneficial for the United States, and legal restrictions of the 1880s (such as the contract labor law) were therefore directed at artificially induced migration. By the early twentieth century, it had become clear that such distinctions did not capture the reality of mass migration. The new immigrants came from a multitude of countries and cultures, they were not easily classifiable by "race," and their motivations varied, as did their background. The desire to understand what propelled European workers to move abroad, especially to the United States, was therefore fueled by a growing sense that a more effective system of immigrant restriction needed to be built on better knowledge of the emigrants.

The small army of social researchers, officials, and touring politicians who went overseas (mostly to Europe) to investigate the causes and routes of emigration in the early twentieth century therefore had a broad mandate. In a typical case, Terence V. Powderly, formerly an American labor leader but by that time a relatively obscure federal official, was sent to Europe in 1906 by the federal Commissioner of Immigration, Frank P. Sargent, to "get complete facts covering causes of emigration from Europe to the United States for the information of the President." Powderly took this task seriously and spent months traveling through a wide swath of Europe, interviewing officials, observing the inspection of prospective emigrants to the United States, and taking many photographs. Powderly's investigations focused on the "character" of emigration and the impact of migration on the emigrants' home communities.[50]

Powderly was one of at least thirteen inspectors sent abroad by the Immigration Bureau, all of whom filed reports with their superiors. Depending on the talents, temperament, and writing skills of the investigators, some accounts gave a vivid ethnographic portrait of the communities studied, while others focused more on the structure of emigrant flow and the attempts to direct and control it through administrative and legal measures abroad. Powderly's investigation and the resulting report was perhaps the most insightful, but other investigators also provided vivid accounts. Among them was Inspector Philip Cowan's report on eastern Europe, which he visited in 1907. Cowan, a longtime activist and journalist in the Jewish community of New York, brought his considerable energy and investigative skills to bear in a report on Russian Jewish emigration. John Trenor, formerly the chairman of the Immigration Committee at the National Board of Trade and co-author of a book on Italian immigrants, provided an in-depth look at Italian emigration after no less than three visits for the Immigration Bureau. Trenor also visited Greece, Macedonia, and Bulgaria. Marcus Braun, a Hungarian immigrant and friend to Theodore Roosevelt, and Charles Semsey, a veteran of both the Hungarian struggle for independence and the Union army (and a former compatriot of Inspector Marcus Braun), visited Hungary and Austria on separate occasions.[51] Altogether, the Commissioner General of Immigration ordered ten investigations of emigration and emigrants between 1902 and 1914: eight in Europe and the Middle East and two in Mexico and the Caribbean.[52] In addition, seven members of the United States Immigration Commission (the so-called Dillingham Commission) also traveled together to Europe in the summer of 1907.[53]

The American investigations took place with varying degrees of openness. Members of the Dillingham Commission traveled openly and used at least part of their tour for sightseeing, some even bringing along their wives. European bureaucrats, high officials representing local and central government, doctors, and representatives of European transportation companies took the time to show these American visitors around and explain emigration from their point of view. The investigators of the Immigration Bureau, on the other hand, went about their travels more discreetly. Some tried to travel almost entirely incognito in Europe. Inspector Kate Waller Barrett crossed the Atlantic as a steerage passenger from Europe to New York to investigate the moral character of female emigrants. Deputized by the Dillingham Commission, other inspectors also made a total of twelve undercover crossings in steerage, posing as immigrants. Inspector Anna Herkner, for example, traveled the entire route from eastern Europe to New York disguised as an Austrian migrant, and her reports gave a frank picture of her journey from Bohemia.[54] Some inspectors, such as Powderly, blended open investigation with undercover work. At various points in his journey, Powderly walked the European countryside without an interpreter or an escort, posing as an itinerant laborer and knocking on doors to ask for shelter for the night. He was moved by the spontaneous hospitality extended to him on these occasions, even when there was no food to be had and the straw sack that had to serve as a bed was a bit thin.[55]

Whether traveling openly or not, almost all Americans took pains to meet ordinary people. Investigators were struck by the many men and women in the European hinterlands who asked questions about emigration and about America. Some told stories of relatives who had gone there. Many wanted to know how they, too, could make the journey. "Wherever we have gone in Galicia and Hungary, a number of persons have importuned us for information concerning America," reported Inspectors Dobler and Semsey after their trip in 1907.[56] What was it like in America? Did they need more workingmen there? Was there really more respect for the working class? "We all like America, it gives us cheer to think about it! I hope I can come one day," exclaimed an Italian railroad trackman to Powderly.[57] Migration and the desire to leave was everywhere. The continent teemed with people who were about to leave, wanted to leave, or were living off those who had already left. "It is a matter of surprise that we do not receive more immigrants than we do to judge from the effects produced in their native villages by the large number of remittances to their families by those already here," wrote Inspector S. A. Eppler in 1906 after a trip to many European countries.[58] "Some parts of Northern Hungary have been left practically without sufficient men to carry on local activities," observed Kate Waller Barett in 1914.[59] And her colleague John Trenor was even more drastic: "emigration . . . has resulted in the carrying off of so much of the very backbone of certain provinces as to leave them in a state of practical collapse."[60]

American inspectors found very little migration that could be termed artificial. Immigration agents, representatives of ship companies, and labor recruiters might have been important facilitators in the exodus, but they did not have to motivate their clients to leave. Motivation stemmed from structural poverty, the lack of remunerative work, discrimination, and political oppression of working class people and ethnic minorities. "Why does the emigrant leave home?" was the question Inspector John Trenor tried to answer on his trip in 1907. Observing the conditions in southern Italy, a ship doctor turned to him and remarked, "Your query should rather have been: 'Why would they not emigrate?'"[61]

Leaving Europe in the Twentieth Century

Overall, the motivations for Europeans to leave home differed little from those of earlier generations: they sought more and better paid employment prospects, availability of farmland, or the opportunity to escape political and social oppression. But the relative ease with which emigration could be organized and financed in the first decades of the twentieth century made exit a realistic possibility for far more people than in the nineteenth century. Sometimes sheer adventurousness and impatience seemed to be at the root of the decision to leave. Anna Hinitz remembered that her family, near Odessa, simply made the decision to leave in 1912 "because my oldest three brothers all had already escaped from the Russian Army and they settled in the States. In 1912 my folks realized there was no use of staying longer, but to join the sons in the States."[62] Family members had already left and were doing well in North America, and life was better overseas. Leaving was simply easier than staying.

Chains of information and travel were well developed by the early twentieth century for most European emigrants. Letters and personal messages relayed by visitors reinforced the news gleaned from newspapers and the information of immigration agencies. This was not new, but the extent and tradition of migration that existed by the early twentieth century meant that migration chains reached much further into the faraway regions of Russia and the Mediterranean as well as the villages of Scandinavia and central Europe. A more literate population could write and read letters more easily, the letters reached their recipients more quickly, and they might contain ship tickets and money for emigration. Most powerful, though, was the presence of return migrants, even in remote parts of Europe. Traveling in rural Montenegro by horse carriage, Inspector Trenor witnessed a conversation between his coachman and a man they had accidentally encountered on a rural road. The stranger "was well dressed, weighted down with a gold chain and seemed quite content and prosperous . . . He said he had been in California, had done well, saved money and was on his way back home to take his wife and family back with him."[63] Kalman Borko remembered how his father was motivated to leave by a neighbor who had returned to Slovakia from the United States. As Borko remembered many years later, "They teamed up together in 1920 and came over to New York."[64] Even in seemingly isolated places, American visitors found signs of returned immigrants and their footprint of wealth and success. Remittances also told a powerful story. At one bank in rural northern Hungary, Inspector Semsey found the local bank manager unwilling to pay interest on deposits. The bank was already flush with funds from remittances and did not need to pay interest in order to attract more depositors. "What more eloquent appeal could be made to induce the poor unfortunates to leave their unpleasant environment and undertake the arduous journey?" observed Semsey.[65]

Organizing the exit was still complicated, even for those with family ready to receive them overseas. First, the money for the passage needed to be raised. The price of a transatlantic crossing declined in the late nineteenth century to the point that steerage passage from Great Britain to the United States could be had for less than $40.00 in 1912. Additional costs such as railroad tickets, accommodation, and food while waiting for departure could easily double the cost of a ship ticket, especially for eastern Europeans. The passage thus represented a considerable cash layout for poor emigrants.[66] The financial strategy adopted therefore involved the pooling of financial assets and a systematic use of stage migration. The first to go were the family members most likely to find work easily and earn relatively high cash wages (usually young males, but sometimes young women, too).

It could be difficult to raise the money for the passage of the "pioneer" emigrant in a family. Mediterranean farmers had little access to cash, so Italian or Greek families often had to sell land or livestock to finance the trip. Rose Breci remembered how her father, the first in the family to leave, sold his horse to finance the passage. Mauro Rio's family sold the little plot of land the family owned in order to finance their son's passage.[67] If the family was landless, borrowing from kin or wealthier persons at home was a way out. Once the first family members were settled, others could follow with the help of prepaid tickets sent from America. By the early twentieth century, prepaid tickets were the single most important source of funds for the passage to North America. They enabled families to reunite on American soil. Ethnic communities that had started small grew, and the flow of migration from home could continue even when times were hard.

Once the funds for the trip had been raised, the next steps involved gaining the necessary permits to leave and organizing the travel route. In western and central Europe where emigration was long established, permits were easy to come by, and transportation was predictable. Indeed, as members of the Dillingham Commission soon learned on their trips to Ireland, England, France, and Belgium, these western European nations sent relatively few of their own citizens to the United States by the early twentieth century. Instead, they had become countries of transit migration, with well-established networks ferrying migrants in and out through their port cities. Few official government agencies kept track of the transit migrants or enforced any migration controls. Supervision over the departing passengers in western European ports was largely delegated to the transportation lines and local port administrators.[68]

Transit migration was too lucrative a business to endanger with overly restrictive government oversight in western Europe. To understand early twentieth century European migration and to control it at the source, investigators had to focus their attention on eastern and east central Europe, Italy, and the Eastern Mediterranean. In those regions, the logistical hurdles were still high for many emigrants, and political corruption and a generally inaccessible bureaucracy made organized exit difficult even though controls were largely unenforceable by official agencies. Understanding and controlling exit from Eastern Europe and the Mediterranean, the investigators learned, was the key to understanding emigration and immigration to the United States in the early twentieth century.

Leaving Russia

Emigration from western Russia reached unprecedented heights by the turn of the twentieth century. The causes of this exodus were not difficult for American observers to discover when they traveled in western Russia and Ukraine in 1908. Underdevelopment was a problem for nearly all rural Russians, and Jews were prohibited from taking advantage of even the sparse opportunities that did exist in the pale of settlement (the area to which most Russian Jews were restricted).[69] "Lechowicz was a small town and it was really bad. We couldn't make a living over there. My father was working for only about two dollars a day," was Frank Shelibovsky's memory of his childhood in a village near Minsk.[70] Restricted economic opportunities were closely tied to discrimination and political persecution for Russian Jews in particular. The personal violence of pogroms motivated many to leave beginning in the 1880s, as did the prospect of obligatory three-year army service. Escaping the Czar's army played an important role in the emigration of young men without families, and it fostered the migration of family members who might not have wanted to leave otherwise.[71]

The suppression of political dissent was a third strong ground for leaving. Especially after the unsuccessful revolution of 1905, active members in revolutionary groups needed to flee in order to escape the penal colony. The American historian Morris Schappes remembered how his father had to leave Russia precipitously in 1905. With the help of sympathizers, he stole across the Romanian border and soon found himself on a boat to Argentina.[72] Inspector Cowan got a firsthand taste of the repressive regime as the secret police trailed him during his investigation and regularly intercepted his mail. "The whole atmosphere in Russia is such that it is difficult to win the confidence of people high or low, and to get them to speak freely. There is a feeling of repression," he noted after his trip in 1906.[73]

Even though the pressure to leave was great, the passage from Russia for the United States was among the most difficult in pre-

World War I Europe. "Russia does not recognize the right of her people to leave the country except temporarily," noted the Dillingham Commission in 1911. The only groups who were granted the permission to leave were ethnic minorities. Jews, ethnic Poles, Lithuanians, Finns, and ethnic Germans made up more than 95 percent of those seeking to leave. Altogether, about 1.5 million Russians emigrated to the United States in the first decade of the twentieth century. Russia was the third largest country of emigration worldwide, the American observers noted.[74]

Migration chains out of Russia were shaped by the official disapproval of emigration and by the poverty and multiple motives of emigrants. Poles, Jews, and Germans, who were concentrated close to the western border of Russia, left by crossing into Germany, although some of the northwestern emigrants departed via the Baltic port of Libau. Exit via Russian harbors had the advantage that health inspections were minimal, though police controls were tight and deterred those without passports. For Jewish emigrants from southeastern Russia (Bessarabia) or Ukraine, direct departure via Odessa was possible but expensive. Instead, a train trip across the Austro-Hungarian border was usually arranged, followed by a railroad trip across Austria and Germany to the port cities of the North Sea.[75]

Because emigrants from Russia labored under the double handicaps of poverty and official disapproval of emigration, and because of the distance to ports of departure, organizing the exit was a formidable task. A passport, necessary for legal exit, was expensive. It cost eighteen rubles, reported Inspector Cowan, a large sum for a working-class family. Alternatively, would-be migrants could apply for an emigrant passport, which did not allow for return—this was risky, because it rendered those deported or not admitted to the United States effectively stateless. Internal passports (for travel within Russia) were cheaper and often were the only documents that aspiring emigrants could come by.

The help of licensed and informal agents or facilitators was crucial to organizing an exit, whether documented or not. Facilitators helped emigrants plot a safe, practical route and organized passage along these routes. Fourteen-year-old Polly Adler remembered how her father took her to the railroad station in the neighboring town and "after embracing me solemnly, turned me over to the travel broker and departed." The agent put Adler and her cousin together with a group of young men escaping the draft. They traveled without passports by train to the German border where the train line ended. The group "left the train and sneaked into Germany through dark muddy tunnels. The tunnels were scary, but we were in no danger, as the travel broker had paid the necessary bribes when he arranged our passage."[76] For Rose Cohen and her aunt, the agent organized an illegal border crossing on a horse cart with young Rose hidden under sacks of hay.[77] Samuel Nelson remembered how agents had instructed him and other passport-less emigrants to run across the border, ignoring "guards shooting in the air . . . they were probably also bribed to let you cross."[78]

American observers, too, noticed the well-organized network of what they called "runners" or agents, whom they saw not as unavoidable facilitators of Russian Jewish emigrants but as a highly problematic class of men out to fleece hapless emigrants. Immigrant inspector Maurice Fishberg observed in 1905, at the Russian border towns with Germany, "The emigrant passing through Germany is considered the legitimate prey of the German steamship companies and their agents."[79]

Crossing the border out of Russia into Germany or Austria-Hungary was just a first step. Transit through Germany or Austria (or both) came next, and this part of the journey could be lengthy. Austrian authorities were apparently lenient, and train travel through Austria, though lengthy, was usually not a problem. But most Russian, Galician, and Polish Jews had to leave via German ports, or they traveled through Germany to ports further west; dealing with the German authorities was a necessary second (or third) step, and this was not a straightforward affair. Germany, especially the Prussian provinces, had become a country of immigration by the early twentieth century, and Prussia had instituted a tight control system for migrants, whether transit migrants or seasonal laborers.[80] "Of all the countries named, Germany is very particular as to who shall immigrate," remarked Terence Powderly perceptively.[81] For the Prussian authorities, the rampant smuggling of migrants, false passports, and bribed border guards on the Russian side were a perpetual source of tension. In the early twentieth century, officials were also concerned with the prevention of epidemics, which Russian emigrants in particular were suspected of importing. At the same time, the German imperial government was reluctant to spend money on stringent border controls.

What had emerged by the time American observers visited the border stations in the German east in 1906 and 1908 was an ingenious way to shift most control functions (and costs) to private businesses while maintaining national sovereignty over the border crossing. Emigrants from the east were inspected at the German crossing points by Prussian authorities. If they had passports and tickets to travel overseas or to England, they were permitted to pass and then directed to the inspection barracks of transportation companies such as the Hamburg America Line or the Bremen based North German Lloyd. If they did not have passports but prepaid tickets, authorities would also let them pass so long as they went to the transportation companies' checkpoints directly. Those without tickets or passports were only let in if they bought tickets for their overseas passage immediately at the border. Steamship companies had many freelance agents stationed at the border crossing and paid a commission to each runner for steering a customer in their direction.[82] The elaborate inspection system that followed was, of course, costly for transportation lines. But in return for their investment, the lines held a monopoly on the North American immigrant traffic from Germany. Ultimately, passengers paid for the inspections in the form of higher ticket prices.

If everything worked according to plan, German (usually Prussian) border authorities did little more than divide the migrants into groups of legal, illegal, and unorganized migrants and directed them to the appropriate place at the border. The inspection proper was then handled by the ship lines. Through far from their actual base of operations in Hamburg and Bremen, the transatlantic ship lines had by 1906 erected transit migrant barracks for this purpose in nine different border towns in Prussia. These barracks were periodically inspected by Prussian public health authorities. There, emigrants were examined carefully by physicians (employed by the ship lines) for scalp diseases, physical frailties, and trachoma, all according to criteria that were used by immigration inspectors at North American ports of arrival. Migrants had to shower, and their baggage was disinfected. A quarantine area housed those considered too ill to travel for a maximum of five days, after which they were deported back east or allowed to journey on.[83]

Once the transit migrants had passed this part of the inspection, the passengers were put on special trains or special wagons to take them to their port of embarkation. The train lines from the eastern border would normally go through Berlin, but transit migrants were instead directed to Ruhleben, a small town west of the city, where another inspection point was located. All migrants were taken off the train there, and those who had not been inspected at the border (because they had crossed elsewhere, or because there had not been space in the smallish border barracks) were now inspected again, this time by physicians in the employ of the German railroad lines, before they could board the train for Hamburg or Bremen where the ships were waiting for them.[84]

Hamburg and Bremen processed emigrants slightly differently. In Hamburg, beginning in 1902, all emigrants were housed in spacious *Auswandererhallen* (emigrant halls), separated by country of origin. In Bremen, emigrants were put up in four boarding houses run by a contractor who also ran the largest network of Lloyd Line ticket agencies over central and eastern Europe. At both ports, more inspections and observations occurred. Emigrants who had made their own way to these cities or passengers who did not appear healthy were examined by yet another group of doctors. At this point, the inspection took place under the authority of an American consul, who signed off on the physicians' reports. The report of the transportation line (forwarded to the city authorities of Hamburg or Bremen) noted men and women rejected for mental illness, tuberculosis, pregnancy, or indigence, just as at the U.S. border.[85]

To Terence Powderly and the members of the Dillingham Commission who visited Prussia, the emigration inspection at German borders and ports was a marvel of thoroughness and efficiency. The Americans assumed that the German imperial government was ultimately in charge of the entire process, and it was seen as a perfect example of the desirable cooperation between government authorities and private companies. The inspections in Germany seemed to follow the regimen prescribed at the American border: screening focused on trachoma, skin disease, and general physical health, just as it did at Ellis Island. Many would-be emigrants were rejected for physical defects and sent back to the border crossing where they had entered. On the other hand, the German inspections were not likely to reject migrants who were simply poor but otherwise in good physical shape. To the chagrin of American observers, the American "likely public charge" exclusion had little currency for the Prussians.[86] Although the legal power of American consuls was limited to inspecting and approving the baggage and freight carried by the ships, the ship line's deference to U.S. rules assured observers that American standards for immigration were met to a large degree without the direct involvement, responsibility, or investment of the U.S. government. With the cost borne almost entirely by private businesses (in exchange for a lucrative transportation monopoly), the system also benefited the Prussian authorities who retained indirect control. The port cities of Hamburg and Bremen profited handsomely from the business of emigrants, as did the ship lines with their monopoly in the trade.

For the emigrants who had saved, bribed, and strategized their way to the Russian-German border and across into Germany, the rigid and dehumanizing sequence of controls added to the already considerable psychological strain they had to endure. "I have seen persons who have successfully passed the examination at the border collapse under the excitement induced by their anxiety and suspense," reported Inspector Eppler about the German ports.[87] Polly Adler's cousin, with whom she had traveled from Minsk through the mud tunnels of the Russian-German border and finally on a German train to the port of Bremen, lost her nerve during this last transit passage. "My cousin became increasingly confused and at last broke down completely. 'I am afraid,' she wailed. 'I cannot go to a strange land.' . . . The one thing on her her mind was getting the hell out of there and back to Russia, so it wasn't long before she kissed me goodbye and went her dim and distracted way." Adler traveled to New York on her own.[88]

Leaving Austria-Hungary

Posing as an itinerant foreign laborer on his travels through parts of Austria-Hungary in 1906, Terence Powderly was struck by the great poverty of the friendly Hungarian peasants he encountered. "Argument is not required to prove why these strong, healthy looking men left their country to come to us," he mused in his report.[89] More remote parts of the Empire, like Galicia, were even worse off: "in Galicia hopeless poverty is everywhere to be seen," reported Inspectors Dobler and Semsey in 1907. "The burning desire to escape from such an environment of hopeless poverty is the sole cause of this unusual exodus from Austria Hungary."[90] Some provinces were not just poor but also very isolated. Because there was no railroad system, Inspector Trenor had to cross Montenegro by carriage and on horseback. "To properly describe the country and its people would involve more of pride and poverty than one is usually prepared for," he stated laconically.[91] Other parts of Austria-Hungary that sent emigrants— Ruthenia and the Carpathian Mountains—were considered inaccessible and were never visited by any American observers.[92]

Social connections to migrant communities in North America were strong in central and southeastern Europe, despite their apparent remoteness.[93] They helped orient emigrants and directed their exit though Germany, France, or the Mediterranean. While leaving a home in the Austro-Hungarian Empire was easier than leaving Russia, emigration was still hampered by contradictory government regulations and bureaucracy, which both hindered and promoted migration. To leave legally, prospective emigrants had to acquire a local passport from the police. This document was only issued to men if they had fulfilled their military service and to women if they could submit a *Moralitätszeugnis* (a certificate of moral conduct). The passport then needed to be stamped or signed by a local physician, who was certifying that the emigrant did not suffer from contagious diseases or physical illnesses or handicaps. Terence Powderly noted that it was not difficult to get permission to leave, and that the Austrian authorities seemed to encourage temporary migration of poor rural citizens to the New World in expectation of the remittances that helped impoverished rural families.[94]

But the imperial government did try to prohibit the emigration of people without the required permits. Single women wanting to travel by themselves were detained in police checks at railroad stations, for example. Women under the age of eighteen and traveling without a relative were sent back to their homes, as were men without a military record and those likely to become a public charge.[95] But, at the same time, little was done to halt undocumented migration across the Austrian-German border. All in all, the system of population and migration control that the Austro-Hungarian Empire had on its books worked unevenly, and the control the government had over its emigrant population was tenuous.[96]

Emigrants from Austria-Hungary could organize their exit and travel on their own, but the departure was usually arranged by emigration agents, who were numerous even in the rural parts of the Empire. "These mountain regions and agricultural valleys are swarming with agents," commented Charles Semsey.[97] The government licensed the major agencies and assigned them to certain territories, providing lucrative de facto monopolies. American observers noted that the main Galician agent, a man named Sigmund Resch, was a royal councilor, and the main Hungarian representative was a banker. These agents had subagents who actually sold the tickets and arranged the journey for villagers and small-town inhabitants. The subagents organized both legal and undocumented exits: like elsewhere in eastern Europe, they arranged for illegal border crossings, put groups together as families, plotted routes across Europe, and sometimes accepted in-kind payments such as livestock instead of cash. The American inspectors were also convinced that some subagents worked directly with American-based labor contractors to organize groups of men to come to the United States.[98]

Because of the high price of tickets and the strict exit controls at the Austrian harbors of Fiume and Trieste, and also because of their geographic distance from regions of emigration, many emigrants from the northern and western part of the Empire choose to travel via Germany, where they were subject to the same inspections as Russian emigrants. Others took a lengthier, less policed route through southern Germany and France. A Hamburg-based agent named Morawetz advised emigrants from Galicia as follows: "buy a dark suit, so that you will look like a nobleman and do not take a direct train to see me but take a train via Cracow, Prerau [Bohemia], Prague, Magdeburg and buy tickets for only segments of the trip. Take the fast train to Bohemia and do not travel fourth class until after Magdeburg. If you are asked where you are going before you have reached Cracow, say Cracow. After Cracow, say that you are going to Prague for business reasons and after Prague you can travel undisturbed and in this way do without a passport entirely."[99]

Alongside these alternative routes, the final exit for thousands of emigrants from Austria-Hungary were the two Austrian ports of Trieste and Fiume. Both cities had grown in importance as locations for business and commerce, and had increased their emigration traffic considerably in the early twentieth century. The imperial government rewarded immigration agents for steering traffic to these ports, and made licensing arrangements for ship lines that limited competition there. The Austro Americana Line and the White Star Line (and, in the early years, the Cunard Line) ran boarding houses there and organized medical inspections. By "invitation" of the lines, U.S. consuls personally screened all passengers who sailed for the United States before their embarkation. They also worked closely with a medical officer employed by the steamship company. One of these consuls was Clarence Rice Slocum, an unusually active American official, who voluntarily filed monthly reports on his activities to the Immigration Bureau. Slocum personally inspected each passenger and rejected many of them, not just for physical ailments but also for being likely public charges or suspected prostitutes. Slocum was ardent in his pursuit of participants in the "white slave traffic." While Slocum had no legal power to reject prospective immigrants, his recommendations to the ship company were usually followed.[100] Altogether almost 4,700 prospective emigrants were rejected in Fiume in 1907 alone (about 20 percent of those who had already purchased tickets and passed Hungarian government controls).[101] The American consul at neighboring Trieste made similar decisions.[102] Ironically, these screenings did very little for passengers who wanted to be sure of admittance in the United States. In general, passengers from the Adriatic harbors continued to experience a high rejection rate at Ellis Island in the years before World

War I. Leaving directly from Austria-Hungary provided no guarantee of crossing the next border successfully.

Leaving Italy and Greece

Italians were the largest nationality group among emigrants from pre-World War I Europe. During the first decades of the twentieth century, the Italian economy was dependent on emigration and Italy's social and legal systems were organized around regional and international migration of Italian citizens. The destinations varied: Italians went to neighboring countries such as France and Switzerland; to more distant destinations in northern Europe such as Germany and Belgium; and finally overseas, with Argentina, the United States, Canada, and Australia as their primary destinations.

In the United States, Italians made up the largest nationality group of immigrant arrivals during the decade and a half before 1914. Over 2 million arrived during the first decade and 1.1 million in the second decade of the twentieth century. But many of these were return migrants who were entering the United States for the second or third time. Thousands even made the journey on a seasonal basis. Between 1908 and 1924, 60 percent of the total number of southern Italian immigrants returned back to Italy at least once.[103]

Like Italians, Greeks had a tradition of regional and transnational migration well before they became a significant group among emigrants to North America. The 1900 census counted only 8,655 people of Greek birth in the entire United States; in the following decade, over 167,000 emigrated to the United States. Like Italians, Greeks had a high rate of remigration: 53 percent of Greeks returned from the United States to their homeland before 1924.[104]

Agricultural failure, rural underdevelopment, and political crises in the Ottoman Empire were the most important factors in feeding the emigration stream to North America. In addition, Greece was rapidly becoming a transit country for emigrants leaving the Ottoman Empire in the early twentieth century. Large numbers of Armenians and so-called Syrians (that is, Christians from Mount Lebanon) emigrated via Greece to the United States before and after World War I.[105]

Greek, Middle Eastern, and Italian emigrants were viewed with hostility by Americans. Many were not considered whites; citizens of the Ottoman Empire (such as Lebanese and Syrians) had to battle the designation "Asian" by immigration officials.[106] Their poverty rendered them vulnerable to suspicions of criminality, illness, and dependency by American authorities. The fear of rising numbers of Italians, Greeks, and Syrians was one of the reasons for sending many American observers to Italy and Greece in the early twentieth century, and numerous, lengthy reports were filed from these countries. Members of the Dillingham Commission investigated Greek emigration, and as part of their research tried to trace the suspected routes of Greek contract laborers and indentured workers from the eastern Mediterranean to North America; members of the congressional committee were hampered in their efforts by their limited knowledge of Greek and Greek migration.[107] A few officers of the Bureau of Immigration were more knowledgeable. Inspector Marcus Braun wrote a report on the "export" of young Greek men and boys to the United States. Inspector Andre Seraphic, a career officer of the Bureau who spoke Greek and (apparently) Arabic, followed up Braun's account with his own investigation of the lives of young Greeks in eastern cities of the United States. Seraphic also conducted a far-flung undercover investigation to trace the flow of emigrants from the Middle East to North America. Unlike the more differentiated reports that Powderly and Trenor filed from Italy, Braun and Seraphic's investigations of Greek and Syrian migration painted a dark picture, usually confirming American officials' worst fears about the degraded nature of emigrants from the eastern Mediterranean.[108]

To the American investigators, poverty and its everyday manifestations were only too visible among the beautiful landscapes of Italy. Taking off on one of his customary hikes into the countryside near Naples, Terence Powderly observed, "Many of the people looked hungry, the women appear listless and indifferent to life." Powderly also noted the low wages paid to the workers he encountered.[109] Inspector John Trenor, a specialist on Italian affairs, provided a more structural analysis of the causes of emigration from Italy, citing the underinvestment in the southern part of the country, the corruption of the public officials, and the well-established communication network among emigrants and those who were still in Italy. He understood that Italian migration streams were fed by the desire to return to Italy but that nonetheless there was nothing artificial about Italian emigration, that agents were not needed to induce people to leave.[110]

The history of Italian emigration to the United States reached back to the early nineteenth century, but as a mass phenomenon the migration of southern Italians was of relatively recent origin. Because of the frequent back and forth of migrants, family and village networks between home and overseas were dense by the early twentieth century Italy. By the time American inspectors came to visit, some networks already spanned multiple generations. Rocco Morelli was born in the United States in 1906, but his parents returned to Sicily when he was a year old to join his grandfather, who had returned from his transatlantic migrations earlier. Within this community of migrants, the young boy remembered how his grandfather had told him, "Grandson, you will never come back to Italy once you land in the United States . . . Because in the United States, you have a lot of everything." The younger Morelli was dubious: "What do you need a lot of everything?" A few years later Rocco Morelli would leave Italy for good, fulfilling his grandfather's prediction.[111]

The decades before World War I were the years when, as Donna Gabaccia notes, Italian overseas communities changed from camps to *colonias,* from groups of male temporary workers to permanent neighborhoods of Italian immigrant families in North (and South) America. Letters home told the story of employment, modest well-being, and the need for more workers. "Each letter that tells of favorable conditions in the United States is read, re-read, handed round and devoured by the poor hungry people who long for an opportunity to leave their native land for a place where they can earn more than bread and insult," wrote Powderly.[112] Workers seemed to be well informed about opportunities and wages in North America. Powderly usually found someone with rudimentary English, even in relatively remote villages. Trenor saw that "in many sections of the Basilicata, Campo Basso, Calabria and Sicily one sees rows of small but neat and commodious houses built by either those who have returned permanently or for the Old Folks left at home."[113] Most impressive was the juxtaposition of emigrants and returnees witnessed by Trenor in

Naples in 1906. "On one side the [return] passengers from steerage, all neatly attired, were unfastening their well-filled trunks preparatory to Custom-House inspection. On another were the thousand or more awaiting embarkation to the, to them, 'Land of Promise.' The keen and wishful look in many an eye made a strangely pathetic picture."[114]

The overseas migration of the Greeks was less established than that of the Italians, but the threads of family migration developed steadily after the first few years of the twentieth century. By 1909, Grace Abbott, a keen observer of the growing Greek community in her neighborhood around Chicago's Hull House, had noticed how the formerly all-male Greek colony in Chicago had become more diverse, as an increasing number of women and children were brought over by their husbands and fathers. Greek emigration was therefore just beginning to become a permanent migration of families when first the Balkan War (1912–13) and then World War I broke out, interrupting the flow.[115]

Emigration of Greeks and through Greece continued and increased right after World War I as family networks revived and conditions in Greece and the eastern Mediterranean deteriorated. Maria Alexaki, for example, was separated from her husband (who had left for the United States in 1912) for eight years before she could join him in New York in 1920. Yet, even then, Maria was told that their migration would be temporary: her husband planned to return to their native Crete within four years. Harry Apanomith shared the motivations of many of his fellow Greeks when he remembered other emigrants as "big show-off Greeks." Like them, he wanted to make "five thousand dollars and go back." Following the pattern of a growing majority of Greek emigrants, Apanomith ended up staying away from Greece for decades to come.[116]

The expectation of return and the high remigration rate for many Mediterranean men in the first decade of the twentieth century not only shaped the image and expectation of *La Merica* for Italians, it also structured the organization of exit for both Greek and Italian migrants. Stage migration was the rule for both groups, in contrast to most eastern European Jews and many Germans and Irish of earlier times. Men almost always left first and separately from their families. Even if wives followed with the children later, they, too, expected to return at some later time. Helen Nitti remembered how this shaped the departure of their family: "We left everything, all the beds made, food in the house, everything we owned, just close it. Because people used to say that they used to be back."[117]

Italians were almost the only large nationality group in early twentieth century Europe who left for their overseas destination directly from home without transit migration through other countries. Yet agents and facilitators abounded there as well. Emigration agents were licensed by the government and the ship lines, but supervision was minimal, and the business was poorly regulated. Ercole Sori found that after the Italian federal government had passed a comprehensive licensing law in 1901, 9,000 agents were licensed, surrounded by uncounted subagents who acted as intermediaries, providers of information, and facilitators in a variety of ways. The agents came from many backgrounds, from local notables like mayors, priests, and even aristocrats to men of less certain standing.[118] Terence Powderly stumbled into the family of such an agent in central Italy. The father of the family, an employee of the railroads, seemed to be well connected in the village and ran "an information agency," with numerous correspondents overseas who reported to him regularly on the conditions. The man's business focused on facilitating emigration for laborers by providing information about labor contractors in the United States, sending men over in groups suitable for these contractors, and organizing the bureaucratic aspects of the departure.[119]

Similar to the Chinese system, local Italian agents issued tickets on credit, to be repaid with the help of middlemen in the United States, or they enlisted a contractor at the other end to return them the money.[120] Such arrangements were illegal under the United States Contract Labor Law of 1885. But Italian agents, well aware of the American law, usually operated too informally and unbureaucratically to be identifiable to the American apparatus of enforcement. Italian facilitators were men of a certain social standing in the community, and their word and expertise was what was mattered to their clients, not their written contracts, license, or transparent business practices.[121]

Agents also helped with passports and exit permits. Though Italian officials assured American visitors again and again that under Italian law the government did its best to prevent "undesirables" from leaving, the existing provisions that prohibited young men who had not served in the military or those with criminal records from emigrating were often not enforced. The Italian government's presence in the lives of emigrants resembled the situation in the Austro-Hungarian Empire: it was more theory than fact. If passports were hard to come by, emigrants could simply leave for other ports where passports were not necessary (Marseilles was one such destination). It did not help that under Italian law citizens who left for overseas were merely temporary labor migrants whose primary residence continued to be in Italy. In the eyes of government authorities, leaving Italy for overseas did not constitute permanent emigration.[122]

Greeks faced similar problems to the Italians, although the Greeks were poorer, had less-developed migration networks, and had fewer ports of departure to leave for the United States. Raising the money to pay for the passage was often the main problem for the cash-poor rural farmers and fishermen. Land or animals were sold to finance the passage of the pioneer. If that was not possible, a relative or an agent might loan the money, which would then be paid back with the first paychecks in the New World.[123] It was in this context that agents became labor contractors (as defined by American observers), who organized and financed both the exit from Greece and the entry into the United States and who connected their clients to a well-organized network of labor recruiters in the North American West.[124]

Family members who followed the pioneers almost always relied on prepaid tickets. Persephone Milos left as a young child from her northern Greek home with her mother because her father, a long-time emigrant, had sent them money for the passage. "How else would we pay for it?" she asked.[125] The older children who followed their fathers on these prepaid tickets also received "a little package," as Anna Sofranos remembered. The pack contained $25, the required amount of cash needed to pass through immigration control at Ellis Island. Once a new immigrant was established in America, the money was refunded to the family member or facilitator who had issued the package. A new ticket, earned by the new arrival, would also be sent to the remaining family members.[126]

Depending on how close Greek emigrants lived to the major ports of Piraeus or Patras, they could leave directly for the United States, or they could travel via Italy and depart from Naples or Palermo. When Maria Spanos left with her mother in 1915, a year after her father had last left their Greek home and nine years after he had first emigrated to the United States as a skilled tailor, the family had to travel via Italy. In Naples, mother and daughter passed health inspections and went from there to the United States.[127] Constantine Moschos, too, had to go via Naples with his mother. There, he was kept in quarantine for days; his impression was that this was just a way to supervise passengers while they were waiting for the scheduled boat to arrive.[128] Panagiotis Chletsos had a more difficult time: in 1904, he and relatives took a complicated route from Asia Minor to Italy and from there with trains to Belgium, where they finally boarded a Cunard Line steamer that brought them to New York.[129]

Taking a route directly to the United States became more popular (and more profitable) for Greeks after the first decade of the twentieth century, as transportation networks from the eastern Mediterranean became denser. This direct passage to the United States was preferable because the exit controls were less rigorous in Greece and passengers were unlikely to be kept in quarantine or rejected because of a lack of passports. There were health inspections, organized by the ship lines, but these were considered more a bureaucratic hurdle than a true hindrance to leaving. In general, the Greek government supported emigration, for the Greek economy depended on the cash remittances the migrants would send to support their families.[130]

American observers knew that Italian exit controls were loose. Beginning in 1894, after a cholera outbreak in Europe raised the fear of an epidemic in American port cities, the U.S. Immigration Bureau had posted physicians of the Marine Health Service to select Italian ports with the right of inspecting prospective emigrants before they could board the ships for the United States. In Naples, three physicians of the Service (predecessor to the U.S. Public Health Service, the agency that fielded physicians for health inspections at Ellis Island, Angel Island, and other U.S. immigration stations) examined emigrants with the approval of the Italian authorities and under contract with the steamship companies (who paid for their services). The American doctors checked all passengers, even first-class travelers, for trachoma and other illnesses according to the same standards that were applied to immigrants at U.S. ports of arrival. That way, the steamship companies hoped to minimize the rejection of their passengers at the U.S. border and avoid the cost of transporting those passengers back.[131] The members of the Dillingham Commission were impressed by this system, which combined the public control function of U.S. authorities with a profit incentive that motivated the steamship lines to pay for the service. Despite the official nature of the health inspection, the American doctors issued merely a recommendation to the ship line. In fact, the immigrants who arrived at Ellis Island from the port of Naples continued to be rejected at a far higher rate than immigrants from most other ports.[132]

American observers did not like what they considered the Greek government's lack of control over emigration. But in contrast with their success with Italian authorities, American efforts to enlist the Greek government in a campaign to control emigration from Europe were not successful. A combination of nationalism and strong commercial interest by Greek ship lines made it impossible to find local allies. Even the American consul in Greece was considered by the Americans an ally of Greek ship lines rather than of U.S. interests.[133]

The nationalism of the Greek government played out in different ways when it came to dealing with its own migrant populations. Like the Italian government, the Greeks had an expansive view of Greek citizenship. Ethnic Greeks who lived in the Ottoman Empire or elsewhere were always considered to be Greek citizens, regardless of their place of residence. They could always "return" to Greece, and they had the right to emigrate without exit passports. Thus, Greek citizens could move abroad via Greek harbors unhindered, unless they were subject to military duty, and the ship lines that sailed directly for the Americas did not enforce a passport requirement. The Greek government also considered preinspections by American health inspectors an interference with its sovereignty. Entreaties by the Americans to impose a system of exit controls were met with refusal. Free movement of citizens was central to Greek national identity, and any attempt to regulate exit from afar was seen as interference from a foreign power.[134]

Overall, the early twentieth century reports on emigration from Europe were among the most detailed statistical and ethnographic portraits of migration ever produced by members of the U.S. government. While the views of some investigators, especially the members of the Dillingham Commission, did little more than underscore their prejudices, others were insightful. Terence Powderly and most of his colleagues in the Immigration Bureau delivered highly nuanced portraits of various emigrant communities. But with insight and differentiation came an inability to recommend ready ways to fix the system of selection and examination of emigrants in Europe, even though many investigators considered it faulty. The silence of the Dillingham investigation is particularly noteworthy. Although Congressman Dillingham and his colleagues criticized the shoddy inspection practices and uneven enforcement of emigration provisions in Europe, the commission could not agree on a system of emigration control that would go beyond the existing process, which was dominated by commercial operators and relied on financial incentives for them to preselect their passengers. There was no discussion of enhanced powers for U.S. consuls or any recommendation to post representatives of the Immigration Bureau at the European ports of departure.

Moving the control over departing emigrants directly into the hands of the U.S. government—as was attempted in China—seemed but a remote possibility in 1911. Within a decade of the publication of the Dillingham Report, however, this was the system that would be realized: through a quota-visa system, the U.S. border would be moved abroad for most immigrants to the United States.

Leaving Europe in the Interwar Years

European migration to the United States was interrupted by World War I. The Great War, which began in Europe in August 1914, led to some dramatic departures for emigrants already en route to the United States. Rae Levin's family had to travel in the darkened cargo hold of a freighter that late summer, a very uncomfortable trip.[135] Rebecca Gold remembered how, when she and her family boarded the ship in the Latvian harbor of Liepaja (Libau), "the war broke out already and they stopped young men of age that . . . were supposed to serve in the army . . . hundreds of families came to the port without reservations on the boat. They figured they will take a chance and they will come to the port and maybe they will be lucky to get on a boat and then run away."[136] But for many emigrants, plans to leave Europe, to return to the United States, or to reunite with families on the other side of the Atlantic were put on hold indefinitely. Leaving Europe for North America was nearly impossible between the summer of 1914 and 1919.

When the fog of war began to lift after 1918, the landscape of emigration had changed profoundly for Europeans who wanted to leave for the United States. On the American side, the border had been redrawn by the passage of a number of laws and executive orders limiting admission of immigrants: a literacy test was the most hotly contested and important measure passed (in 1917) to exclude illiterate adult immigrants. A passport requirement for all immigrants was another new measure, imposed in the same year. Beginning in April 1917, passports, which had to be issued by an emigrant's country of origin, also needed to be stamped ("visaed") by a U.S. consul before departure. The consul could withhold his stamp if he decided that an emigrant might pose a security risk for the United States. Emigrants from "enemy alien" nations fell under this provision. Although immigration to the United States remained free of quotas or numerical limitations until 1921, these measures cast a shadow on European immigration. They also signaled an end to the period when the United States in practice delegated all emigration control to commercial ship lines and to foreign governments in the countries of departure.

But immediately after 1918, it was less U.S. law than European circumstances that made crossing the border from home so difficult for would-be immigrants to the United States. Europe and the Middle East remained in turmoil long after the official cessation of war hostilities. Emigrants found themselves displaced, persecuted by new regimes, trapped in the midst of continuing civil wars, stateless, or citizens of newly emergent nations.

Among the major powers, Germany had been reshaped, and the Austro-Hungarian and Ottoman Empires had dissolved.[137] Vera Kaplan, the daughter of a wealthy Jewish family in Kiev, later remembered the deprivations of World War I. When Ukrainian nationalists and Russian revolutionaries began a civil war and cholera broke out in her home town, she and a friend decided to flee into Bessarabia and Romania. In Romania, they managed to get a Romanian passport, American visas, and ship tickets to the United States, all with the help of a humanitarian organization.[138] Rose Krawetz and her large rural family of Russian Jews had to leave their home early in the war and barely survived by moving between the changing eastern fronts, while family members succumbed to epidemic disease; finally they were able to make their way out via Danzig to join the rest of their family in America in the early 1920s.[139]

Men were caught in the machinery of military mobilization, and some had to serve lengthy enlistments. Irving Markman remembered how the newly formed Red Army took every teenager in his Russian village in 1917. He was sent first to Siberia and then to fight against antirevolutionary forces until his mother finally got him out in 1922. Only then could he emigrate with his mother and join his father in the United States.[140] David Thulin, a young opera singer with a traveling company in Russia, experienced a truly global migration before arriving at the U.S. border three years after the war had ended. The young man and his fellow performers were surprised by the outbreak of the war east of the Ural Mountains. The little company remained together through wartime and revolution, but shifted their engagements eastward. By the time the civil war had broken out in Russia, the company was touring in China, Japan, Indonesia, India, and the Philippines. Thulin and his company landed in Seattle in late 1921 by way of Japan, and they continued to perform for opera lovers in the United States before settling as vaudeville performers in 1924.[141]

The worst conditions were endured by inhabitants of the Ottoman Empire, especially Armenians. Wholesale expulsions, community massacres, and a lengthy search for a safe place to survive took up years before emigration to the United States became possible. Harry Abrahamian fled his native Turkey disguised as a woman for the temporary safety of Syria. He later returned from Beirut to Turkey with his family to get the passport that allowed him to gain admission to the United States as a student. Mary Assadourian was not so lucky: her entire family perished before she found refuge in a Syrian orphanage. Relatives in the United States sponsored the young girl for emigration to the United States in 1921. The stories of Armenian refugees highlight another development in the stories of exit after World War I: the role of refugee agencies and voluntary organizations. These groups aided men, women, and their families in navigating the highly bureaucratized process that now dominated American immigration requirements, including the visa, health examinations, and affidavits of financial support.[142]

Most emigrants who succeeded in leaving for the United States in the interwar years had neither the harrowing experiences of Armenian refugees nor the colorful career of David Tulin. They simply had to wait an unexpectedly long time to join the husbands or fathers who had preceded them to the United States. For these families, exit was not significantly changed between 1919 and 1921. After much debate, in 1917 the U.S. government had introduced a literacy test for all immigrants over the age of 16. But since the test was administered in a language of the immigrant's choice it turned out to pose a low threshold for adults from most European countries. The requirement for a visaed passport added to the hurdles of would-be emigrants, especially in the countries that were in political disarray.[143] Despite these restrictions, immigration from Europe to the United States soared once again, as soon as the transportation infrastructure for transatlantic passenger traffic was substantially rebuilt. Emigration from Poland and Russia continued to be difficult—and, in the case of Russia, at times almost impossible because of the civil war conditions.

The resumption of emigration from Europe proved to be a brief hiatus for many European emigrants. In May 1921, the U.S. Congress passed its first quota law that covered all European immigrants. The law, called the Emergency Quota Act, went into effect on June 2, 1921, and determined that only a fixed number of emigrants from each country (equal to 3 percent of that immigrant group's representation in the 1910 U.S. census) could enter the United States as immigrants each year. Originally passed for only one year, the 1921 law was extended twice until it was superseded by the 1924 Johnson-Reed Act. The Johnson-Reed Act permanently limited European immigration based on a fixed nationality quota for immigrants from each country. The annual quotas were based on 2 percent of the estimated number of U.S. inhabitants from each immigrant group in 1890. Descendants of immigrants from earlier eras in North American history were included in this apportionment, which lifted the number of British and German immigrants admissible under the quota but depressed the number from the most recent countries of immigration. Italians, Greeks, and eastern Europeans were assigned small nationality quotas. As a result, emigration from Europe to North America greatly declined after the summer of 1921.[144]

The sudden implementation of the 1921 Emergency Quota Act threw virtually all European emigration into disarray. Because the Emergency Quota Act made no provisions for emigration or departure control, U.S. authorities had to deal with the new restrictions solely at the ports of arrival in North America. At first, the quota allocations not only were divided up by port of arrival, but also were separated into twelve monthly allotments at each port. Arriving passengers were counted against their nation's quota as they landed, and those who were above quota in any particular month were supposed to be sent back. This led to chaotic scenes, especially at the beginning. Within one day of the new law, for example, more Italian immigrants had arrived in New York and Boston than were permissible under the quota system for the entire month.

Emergency legislation allowed the Immigration Bureau to "mortgage" the number of arrivals against next month's quota, but the system remained unpredictable for departing passengers in Europe. Ship companies were unable to calculate whether their passengers would be admitted, so they raced across the ocean to beat the competition as soon as a new quota period opened, then ceased transporting immigrants after the quota was filled.[145]

In 1922 and 1923, quotas were allocated for the entire year, beginning in June; this system limited transatlantic migration traffic to a few months per year. Gradually, the American authorities also instituted an informal system under which certain groups of emigrants were given preference at the port of arrival, even if the law did not specify this. This could lead to heartrending scenes and wrenching decisions about when to leave. In December of 1922, just a few days before Christmas, three steamers arrived from Italy in New York harbor with a total of 1,486 Italian passengers on board—386 more than the yearly quota for Italians (in force since June). Immigration officials let the wives, young children, parents, siblings, and brides of long-time Italian residents land first. Four newlywed women were the last ones to make it. "It was just before the gates slammed shut against Italy, her yearly quota exhausted, that [four] girls were 'safe' and passed to the accompaniment of Bravas from waiting onlookers as they flung themselves into the arms of their anxious bridegrooms," wrote the *New York Times*. Over 300 others had to depart back home.[146]

In Europe, Irving Markman had finally succeeded in leaving the army and war-torn Russia in the spring of 1923, but by the time he reached his port of embarkation, Cherbourg, the White Star Line informed him that the quota for Russians would be exhausted by the time he was scheduled to arrive in New York in June 1923. Though he must have been one of the first in line for the 1924 quota, the change in the law that year, which set a lower quota, resulted in further delays for this Russian Jewish refugee. He and his family had to live in France until 1927, when they were finally able to leave for New York.[147]

The vise of nationality quotas and stricter entry requirements tightened further with the passage of the 1924 Johnson-Reed Act. The new law connected immigrant admission to emigration control by U.S. authorities. In order to buy a ticket for the transatlantic passage, emigrants needed to get an immigrant visa issued by a U.S. consul before departure. The consulate examined the applicant, and, if he or she qualified under U.S. immigration law, assigned him or her a numbered spot on the quota list. Emigrants could leave once their number had reached the top of the list. The U.S. federal government also introduced a system under which veterans of the U.S. army in World War I as well as wives, children, and parents of prior immigrants who lived in the United States could get visas first. Exempt from the quota were wives or children of U.S. citizens. The 1924 law also created separate visa categories outside the quota limitations: students and university professors could enter under separate categories, as could clergymen and diplomats. These exemptions were modeled after the Chinese exemptions in the nineteenth century, which also allowed "nonlaborers" to enter for specific purposes. Lydia Hartounian remembered how only four members of her family of five were able to enter under the Turkish quota. "Mother was almost sent back because she was born in Syria, and the Syrian quota had been full . . . But fortunately she was permitted to stay here when they found out that she had been a teacher in the old country, and she entered the country as a professional."[148]

The Johnson-Reed Act made emigration more difficult but also more predictable for many Europeans. Now the decision over admission was made by two different sets of U.S. officials: consuls prior to departure and immigration officials upon arrival at the U.S. border. The role of transportation lines in determining exit was virtually eliminated. Everyone, from the wealthy to common laborers, both men and women, stood in the same "line" because the quota system applied to all would-be immigrants.[149] From the American viewpoint, this system worked well during the 1920s: while it increased the workload of foreign service personnel abroad, immigration admission was coupled with exit control and both were in the hands of the federal government.

During the 1930s, as the Great Depression became a long-term feature of the American social and economic landscape, American consulates in most European cities granted almost no visas at all. Because of high unemployment in the United States, almost any visa applicant was deemed a likely public charge, and directives from the State Department and the President himself warned consuls from issuing immigrant visas. The strict new policy meant that even quota-exempt family members could not join their loved ones overseas, as sponsoring U.S. family members were usually not deemed secure enough to support a prospective newcomer. The gates to emigration to the United States were practically shut throughout the 1930s by the U.S. government's representatives abroad. Return migration exceeded new immigration from 1932 to 1935; for a few years, the United States became a country of emigration.[150]

The difficulty of departure for North America brought on first by the quota law and then by the Great Depression changed strategies and migration routes for more than a generation of migrants. Emigrants from some European countries simply shifted their destinations: Italian and French migrants went to the colonial possessions of their home countries in Northern Africa. Italians also went to South America in large numbers, and Armenians and Lebanese flocked to other Mediterranean countries as well as to Mexico, Brazil, or coastal Africa. Eastern European Jews went to France, Germany, and, increasingly, to Palestine.

Under U.S. quota laws, other entry strategies included leaving for the United States with a student visa or as a visitor then staying on, or hiring on as a sailor and jumping ship. Some migrants attempted—sometimes successfully—to enter the country as stowaways. Otto Heinemann, a waiter from the port city of Bremen, tried this three times before crossing the border successfully and settling in New York City. In general, illegal immigration from Europe rose drastically after 1924, an inevitable development that was little commented on by defenders of immigration control at the time.[151]

For U.S. officials concerned about immigration, the 1920s and 1930s were difficult but successful years. Low numbers of visas and strict control at the source were the price that needed to be paid for the federal government to assert meaningful control over immigration. Meanwhile, stories of heartbreak, divided families, and interrupted migration chains loomed large in the memory of emigrants from Europe from the 1920s and early 1930s. On the eve of World War II, tens of thousands of Europeans tried to flee to safety in North America from the onslaught of Nazi expansion, but the United States had successfully built a system of "Paper Walls" around the nation, with consular offices abroad representing the heavily fortified outer wall of the system. Once again, the most difficult border to cross for many emigrants was not the point of entry into the United States but the exit from home.[152]

CHAPTER **2**

Landing in America

In the American imagination, the history of immigration is always tied to the port of arrival: Ellis Island or Angel Island, the dusty border towns of Texas or the verdant Canadian border. The writer Mary Antin remembered how as a young child she reacted to seeing the North American shoreline after a sixteen-day crossing: "What are the feelings these sights awaken! They can not be described. To know how great was our happiness, how complete, how free from even the shadow of a sadness, you must make a journey of sixteen days on a stormy ocean. Is it possible that we will ever again be so happy?"[1] Arrival at the border of the United States signaled for many the potential for transformation, but it also highlighted the power of the American state and the powerlessness of the individual immigrant.

The border station also symbolized the power of the American state and highlighted the powerlessness of the individual immigrant in a very public way. "We were being marshaled through the gates there as if we were . . . going into prison. The people who were in the role of authority were not particularly gentle," remembered one immigrant.[2] Images of landing at Ellis Island still help us visualize the contrast between the reach of government and the helplessness of immigrants.[3] But compelling as this contrast may be in the nation's imagination, the reality of crossing into the U.S. border was always more complex, for it reflected shifting power balances and constant negotiations between immigrants and the officials who represented the United States.

Between the early nineteenth century and the mid-twentieth century, the nature of arrival in the United States and with it the border crossing experience changed in profound ways. This reflected the shifting power of the federal government in relationship to the newcomers, and it also mirrored a change in the importance of fixed physical borders. As the significance of formally crossing into the territory of the United States increased, the comings and goings across the border were increasingly documented, and an apparatus of border administration grew around a growing number of tasks: first came the need to document, then increasing tasks of inspection, and finally the power to exclude. As the bureaucracy at the border grew, so did the reach of federal immigration law. When the nineteenth century came to an end, it became clear that no immigration law would be effective without a nationwide apparatus at border stations to enforce it.

Over time, the physical borders of the United States existed in a field of tension that arose between their highly regional character, especially in the early years, and the desire for a unified federal border administration. Ideas about race and nationality, about fitness for citizenship, about labor needs and foreign interests varied greatly at the different borders of the United States. This chapter will first examine the changing shapes of borderlands in the nineteenth century and the transition to the more heavily regulated borders of the twentieth. Our examination will then focus on the different geographic regions in order to discern more accurately how the border looked to both immigrants and border administrators during the first thirty years of the twentieth century. Race and gender played out differently at different borders, for example. Poverty and class were also assessed in ways that changed from one part of the country to another. In short, regional practices and perspectives defined the negotiations between immigrants and the authorities fundamentally at all border stations.

For most of the nineteenth century, North American ports of arrival were not organized to receive large numbers of European immigrants. Almost no port had a central immigration station for landing passengers before the late nineteenth century. Up to the mid-1800s, most larger ports had only a quarantine station—often at a distance from the port proper; some ports of arrival did not even have that much. Besides the quarantine station, the ports had only a customs house. Customs officers were the only representatives of the federal government at immigrant arrival stations until the 1880s, and they were interested in the arrival, inspection, and taxation of goods, not people.

Later immigrants' first encounter with officials came usually during the quarantine or health inspections, performed by physicians employed by the city where the ship was landing (or in the Canadian case, by government-employed physicians). These inspections were not mandated by the federal government until the National Quarantine Act of 1893. But well before then, they had been introduced by municipal or state authorities in certain ports of arrival (Boston in the early nineteenth century, and New York and Philadelphia in the mid-nineteenth century).[4] In most instances, passengers were inspected on board their ships for signs of contagious disease, ranging from measles and cholera to skin diseases; only then were they released for landing. Often the inspection was cursory, but those who were identified as sick could be detained for weeks or even months in the quarantine hospital. Lengthy stays in these sometimes overcrowded and unsanitary facilities could be a traumatic introduction to the new country.[5]

The largest and most infamous of the early quarantine hospitals was located on Grosse Isle, in the St. Lawrence River near Quebec City. Grosse Isle at times housed tens of thousands of Irish famine migrants, many of them deathly ill, many of them dying. For New York arrivals, a hospital on Staten Island and the Wards Island Quarantine Hospital housed immigrants during much of the nineteenth century. Essington, eight miles downriver on the Delaware, served this function for passengers destined for Philadelphia. In some quarantine hospitals luggage was also inspected and disinfected. Olof Olsen, who arrived as a young Swedish immigrant, later remembered his parents' concern over the health inspection because he had had measles during the voyage. But the inspectors paid no attention to him; instead, they took another drastic measure upon the family's arrival in New York: they burned everyone's bedding, presumably to eliminate a source of infection.[6] After passing health inspections on board or after their stay in the quarantine hospital, most nineteenth-century passengers were let off at the docks where their passenger ship landed.

Upon landing, the ship's captain was required by law to give a list of passengers to local authorities, who would then report it to the Department of the Treasury for record-keeping. In some cities, the captain also needed to furnish a bond for each passenger, while in others the landing passengers themselves had to pay a "head tax." These payments were enacted by various port cities beginning in the 1830s. The federal government also instituted a federal head tax of fifty cents in 1882 to pay for the care of indigent immigrants after their arrival.[7] The passengers themselves were not required to report to officials, though their luggage could be inspected; no passports were required, and no documents had to be shown after landing. Indeed, except for customs officials, no representatives of the U.S. government were present at the port of arrival until the 1880s. Instead, a large and motley group of commercial "helpers" greeted immigrants as they stepped on land. A 1848 inquiry by the City of New York revealed chaotic scenes on the docks where immigrant ships landed; the report found much fraud and corruption among the "runners," and a complete lack of regulation or oversight by the city.

In response, the City of New York built Castle Garden immigration station, the first such building designated for newly arrived immigrants. The Commissioners of Immigration of the State of New York, officials appointed for the first time in 1849, were to keep watch over conditions at the station. Most of the services offered at Castle Garden were provided by businesses and benevolent societies: there was an employment bureau, a ticket agency that sold railroad tickets, and permission for those who needed shelter for the night but could not pay for it to stay in the building for free. The indigent were shipped to the Poor House on Wards Island.[8] "All is well and wisely done for the protection of the emigrant who would otherwise if left to himself, become the prey of sharpers, boarding house 'runners,' scalpers, loafers . . ." commented an observer hopefully to the *New York Times*. The Commissioners, however, were volunteers, and day-to-day management of Castle Garden remained lax.[9]

In Philadelphia, commercial interests were even more dominant than in New York. Next to the Washington Street Dock, where the two ship companies involved in late nineteenth century transatlantic immigration traffic docked, the Pennsylvania Railroad offered a convenient, direct connection to the American interior, and, as it happened, this railroad company was also the sole owner of one of the ship lines (the American Line).[10] In Baltimore, arrangements were more makeshift though not necessarily less efficient. Quarantine inspection took place aboard the ships, with doctors boarding as the steamers entered the Chesapeake Bay. By the time the ship docked on pier eight or nine in Baltimore harbor, the quarantine inspections had been completed, and passengers could disembark directly to the terminal of the Baltimore and Ohio Railroad. Other new arrivals stayed at Mrs. Koerber's, a boarding house with 350 beds run in a special arrangement with the ship lines. Her establishment was not supervised or in any way licensed by the city or state, although it would later serve as an informal detention center for rejected immigrants. Other port cities such as New Orleans and Providence had virtually no facilities for immigrants at all prior to the 1890s.[11]

At land borders, the markers for border crossers were even fewer. Customs buildings, sometimes no more than a shed, sometimes grander, existed at most border crossings. The border itself was usually unmarked across Canada and Mexico before the 1890s. Border crossers were not registered, and immigration statistics did not record them unless they arrived directly from overseas.[12]

In contrast to their encounter with a regulated and controlled departure from Europe, nineteenth-century immigrants to North America experienced their border crossing into the United States as a journey in which government presence was minimal. Indeed, the physical border of the United States, though contested, marked, and recognized, was not an important hurdle for immigrants' arrival. Crossing the ocean and enduring the hardships of the newly arrived were seen as the primary hurdles to overcome for immigrant settlers. Government intervention was only important when something went wrong that would have costs for the city or community of arrival, such as when newcomers were too ill or too poor to fend for themselves or if they carried contagious diseases. The principle that government should stay out of the way of immigrants was only tested for the first time by the arrival of large numbers of poor Irish immigrants in the 1840s. Overcrowded vessels, a quickly growing class of urban poor, and the fear of epidemics resulted in the passenger laws of 1847 and 1855, which governed the conditions on board ships regarding space and provisioning. But many of these laws' provisions were aimed at remedying conditions encountered before the immigrants landed in the United States, and enforcement of the federal measures was delegated entirely to local agencies, transportation companies, or U.S. government representatives abroad. Even at the largest ports of arrival such as New York, no government agency existed that was devoted to controlling, counting, or in any organized way receiving immigrants.

The first hints of systematic change occurred not in the wake of continued Irish immigration but in the context of the first laws regulating Chinese migration to the United States—the "anti-coolie law" in 1862 the Page Law of 1875, and the Chinese Exclusion Act of 1882. These laws established the port of arrival as the station where immigrants were not just counted and checked for epidemic diseases but also inspected to see whether they fell under one of the prohibited categories and were therefore excludable (i.e., Chinese coolies, prostitutes, or criminals). The passage of these laws established the first set of active border controls by the federal government. Only Chinese were subject to these exclusions, but a growing movement to institute similar controls for Europeans gathered force almost immediately.

In August 1882, just three months after the passage of the Chinese Exclusion Act, Congress passed a law barring the admission of "any convict, lunatic, idiot or person unable to care for himself without becoming a public charge." Such persons were to be returned to the "countries from whence they came," with the cost borne by the ship line that brought them.[13] This law was the first to exclude immigrants not by race but by personal characteristics, as determined by a representative of the federal government at the port of arrival. The Foran Act, a federal law passed in 1885 (amended in 1887), added contract laborers to the list of excludable immigrants. The contract labor law was an important part of solving the problems associated with poor immigrants by "picking out the 'defective' element," as Kitty Calavita formulated it.[14]

The passage of these exclusionary laws set a precedent for all immigration regulation to come for the next forty years, for they established the physical border of the United States (usually the port of arrival) as the point where screening took place, and they created certain classes of immigrants whose personal characteristics excluded them. Immigrants who did not fall under these categories were to be admitted. For Europeans admission as immigrants remained the "default" option for the federal government.

In practical terms, the laws of the 1870s and 1880s necessitated the presence of government officials at all borders. At first, customs agents were deputized to enforce laws, but soon this proved to be inadequate. Local and state officials, such as the New York Commissioners of Immigration, were then called on to make sure the provisions of the contract labor law were observed. But nationwide enforcement of immigration restriction remained a haphazard affair. In some smaller ports inspections were virtually nonexistent, and even in larger centers of immigration the competence of officials and the efficiency immigration inspections varied greatly.[15]

In New York, problems abounded during the 1880s.[16] The five-member Board of Commissioners of Immigration had twenty-five employees to run Castle Garden, just as they had had during the 1860s when immigrants were less numerous. These men inspected up to 6,000 immigrants who arrived each day, determining if they were to be excluded, making arrangements for sending them back, or processing them as newly admitted.[17] In response to this untenable situation in New York, the first decisive step toward the complete federalization of border control was taken in April 1890, when the Secretary of the Treasury decided unilaterally to withdraw from his cooperation with the New York Commissioners of Immigration and take over the immigration inspection directly at the largest point of entry to the United States.[18] Federal authorities quickly appointed two federal Commissioners of Immigration (both political appointees) who proceeded to hire staff and conduct business from a barge office in New York Harbor. Within a year, the first facilities on Ellis

Island (originally a Navy depot and therefore in federal posses-
sion) were ready to process all arriving immigrants directly under
federal auspices. The Marine Health Service took over the screening of immigrants for physical "defects" and diseases at the same
time.[19]

This precedent-setting move, cemented by an 1891 law that created the Federal Bureau of Immigration, served as a model for building an entire federal inspection system at the nation's borders.[20] The
Immigration Act of March 3, 1891, provided for a federal inspector of
immigration and authorized federal employees to take over the inspections of immigrants at all of the nation's ports of entry. The law
also added to the "excludable classes": men and women who had committed a crime or misdemeanor of "moral turpitude," polygamists,
and those suffering from a loathsome or dangerous disease were also
to be excluded thereafter. An increased head tax of $1.00 per immi-
grant and fines levied on transportation companies if they know-
ingly transported excludable immigrants to the United States were
also part of the law. The actual number of immigrants excluded under these provisions proved not very high (especially in comparison
with the rapidly rising rate of immigration), but the direct involvement of the federal government in the screening of immigrants anticipated the centralized system of federal control of border crossings
in the twentieth century.[21]

The effect of the laws of the 1880s and early 1890s on the border-
crossing experience of immigrants varied greatly. Europeans were
rarely scrutinized. Fifteen-year-old Goldie Tuvin remembered her
1889 arrival in ways that differed little from the immigrant experience of earlier decades. After leaving the ship on New York's South
Street piers, "we were caught in a stream of people struggling down
the gangplank and found ourselves among trunks, bags, bundles all
strewn about, helter-skelter. Several men in uniform were examining one trunk minutely tapping the bottom and the sides. We had
nothing to declare and oddly enough the customs man seemed to
realize this, because he asked aunt Emma to open the smallest of
bags and almost at once told her to close it." Goldie remembered no
questioning of her parents or examination of the family's circumstances.[22] Like Tuvin, most Europeans were admitted without much

ado. They made their border crossing into the United States largely without interference from officials.

Only Chinese immigrants were subject to strict scrutiny by federal officials. In a mirror image of their complicated departure, Chinese passengers had to present the documents that they had secured upon departure for examination at the port of entry, which certified their status as merchants or as members of other exempt groups; these were the so-called section six certificates, or the return certificates if they had been in the United States before 1882 and were merely returning after a temporary absence. All U.S.-born Chinese had to furnish proof of their U.S. citizenship. In the encounter with officials, having the proper documents and having them accepted as authentic was critical for gaining admission. For Chinese immigrants after 1882, complicated and often changing paper requirement and hostile officials made crossing the border into the United States a process fraught with uncertainty.[23]

Contexts of Arrival in the Twentieth Century

Immigration law was the most prominent and visible of the instruments of border control and negotiation. The law served not only immigration officials but also was used by immigrants to make a valid claim for admission. Other forms of codified controls (internal rules, expert opinions, scientific reports, and statistics) were less accessible to immigrants though they shaped the behavior of immigration officials in important ways. For immigrants, help came from experts and groups who had an interest in immigrant admissions: immigrant societies, lawyers, and employers of immigrants. These were the troops, often invisible, aligned on the immigrants' side. Overall, immigration officials had disproportionate legal and police powers on their side, even though no separate enforcement agency existed until 1924 and they had limited political and financial resources to enforce their actions.

At the beginning of the twentieth century, immigration law sorted newly arrived passengers and border crossers into two groups: Asian immigrants, who were not admitted unless specifically exempt from immigration bans, and American and European immigrants, who were admissible unless they belonged to one of the excluded classes. In 1917, this basic principle changed: all immigrants over the age of 16 had to have a passport and pass a literacy test to be admitted. Still, every newly arrived person was considered a potential immigrant who was supposed to be examined accordingly, although in practice immigration inspectors often treated border crossers differently if they lived close to the U.S. land border and were thought to cross into the United States frequently. Beginning in 1921, a quota-visa system limited entry for Europeans.[24]

Within this rough framework of admissibility and exclusion, immigration law grew in complexity during the first three decades of the twentieth century. Even at the beginning of the twentieth century, a period which is often considered the "open door" era of immigration, immigration restrictions were numerous and complex. Asians were sorted into exempt classes (merchants, diplomats, and students) and nonexempt (everyone else). European immigrants were excludable for an ever longer list of causes, ranging from highly specific to very broad categories. The laws regulating admission of immigrants were accompanied by a number of court decisions which, for the most part, affirmed the right of Congress to regulate immigration and naturalization. During the twentieth century, immigration policy was less influenced by judicial modifications than other parts of civil law and procedure.[25]

Immigration law acquired meaning and specificity because of debates and information provided by experts aligned on both sides, the government and the immigrants. Restrictionists and those in support of continued open immigration formed well-known and well-defined opposing camps among voters, their political representatives in Congress, and immigration officials. The two sides in this struggle relied on somewhat different kinds of arguments and organized their supporters in different ways. Those in support of continued open immigration (at least from Europe) relied mostly on traditional electoral politics. Immigrant groups held rallies, published articles in the ethnic press, and sent petitions and letters to make their opinions known. The Immigration Bureau, especially its stations at Ellis Island and San Francisco, were recipients of these unsolicited letters and communications. At times, local immigration officials were (not unjustly) accused of being partisan themselves and felt under siege from such political activism. Their public image as neutral arbiters of the law and compassionate administrators of immigration was endangered by open partisan lobbying.[26]

In contrast to the visible and sometimes noisy partisanship of immigration advocates in the early twentieth century, restrictionists marshaled the quiet expertise of social scientists to make their case and found a receptive audience in the Immigration Bureau. Credentialed academics and self-taught advocates gathered materials and wrote academic publications in the late nineteenth century. In the early testimonies before Congress, the practitioners of border control in the Bureau outshone the academic representatives of immigration restriction such as Prescott Hall, but this changed as the methods and presentation of restrictionists became more nuanced and better informed. The most famous scientific inquiry about immigration in the early twentieth century was the Dillingham Commission's forty-two volume report, which contained a detailed (if biased) study of many aspects of immigrant communities in the United States. The commission's research ultimately resulted in the passage of the Immigration Act of 1917, which contained a literacy test, and the 1924 Johnson-Reed Act. Both laws were explicitly based on the work of social scientists of the time.[27]

Experts continued to influence immigrant officials and immigrants long after the publication of the Dillingham Report. Academic expertise and research informed the Immigration Bureau primarily in three areas: racial classification, illness and disease, and human trafficking. The files of the Immigration Service reveal how avidly bureaucrats collected scientific research and referred to it, even when it contradicted the day-to-day experience of officials on the ground. For expert opinions on race, the Bureau had the Dillingham Commission's "Dictionary of Races and Peoples" on file, and sometimes turned to it for advice on the racial classification of Mexicans.[28] Notions of "blood" and race, not nationality law, guided officials when they had to determine the racial classifications of immigrants from Asia and their sometimes biracial offspring.[29]

The Immigration Bureau also encouraged and used the latest research on intelligence and mental illness. Because the Bureau had to screen for "imbeciles," "feeble-mindedness," and epilepsy, inspectors had to devise ways to sift out nonadmittable immigrants. They fashioned their own simple intelligence tests, but also accommodated researchers who developed such tests and tried them out at immigration stations.[30] Most officers on the ground found the categorizations and testing mechanisms of formal science of limited use for their purposes, and they preferred to rely on their common sense in making their judgments. But because they worked in the context of scientific testing as an emerging science, they still needed to justify their stance and accommodate alternative views.[31]

Administrators made especially extensive use of expertise to fill in the cultural and social background of immigrants. From thick files on Japanese picture brides, which included assessments of Japanese cultural views regarding marriage, to a comprehensive attempt to map out the prevalence of organized prostitution in U.S. cities, the Immigration Bureau collected and generated large amounts of information that could give a context to the work of immigration admission officers. Some of this information, such as data on prostitution, was rarely put to use; other parts were controversial, such as the information on the legitimacy of Japanese proxy marriages. But together they provided a crucial basis for immigration policy in the early twentieth century.[32]

As we saw, inspectors of the Immigration Bureau also were sent to investigate the backgrounds of the specific immigrant groups themselves. It helped that quite a few employees of the Bureau, especially on the East Coast, came from an immigrant background.[33] Just as the inspectors, especially in large stations, were encouraged to see themselves as part of a web of knowledge and science, so too the Commissioner General of Immigration himself began to cast the service in the light of objective social scientific research. Between 1902 and 1918, the *Annual Report* of his office, formerly a brief recitation of arrivals, departures, money spent, and letters sent, became a compendium of social statistics on immigration that included maps, color graphs, and photographs of "typical" immigrants.[34]

Expertise was not an instrument available only to one side in the border encounter. The Immigration Bureau did some of its research in part to counter the informally accumulated expertise of immi-

gration networks, smugglers, labor contractors, and governments promoting emigration. But although expert knowledge was wielded by
both sides, publicly recognized expertise and professionalized and
systematically distributed knowledge belonged almost entirely to
the U.S. government and its representatives. Only in the post–
World-War I era would immigrant advocacy organizations make
more systematic use of research and its results for their communities. During the prequota era, science and demographic knowledge
served the forces of control, not those who wanted to enter the
United States.[35]

For immigrants and immigration authorities, immigrant advocacy
organizations played an increasingly important role in negotiating
border crossings during the early twentieth century. Immigrant advocacy groups, some of them with a commercial interest in immigration, had important influence in shaping admission policies and
intervening in individual cases as well. The most effective assistance
for immigrants came from the immigrant aid organizations head-
quartered in New York and other East Coast ports that had been set
up to help immigrants with housing, work, and emergency charity.
On the West Coast, the immigrant aid network was much weaker,
limited to a few Protestant missionary societies as well as Chinese
and some Japanese benevolent organizations. The Chinese groups
were important for the legal assistance they extended to some Chinese arrivals who could not gain admission to the United States on
their own. At the southern border and in the north, immigrant aid
societies were largely absent at the border stations.[36]

To the inspectors of the Immigration Bureau, the presence of the
immigrant advocates was both a political threat and a nuisance in
their day-to-day work. In response, the Immigration Bureau tried to
delegitimize immigrant advocacy groups as partisan, not working for
the "true interest" of immigrants, riddled with commercial interest,
and influenced by "outside" agitators. At some immigration stations,
representatives of immigrant groups were banned from the station
or strictly limited in their activities. In New York and elsewhere,
they were not allowed to offer immigrants legal counsel except in
writing, a prohibition fought tenaciously. At Ellis Island, where advocacy organizations were most active, the Bureau even launched

an investigation into the organizations and individuals seen as particularly problematic in this respect.[37]

The most potent influence of immigrant advocacy groups came from their growing expertise at using political pressure and legal advocacy to fight for their clients and for immigrants in general. Immigrant advocates could mobilize political patrons, the courts, and public opinion for immigrant rights. Well aware of the potential voting power of immigrants, presidential administrations rewarded prominent members from European immigrant groups with leadership posts in the Bureau of Immigration, the Bureau of Naturalization, and the Department of Labor. As a result, conflicts sometimes surfaced between the more proimmigrant heads and the more restriction-minded civil servants on the ground.[38]

It was the presence of lawyers and their real or imagined ability to take immigrant admission cases to the courts that had the most profound effect on the negotiations between immigrants and immigration inspectors at the border. Lawyers were successful at gaining the right to admission for many Chinese and some Japanese. Lawyers challenged the right of the Immigration Bureau to detain immigrants, calling for habeas corpus proceedings and fighting "likely public charge" exclusions. They also challenged politically motivated deportations during and after World War I. The increasing success of immigrant advocacy groups, including immigration lawyers, ultimately furthered the movement of immigrant admission away from the physical border and its immigrant advocates.

Inspectors and Immigrants

In the encounter at the border, the immigration inspectors played the central role as representatives of the state at the border crossing. The inspectors were employees of the Bureau of Immigration (as it was called until 1932), a new agency that had started out within the Department of the Treasury with only five employees in Washington in the early 1890s. By the 1920s, it had grown to a federal bureaucracy with over 2,400 employees in thirty-five districts and a far-flung network of examiners, inspectors, and special agents within the Department of Labor.[39] Immigration inspectors had a wide array of legal powers, both judicial and executive, over immigrants. Bureau officials functioned as both administrators of the law and as judges who decided on the appeals of immigrants at border stations where lawyers were rarely present. In cases of disagreement among the hearing officers, the Commissioner General of Immigration in Washington made the ultimate decision about admission. Only rarely did immigrants succeed in bringing an admission case to court. The rights of immigrants to have their future decided in an American court of law was (and is) very limited, for immigrants were not U.S. citizens and could not appeal to the courts until they were officially admitted to the United States.[40]

In the larger setting of American politics, the immigration inspector belonged to a modest outfit. In Washington, the Bureau of Immigration and its successor, the Immigration and Naturalization Service, struggled for recognition, money, better staffing, improved infrastructure, and political influence. Almost every year, the Commissioner General prefaced his *Annual Report* with an appeal for more money, more employees, and better facilities. On many parts of the southwestern border, immigration officials were housed in structures little better than shacks. Immigration inspections in large port cities such as Baltimore or Boston had no permanent facilities until around World War I.[41] Complaints by inspectors about long days without a day off for many weeks, crumbling facilities, unqualified personnel, and low wages were a regular part of their correspondence with Washington headquarters. "In the continuous battle with the high cost of living, employees are under the absolute necessity in many cases of eking out a livelihood with outside work" reported the commissioner in charge of New England to the Washington headquarters in 1920. His employees included "several engaged in teaching night school, shorthand reporting, insurance soliciting, clerking in provision store, athletic coaching, packing and shipping and poultry raising" to make ends meet.[42] The power of the Immigration Bureau over its clients was considerable, but in contrast to other agencies of the growing federal bureaucracy, its employees and leaders were penurious and without much political clout in Washington.

Part of the reason for the political powerlessness of the immigration agency stemmed from its inherently contradictory mission, which made it difficult to find permanent allies in Washington. As an agency founded to make border inspections and controls consistent and regular throughout the country, the Bureau was seen as a law enforcement body whose natural political alliance was with restrictionist forces.[43] But the Bureau's leaders and employees wanted to see themselves as mediators between the American state and immigrants, as teachers to both sides, shaping immigration policies in large ways and day-to-day actions. In Congressional testimony, interviews, and letters, the immigration commissioners argued that they were more than just managers of the border; beyond that, they served as stewards of the American people's desire to let in only the truly deserving immigrant and as protectors of all immigrants from the vicissitudes of life in America. Buffeted between its conflicting demands and squeezed by slim budgets, the Bureau's efforts to present itself to the public as an agency that served immigrants and the nation came across as half-hearted.[44]

The position of the immigration agency did not improve as restrictionist forces gained the upper hand in Washington during the first two decades of the twentieth century. Even though some officials, such as Ellis Island Commissioner William Williams and Commissioner General Anthony Caminetti, aligned themselves openly with the restrictionist camp, immigration restriction laws diminished the power of the Immigration Bureau because they eliminated the inspector's decision-making leeway. In theory, the Immigration Service retained authority over immigrants long after arrival because of its deportation power, but in practice the reach of the immigration inspector ended at the physical border of the United States and indeed became weaker after the visa and quota laws of the 1920s.[45]

Immigrants, the central actors in the drama of the border crossing, seemed nearly without power at the border station. True, the law let them enter almost by default, with minimum restrictions, if they were from Europe or the Americas. But the power to influence the decision in their favor seemed to be indirect only. Wracked by the physical discomfort of the sea journey or the hardship of crossing the arid border in the south, immigrants arrived physically exhausted and disoriented, unable to express their plans and needs to the uncomprehending English-speaking officials. "Rumors were current among immigrants of several nationalities that some of us would be refused admittance into the United States and sent back to Europe. For several hours I was in cold sweat on this account," remembered the writer Louis Adamic as he looked back on landing at Ellis Island in 1913.[46]

Despite their feelings of helplessness at the border, from the viewpoint of the immigration inspectors immigrants did have power. It lay in their sheer numbers and the diversity of their backgrounds. By the early twentieth century, the largest ports of entry landed many large passenger ships daily, with hundreds, sometimes thousands of immigrants disembarking from the steerage class alone in a few hours. With the exception of Ellis Island and Angel Island in San Francisco Bay, port stations were not equipped to handle large numbers of people. Land borders were even less likely to be ready for large numbers of immigrants. Immigration employees tried to keep the new arrivals in order in a military fashion: having them line up, moving them quickly in single file, and barking orders at them. As they were waiting for inspections and examinations, the new arrivals were sometimes kept in prisonlike conditions: fenced in, kept in basements, or in locked facilities with barred windows. But such displays of state power could not contain the chaos of immigrants slipping in without the inspections, the improper classification of unrelated children traveling with an assumed "mother" under one passport, adults masquerading as children of identified travelers, men and women hiding in carriages or trains on the land border, and immigrants simply running away from the inspectors. Every border crossing presented its own set of challenges: the lack of manpower in the southwest and rural north, the sheer number of arrivals in New York, the mingling of natives with immigrants on ships from the Caribbean, and the difficulty (for Americans) of ascertaining the identity of Asian immigrants in the west. At all border crossings, their numbers and their cultural distance could work to the immigrants' advantage.[47]

Immigrants were only sometimes aware of these advantages. Only a few saw opportunity in the chaos and lack of supervision that often reigned. For the most part, immigrants valued meticulous preparation and self-presentation at the border. They had plotted their routes carefully to get this far; now they took care to appear respectable at the border. Steerage passengers put on their best clothes and presented officials with their possessions, deeds to land they held, and cash. They showed proof of social respectability: a marriage certificate, work books, certificates of professional qualifications.[48] This did not detract from the fact that most immigrants were understood to be working class, something the newcomers understood very well. Inspectors liked to admit working-class immigrants, as in these cases physical health was the all-important criterion. Men and women who stepped beyond their assigned class confines could run into trouble. If they traveled second class instead of steerage, this could get them around the Ellis Island inspection, but it could also render them suspicious as impostors, criminals, or people involved in the sex trades.[49]

The photographs of Augustus Sherman document this self-presentation magnificently, in part because the photographer himself took up the immigrants on their offerings and complemented them with his own staging: a dignified pose, lighting that emphasized the seriousness, even solemnity of the occasion, a display of the folk costume or the tools of the trade for some immigrants.[50] In the self-presentation, perceptions of race, gender, and morality represented treacherous shoals as immigrants faced officials. What constituted virtue and made for an unproblematic border crossing for women in the United States could be difficult to fathom for female immigrants. Japanese women sometimes arrived heavily powdered, a sign of status for them but an alarming characteristic for immigration officials, who considered such makeup a characteristic of prostitutes.[51] Women from the Caribbean sometimes seemed too richly dressed for their working-class status.[52] The countess Vera Cathcart flaunted her aristocratic origins and artistic interests to immigration officers in 1920s New York, who were not only turned off by her manner but also by her declaration that she was a "divorcee"; as a result, she was detained as a "loose woman" at Ellis Island.[53] Men faced different categorizations. A Scandinavian might be admitted with little money in his pockets, but a similar man from Italy or Greece would be scrutinized as a contract laborer, an illiterate, or a likely public charge.

Even though immigration officers prided themselves on their ability to decode the appearance of class and gender proper to the culture of origin, immigrants had to be active and alert as they faced the inspectors. The constraints of knowledge about America and their poverty limited their position, but their numbers, their informal networks of knowledge, and their social networks were a valuable counterbalance. Immigrants also knew that immigration stations varied enormously in their practices. Knowing the ins and outs of a specific border zone could be a critical aid to successful passage for immigrant women and men.

The East and Ellis Island

East Coast ports of entry dominated immigration politics because they processed so many newcomers every year. During the nineteenth century, almost all immigrants landed on the East Coast. Between 1900 and 1914 at least 90 percent of all officially enumerated immigrants to the United States entered through the ports of the Atlantic seaboard. During the same period, the vast majority (80 to 85 percent of those who arrived on the East Coast) entered through New York harbor. In fact, over the late nineteenth and early twentieth centuries, the importance of New York as an entry station increased, while the status of other northeastern ports of entry decreased markedly. This was the result of growing international and national transportation networks that favored New York as a hub with good connections to the rest of the United States. In other words, immigrants chose to arrive in New York because of convenient transportation schedules and lower ticket prices in the nineteenth and early twentieth centuries.

The ports of Boston, Philadelphia, and Baltimore offered immigrants some regional advantages. For example, kinship connections made the direct trip to Boston a preferred choice for Irish and some English emigrants. Portuguese and Italians flocked to the United States via New Bedford, Massachusetts, which offered jobs in fisheries, textiles, and transportation. Europeans were attracted to Philadelphia and Baltimore because of their relatively lax inspections—these ports of arrival had the lowest debarment rates among East

Coast harbors as well as the conveniences associated with smaller entry stations.[54]

Few immigrants tried to enter any southern ports except Florida. As for southern ports such as Savannah and Charleston, their sparse railroad connections to the hinterland, the laggard economic development of the southern states, and the lack of regular connections with Europe served as disincentives. Occasional attempts to systematically promote the immigration of Europeans, especially skilled workers to southern states, usually misfired: the arriving workers found working conditions and wages below their expectations; for their part, Immigration Bureau inspectors, originally in favor of diverting white immigrants to areas with little white immigration, were tipped off by the dissatisfied immigrants and moved against these attempts at "assisted immigration."[55] Immigrants arriving in Puerto Rico and Florida were usually not considered permanent immigrants in the early twentieth century; they became part of a permanent class of border crossers, who lived between nations with no aspirations to citizenship and permanence. Like Mexicans and Canadians, the Caribbean migrants were only occasionally and randomly scrutinized by officials of the Immigration Bureau.[56]

The place that symbolized the arrival station most poignantly to immigrants and observers was Ellis Island, New York's arrival station since the 1890s. The "Isle of Tears" stood for the painful transition into a new life, the fear of rejection, and the uncertainty and chaos surrounding the newly arrived. For immigration officials, too, Ellis Island set the tone for border administration. With its many employees and facilities, the Ellis Island immigration station became the place to forge a career in the service. It set the standard for practices of interpretation and border administration, and its head, the Commissioner of Immigration at the Port of New York, became by far the most influential official in the Bureau after the Commissioner General and, indeed, was occasionally more influential than his superior.[57] Decisions and ideas generated at Ellis Island set the norm for the Immigration Bureau during the early twentieth century.

Its size and the great number of immigrants also turned Ellis Island into a magnet for commercial interests as well as corruption, which accompanied the businesses trying to profit from immigration. Because the local commissioner was a political (presidential) appointee, the station easily, ended up in the hands of well-connected local bosses such as the Republican ward boss Thomas Fitchie (who served as Commissioner from 1896 to 1902); the bosses in turn doled out lucrative contracts (for food, transportation, and luggage delivery) and jobs to their friends. Extortion, graft, and outright swindling of immigrants were endemic at Ellis Island in 1900 and led to a large-scale investigation in 1902; nonetheless, problems continued for decades.[58] Commissioners, from the iron-fisted Wall Street lawyer William Williams to the more flexible William Watchorn and the reform advocate Frederick Howe, had to contend with shifting political winds in Washington, unwieldy rules, huge numbers of immigrants, and endemic corruption among lower level administrators on the island.[59]

Ellis Island was not only the largest arrival station but also had the most elaborate routine procedures for admitting immigrants (with the exception of Angel Island's screening of Asian immigrants). Up to 5,000 immigrants a day had to be processed in a system with many stages that had been designed to impress on immigrants the thoroughness of the federal inspection system and the powerlessness of the individual immigrant.[60] The inspection began with officers of the Immigration Bureau boarding each arriving ship for the quarantine inspection and a look at first-class and second-class passengers who—if everything was to the inspector's satisfaction—would not be subject to further inspection. After World War I, only first-class passengers were exempt. These more privileged passengers could then proceed directly to Manhattan on a barge, avoiding Ellis Island entirely. Class privilege, as expressed by the ability to pay a higher fare, thus trumped everything else in determining the admissibility of immigrants.[61]

Immigrants knew about the special treatment of first- and second-class passengers in New York (special treatment was not necessarily available elsewhere). Some would pay extra money for a first-class ticket in order to escape the close scrutiny of an investigation at Ellis Island. Others did not need to invest money to get first-class treatment. Twelve-year-old Clara Larsen remembered how she crossed the ocean as an unaccompanied girl to join her family in New York in 1913. Even though she was in steerage, she befriended a fellow Russian who was a second-class passenger. Before arrival, the Russian woman invited young Clara into her cabin because "I could get out there easier"; upon arrival in New York, "she took her luggage in one hand, and the other hand she gave me and we went all the way through like ladies."[62] Immigration inspectors were alert to such strategizing, and they were always on the lookout for immigrants whose visible class status did not seem to fit their first- or second-class ticket. Such immigrants were suspected of harboring hidden illness or, in the case of female travelers, of being prostitutes whose traffickers had paid for the tickets. Inspectors were free to order such suspect passengers to join the steerage passengers for inspection at Ellis Island, often much to the indignation of those singled out.[63]

The vast majority of passengers could not bypass Ellis Island because they had third-class or steerage tickets. They were ferried from their ship by a small cutter to the Immigration Station at Ellis Island after their initial quarantine inspection on board ship. All subsequent examinations took place on the island, most of them in the Great Arrival Hall. The entry to the Great Hall led up a large set of steep steps, which the new arrivals had to climb under the observation of immigration officials. Those who had trouble mounting these steps were marked for further examination of their health and ability to do physical labor. In the Great Hall, an overwhelming number of people greeted the new arrivals. "It was immense. To me it looked like it was everything; the whole world was there," remembered Estelle Schwarz of her arrival from Romania in 1910.[64]

Recent passengers were lined up for examination by officers of the Public Health Service, who checked all passengers against the catalogue of diseases that made immigrants ineligible for entry. The preferred method of this physical examination was what Amy Fairchild has called the "medical gaze," a brief survey by the physician-officer of an immigrant's scalp, eyes, and posture. Only the unfortunates singled out for further scrutiny were segregated into examination rooms; otherwise, the review took place in public, though men and women were separated.[65] The examiners did their work in near silence, the refusal of communication magnifying the passivity and powerlessness of the applicants. The most feared part of the physical examination, the inversion of the eyelid to check for trachoma, was done with near-brutal speed. Because trachoma was widespread in southern and eastern Europe, and was often transmitted on board ship and easily recognized, it was the reason for most medical exclusions. About one-half of 1 percent of arriving passengers nationwide were debarred from entry because of trachoma every year in the decade before World War I.[66]

Immigrants who failed the physical examination were kept at Ellis Island briefly and sent back with the first returning ship to their country of origin—unless they could gain the help of immigrant aid societies or family and appeal the exclusion decision from Ellis Island. Minnie Edelman remembered how her mother, detained at Ellis Island for an unspecified illness, was able to get released: "because my father worked with the HIAS [Hebrew Immigrant Aid Society], and finally the HIAS worked it out with the government, and my father posted a five hundred dollar bond. God forbid if she has to go back!"[67] Such cases were rare, and successful appeals were even rarer.[68] Rosa Semiana arrived at Ellis Island as a 71-year-old widow from Italy to live with her adult sons, both men of substance in New York's Italian community. Because of her supposed senility (a catchall phrase for physical frailty and disorientation), she was judged a likely public charge and debarred, despite the protests of her sons.[69] Special hardships awaited the families who were collectively sent back because one member of their family had trachoma or some other illness—a policy first initiated systematically at Ellis Island in 1910 and afterward made standard procedure nationwide.[70]

After the medical inspection, immigrants were grouped by ship and put in line for questioning by immigration inspectors. The information on the passenger manifests, recorded on board the ship by the ship's employees, was the only standard information available about arriving passengers, most of whom were not required to present a passport or other standardized identification from their country of origin before 1917.[71] The immigration inspectors checked the information on the manifest against the information the passengers provided under separate questioning, including age, name, family status, occupation, and destination. If there were any discrepancies, as there often were (as manifests could be wrong, arriving passengers could be confused, and translation problems could arise), they could lead to further interrogation.

The inspectors especially wanted to find out if the passengers had come to the United States with financial assistance from anyone besides family members and whether they would be able to earn a living in the United States. Groups of men (and more rarely groups of women) who traveled to the same destination without a sufficient amount of money in their pocket were often suspect under the contract labor law and were sometimes inspected by a special set of officials. Those with vague plans, few skills, and fewer dollars in their pockets were automatically considered candidates for exclusion under the likely public charge clause, the major reason for exclusion at Ellis Island and elsewhere.

After this second examination—often performed by a multilingual inspector, sometimes with the help of an interpreter—about 80 percent of the arriving passengers at Ellis Island were sent on their way to enter the United States. Another 20 percent or so underwent further examination before a Board of Special Inquiry consisting of three inspectors and an assistant. The vast majority of immigrants who had to appear before such a board were admitted, often after some further investigations and sometimes on bond. Altogether, only about 1.5 to 2.0 percent of newly arrived immigrants were debarred for any reason in New York in the early twentieth century, two-thirds of them as likely public charges.[72]

The low percentage of rejections did little to alleviate the immigrants' anxiety about the personal examination of their bodies and their lives at Ellis Island. Young Louis Adamic remembered that when he landed at Ellis Island on New Year's Eve of 1913 he "gradually worked up a panicky feeling that I might develop measles, or smallpox or some other such disease."[73] Many of the fears concerned the Board of Special Inquiry. The encounter with the inspectors on the board would determine an immigrant's entire future. In the interview, immigrants were mere applicants with few rights, while inspectors seemingly had the exclusive knowledge and the power to interpret the law. But immigrants were not completely without power and knowledge: there were ways to turn the crude categories of gender and family status employed by the Immigration Bureau to their advantage. Male immigrants were primarily inspected for their ability to earn a living through physical labor. Therefore, the appearance of health, and the willingness and ability to do physical labor were most important for male immigrants. Formal ties to organizations or individuals that might hinder an individual's success as an independent wage earner (labor contractors, groups that provided financial assistance with immigration, or radical political groups) were seen as serious impediments as well.[74]

Inspectors frequently racialized their inspection of male fitness. They often considered Jews doubtful candidates for physical work. In 1911, what the immigration authorities called "the Jewish Immigrant Society" at Ellis Island (HIAS) complained that immigration officials were systematically rejecting Jewish tailors as likely public charges on the grounds that tailoring was an overcrowded trade. But if Jewish tailors claimed to be laborers, they could also be rejected under the same clause because such workers were unskilled. If they claimed that jobs were waiting for them, contract labor charges led to exclusion. This situation was clearly designed to keep eastern European Jewish men from landing in New York. Italian and Greek men were often vulnerable to charges of being contract laborers and were sometimes excluded after flimsy investigations. These workers had to overcome officials' widespread prejudice that Mediterranean men were by nature dependent personalities.[75]

Women immigrants were admitted under different criteria: physical health mattered, especially for single women, but inspectors judged it in the context of women's "moral health." Social and economic support structures were of primary importance for the admissibility of women immigrants. This was most clearly visible if the women traveled without male family members. Helena Stucklen, an Ellis Island "matron" (or female supervisor), testified in 1899 before a Congressional commission that she was always on the lookout for pregnant women who traveled unaccompanied by a husband. This kind of discovery would almost certainly lead to exclusion as a likely public charge or as a person of "moral turpitude." A pregnant woman who expected a child from someone other than the man she was about to join could be admitted if the husband and wife "reconciled" before eyes of the officials, but only then could the woman land permanently. In other cases, single women were asked to marry their fiancé on the spot.[76] Unaccompanied women immigrants were usually held until their male family members arrived at Ellis Island to pick them up or until immigration officials were satisfied that a family was ready to receive and support them in the interior. A prepaid railroad ticket and the help of an immigrant aid society could replace the personal escort. Women who arrived with young children but had no obvious marriage partner with them or waiting for them were debarred, sometimes after many days of waiting at Ellis Island.[77]

Women traveling alone, even when not pregnant, were always vulnerable to suspicion of being immoral or a likely public charge without visible ties of family or community to keep them within the world of domesticity and morality. Many women tried to arrange their journey to evade this sort of suspicion by making specific travel arrangements or "disguising" themselves as domestics (even though they intended to work in factories). In the summer of 1908, a group of four young women from Austria-Hungary had planned their arrival in such a way as to not attract special attention from the Immigration Bureau. The young women, all from the same village, planned to settle in western Pennsylvania and work as domestics. They traveled with an escort, an older man who was a laborer from the same village and was returning from an extended visit back home to his residence in Pennsylvania. But to U.S. officials this arrangement looked suspicious. The American Consul in Fiume, Italy (their port of departure), alerted Ellis Island officials to the arrival of the small group "suspected of intended violation of the laws intended to govern and prevent the white slave traffic." An investigation by the Ellis Island officials revealed the women's perfectly ordinary migration story; though the man was sent back as a likely public charge because he had only $30 in his possession, and a 15-year-old girl was also debarred as a minor, the rest of the small group was admitted after a lengthy series of interviews. A full investigation a month after their admission did indeed find the women working as domestics and "all

respectable." Similar cases of women from eastern Europe who traveled in groups but without close family members were also pursued
by the Bureau, all with the same results. In a related case, the Immigration Bureau investigated the admission of a 35-year-old Sicilian
woman, whom immigration inspectors apparently considered too old
to work as a domestic as she claimed she would. When a subsequent
investigation into her life revealed that she had quit her domestic
employment and worked as a seamstress, inspectors were only satisfied after the woman brought character witnesses to testify to her
virtuous lifestyle.[78]

Immigrants could negotiate their entry as individuals or families,
as most did in the early twentieth century. Increasingly, in the years
leading up to World War I, organized intervention by immigrant advocacy organizations took the place of individual negotiations. The
German Society and some German Protestant charities had been active at the New York immigration station since the mid-nineteenth
century, finding work, housing, and occasionally charity care for
newcomers from Europe. Some of these groups also had a business
interest in providing aid, for their representatives steered immigrants
to boarding houses or work from which members would profit. At
least two investigations of the Bureau of Immigration uncovered
such activities at Ellis Island and led the Immigration Bureau to ban
some organizations from the station.[79]

By the early twentieth century, the traditional charity role of immigrant organizations was eclipsed by more open advocacy for the
newly arrived. In early 1903, the *New Yorker Staatszeitung,* beacon of
German American Republican respectability, led an investigation into
the discriminatory and rough treatment of immigrants. The Hebrew
Immigrant Aid Society (founded in 1904) and the German Society
protested the harsh conditions and discrimination faced by the newly
arrived immigrants from Europe. Lawyers, especially those working
for the HIAS and the Union of American Hebrew Congregations,
remained concerned about random exclusions and discriminatory
enforcement.[80] In September 1909, the editor of the *Jewish Morning
Journal* led an antidiscrimination campaign that soon involved the
editors of major newspapers for Bohemians, Hungarians, Italians,
and Polish immigrants. The immigrant advocates' focus was Ellis

Island Commissioner Williams's policy of denying admission to all immigrants whose American relatives had prepaid their passage (they were excluded as "assisted immigrants") unless they could somehow prove that they could have paid for the tickets themselves but had elected not to do so. The newspapers also criticized an openly enforced minimum of $25.00 in cash that every arriving adult had to possess in order to be admitted.[81]

Commissioner Williams, to the chagrin of his superiors in Washington, brushed off the immigrant advocates and refused to change his policies. As the campaign to have Williams removed from office continued for the next two years, the congressional Committee on Rules passed a resolution condemning these Ellis Island practices and held hearings on the matter in the summer of 1911.[82] Despite fiery speeches from German American Republicans, Williams kept his job for two more years. He resigned in 1913 after the election of Woodrow Wilson.[83]

For the next ten years, as Ellis Island was administered by commissioners whose restrictionist leanings were less obvious, the island continued to be the focus of much national attention as hundreds of thousands of European immigrants arrived before and after World War I, and immigration officials had to administer ever more complex exclusion laws. The power of the Ellis Island officials increased with the institution of the literacy test in 1917. The beginning of the quota era, however, spelled the decline of their power, as the most important admission decisions shifted away from Ellis Island and into the offices of consuls abroad.

The North: Canada

At the turn of the twentieth century, if Ellis Island and other eastern seaboard ports represented the crowded urban side of the immigrant nation, the long Canadian land border stood for the vastness of the American frontier. The physical border between Canada and the United States was fixed by various treaties between the Dominion of Canada (also called British North America in immigration statistics) and the United States. For much of the continent, the northern border was (and is) marked by the 49th parallel, a line agreed upon by statesmen and military commanders in the eighteenth and nineteenth centuries that had little relevance to most people's lives until the twentieth century. Just as the earthen mounds that marked the border along the prairie could be washed away in a strong rain, so the border itself could be invisible or imperceptible to those who lived alongside it.[84] But migration was an ever-present part of this frontier. "The United States and Canada have been spilling great waves of men and women into each other's territories," observed historian Marcus Hansen in 1938; "here is a continent where international boundaries have been disregarded by restless humans for almost two centuries."[85] Canadians and Americans would cross the border to work in the United States for a season, a day, or the rest of their lives, in patterns that varied throughout the nineteenth century. Economic cycles and the seasons influenced these flows back and forth, not political power or legal changes.

For much of the nineteenth century, this cross-border flow attracted little political attention. It was not until the 1890s that the U.S. government instituted regular controls for everyone entering from Canada. By that point, the intermingling of populations across the border had assumed a more one-sided character than in earlier decades, as the emigration from the Maritime provinces, Quebec, and Ontario far outnumbered the migration northward from the United States. Better prospects awaited Canadians in the labor markets of New England and the industrializing Midwest than in the Canadian borderlands.[86] At the same time, the overseas migration into Canada was increasing as a result of good transatlantic ship connections and the conscious attempts of the Canadian government to further European immigration into the Dominion. Many Europeans arrived in Newfoundland, Halifax, Montreal, or Ottawa, then continued on to the United States by rail, crossing the border at Vermont or Michigan. Canada and the Canadian U.S. border had changed character by the end of the century, for the Dominion had become a country of transit migration from Europe as well as a country of emigration for residents of the Maritime provinces.[87]

Concerned about the prospect of nearly unchecked immigration via Canada, the U.S. Immigration Bureau negotiated a bilateral agreement in 1894 with the Canadian railroad companies that were bringing immigrants from Canada to the United States. This was a crucial step in the attempt to move the admission to the United States away from the physical border with Canada. Legal admission to the United States would happen according to American law but on Canadian soil. The contract with the Canadian railroads held that passengers destined for the United States but landing at Canadian ports could land only if they were admitted by both Canadian and U.S. authorities. In practice, this meant that at the port of arrival (Halifax, St. John, Montreal, or Quebec City) immigrants were first inspected by Canadian health officials and then by inspectors of the U.S. Public Health Service for excludable illnesses and "defects." Canadian authorities also noted immigrants' origins, age, family status, and intended destination. If immigrants were destined for the United States, the Canadians forwarded a separate copy of their ship manifest to U.S. immigration inspectors in Montreal or other railroad hubs from where trains departed for the United States. The costs of this extra screening were borne by both the Canadian railroads and the Canadian government.[88]

Transit migrants faced a second border crossing as they boarded the trains that would take them to their U.S. destinations. Here the "class A immigrants" (as transit migrants to the United States were called by American officials) would be joined by other groups, such as the men and women who had arrived from Europe weeks, months, or even years earlier as well as native Canadians who were also migrating to the United States. At the railroad departure point, inspectors of the U.S. Bureau of Immigration examined the immigrants to see if they belonged to any of the excluded classes. Other groups were merely asked about the length of their stay in Canada and if they turned out to be only short-term residents of the Dominion, they were also inspected for possible exclusion from the United States.

The number of class A immigrants who were rejected at the Canadian railroad station was low; after all, they already had been inspected at their (Canadian) port of arrival, according to U.S. law.[89] On the other hand, immigrants who had spent some time in Canada but were still considered Europeans had a higher rejection rate than almost any other group of border crossers: between 8 and 14 percent of immigrants from Canada were debarred at the border between 1900 and 1921. Only after the Immigration Bureau had approved the prospective immigrants before their departure from Canada did the Canadian railroad companies sell tickets to these passengers to enter the United States. All passengers were once again checked (against the original ship's manifest) at the U.S.-Canadian border town (St. Albans, Vermont, for example), but this examination was usually superficial. This triple-inspection system reflected the U.S. authorities' desire to strengthen border controls but to do so in a place invisible to the American public and with a minimum of additional costs. By moving the border into a foreign territory, the system also minimized the help immigrants could get from immigrant aid societies or kin.[90]

The new system had some weak points: Canadians and long-term residents of Canada were not rigorously inspected, and the Immigration Bureau's system only caught those who were willing to declare their intentions openly. Assumptions about race and the general fitness of Canadians to fit into the United States as future citizens also limited the Immigration Bureau's attention to Canadian immigrants. For example, U.S. authorities were quite fixated on catching illegal Chinese immigrants at the northern border and employed special personnel to look for them. The Bureau viewed all of the 28,000 Chinese residents of Canada as potential future immigrants to the United States. "A task of gigantic proportions" is what the Chinese Inspector for the Canadian border called the perceived threat of Asian migration in 1913.[91] On the other hand, officials were unable to sort other migrants across the northern borders into neat categories, for often the passengers themselves were vague about their plans or had changed their minds. During the first years, the network of inspection also only extended from Halifax to Toronto. From the mid-1890s to 1908 the Bureau expanded, establishing inspection stations all along the Canadian border. But a border that spanned many thousands of miles still had countless holes that immigrants could pass through without encountering border inspectors, only 180 in all, who were stationed all the way from Newfoundland to Vancouver.[92]

Immigrants to the United States were aware of the peculiarities of the Canadian border and the special problems of crossing it. But the northern border also held some advantages for European immigrants. British immigrants could relatively easily disguise themselves as Canadians entering the United States as their accents and "ethnic characteristics" made them indistinguishable for the American officials. Labor agencies also operated relatively undisturbed across the border well into the 1920s and even the 1930s. Special exemptions existed for domestic servants and nurses brought in on contract from Canada.[93]

As with Mexican migration in the south, both a tradition of cross-border migration by Canadians and Americans and strong economic interests on both sides continued to make the border porous in the decades after 1915. Migrants, even if they came from distant parts of Europe, knew this and used it to their advantage to negotiate their border crossing: they became "Canadian," or at least Canadian residents, or crossed the border undetected altogether. In 1914, the Immigration Bureau counted only about 45,000 immigrants who were Canadian or long-time residents of Canada, though an immigration inspector commented that well over 50,000 men and women crossed the Canadian border without inspection by taking ferries to the United States on which no inspection occurred.[94] In an acknowledgment of such realities, the Immigration Bureau introduced the category of "non-statistical immigrants" for Canadian border crossers in 1915, just as it had on the Mexican border. Nonstatistical immigrants were not considered permanent migrants or possible future citizens of the United States. Even though these men and women had crossed the national border into the United States, their arrival was classified as something less than an entry of immigrants.[95]

The easy border crossing for Canadians and those who managed to pass as Canadians carried a price. As the stay of many border migrants lengthened and turned into a permanent life in the United States, many would lack the needed documents to legalize their residence—a problem that also surfaced if Canadians wanted to become naturalized U.S. citizens. The Immigration Bureau had to grapple with this question hundreds of times, especially in the 1920s and 1930s as long-time residents from Canada sought naturalization. In the end, naturalization law favored those who had submitted to the rigidities of crossing at the first and second borders in a documented fashion, while it disadvantaged the border dwellers and frequent border crossers.[96]

In contrast to the busy border stations on the East Coast, the Canadian border with its spread-out and often isolated border stations and low levels of immigration was a relative backwater. Its dual character as a land border crossed by both overseas immigrants and neighbors reflected the dilemmas the U.S. government faced: increased political pressures for tighter and comprehensive border control in tension with a readily available supply of immigrant labor from across the border. It was up to individual immigrants themselves to negotiate which slot they would try to fill. Often they had the choice between submitting to strict border controls and screenings or crossing the border as undocumented, nonstatistical immigrants with little immediate risk but problems in the long term. Such dilemmas would characterize immigrant entry for much of the rest of the twentieth century at all land borders of the United States.

The Mexican Border

In contrast to the Canadian border, the Mexican border was a more openly contested space, especially in the nineteenth century. The 1848 Treaty of Guadalupe Hidalgo fixed new borders between the two nations and turned all Mexican inhabitants of the newly incorporated territories of the Southwest into U.S. citizens.[97] Much of the new border line ran through empty and arid lands, though some of it also cut across cities such as Nogales, a settlement older than the nations that divided it.[98] To Mexicans and indigenous Indians, the U.S. government's attempt in the nineteenth century to impose a border and regularize its crossing seemed irrelevant and intrusive. It had little impact on the lives of the men and women whose economic and social ties stretched overland across the two nations and whose culture and language was the same on both sides.[99]

In general, the Southwest remained a backwater for the rest of the nineteenth century, different from the major ports of entry for immigrants into the United States. The physical markings of the border were neglected, administrative infrastructure was weak, and U.S. officials had a quasi-colonial relation to migrants. In the late nineteenth century, the border with Mexico was considered peripheral to national concerns and immigration policies.[100]

However, the economic development of the border zone changed rapidly on both sides in the early twentieth century. Railroads entered the Texas, Arizona, and Southern California borderland: by 1900, Laredo was served by five railroad lines from the north. Ciudad Juárez, the only Mexican border city with railroad connections to central Mexico at that time, was also developing fast. With the railroads came the need for unskilled labor, first on the railroad itself and soon thereafter in the diversifying agriculture of southern Texas. As a result, Laredo, Brownsville, and El Paso became centers for labor migration from the south.[101]

Mexico itself was in the throes of early industrialization, which brought displacement of small farmers and urbanization to some parts of the country. The Mexican government encouraged immigration from overseas in the early twentieth century to help along these developments. But compared with the United States, the country offered limited economic opportunities to newcomers. As a result, Mexico became a transmigration area for immigrants from Europe, the Middle East, and Asia, some of whom stayed in Mexico, others of whom were trying to cross into the United States. By 1910, Mexico was a country of immigration and emigration. The Immigration Bureau investigated the transmigration through Mexico in 1906 and after, and found networks of organized migrant smuggling throughout the Southwest, serving both Chinese (and later Japanese as well) and Middle Eastern migrants. None of these migrations was large, but they made a reorganization of border control politically more urgent.[102]

Reform proved to be difficult. The absence of inspectors, facilities, and infrastructure made it impossible for U.S. officials to maintain much of a presence at the border. Salaries were too modest to induce even the lowliest watchmen to sign up with the federal government, and physicians and inspectors who knew Spanish were nearly impossible to find, especially if they needed to be recruited from the list of those who had passed the civil service examinations. Geographic and social isolation, and the lack of career opportunities added to these problems and furthered corruption at southwestern border stations.[103]

From 1891 to 1907, the entire Mexican border formed one district of the Immigration Bureau with its headquarters in El Paso. In July 1907, this gigantic territory was divided into two districts: distict 23, with headquarters in San Antonio (with jurisdiction over western Texas, all of New Mexico and Arizona, and Southern California), and district 9, with headquarters in Galveston (with jurisdiction over east Texas and the Gulf Coast).[104] Because east Texas and the Gulf Coast had relatively little immigration from Mexico, district 9 with its newly appointed head, F. W. Berkshire, administered virtually all Mexican immigration. Berkshire tried to establish a system of inspections and border administration modeled on the East Coast, but the huge territory and lack of resources made this a Sisyphean task. Berkshire, admitted openly in 1913 that many immigrants were never recorded when they crossed the border.

Like their counterparts at the Canadian border, many Mexican border crossers were not counted as immigrants. "Because of the peculiar, and, it may be said, unparalleled conditions obtaining along the Mexican border, most of the Mexicans who crossed this border fall within a class known as non-statistical," Berkshire wrote in his contribution to the 1913 *Annual Report*.[105] Immigration officials thought that about 80 percent of those who entered the United States from Mexico were in this class. Such immigrants were considered to be temporary sojourners who had no interest in settling in the United States and becoming U.S. citizens. Mexican immigrants were marked from the beginning as falling outside the trajectory that led from the physical border crossing to the social and eventually political integration into the United States as citizens.

An alternative to a tightly controlled territorial border, the externalization of immigration control according to the Canadian model, was also attempted by the U.S. government in the Mexican case. But unlike Canada, Mexico was slow to build a cohesive and effective administrative state backed by a functioning central government. Economic dislocation brought political unrest and then revolution and civil war during the early decades of the twentieth century. A tradition of aggressive regional expansionism on the U.S. side also meant that Mexican authorities did not see the Americans as "partners" in administering the border. In turn, federal authorities considered the Mexican borderlands wild and anarchic, especially during the years of the Mexican revolution (1912–1918) and the ensuing civil war. It comes as no surprise then that the U.S. government's attempt to negotiate a Canadian-style agreement with the Mexican state railroads failed. The lack of functioning allies within the Mexican government was a source of great anxiety to the Immigration Bureau, which considered Mexico to be a wide open gateway for racially and economically undesirable immigration.[106]

Judging from the reports of U.S. officials and the lively cross-border economy that emerged, especially in the years of the Mexican revolution and World War I, we can conclude that migration from Mexico to the U.S. was considerable but that most of it was unrecorded, nonstatistical, and (by later definition) illegal. A 1907 report of Immigration Inspector Andre Seraphic showed how undocumented border crossings (at border stations) could work. Seraphic, who looked Mediterranean to his contemporaries, posed as a Mexican laborer when he entered the United States. Immigration inspectors treated him like any other Mexican border crosser: they ignored him and waved him through. Nobody noticed that he apparently spoke no Spanish. Seraphic also described border crossers who walked across the international bridge in El Paso and were never searched or inspected, and those who forded a river nearby while being waved through by officials from the bridge above. Inspectors were unlikely to step out, away from a warm fire or a nap in the middle of the night. Seraphic also noted the kinds of corrupt officials who helped undocumented border crossers: physicians who were alcoholics, Arabic interpreters who spoke little or no Arabic, and officials who could be bribed to ease the passage or were so incompetent as to make bribes superfluous. Arriving passengers who came to the Brownsville station at night were told to come back in the morning, but inspectors might also let them through if they looked clean enough and ask them to come back the next day for the health inspection.[107]

The reports about the dismal state of inspections on the Mexican border attracted no wide attention (unlike the conditions at Ellis Island or the arrival of Chinese in San Francisco). But by World War I, with the Mexican civil war and refugee migration at its height, the Immigration Bureau and the U.S. Public Health Service attempted to tighten control by introducing a system of health inspections at some southwestern border stations in 1916. For the immigrants who submitted to these inspections (because they wanted an official record of their entry), the inspection and screening were quite invasive: officials disinfected immigrants' luggage, made immigrants disrobe and take showers, and—if officials suspected lice—shaved their heads or had their scalps "bathed" in a kerosene solution. Public Health Service physicians then examined everyone for diseases and "defects." While these routines resembled the inspections at Ellis Island and in San Francisco, southwestern immigration stations did not have the hospital or clinic facilities found on the coasts. Mexicans were sometimes held in cellars of the (often small) immigration stations or in rooms that resembled pens while this health inspection occurred. Officials took great pains to separate Asian from non-Asian immigrants during the inspections. First-class passengers (on trains) were exempt from these procedures. In addition to the health check, Mexicans were also interviewed and had to pay a head tax. At $8.00 the head tax was low but for poor Mexicans it represented a considerable cash outlay. Beginning in 1917, officials also administered a literacy test.[108]

Interviews could be quite detailed in some cases, rivaling those at Ellis Island, at least according to the preserved records of the Immigration Bureau. Prospective immigrants were asked about their background, their plans to earn a living, and their intended residence. Inspectors wanted to know, for example, if a relative really did have enough space to put up extra family members in a two-bedroom house. What were the plans for the children's schooling? The records of detailed examinations show that inspectors decided on Mexicans' ability to earn a living from their physical appearance; class and race also were important factors in this assessment. "Applicants are part of the better classes of Mexico" noted officers with approval in certain cases.

The concept of class was a flexible one and used differently on the Mexican border from elsewhere. Guadalupe and Manuel Munoz presented themselves at the El Paso Station in 1918. Guadalupe was only 13 years old and her brother was 21, and they stated that they were orphans destined for their uncle's home on the American side of the border. A detailed examination showed that Manuel had no skills and only $2.00 in his pocket; he and his sister expected to live with their uncle in a two-room house. These circumstances might have prevented a European immigrant from landing on the East Coast, but in this case, the inspectors were impressed by the siblings' well-dressed appearance. The girl looked well cared for, and apparently both brother and sister were articulate. Manuel had already checked out his future home that morning before present-ing himself to the inspectors, and even though "we did not talk about work because it was Sunday," he expected to find a job with his uncle. It took a bit of coaxing to get them to agree that the girl would go to school and not work. The inspectors let the two young people in.[109]

Officers were also interested in the racial origins of immigrants. Chinese and Japanese illegal immigration occupied much of their time in the early decades of the twentieth century. The smuggling of Syrian immigrants and their racial status as below that of Mexicans was also subject to discussion.[110] Immigration officers noted when people who called themselves Mexican did not appear to be so. "What is this name Lyncet?" they asked Salvador Lyncet, a young man at Nogales in the winter of 1917. When the immigrant answered that it was a French name but that he was Mexican, the officers wanted to know more: "How much French blood do you have?" "I suppose that I am of the French race but I am a citizen of Mexico" was the answer recorded. Mexican was a political designation this immigrant ac-cepted, but he did not dispute the inspectors' insistence on making him racially a European.[111]

The intentions of the Mexican border crossers were also important to officers. A plan to stay permanently in the United States was not necessarily a positive sign for Mexicans as it was for Europeans. When Carmen Moctezuma and her nephew Alfonso arrived in Laredo in February 1918, she could produce ample tuition money for the child and made a good impression on the inspectors, who noted that the family had some assets in Mexico. It was not important that she had lived in the United States before and had a house in Laredo; rather, her declaration that she had no plans to live permanently in the United States and had no intention of becoming a U.S. citizen swayed the officers in favor of admitting them. Impermanence, always a negative factor when it came to judging Europeans, worked in favor of Mexicans. Their future fitness as American citizens was not at stake if they merely wanted to stay in the United States for a limited time.[112]

The border examinations showed a much higher rejection rate for Mexican immigrants than for those who arrived on the Atlantic Coast. About 10 percent of the inspected Mexicans were debarred, usually because they were considered likely public charges or because they failed the health examination. Undocumented migration was the silent, anonymous way around the likely exclusion for those who were unwilling or unable to pass inspection, pay the head tax, and pass the literacy test yet were able-bodied and had the necessary information to make the crossing clandestinely.[113]

Another way across the border for Mexicans was to enter as contract laborers. Since 1911, Mexicans had crossed the border with the help of officially approved labor contractors for railroad companies, which were exempted from the Foran Act. During World War I, railroad companies and large agricultural growers successfully lobbied the Secretary of Labor to authorize the suspension of the literacy test and other restrictions for Mexicans who entered as contract workers.[114] Growers continued to import temporary workers from Mexico unhindered by border screening until 1921. Immigration inspectors, who were charged with facilitating rather than controlling this migration, counted more than 21,000 temporary laborers from Mexico in 1919 alone. They noted that about half of those who applied for contract labor permits were illiterate. The early contract labor programs dulled the effectiveness of the literacy test and high head tax as restrictionist tools at the Mexican border.[115]

The high percentage of Mexicans who made undocumented border crossings or came as contract laborers had fateful long-term consequences for the Mexican immigrant community in the United States. Temporary worker programs and undocumented migration favored the border crossing of able-bodied young men with little intention of staying in the United States permanently. The U.S. government's expectation was that these migrants would not truly leave their homeland behind, would never become American in any sense, and, most importantly, would never turn into U.S. citizens. No Mexican immigrant support organizations existed at the border during the first two decades of the twentieth century. Mexican American immigration lawyers were also rare. Support networks were largely limited to smuggling operations and over time to commercial interests that wanted to gain regular access to large numbers of Mexican laborers regardless of literacy tests, head taxes, or other qualifications.

The Western Border

The western border of the United States received the most diverse immigrant populations, and its border stations were part of highly varied regional contexts. The southern part was sparsely populated and resembled the U.S.-Mexican border elsewhere. Smuggling of goods and people flourished, and supervision at land crossings was minimal. As district 23 Commissioner Frank Berkshire, whose jurisdiction included Southern California, stated dryly in 1910, "incompetence, inefficiency and a lack of system and organization was rife in this territory."[116] North of San Diego, the western border was administered in four separate districts: San Francisco, Honolulu, Portland, and Washington (which included the border stations of Port Townsend/Seattle, Portland, Victoria, British Colombia, and later Ketchikan, Alaska). The northwestern part of the border was the entry point for a mixture of native-born Canadians, Europeans, and Asians. Smuggling and illegal entry were a perpetual concern for immigration officers just as they were in the Southwest.[117] But the largest number of immigrants entered the West through San Francisco and Honolulu. Honolulu received primarily immigrants and contract laborers from East Asia, and Asian immigration (and its exclusion) also dominated the agenda at Seattle and San Francisco.[118]

The western border had far fewer immigrants than other parts of the country. In 1907, about 8,000 immigrants (out of a total of over 1.28 million) entered through the Pacific ports of the mainland and

24,000 in Hawaii. An additional 1,400 were admitted via the Pacific borders in Canada (mainly through Vancouver). Over the coming years, the percentage of immigrants who entered via the Pacific Coast stayed below 10 percent, although in 1920 it was a bit higher. The actual number of immigrants who arrived in the West was higher than the officially recorded number because so many Chinese immigrants entered as "paper sons" (that is, as U.S. citizens) and were therefore not counted as immigrants.[119]

The political and administrative focus of the western border was on Asian exclusion. Asian exclusion gave these border stations a unified purpose, political weight in Washington, and relatively ample budgets. In 1915, for example, Ellis Island spent an average of $1.30 per immigrant, but Portland, Oregon, had $8.70 per immigrant in its budget. San Francisco—processing over 13,000 immigrant applicants the same year—still had over $3.30 per immigrant to spend.[120] The officials who worked at western ports of arrival were united by a mission of exclusion. At least in the first decade of the twentieth century, San Francisco immigration officials were selected for their jobs because of their closeness to the anti-Chinese movement.[121] At the Seattle station, too, inspectors were openly anti-Asian and made no attempt at impartiality. These officials spent most of their time on investigative work that focused on verifying the background information of Asian applicants for admission.

But, unlike at the Eastern border, expertise did not mean knowledge of Chinese, Japanese, or local Asian communities. Instead, detailed knowledge of legal and administrative precedents regarding Asian exclusion and investigative and interrogation techniques were most valued. None of the western inspectors had traveled to Asia or investigated conditions of emigration.[122] Stations hired bilingual personnel only as translators, and they often treated them with suspicion. Only one of the San Francisco translators, John Endicott Gardner, the son of a Chinese immigrant mother and an American father, was eventually promoted from translator to "translator inspector," a position he retained despite accusations of being pro-Chinese and too lenient.[123]

Among the western border stations, the port of San Francisco had special significance. Of all entry points in the West, it had the highest number of immigrants; it was the focus of Asian immigration to North America and the center of the anti-Chinese movement in the United States. San Francisco was second only to Ellis Island in its reputation as an example of efficient immigration control and expertise during the Progressive Era. Because the city had a sizable Chinese and a Japanese community, a growing network of ethnic organizations, and a Chinese and a Japanese consulate, Asian immigrants had institutional resources to help them fight for their right to enter the United States.[124]

In the first decades of their arrival, Chinese immigrants in San Francisco did not receive different treatment from that accorded to Europeans. Before the 1870s, the new arrivals from China were no more monitored by representatives of the U.S. government than Europeans. But in contrast to Europeans, the Chinese were not free to leave San Francisco and find work wherever they wanted after they had been admitted. As ticket credit travelers, they had no choice but to remain within the Chinese merchant community to which they were beholden until the debts for their passage had been paid off.[125] After passage of the anti-coolie law and the Page Law, customs officials were supposed to examine Chinese arrivals, though their examinations did not cut down perceptibly on the rate of admissions. Special "Chinese inspectors," also working for the Treasury Department, were put in charge of the arrivals from East Asia after the passage of the Chinese Exclusion Act in 1882 until 1893, when these special officers began to work within the newly formed Immigration Bureau.[126]

Inspection of immigrants at San Francisco occurred in the context of segregation by race and gender. After the on-board quarantine inspection of arriving passengers, U.S. officials separated them: European first-class passengers and white Americans did not have to go through inspection off the boat. Other European immigrants who arrived directly from overseas were examined much like European immigrants on the East Coast. Most of them were released after a brief stay of a few hours, a medical examination, and a brief interview. Only a few were detained at the immigration station for a few days. May Zhouyi remembered that when she landed in 1903 "Europeans, Japanese, Koreans were allowed to disembark almost immediately. Even blacks were greeted by relatives and are allowed to go ashore. Only we Chinese were not allowed to talk to our loved ones and were escorted by armed guards to the wooden house."[127] After the 1907 Gentlemen's Agreement, this missionary wife would have shared her detention with Japanese and Koreans, who by then were also routinely detained. The separation of Asian newcomers from whites occurred regardless of the citizenship status of the new arrivals. San Francisco and other western ports did not distinguish between U.S. citizens and immigrants; officials made their inspection entirely according to racial criteria.

In the late nineteenth and early twentieth centuries, the inspection of Asian arrivals took place in the warehouse of the Pacific Mail Company, which the Immigration Bureau rented for this purpose. This shed also served as a detention facility for Asian immigrants, often for more than the one hundred it was built to accommodate.[128] John Jeong remembered his detention there in 1900: "I had to stay in the place on the pier for about two weeks . . . There was a big room there for everyone to sleep in. And then a big eating hall with long tables. I remember we ate our meals standing up." Chronic overcrowding and lengthy detentions led to illness and protests from the detainees.[129] Except for a quarantine station (already at Angel Island), the San Francisco immigration station had no other permanent facilities until 1910, when it moved to a new set of buildings on Angel Island. There, facilities were less crowded and primitive than at the Pacific Mail shed, though immigration officials began to complain in the early 1920s that the buildings were fire traps and inadequate in the long run.[130]

The new buildings enabled the Immigration Bureau to hold immigrants longer, often months, as the federal authorities examined, questioned, screened, and researched the background of all Asian immigrants to determine their eligibility for residence in the United States as merchants, wives of merchants, students, or U.S. citizens.[131] Unlike Ellis Island, the immigration station at Angel Island was primarily a detention facility, as Asian immigrants knew full well. One anonymous detainee remembered in a poem:

> Our ship docked,
> and we were transferred to a solitary island . . .
> Built firmly as the Great Wall

Room after room are but jails,
And the North Gate firmly locked.[132]

Although detention lasted only a few days for most arriving Asian passengers, for a minority of immigrants from China and Japan it could last for weeks or months, especially for Chinese suspected of being paper sons. In the isolated setting, Chinese and Japanese immigrants had to press their claim to land in the United States away from family, immigrant organizations, and lawyers. Katherine Maurer, deaconess of the Methodist Episcopal Missionary Home of San Francisco, was the only outsider allowed on the island for decades. She provided necessities, mailed letters, and occasionally missionized. Later, visitors from the city's Chinese YMCA were also admitted. But by and large, Asian immigrants at Angel Island led the lives of prisoners who were confined to their barracks most of the time, guarded by watchmen.[133]

For most Asian arrivals, the stay at Angel Island began with a physical examination. In contrast to Ellis Island where this was a quick line inspection with only specially marked cases separated for a secondary health inspection, immigrants at Angel Island were thoroughly examined in a clinic-like setting. The "medical gaze" was not sufficient for Asian immigrants.[134] Stool samples (to check for parasitic infections) and a detailed look at the undressed immigrant were part of the routine. "The doctor told us to take off everything," remembered one immigrant, "really though, it was humiliating. The Chinese never expose themselves like that. They checked you and checked you. We never get used to that kind of thing".[135] The embarrassment was particularly great for Asian women, who were even less used to disrobing than males. Medical examinations with laboratory tests meant at least an overnight stay. Until 1917, parasitic infections were considered incurable and reason for deportation, although some immigrants were allowed to stay for treatment.[136]

After the medical inspection came the interview with an immigration inspector (after 1918, before a Board of Special Inquiry) to establish an Asian person's right to land in the United States. In the early years, it could take months until inspectors were ready to hear a case. The hearing was the most important part of the border crossing from the perspective of both Asian immigrants and immigration officials. The inspectors had already classified and detained immigrants by race, and they were prepared to exclude the newcomers according to specific racial exclusions—as Chinese prostitutes or Japanese laborers, for example. For many Asian immigrants (especially men), a successful interview had to establish an identity beyond race: as a U.S.-born Asian American, a son of Chinese Americans, a Filipino national, or a wife of an American citizen. This was the interview that Asian migrants so carefully prepared for before they left their homeland.

Chinese applicants in San Francisco had to make a case that they were either merchants exempt from the Chinese Exclusion Act, or that they were in fact not Chinese immigrants but U.S. citizens. Often the interrogation focused on the Chinese American family ties of applicants who claimed to be American because they had American fathers. Two family members (father and son, but sometimes husband and wife) were interviewed separately and asked the same detailed questions. If the family ties were legitimate, the answers were expected to be the same. Mr. Low remembered how he was asked "my name, village, population of the village, number of houses in the village lane, the neighbors living up and down the lane and their occupations."[137] Sometimes the questions went into absurd detail: "They even asked me where the rice bin was kept. Can you imagine? If your father had said the left side and the son the right side, that won't do," remembered a Chinese man who arrived in 1927.[138]

Because the interviews of both the American relative (who was asked to appear on Angel Island or was interviewed at another immigration station elsewhere in the United States) and the Chinese immigrant were so detailed, both immigrants and sponsors, fearful of making a mistake, memorized "coaching books" during the lengthy passage across the Pacific and during their detention at Angel Island. Officials were always on the lookout for these books, with Chinese employees who worked in the kitchen on Angel Island being perennial suspects as smugglers of such notes.[139]

Asian immigrants who tried to enter as a merchant needed to submit so-called "section six certificates," from the American consulate in China, to support their claim. These certificates were examined in detail at Angel Island. If they were judged to be authentic and representative of the immigrants' status, merchants were not subjected to further examination. But if there were any doubts about their authenticity or the background of their bearers, witnesses (preferably non-Chinese) were called in, and the interrogation centered on the merchants' status as businessmen, their financial capital, and other signs of their social class. Especially at the larger ports such as San Francisco or Honolulu, immigration officials delved into the business relationships among Asian merchants at the port, called Chinese witnesses, and maintained a certain level of expertise on Asian immigrant businesses. In Honolulu and Seattle inspectors tried to cultivate local contacts to help them in their investigations. Immigration officials were interested only in "high class" merchants, those with international connections and contacts with non-Chinese business communities. Small businessmen had much more difficulty winning recognition as bona fide merchants.[140]

It was the immigration inspectors' examination of such transnational and transracial business connections that became a problem when Filipino immigrant Fernando Villareal tried to be admitted as a merchant in 1913. Villareal had brought with him a section six certificate issued by the U.S. consul in Manila. In interviews, it turned out that Villareal had connections within the Chinese-Filipino community in Manila and had been involved in various small business ventures there. But none of these activities seems to have resulted in contacts with the Chinese or Filipino community in San Francisco, as the Immigration Bureau could not locate any of the required character witnesses. On the other hand, Villareal had also worked as a tailor and was apparently skilled in this profession. This doomed his application as a merchant. Immigration officials considered Villareal's manual skill a sign of his status as a "laborer." As in other Chinese merchant cases, a past as a manual laborer, however skilled, led to automatic exclusion. In contrast to East Coast European immigrants, who often had an advantage if they could demonstrate a past as skilled workers, Chinese merchants had to demonstrate the absence of such skill in order to be admitted. Immigration inspectors used their ideas of class (a rich wardrobe, light skin, fine handwriting, and—for women—bound feet) to determine merchant status. Villa-real failed to persuade officials of his standing as a member of the merchant middle class.[141]

For Asian women, gender discrimination added formidable hurdles to Asian admission. Beginning in 1882, Chinese women could only gain admission if their husbands were U.S. citizens, students, or merchants. Between 1924 and 1930, only merchant wives were admitted, although successful litigation reestablished the admissibility of wives of Chinese Americans thereafter. Therefore, inspectors always determined the status of a woman's husband before the interrogation about a woman's admission could even begin. If a husband did not appear, could not be found by the Immigration Bureau, or was found inadmissible, his wife had no chance of admission. If husband and wife were both present, they were interviewed separately; no contact was allowed before the Bureau had made its final decision. This contrasted with the interviews of married couples on the East Coast, where the partners were interviewed together.

The central point of the interrogation of husband and wife was the legitimacy of their marriage and the nature of their domestic life. Domesticity was defined by Western notions of household chores and husband-and-wife intimacy, and the interrogation also tried to establish a shared life history of the partners. This was a difficult standard to meet for many Chinese and Japanese women at Angel Island. Chinese families had often been separated for years, if not decades; life circumstances had changed for the women at home, and the interviews would then depict a different reality in the memory of husband and wife. Helen Wong Hong married her husband, a long-time Fort Wayne resident from the same Chinese village, at age 18 and arrived with him at Angel Island shortly afterward, around 1937. "They asked all kinds of questions about the type of stove we used in the village, how many tiles on the floor, even how many steps in the stairs. I had lived in Hong Kong all those years and didn't remember anything about the village. They asked us where you lived, where is the kitchen, and your lineage going back generations. How could anyone remember all that? . . . I answered wrong and they would not let me land."[142]

The claim to a married life of domesticity and shared intimacy in the Western sense was especially challenging for Japanese women who arrived as picture brides in San Francisco and other Western ports. These women had never met their husbands. Because this was a legally binding marriage under Japanese law, the United States was obliged to recognize the women as wives and admit them on the strength of their husbands' claim for them. When confronted with picture brides, immigration inspectors at many western ports none-theless refused to recognize the legitimacy of their marriages; some organized Christian wedding ceremonies between the spouses at the port of arrival before releasing the women. The head of the San Francisco Station, Samuel Backus, however, recognized the need to acknowledge Japanese law and custom, so he rejected few picture brides. Over two-thirds of all Japanese women who arrived in San Francisco in the years before World War I came as picture brides, and over 99 percent of them were admitted.[143]

When problems occurred for these women, it was usually not be-cause of their individual presentation or testimony but because of circumstantial evidence against them. Many Japanese and Chinese women, even some whose husbands did appear at Angel Island, had to fight the suspicion that they were prostitutes. If wives were very young or if the age difference between husband and wife was large, this, too, cast doubt on their claims to a proper married life. Very young women were sometimes not released to their husbands but rather ended up in the rescue mission run by Presbyterian activist Donaldina Cameron in San Francisco.[144] Other women were suspect because they did not exhibit the signs of class that officials expected of the merchant wife. Photographs of Western-style weddings could bolster the claim of women being of the right class, as could—paradoxically—the inspector's notice of their "tiny" (bound) feet. Heavy makeup, on the other hand, could be perceived by inspectors as a status marker for "low class" women.[145]

Because the ban on Asian immigration was so complete, and the possibilities for the immigration of women outside marriage were practically nonexistent, women from Asia could almost never make a claim for admission in their own right at the Angel Island border station or elsewhere. They could only hope to indirectly influence the decision by presenting a carefully groomed, demure image of domesticity and fidelity.[146]

Male and female immigrants from Asia fought their harsh treatment and debarment vigorously with the help of transnational networks of support. San Francisco-based organizations of Chinese merchants, such as the Chinese American Chamber of Commerce, protested against the detentions, mistreatment, and abuse of Chinese immigrants in San Francisco beginning in the 1890s. These protests culminated in a Chinese boycott of American goods in 1905.[147] Officials such as the Immigration Bureau's Chinese Commissioner in San Francisco considered such protests further proof of the difficult character "inherent in the Mongolian race."[148] But diplomats and the Immigration Bureau in Washington paid attention and began to permit better access to attorneys for new arrivals on Angel Island, beginning in 1907.[149]

About 75 percent of all Asian arrivals on the West Coast gained admission to the United States despite Chinese and Japanese exclusion laws. This remarkable level of success resulted from well-prepared emigration and successful strategizing for the encounters at the border stations. Isolating and lengthy though the experience on Angel Island was, it was also the vortex of intense efforts on behalf of immigrants by family, home associations, consulates, immigrant brokers, and lawyers.[150] Immigrants arrived at the interview with not only a sheaf of documents and detailed instructions, but also a list of possible witnesses, contact addresses in San Francisco, and the knowledge that a lawyer might have to be contacted. Those with particularly good resources could have white (i.e., non-Asian) witnesses vouch for them.[151] When a young Chinese woman named Woo landed at Angel Island in 1940, she was greeted warmly by Deaconess Maurer, who had heard about her from Woo's husband. "The other detainees said I was lucky to know her, and because of that I would probably get released soon."[152]

Over 90 percent of the Chinese immigrant cases examined by Erika Lee had lawyers in San Francisco.[153] Even Fernando Villareal, who had no relatives in the United States and only $9.85 in his pockets when he arrived, wrote to the San Francisco commissioners, "If . . . my case is denied I am certainly allowed to communicate with a lawyer in regard to my case." He managed to hire the law firm of Stidger, Stidger, and Kennah, well known for its work in Chinese exclusion cases. The lawyers made a vigorous case for Villareal's admissibility as a U.S. national, pushing his case all the way to the Department of Labor in Washington, where his deportation was finally upheld in February 1914. Had Villareal more money and better connections in the United States, his case might well have wound up in the courts, as did many Asian admission cases.[154]

Even though the Supreme Court and increasingly stringent administrative practices had made it more difficult to challenge Chinese exclusion decisions by the Immigration Bureau in court during the early twentieth century, litigation remained the main way Asian immigrants fought their exclusion. Court cases were built on the applicants' claim that they were U.S. citizens, or the children of U.S. citizens, or admissible as wives of Americans. Lawyers, supported by Chinese benevolent associations in San Francisco and elsewhere, fought for their clients to have their day in court or at least for the Immigration Bureau to change its procedures.[155]

Border crossings at the geographic borders of the United States changed greatly with the passage of the 1924 Johnson-Reed Act (see Appendix 1, Figure 1). The quota law changed the function and the location of the border for immigrants in fundamental ways, and it shifted the main zone of negotiation away from the border stations. Thereafter, some of the most important preparations and decisions were made in the U.S. consul's office abroad, before prospective immigrants could leave for the United States. This change was especially pronounced for Europeans, and much less so for Asian immigrants who had been faced with complicated emigration procedures since the 1880s. Immigrants from the Western Hemisphere, exempt from the quota, experienced little change until the 1965 Immigration Act brought them, too, within the purview of immigration visa restrictions.

For immigration officials, the 1924 quota law brought profound changes in their role as guardians of the nation's borders and ports of entry. At the ports of entry, they were reduced to checking the immigrants' visa and determining the veracity of the information on which the visa was based, a function they retain to this day. Although immigration inspectors retained the power to reject even immigrants with a valid visa (the visa is merely a recommendation issued by the State Department, not a document that represents an entitlement for entry), inspectors only determined if the basic information provided to the consular officer was the same as the information given by personal appearance of the passport holder at the border. Admission no longer depended on the officer's assessment of all newcomers as potential future residents and citizens on the basis of their self-presentation at the border.

With the diminishing function of immigration inspectors as selectors of worthy immigrants and future citizens came an increasing reliance on the immigration service as a police agency at the border. Partly in response to the expected increase in illegal immigration, the U.S. Border Patrol, financed by Congress to enforce the 1924 law, began its work in 1926 under the auspices of the Commissioner of Immigration. Over time, the policing function of the Immigration Bureau would grow considerably until it had become primarily an agency of exclusion and deportation by the 1930s.

Border stations, in tandem with these changes, lost much of their function as the place where immigrants presented themselves to representatives of the U.S. government for the first time to be examined in detail. After 1924, Ellis Island, for example, quickly became primarily a detention station for rejected immigrants and deportees from all over the United States who were about to be sent back. The station closed entirely in 1954. Angel Island, partially destroyed by fire in 1940, also closed its doors then, never to reopen. The gradual abolition of Asian exclusion, beginning with the lifting of the Chinese Exclusion Act in 1943, made such a special station no longer necessary.

Today's land border stations and airports retain a great deal of power for prospective immigrants. The drama of border crossing is reenacted in them hundreds of thousands of times a day, as even daily border migrants must present themselves to be evaluated by the representatives of the U.S. government, who retain the right to deny entry to anyone without further reason. Crossing the U.S. border no longer entails a personal examination of one's life by an immigration inspector at the border, or a carefully prepared self-presentation as part of establishing a claim to a future in the United States; today, it is the presentation of papers, documents, photographs, and finger-prints that determines entry. The human drama of coming into the United States is hidden behind an ever more complex electronic and paper trail.

CHAPTER **3**

Forced Departures

When Doukenie Bacos arrived in New York harbor
from her home in Greece in 1913, she was both expectant and frightened. As the ocean liner sailed past the Statue of Liberty, she remembered thinking, "Lady, you're such a beautiful. You opened your arms,
and you get all the foreigners here. Give me a chance to prove that I
am worth it, to do something, to become somebody in America." But
she was also worried about what lay ahead: "It was a very hard, small
road with thorns. Would I be able to pass those thorns and get out to
go to America, or they have to sent me back again?" Bacos was anxious for good reason: she was only 14 years old and traveling by herself. Underage children (younger than 16 years) who arrived without family were usually not admitted into the country by immigration
inspectors and were sent back immediately. In the end, she was
lucky, for family members had alerted officials to her arrival, and
after being held at Ellis Island, she was released to live with them in
New York. While Bacos was on the island, she was between borders
as she witnessed families waiting anxiously for the verdict of officials about admission or rejection. The decisions seemed random and
cruel as some were let in, others sent back. The memory of her short
time in this gray zone and the possibility of deportation still haunted
her as an old woman, decades later.[1]

From the early years of the new republic, admission of most immigrants had been tied to the rejection of others. After all, the state's
power to select whom it admitted was at the core of border control,

as newcomers knew only too well. But selective admission only worked if it was tied to mechanisms of rejection and deportation. For the U.S. government, the power of removal and deportation was only theoretical during the first century of the republic. The federal government's right to deport aliens was not actually invoked, for sending back immigrants was too expensive and administratively cumbersome. This changed in the 1880s as steamship traffic, better railroad connections, and a legal framework that rendered steamship companies liable for the cost of taking deportees back "whence they came" became established parts of the immigration process. The Chinese Exclusion Act of 1882 and the Contract Labor Law of 1885 as well as subsequent laws on restricting admission of immigrants with physical and mental "defects" were all coupled with deportation provisions that were enforceable. Deportation thus became part of immigration policy in a comprehensive way. By 1900, crossing the border into the United States was always linked to the possibility of a forced return from North America.

For Doukenie Bacos and thousands of others held at Ellis Island after their arrival, the threat of exclusion and deportation was a feared outcome of their migration. The process involved a fine legal distinction, which was not apparent to her and most other immigrants. To most new arrivals, "being sent back" was deportation; however, in legal terms, not being admitted into the United States was not the same as deportation. Rejected immigrants, called the "debarred" by the Immigration Bureau, simply were not admitted into the country; instead, they were refused entry at the border and sent back by ship (and at the ship company's expense) from the seaports of the United States or Canada. (Those refused admission at the land border were not sent back whence they came, except in some Canadian cases.) The debarred made up the overwhelming majority of those sent back prior to 1924.

Debarred immigrants could (and often did) try to gain reentry as soon as it was technically and financially feasible—the next day at the land border, by return ship across the ocean, or years later. Sophia Krietzberg, a Russian Jewish woman, remembered how she, her widowed mother, and a sister failed to gain admission in 1904 to join their relatives in the United States. They were sent back to LeHavre where they originally had taken the boat. "But that desire to come to America, to prove herself" propelled the mother and her two young daughters to work their way from France to Russia and then back to Great Britain, as their entry to Canada was relatively easy. "And from Canada she was able to land in the United States," her daughter reported with satisfaction, bringing a three-year odyssey to an end.[2]

Most working-class immigrant families did not have the energy or resources to try again. Rejection at the border devastated such immigrants and the fear of it cast a long shadow—despite the modest number of new arrivals (between 0.8 and 2.0 percent) who were in fact debarred and sent back in the early years of the twentieth century. The stories of the rejected were heartrending in part because the chances of a return, though legally possible, seemed so distant.

Deportation and the Law

Although in the mind of prospective immigrants debarment at the border was a much feared outcome of the journey, deportation after time spent in the United States, though relatively rare, was a harsher punishment and a significant legal sanction in the twentieth century. The threat of deportation was a possibility that hovered over immigrants long after arrival. It made admission conditional for as long as immigrants remained outside the circle of U.S. citizens, and sometimes beyond. As a Progressive Era court saw it, "The immigrant must be taken to have entered subject to the condition that he might be sent out of the country . . ."[3] As public policy, the threat of deportation became an important instrument in the twentieth century, intended to shape the behavior of immigrants for years after their arrival.

Deportation law always mirrored immigrant admission law in the United States. As categories of immigrant excludability grew from the late nineteenth century on, so did the list of reasons for which an immigrant could be deported. Immigrants became deportable if they had or developed certain illnesses or physical or mental handicaps within three years of arrival. These were usually conditions that would render immigrants dependent on the care (and financial support) of others and which prevented their social and economic independence. Economically dependent and socially marginal people, those who would become a likely public charge, were also deportable beginning in the 1890s; in the early twentieth century, deportation law added "professional beggars" and those who had been convicted of a "crime of moral turpitude" (commonly interpreted to mean a felony). Prostitutes and others connected to the sex trades (defined as those "profiting from prostitution") and polygamists also became deportable beginning in 1903 as did anarchists and (later) communists.[4] Most importantly, beginning in 1917, immigrants who had entered the country without inspection could be deported as well (see Appendix 2).[5]

Until the 1920s, a statute of limitations established that most conditions for deportation no longer applied after an immigrant had lived in the United States three or five years (exceptions were Asians, prostitutes, and anarchists who were always deportable). During most of that time, the law assumed that the root causes of an immigrants' deportability had been present before entry into the United States: a prostitute had arrived at the border with experience or at least intention of working in the sex trades; an anarchist had a past as a radical before arriving at Ellis Island. In most cases, such a history could not be proven by the authorities, but the burden of proof of nondeportability was on the immigrant, so this was not necessarily a serious hurdle for the immigration inspectors.[6]

Despite the considerable power of the federal government, the complications and cost of finding, tracking, and supervising immigrants who were candidates for deportation and proving their excludability within three to five years of arrival was a difficult task for the undermanned Immigration Bureau (renamed the Immigration and Naturalization Service [INS] in 1932). To begin with, the Bureau needed information from local and state authorities in order to identify candidates for deportation. Lists of aliens arrested by local police, treated by public hospitals, or helped by charitable organizations usually provided the trigger.[7] In a few cases deportations were initiated by the immigration officers themselves, usually as part of a follow up to problematic admission cases or admission on bond.

Once the initial investigation was made, the mechanism to determine deportability followed the same guidelines as decisions over

debarment of immigrants: in a hearing administered by three officers, immigrants were asked to present their case. The officers made
a recommendation on the merits of the case to the Commissioner
General of Immigration, who then forwarded the case to the Secretary of Labor, who then had final authority over the case. Deportation decisions were thus made in a much more centralized manner
than border admissions. Ultimately, the superiors in Washington,
D.C., directed the apparatus for the finding, screening, and deporting of immigrants. This relatively remote (and politicized) decision-
making process rendered the expertise and opinions of local commissioners and inspectors less important than in immigration cases.
On the other hand, local authorities could always not enforce deportation law or assign their limited resources to other parts of border
administration. The dissonance between local opinions and decisions
at headquarters sometimes provided an opening for immigrants and
their advocates to push for change and reversal.

Experts and advocates played a role in deportation decisions, just
as they did in admissions. Immigrants enlisted lawyers and advocacy groups to help in individual cases—by arguing that the law
was being applied falsely, for example, or by showing that a case
was based on erroneous facts. For the most part, the expertise marshaled in deportation cases was either based on narrow legal grounds
or on very broad humanitarian and political ones. Social science
research, ethnographies, and histories were used much less often
in deportation cases than in cases of immigrant admission and
naturalization.[8]

Deportations of men and women who were residents of the United
States were rare before World War I. The proportion of deportations
to (non-Chinese) immigrants was less than 1:1,000 during most years
prior to World War I. Only Chinese immigrants were deported in
larger proportions in the first decade of the twentieth century, but
even for them the numbers, always under nine hundred a year, were
relatively modest.[9] Deportation became a more significant part of immigration enforcement at the beginning of World War I. Amid a background of rising restrictionism, Congress passed a revised immigration and deportation law in 1917 that expanded categories for
deportation and lengthened the time during which immigrants could

be deported after entering the United States. Those who had entered the country without inspection (without submitting to the literacy test and without paying a head tax) were deportable within three years of arrival for that reason alone. This group of people, categorized as entered without inspection (EWI) would soon make up the largest group of deportees, as they still do today. Most other immigrants could be deported for cause within five years, and specific groups—criminals, anarchists, and participants in the sex trade—could be deported without time limits after their arrival in the United States (see Appendix 2).

The effect of the 1917 revision of deportation law was overshadowed by the passage of wartime sedition laws that same year and by provisions passed in subsequent years that increased the deportability of politically active immigrants. The Espionage Act of 1917 and the Sedition Act of 1918 made any public comment or activity that could be construed as antipatriotic a criminal offense. Immigrants who were not citizens and who were convicted under these laws became deportable as criminals (under the "moral turpitude" clause). In addition, laws passed in October 1918 and July 1920 targeted foreign-born communists for deportation.[10]

The effect of the increasing reach of deportation law was gradual. Beginning in late 1914, it became nearly impossible to deport Europeans "whence they came" as World War I spread throughout Europe and unrestricted submarine warfare by the German navy made transatlantic travel hazardous. While the Immigration Bureau still initiated some deportations, it could not enforce them in most cases. A total of over 3,200 deportations were suspended during the years 1916 to 1919. When they did occur, deportations took place mostly at the land border or across the Pacific to Asia. It was not until 1919 that deportations increased once again—in tandem with immigration—only to grow further throughout the 1920s.[11]

The permanent introduction of nationality quotas in 1924 had a profound effect not just on immigration but also on deportation. The immediate scarcity of quota spots for most nationality groups outside the Americas increased the cost of immigrating (in terms of time spent waiting "in line" and investment in visa-screening procedures) for most Europeans and, more importantly, put an immigrant visa out of reach for millions more. Seeing no chance of entering as immigrants, young Europeans resorted to temporary visas (as tourists or students), enlisted on ships then jumped ship. Other immigrants simply walked across the Canadian or Mexican border. Under these circumstances, deportation became a much more important enforcement tool than it had been in the past, for it served as a sanction that was applied to anyone who could not prove legal status as a resident of the United States.

Deportation also became much more costly than it had been in the past for both the U.S. government and the deportees. For the federal government, deporting many who came through third countries could become complicated and costly. Transit countries refused to take deportees; sometimes no country of origin could be found, since nations no longer existed or had changed their borders or their governments after World War I. For those sent back, deportation meant that, under the new laws, reentry would be much more difficult than in the past, as they were unlikely to pass muster before a consul who needed to issue them a visa. Deportation thus came closer to functioning as an exclusion from the United States for life, and immigrants began to fight their removal from the United States energetically.[12]

The life story of Joseph Novel, an immigrant from Yugoslavia who arrived as a sailor in 1929, illustrates how deportation became a severe sanction in the hands of authorities and to what lengths immigrants could go to avoid it. Novel jumped ship in Philadelphia and made his way to the Brooklyn waterfront to work as a teamster in the late 1920s and 1930s. He was arrested three times in the periodic sweeps of the docks and readied for deportation. As he remembered decades later: "There was many aliens picked up. They were picked up left and right from Brooklyn piers and the waterfront all the time . . . When a man used to get hit in the leg and he was sent to the company [office] they just called up the immigration, have them pull him back to Italy. It cost nothing," He managed to stave off deportation each time, once by running away from his guards, another time with the help of friends, and finally by enlisting in the U.S. army during World War II.[13]

Other immigrants were resourceful in different ways. Joseph Vobril entered the United States as an engineering student in 1929 but had to curtail his studies when his money ran out during the Depression. He was able to stay in the United States after his marriage to a fellow Bohemian immigrant—a U.S. citizen—in the early 1930s.[14] In many similar cases, young men on student visas were unable to find this private solution to their dilemma, and some were deported. Others simply acquiesced in their fate, hoping for an opportunity later. "It was in 1933," remembered Otto Heinemann, a waiter from the German city of Bremerhaven. "I never felt so bad in my life, they brought me to Ellis Island, they kept me there for about three weeks. After they found out where I came from, they deported me." Within a few months, Heinemann traveled back to New York as a stowaway, and his marriage to a U.S. citizen and the intervention of a lawyer protected him from later deportation.[15]

The need for these European immigrants to be on guard against police raids and Immigration Service arrests showed that the enforcement of immigration law tightened even in the large metropolises of the East Coast. But, by and large, European immigrants who managed to live unmolested by law enforcement also escaped the reach of the Immigration Service in the interwar years, at least if they lived away from the U.S. land border.

It was at the land borders to Canada and Mexico that the immigration restrictions brought on by the laws of 1917 and 1924 had their most direct effect on people living nearby. Mexicans, Hispanic Americans, and Canadians became subject to deportation in much greater numbers and in much greater proportion than before World War I. The main reason deportation law was more rigorously enforced in border zones was the formation of the U.S. Border Patrol, founded in 1924. From the beginning, the Border Patrol—always insufficiently equipped and undermanned by its own reckoning—took a proactive part in policing the border. The Patrol's job was to stop all illegal activity in the borderlands, especially smuggling. The inspectors were expected to seize "contraband of any kind," which, in the words of the Immigration Bureau, included "aliens . . . intoxicating liquor, animals, narcotics and infested products of the soil."[16] The officers also pursued suspected smugglers and people engaged in revolutionary activities far inland as well as into Mexico. The U.S. Border Patrol also acted as law enforcement agency for the Customs Service, state and municipal authorities, the Narcotics Service, the Department of Justice, and the armed forces in the borderlands of the Southwest.[17] But the main task of the Border Patrol was the pursuit of illegal immigrants and as a result, the number of deportations rose dramatically after the mid-1920s. In 1931 alone the Border Patrol arrested over 23,000 people, most of whom were subsequently deported. In addition, countless immigrants whom the Border Patrol considered illegitimate were expelled without any formal deportation proceedings.[18]

The activism of the Border Patrol also created problems for the border administrators in the interwar years and beyond. Deportations required hearings, background checks, and the opportunity for immigrants to prove their innocence. From the viewpoint of the Immigration Bureau, this was a cumbersome procedure to expel tens of thousands of suspected illegal immigrants arrested by the Border Patrol. The Bureau therefore instituted a "fast track" to deport men and women found to be illegally in the United States, the so-called voluntary departures. These de facto deportations occurred without hearings or appeals and were based on the premise that apprehended immigrants who agreed to leave the country "voluntarily" would organize and pay for their own trip. This had advantages for both sides. It saved the Bureau the time and effort of a regular investigation (which might turn out negatively for the authorities), and it also could serve to cover up the unilateral actions of the Border Patrol, such as their arrests of "suspicious characters." In addition, because voluntary departure did not classify the illegal immigrant as a deportee, he or she could immediately apply for legal readmission to the United States on the other side of the border.[19] For immigration enforcement agencies, voluntary departures remained a popular alternative to deportation for decades to come. Throughout much of the 1930s, the Immigration Service counted about as many voluntary departures as deportations, mainly to Canada and Mexico; in the late 1930s, more immigrants departed voluntarily than were deported.

Europeans were more reluctant to incur the cost of self-deportation. An increasing number of them chose instead "voluntary repatriation," a category added by the Immigration Service to remove dependent immigrants from the United States at U.S. expense.

Immigrants, most of whom were not in U.S. custody for violations of immigration law, had to apply to the INS to get approval for this type of deportation. Between 1937 and 1939, almost 4,000 poor immigrants, mostly Europeans who had fallen on hard times many years after their initial entry, were sent back under this program.[20]

The outbreak of World War II made deportation to countries overseas practically impossible. Some governments in Europe or Asia could not or would not issue passports to the prospective deportees, and the dangers of crossing the Atlantic and the Pacific made deportation "a sort of contingent sentence of death," in the words of the U.S. Attorney General.[21] Therefore the Immigration Service began to order fewer deportations, and in many cases deportation orders remained unenforced. In 1941 alone, about twice as many deportation warrants were unenforced as there were actual deportations. Altogether, the number of deportations ordered for all reasons declined greatly between 1939 and 1946. The deportations that did occur during the war years were mostly to Mexico, Canada, or other Western Hemisphere countries.[22]

Deportations to countries overseas resumed after the end of the war. Just as in the previous decades, the majority of deportees leaving in the 1940s and 1950s were classified as having entered without inspection, having false documents, or overstaying their visa.[23] Most of those caught were found at the southern land border of the United States and were Mexican aliens. Operation Wetback, an enforcement strategy of the Immigration Service at the southern border, focused on this target group from 1954 to 1955: almost a million and a half Mexicans were deported after their arrest in the southwestern borderlands. With the exception of these years, the number of deportations and voluntary departures remained modest and reflected the political counterpressures from western and southwestern agribusiness to accommodate all Mexican agricultural labor migrants during a time of full employment. Multiple arrests and deportations of the same persons were assumed to be routine by the 1950s, as most immigrants were able to reenter the United States if they wished to do so. More than ever, deportation was a blunt instrument for the regulation of southern border crossers and would remain so for the rest of the twentieth century.[24]

Deporting the Socially Marginal

As a legal instrument, deportation served to define the American nation's citizenry by separating immigrants worthy of residence and future citizenship from those who had failed the explicit and implicit conditions set for them: economic independence, an adherence to certain social norms, and a certain degree of political conformity. In the eyes of the law, immigrants who failed in even one of these categories rendered themselves vulnerable to deportation. But the law itself and its loose, sporadic enforcement left the definition mutable: deportable aliens were a constructed class whose contours changed considerably over the twentieth century, at times reflecting legal change but often independent of it. Ideas of social conformity and moral standards, rigid and elaborate at the beginning of the twentieth century, were supplemented by definitions of race and racially inflected notions of economic independence. Political conformity was a third category that played an important part in defining a class of noncitizens who were deportable throughout the twentieth century.

In the nineteenth and early twentieth centuries the vast majority of deportees were socially and economically marginal immigrants, mirroring the immigrant exclusions.[25] Deportable immigrants in this class had tried but failed to make it as immigrants and residents in the United States, usually because of illness, advanced age, prolonged unemployment, sudden widowhood, or abandonment by a male breadwinner. In some cases, the reasons for deportation were an individual's behavior: women who had been caught as prostitutes, or men who were engaged in criminal activity, for example. In most years, prior to 1924, between 2,400 and 12,000 immigrants were deported because they fell in one of these groups. Illness and destitution (i.e., classification as a likely public charge) were the largest categories. Immigrants in the sex trade only made up less than 1 percent of deportees in any given year. The demographic picture changed gradually beginning in 1917 as restrictive visa and quota laws were passed. In the late 1920s and 1930s, deportation for poverty and social marginality decreased relative to other reasons.[26]

As so often, the elderly, the very young, and women in general were more vulnerable than men to charges of social deviance and marginality. Because their economic dependence on family support was so great, immigrant women were more likely to be classified as public charges or morally suspect if they lived without family and in poverty. Women had trouble shedding the suspicion of either economic dependency (as a public charge) or socially unprotected economic independence (which made them potential targets for accusations of prostitution or immorality). Sometimes the mere suspicion that a woman could not independently support herself in an honest manner was enough to render her deportable in the eyes of immigration officials.[27]

In early 1908, Maria Raciti, a working-class woman from Sicily, arrived in Philadelphia with her young child to join her husband. After a short time together, the marriage went sour, and Raciti got a divorce. The court ordered her ex-husband to pay child support of $2.50 a week. To the husband, this was unacceptable, and "in order to restore his honor" he enlisted the help of friends in Philadelphia's Italian community, who denounced his wife as a prostitute to the Immigration Bureau.[28] The Bureau promptly deported Raciti and her daughter without further ado. After Raciti was unable to make a living and to support her child in Italy (her husband's support payments had stopped as she left the United States), she returned to the United States without her daughter a year after the first deportation and resumed her life as a textile mill worker. Word traveled fast, however, and friends of her husband saw to it that she was again arrested as a suspected prostitute, about five months after her second arrival. This time, Raciti was better prepared, and she refused to testify without a lawyer. Their curiosity piqued by the convoluted tale of intrigue and betrayal, the immigration inspectors launched an intensive investigation. Raciti, her landlords, and her acquaintances were interviewed about her means of support and her behavior toward male and female members of the Italian community of Philadelphia. Inspector McLaughlin even visited her former boarding house to measure and sketch her room and concerned himself with the construction and size of her bed and the number of pillows on it in order to ascertain whether Raciti could have followed an immoral lifestyle. Raciti was able to portray her life as entirely appropriate for a working-class woman whose family bonds, while frayed in part, were still strong in many respects and who had earned the respect of friends through her quiet self-reliance. After two months of investigation, the Bureau of Immigration annulled the original deportation decree. Raciti had succeeded in renegotiating her border crossing and could remain in the United States in her own right.[29]

Christina Bycroft, an Englishwoman, had fewer informal networks than Maria Raciti, but she was able to fight deportation by mobilizing formal advocacy groups and networks outside of kin and ethnic circles. Bycroft arrived from Canada in Seattle with her husband William and 9-year-old stepdaughter Edith in the fall of 1913. December found the small family in problematic circumstances in a hotel on Seattle's skid row. While her husband had no work, Bycroft had taken a job as a cook in the private home of an upper-class family. Little Edith occasionally earned a dollar for singing to customers at the saloon run by the hotel's proprietor, a well-known figure in Seattle's underworld. Bycroft was apparently uneasy enough about this state of affairs, and the interest of the saloonkeeper in her little girl, to get in touch with the Juvenile Bureau of the city. The effect of this call for help was unintended: in December, Bycroft herself was arrested for public drunkenness at the behest of the saloon's proprietor and her husband. Such a charge made her liable to deportation under the moral turpitude clause. From jail, the distraught woman was befriended by representatives of the city's reform society. With the help of these members of Seattle's middle class, she mounted a defense which, in the end, proved effective. A lawyer gathered convincing evidence that Bycroft was abused by her husband rather than drunk, and members of the reform society as well as the matron of the Seattle jail attested to her good behavior. With her health restored and her employer willing to take her back, she was allowed to stay in Seattle. Her husband was deported, but her stepdaughter remained with the sister of the saloonkeeper, who had taken her in at the beginning to the proceedings. With the help of her middle-class allies, Christina Bycroft had succeeded in presenting herself as a worthy candidate for residency and eventual citizenship, but the power of her self-presentation did not extend to her role as the mother of the little girl.[30]

The files of the Immigration Bureau contain other cases in which women accused of being prostitutes successfully fought deportation orders.[31] Because it turned out to be difficult for the Immigration Bureau to deport women for prostitution, suspicions of morality were articulated indirectly, at least when it came to Europeans. In many cases, women were accused of sexual transgression but were deported as economically dependent, pregnant, or likely public charges.[32] Deportations of women (and men) for these and other social failings continued unabated during the 1920s. Conditions such as pregnancy out of wedlock, poverty of widows with children, or unexpected illness continued to trip up female immigrants, especially if they were single. With the end of 1920s prosperity, an increasing number of long-time unemployed women and men also fell under deportation orders as public charges.[33]

If collapsed families and suspicion of sexual transgression dominated the cases of women, immigrant men were sometimes caught in the investigation of contract labor and were sent back as convicted criminals. Yet deportations of European immigrants for violating the contract labor or assisted immigration law were rare during the early twentieth century. When caught, such immigrants almost never tried to make the case for their right to stay.[34] Criminal activity proved the downfall for a larger number of men who were deported from the early twentieth century on. In the post–World War I era, narcotics and prohibition laws made criminals out of immigrants involved in the moonshine trade. The prosecution of organized crime tripped up a number of Italian men. In combination, these factors were probably decisive in the rise of deported criminals, from 316 in 1921 to 1,773 in 1931. Convicted felons were easily deportable because the prison authorities routinely reported the names of incarcerated aliens to the Immigration Bureau.[35]

As deportations occurred increasingly because of routine reporting by other government institutions to the Immigration Bureau, both male and female immigrants fought back with the help of legal professionals. Instead of individuals pleading their cases in person, lawyers, immigrant advocates, police, and judicial authorities took up their cause. Immigrant aid societies were among the first to organize the defense of their members in formal deportation proceedings. Sometimes this meant a last-minute intervention when an immigrant was being readied for deportation,[36] Increasingly groups such as the Hebrew Immigrant Aid Society (HIAS) adopted a formalized, procedural approach to fighting deportations, which focused on technical points of the law. Lawyers wrote up memoranda and filed the papers with the Bureau. The individual character or the worthiness of an immigrant was not central in such cases. Public appeals were only occasionally part of an organized effort. It is likely that this strategy was responsible for the disproportionate success of immigration appeals in New York. The Immigration Bureau reacted testily to the aggressive procedural way of fighting back. Its officials circulated a series of memoranda regarding the activities of the HIAS on behalf of Jewish immigrants and secretly copied the minutes of the National Jewish Immigration Council, which members of the Bureau analyzed in detail, criticized, and used to defend their record to the Secretary of Labor.[37]

The HIAS was not alone in its role as an immigrant advocate. By the 1920s, it was joined by other advocacy organizations that represented immigrants in the appeals process and raised concern over the social cost of deportation in a wider public forum. These advocacy groups, such as the American Civil Liberties Union (ACLU) and the Foreign Language Information Service (FLIS), were not affiliated with one ethnic group or even specifically concerned with immigrants, but they were effective in drawing attention to the high social cost of expulsions for European immigrants and their families in the United States. They emphasized that as citizens they were concerned that the deportation process was structured in ways that contravened the traditions of American law because deportations were decided by panels that served as prosecutors, investigators, and judges all in one and because prospective deportees were considered guilty until proven innocent. The advocacy groups argued that the random and ad hoc character of many of the deportation proceedings, and the decisions and the power of the immigration authorities to deport even long-time residents of the United States, were detrimental to the image of the United States and contrary to the identity of the nation as a country of immigrants.[38]

But it was an uphill battle to fight deportation practices during the 1920s and much of the 1930s on more than a case-by-case basis. Not only did restrictionists dominate Congress, but the traditional clients of immigrant advocacy organizations, European immigrants, showed up in much smaller numbers. New, non-European constituents— Mexicans and Filipinos, for example—faced related problems, but immigrant advocacy groups rarely reached out to them.[39] Racial and cultural divisions created a widening gap between the groups that needed help and the organizations that continued to rely on traditional constituencies. By and large, immigrant advocacy remained focused on Europeans, including refugees, displaced persons, and traditional European immigrants.

Race and Deportation

Deportation law and policy was deeply racialized in the twentieth century. Racial categories defined deportation law and practice, sometimes in obvious ways, other times more subtly, for much of the hundred years after its inception. Deportation law originated in the Chinese Exclusion Act, and the administration of deportations was originally developed to deport Chinese long before any Europeans, Canadians, or Mexicans were sent back in appreciable numbers for any reason.[40] The so-called Chinese Inspector assigned to every immigration district was the first immigration official in charge of deportations.[41] As deportation became a widespread means of immigration control in the twentieth century, the Immigration Bureau shaped its enforcement practices according to racialized expectations and interpretations of who counted as a suitable immigrant. Non-whites were vulnerable to deportation when white immigrants in similar situations would not have been threatened.

During the late nineteenth and early twentieth century, the vast majority of Chinese deportations occurred after Chinese immigrants were denied admission at the border of the United States. Chinese men who were admitted to the United States needed to register within one year of arrival, and any failure to register or carry a registration certificate was grounds for deportation. Chinese who were admitted as merchants or students but were found to be laborers, for example, were deportable as well. Most Chinese who were deported after entry belonged to these categories.[42] Mistakes did sometimes occur, though the Bureau was loath to admit this. In 1902, Hui Sing, who seems to have been a well-established merchant in Brooklyn, was "caught" by the Chinese Inspector in upstate New York, and the Bureau fought an extended battle to have him deported as a laborer. Sing managed to raise $500 in bail and hired Max Kohler, who within a few years became one of the most prominent immigration lawyers in New York City. Kohler prepared an appeal, but Sing decided to leave on his own rather than endure the continued harassment of the Bureau.[43] In other cases, too, Chinese immigrants fought against deportation in the same way they fought debarment: on procedural grounds by emphasizing their conformity with Chinese exclusion law or by claiming status as U.S. citizens. Many of these claims—if supported by lawyers—were successful.[44]

Between 1902 and 1907, almost 4,800 Chinese were deported under the Chinese exclusion law.[45] As the Chinese community shrank in the twentieth-century United States, fewer deportations occurred. The numbers rarely reached 500 a year after 1910 and fell to below one hundred between 1918 and 1924. The annual number of deportations would rarely exceed 200 until the 1960s.[46] Stringent as the deportation law was for Chinese immigrants in theory, in practice it barely lowered the actual number of Chinese immigrants in the United States.

The effect of deportation law on Japanese immigration was even less pronounced. Japanese immigrants were less vulnerable to deportation than the Chinese, in part because their emigration was so tightly controlled by the government of Japan before and after the Gentlemen's Agreement of 1907.[47] After the agreement halted virtually all immigration by Japanese men to the United States, the Immigration Bureau began to focus on illegal Japanese immigration, especially at the land borders. As a result, more Japanese were deported than before, though the number rarely exceeded a few hundred a year. The number of other Asian deportations was smaller still.

Ultimately, the numerical impact of deportation on Asian immigrant communities was not large. But placing Chinese (and later Japanese) immigrants nearly always within the reach of deportation law had a singular effect on these immigrant communities. Regardless of their individual behavior, their length of stay, or their aspirations for life in the United States, their immigrant status was always tenuous. Deportation law and its enforcement signaled to Asian immigrants and the American public that Asians were not welcome in the United States.

Deportation practice retained a racialized character for all immigrants of color, not just Asians, through much of the twentieth century. As the number of Asian deportations diminished, West Indians and Mexicans began to make up a growing percentage of deportees beginning in World War I. Black immigrants from the West Indies, a growing group after 1900, were expected to fit not just into the American mainstream economically and socially, but also into the inferior position assigned to African Americans in the United States. Economic independence remained a requirement, but social submissiveness was needed as well for these immigrants, at least when faced by white officials.

In 1913, the Immigration Bureau investigated a group of Barbadian families because their passage had been paid by an emigrant assistance group, the Victoria Emigration Society of Barbados. Similar mutual assistance groups had operated in Europe during the nineteenth century without attracting scrutiny. As "assisted immigrants," the immigrant members of the Society were deportable in 1913. When immigration inspectors made home visits to these black families in Harlem, they were touched by their respectability and economic self-sufficiency. "These persons impress me very favorably," wrote Inspector Stone after concluding his investigation, "from observations and interviews I am satisfied that they are industrious people and able to get along." The West Indian immigrants, all working in menial occupations as porters or household servants, appeared deeply respectful toward the inspectors and mindful of their socially inferior position as black Americans. The inspectors spared them from deportation.[48]

No racial classifications in immigration law listed Mexicans separately from white immigrants, nor were there special "Mexican inspectors" for Mexicans or the Mexican border. Rather, as Kathleen Lytle has shown, the U.S. Border Patrol was organized in 1924 as a militarized police force specifically in charge of the Mexican border in 1924. Policing the Mexican border was in many institutional and ideological ways built on the tradition of Chinese inspectors, and the Border Patrol saw its mission as one of preventing border crossings by those designated as racially inferior.[49] Border Patrol officers' deportation practices focused on the darker-skinned Mexican "peons." Treatment of such border crossers, the attempts to classify them by race at entry, and the ease with which they were deported presumed that these immigrants were not just poor and unskilled and therefore unable to be self-supporting as workers but also racially inferior and incapable of articulating their right to stay in the United States.[50] Unlike Europeans, who usually came to the attention of the authorities when they used public institutions, were arrested, were imprisoned, or encountered social service agencies, Mexican candidates for deportation in the U.S. border areas were usually identified by local residents as well as by the police or Border Patrol officers during random searches and interrogations. Such activity seemed to make up the bulk of the Border Patrols' work in the 1920s and 1930s, even though its effect was more to intimidate than to arrest and deport.[51]

The authorities did not expect Mexicans to fight for a hearing, contest deportation, or enlist the help of advocacy groups the way Europeans sometimes did and Chinese often tried. But Mexicans were not entirely without help when it came to deportations. Mexicans identified as deportable sometimes appealed to Mexican consuls in their area for help. More importantly, whites in the borderlands were also among the supporters of Mexican migrants—though they did not act out of altruism. In the spring of 1928, the citizens of Donna, Texas, sent a letter of protest to their Congressman complaining about the harassment and mass deportation of Mexicans in their community by the Border Patrol. Prompted by Washington, the District Inspector of the San Antonio office launched an investigation, which revealed that the number of deportations was no higher than usual (72 Mexicans had been deported in one month). The Inspector refuted the accusations by the white citizens of Donna of harassment of Mexicans, claiming that they were just worried about their labor supply for the annual cotton harvest.[52]

In general, the Immigration Bureau knew that ranchers were reluctant to inform on Mexican border crossers and illegal immigrants in local communities because they depended on a freely available labor force, especially at harvest time, and disliked the Border Patrol's efforts to limit the number of Mexicans through deportation.[53]

The Border Patrol's mission was less controversial when it came to the deportation of Mexican women. In some border towns, inspectors and police went around Mexican neighborhoods to identify and arrest Spanish-speaking women who lived by themselves and were reputed to receive unrelated men into their homes. Sometimes the women were held as material witnesses to make prosecution of their pimps more likely. The women could deny the inspectors' accusations, though some admitted to having a few boyfriends. In either case, they usually lost at the hearings. No immigrant aid agency was mobilized, no lawyers were present, and no family members showed up to vouch for them. The case of Cecilia Bustillos is typical of how a Mexican immigrant woman could be ensnared in the net of deportation at the border. She was arrested as a suspected prostitute in El Paso in 1909 by the local police and reported to the Immigration Bureau. Unlike most Mexican women, Bustillos filed an appeal with the Bureau, claiming to be a U.S. citizen by marriage. But she could not validate her marriage to the satisfaction of the authorities, as her husband lived in Arizona and no family members could vouch for her story.[54] Like many Mexican women, she was deported as an illegal immigrant. Although Mexican women were much more likely to be deported as prostitutes than European women, the suspicion that these were "loose women" was often not openly stated. Racial suspicion as well as gender prejudice made the lives of single Mexican women subject to scrutiny and sometimes resulted in expulsion.[55]

After passage of the 1917 literacy law, the majority of all deportees from the United States were Mexicans; by the late 1920s, deportation in general became associated with Mexicans who had entered the United States without inspection.[56] Greatly facilitated by the Border Patrol, formal deportation of Mexicans increased to well over 5,000 in 1929. By 1936, when the figure was approaching 9,500, almost half of the deportees from the United States were deported to

Mexico, twice as many as were deported directly to Europe. All in all, almost 60,000 deportations to Mexico took place between 1928 and 1938.[57]

But these figures only tell a small part of the story. While the proportion of Mexicans among all deportees was high during the 1920s and the Depression decade, the actual number of deportees to Mexico fell after 1930—in tandem with the number of deportations in general. This decline masks the fact that a very high number of Mexicans, almost half a million, left the United States for Mexico over that decade. The vast majority of them were not counted as deported but rather were classified as voluntary departures or participants in repatriation. People who returned voluntarily usually had been arrested as illegal immigrants but had waived their right to a hearing by the INS. No illegal entry was put on their record permanently if they agreed to leave the United States on their own, and they retained the right to reenter the United States in the future. The Immigration Bureau presented this as a humane and cost-efficient solution to the problem of illegal immigration into the United States.[58]

More than 8,000 Mexicans were induced to leave in the early years of the Depression, and around 5,000 left "voluntarily" in the mid-1930s. The possibility of being forced into voluntary departure became part of the risk of border crossing for many Mexicans. The predominance of voluntary departure also meant that the struggle against deportations was almost entirely an individual one for Mexicans, fought outside the institutional advocacy and judicial systems of immigration regulation.[59]

The vast majority of Mexicans who left the United States during the 1930s, however, were counted neither as deportees nor as voluntary departures. Their return to Mexico was either part of the large informal return migration during the Depression or part of a so-called repatriation program of Mexicans (and Mexican Americans) that occurred in Southern California, Arizona, Nevada, New Mexico, Texas, and some midwestern states during the early 1930s.[60] Cities and towns along the border as well as further inland organized these expulsions of Mexican and Mexican American residents in the early 1930s in order to trim local relief rolls and to get rid of the

unemployed. In border towns, the expulsions resembled police actions: they were initiated by police and municipal governments and
were not coordinated with the Immigration Bureau or federal authorities. Further inland, deportations were organized by U.S. counties and municipalities in cooperation with the Immigration Service
and Mexican authorities, especially the Mexican consulates.[61] The Immigration Service kept no figures on these repatriations and did not
mention them after its 1933 *Annual Report.* According to Mexican
authorities, over 450,000 repatriations from the United States to
Mexico took place between 1929 and 1937.[62]

In the long run, the exodus of Mexican immigrants during the
Depression proved temporary. Those with long-established ties in
the United States returned to their U.S. homes within a short time,
or at least as soon as employment prospects improved around 1940.[63]
"On the southern border the utmost vigilance is now demanded to
prevent the illegal re-entry of those Mexicans who during the Depression either returned to Mexico on their own initiative or were repatriated at the expense of American communities," stated INS Commissioner MacCormack in his 1936 *Annual Report.*[64] The substantial
remigration of Mexicans thus defied the stereotype that Mexicans
were not future citizens and permanent settlers. At the same time,
the insecurity of status that was a nearly permanent feature of Mexican immigrants' lives was underlined by the large number of deportation and repatriations Mexicans endured during the 1930s. Operation
Wetback in the 1950s and similar mass deportation measures from
the 1980s on cemented the image of these non-European immigrants
as impermanent, uncommitted to the American order, and uninter-
ested in citizenship.

Political Deportations

Immigrants who were expelled from the United States because of
their political beliefs or associations were a small group of deportees
in the twentieth century. But throughout this time political deportation attracted a large amount of public attention. In a fundamental
way, political deportations raised the question of why, in a country
that so highly valued political freedoms and freedom of speech, a

person could be expelled for making use of these freedoms. More than with other policies and laws of exclusion, the deportation of politically objectionable immigrants was at the center of the debate over who deserved to remain in the United States and become a citizen.

Concern over radical immigrants dated back to the era after U.S. independence. In 1799, Congress passed the Alien and Sedition Laws; directed against French royalists, the laws limited the political activities of foreign nationals and threatened violators with deportation. But the Sedition Laws lacked enforcement mechanisms and were not, in fact, used to deport alien radicals during the nineteenth century. It was not until the 1880s that Congressional hearings contemplated measures to control foreign-born radicals in the United States through deportation.[65] In the aftermath of the assassination of President McKinley (by a self-confessed anarchist who was a native U.S. citizen), exclusionary laws were directed specifically against immigrant radicals. The Act of March 3, 1903, forbade the entry and naturalization of "anarchists, or persons who believe in or advocate the overthrow by force or violence [of] the Government of the United States."[66] The 1903 law also rendered political radicals deportable within three years of arrival in the United States. Radicals who did gain U.S. citizenship could be stripped of their new nationality if they had been anarchists before or at the time of naturalization.[67] Central to these provisions was the idea that anarchists brought with them violent ideas that were inimical to American political principles and the belief that such "imports" needed to be excluded from the landscape of ideas and political parties. That anarchists could be home grown and immigrants could acquire their convictions after life in the United States were not seriously considered in the years prior to World War I.

The 1903 law mandating the deportation of anarchists posed a problem for the Immigration Bureau. Unlike Asian immigrants who were socially distinct and easily identifiable or poor immigrants who were often snared by their need to contact and rely on public or private charity, "anarchists" in many parts of the United States could live their lives in obscurity. Their political activism within ethnic communities occurred away from the gaze of government. But from

1908 to 1909, the Bureau of Immigration decided to make anarchists the focus of its fledgling enforcement efforts beyond the border. The initiative occurred in the context of a flurry of restrictionist laws and measures: the naturalization laws of June 1906 and of 1907, the Gentleman's Agreement, and the growing campaign against white slave traffic.[68]

In a series of memoranda, local immigration districts were directed to gather information about alien anarchists with the help of local police. The response from many police chiefs to the Immigration Bureau's request to identify radical immigrants in their communities was a chilly one. "The Chief of Police politely informed me that he would not think of prying into the private affairs of the citizens of Cleveland so long as they kept the peace and begged to be excused from interrogating aliens with whom his department has come into contact in the manner which I suggested," reported the Cleveland representative of the Immigration Bureau to headquarters in Washington.[69] The Chicago inspector reported a similar lack of cooperation, as did other locales.[70] In some cities (New York, Boston, and San Francisco) cooperation was a bit better: immigrants were investigated and apprehended for criminal activities and for vagrancy as a result of this campaign. But none were arrested as anarchists.[71] In most American cities, immigrants' political activism and their open participation in the fabric of political life was not a cause of concern prior to World War I. Police and politicians—whose power was in good part derived from the votes of their immigrant clients—were reluctant to disturb this equilibrium in order to satisfy the curiosity of a far away Washington agency.

The situation was different in the American Northwest, however. There, the local police zealously pursued a campaign to identify and expel immigrant radicals, especially members of the International Workers of the World (IWW).[72] Western industrialists, small-town politicians, and their law enforcement allies were aligned firmly in their militant opposition to leftist workers, many of them affiliated with the IWW. Employers, "leading citizens," and local police pressured the Immigration Bureau in 1909 to initiate the deportation of alien radicals. "They have arrayed themselves against our government and its institutions; they cry out against our flag and demand that it be pulled down and replaced with the red flag of an anarchist. They even encourage women and induce children to join their ranks and attempt to educate them in ways detrimental to the spirit of good government," complained the Spokane Chief of Police to the local immigration officer.[73]

In this case, however, the Immigration Bureau was not eager to become identified as an arm of local law enforcement and did not share the zealotry of the local police. Instead of speedily deporting the arrested "anarchists" brought in by police, the inspectors of the Immigration Bureau went by the book and began a lengthy investigation of each one. Usually the immigrants denied being anarchists and defended their right to be active and organize for a more just political system. The arrested immigrants always stated that their organization wanted to "better the condition of the workingmen," and that, "the IWW does not teach anything about the overthrow of government."[74] In other cases, members of the IWW refused to speak to judges or Immigration Bureau officials. "Various paragraphs from the official pamphlets and books were read to him," wrote one inspector about the deportation proceedings against IWW member James Lund, "but it seemed almost impossible to secure a definite answer from him as to his beliefs. He is below the average on intelligence and, in fairness to him, it may be said that he did not, at the time of joining, realize or understand the principles and teachings of his organization."[75] In Spokane, the local immigration inspector A. F. Richardson found in 1909 that "in no case have any of the men interviewed admitted that the organization is of an anarchistic tendency." Without the will or the means to further investigate the political activities of those arrested, the Immigration Bureau had to let the men go.

Unless immigrants had been convicted of a crime of moral turpitude or had been found personally advocating the violent overthrow of the government the Immigration Bureau did not initiate deportation proceedings. No immigrant members of the IWW were deported before World War I, and fewer than a dozen anarchists were deported from the entire United States during the same time period, to the disappointment of politicians and businessmen in the western states.[76]

The U.S. entry into World War I began a new chapter in the deportation of politically active immigrants. Wartime prompted the passage of both antiradical and immigration restriction laws. The 1917 immigration law made the deportation of political radicals easier. "Any alien who at any time after entry shall be found advocating or teaching the unlawful destruction of property or advocating or teaching anarchy or the overthrow by force or violence of the Government of the United States" was now deportable at any time after entry.[77] The law was amended in October 1918 and July 1920 in order to arrest and deport foreign-born communists more easily. The Espionage Act of 1917 and the Sedition Act of 1918 made any public comment or activity that could be construed as antipatriotic a criminal offense.[78]

These laws were supposed to deal with domestic dissent during World War I, and they affected native and immigrant radicals alike who were active in the antiwar movement. Socialists Victor Berger and Eugene Debs (both U.S. natives) were sentenced to prison terms under these laws as were immigrant anarchists Emma Goldman and Alexander Berkman.[79] The prosecution and deportation of immigrants caught under these provisions led to a confusing maze of bureaucratic infighting and varying legal interpretations by different federal agencies and the courts. The voices of immigrants and their supporters played a role as well, but they were usually drowned out by the noise of wartime patriotism and feverish red-baiting between 1917 and 1920.[80]

As could be expected, immigration officials, local police, and members of the Department of Justice's Enemy Alien Bureau (a new creation) had few problems finding common ground in the Pacific Northwest when it came to using the new laws against immigrant radicals. Reviving the effort that had been abandoned around 1910, officials rounded up hundreds of immigrant members of the IWW and—while they waited for deportation warrants—subjected them to often lengthy prison stays.[81] Local representatives of the Immigration Bureau were now clearly influenced by local politicians and police who believed the IWW men to be "a landless and lawless mob who, having no property themselves, recognize no rights or property no law and no authority save the policeman's stick or physical violence."[82]

Commissioner General of Immigration Anthony Caminetti, a California native sympathetic to restrictionists, was not always a willing ally in the West Coast inspectors' attempts to deport immigrant radicals wholesale. During the war, he insisted on an individual examination of each deportation warrant against an IWW member. As a result, by late 1918, the effort to deport thousands of arrested Wobblies had nearly collapsed. By the time the deportation could be organized, hostilities had ended in Europe, and the number of IWW members imprisoned had dwindled to thirty-six. In the end, only seven men were sent back to Europe.[83]

While immigration officials hesitated, the reins in deportation matters were quickly taken over by officials in the Department of Justice—a rival to the Department of Labor, which oversaw the Immigration Bureau until 1940. During World War I, the Justice Department's newly founded Enemy Alien Bureau registered and supervised foreign nationals who were considered a potential danger to the United States. This new agency turned out to be the proving ground for the young J. Edgar Hoover. With a small staff, Hoover amassed files on thousands of aliens in the United States, using this information in an attempt to increase federal oversight over immigrants outside the Immigration Bureau. Despite these extensive registration and surveillance efforts, the federal government did not automatically detain citizens of an enemy nation (enemy aliens) in internment camps or deport them. Nevertheless, over 6,000 enemy aliens were detained during World War I as dangerous foreign agents or spies, at least temporarily. The Immigration Bureau was not involved in these detentions but remained concerned with border security issues such as the clandestine migration of Germans across the Canadian border.[84]

The involvement of the United States in the war was too brief and Hoover's Bureau was too short lived to promote the agenda of immigrant surveillance effectively. After the Enemy Alien Bureau was dismantled in the spring of 1919, Hoover became Assistant Attorney General in the Department of Justice where he continued his investigation of immigrant radicals under the new Attorney General, J. Mitchell Palmer. In this new position, Hoover took the laws of 1917–1920 as a mandate to arrest immigrant radicals and push for their expeditious deportation.[85] Hoover's task was made easier because the laws of 1917 and 1918 provided for deportations through guilt by association. Entire organizations and their publications could be declared enemies of the state by the Department of Justice, and all members, regardless of their individual level of participation, engagement, or belief, became deportable. In its requests for thousands of deportation warrants—usually after mass arrests in late 1918 and in 1919—the Department of Justice made entirely circumstantial evidence the core of its argument. In the occasional hearings about deportation, only the membership of an individual in an organization needed to be demonstrated; the rest of the argument focused entirely on the organization's propaganda, program, and bylaws.[86] The beliefs and life circumstances of individual immigrants were immaterial. For the authorities in large-scale deportations, this approach had significant advantages over the older individual examinations favored by the Immigration Bureau: few moral arguments could be made, and no direct personal engagement with the immigrant and his life had to be entered into. Thousands of deportations could take place within a year, if necessary.[87]

Between 1919 and 1920, Hoover was relentless in pushing for mass deportations from his perch in the Department of Justice. Almost daily, he sent memoranda and letters to Caminetti urging closer cooperation, complaining about lackadaisical immigration inspectors, and asking for the prompt issue of telegraphic deportation warrants for hundreds of immigrants. Occasionally, Hoover would also feed bits of information about the general malfeasance of foreign radicals to immigration officials in order to force them to act.[88] At first, Caminetti resisted this pressure, but over time he and his colleagues bowed to Hoover. Caminetti began to forward a large number of deportation warrants to his superiors at the Department of Labor, Secretary William B. Williams and Deputy Secretary Louis F. Post.[89] Both men were old-school Progressives whose oversight over immigration matters was informed by their past as unionists and reformers. They tried to continue to examine each deportation case individually because they maintained a faith in the potential individual worthiness of each immigrant, though they, too, wanted to deport "malignant conspirators and destructive revolutionists."[90] In the end, they signed hundreds of deportation warrants although Post also cancelled over 1,100 deportation warrants.[91]

Over 700 immigrants were deported to Europe in 1920 and 1921 for their political beliefs, most of them for mere membership in obscure immigrant organizations such as the Federation of Unions of Russian Workers of the United States and Canada, the Communist Party of America, and the Communist Labor Party.[92] None of these groups were anarchist, although they advocated revolution in Russia and argued for radical change in the United States as well. No member was accused of criminal malfeasance or other individual misdeeds. In late 1919, 184 immigrants belonging to the Federation of Unions of Russian Workers were deported aboard the *SS Buford*.[93] In addition, 530 members of the Communist Party of America were also deported under the 1918 law.[94]

Amid the increasingly feverish persecution of political dissidents, the voices of the persecuted themselves were sometimes difficult to hear. As a deportation train that the Immigration Bureau had organized in early 1919 wound its way across the country from Seattle to New York, picking up deportees at stations along the way, a newspaper reporter observed "a motley company of IWW troublemakers, bearded labor fanatics and red flag supporters huddled in crowded berths and propaganda strewed compartments." But few voices, other than those singing "foreign songs" came from the train. In some cities, such as Chicago and Detroit, labor rallies were held in support of the deportees as the train passed by. In Butte, Montana, IWW sympathizers even tried to storm the train. But otherwise neither the deportees themselves nor their supporters managed to be heard.[95]

Only one contemporary study by Constantine Panunzio on the backgrounds of the political deportees of 1919–1920 and the memoirs of Assistant Labor Secretary Louis Post cast a light on the motivations and reactions of political deportees in this period. Panunzio's interviewees revealed the male deportees' profound distance from both American life in general and immigrant communities.[96] Louis Post also remembered that quite a few men "had joined the Communist Party without any knowledge of its program and upon the understanding that he was joining a school for the study of mechanics . . .

because he did not understand English."[97] Many of those singled out for deportation seem to have lived through enough random government-sponsored injustice in Europe that they were not surprised to encounter similar actions in the United States. Elarton Shelig stated to Panunzio that "I did not do anything; if they find it is necessary to deport me because I am not an American citizen, they can do anything they wish to me."[98]

Most of the deportees were caught in the political storm against their will. Louis Post himself recognized that "as a rule, the hearings showed the aliens arrested to be workingmen of good character who had never been arrested before who were neither anarchists nor revolutionists nor obnoxious to the spirit of our laws in any sense. Many were faithful fathers of American children . . ."[99] "I will learn to read and write, get my papers and be a citizen, work hard, get an education for my children and family . . ." hoped one of the deportees interviewed by Panunzio.[100] Tony Smollok was even more disappointed, "When I came to this country and saw the Statue of Liberty I tipped my hat to it and was happy. During my stay in this country I could not find any understanding from the American people toward myself and have been frowned upon all the time as a 'Polack' in public places . . . the final result is . . . I am arrested by the government which I tried to understand and obey."[101] The fact that good workers or, more importantly, men and women willing to consider themselves Americans were deportable just because they belonged to certain organizations, embittered these immigrants.

Not all deportees were disappointed or passively awaiting their fate. Some members of the Union of Russian Workers as well as individual anarchists and members of early communist organizations were in fact vocal in their criticism of the U.S. government. As anarcho-syndicalists, they rejected any form of nationalism or patriotism and refused to seek U.S. citizenship. Many of these radicals were not only willing but demanded to go back to Europe; they protested their lengthy incarceration and their inhumane treatment in prison and demanded prompt release and repatriation to Soviet Russia.[102] A group incarcerated on Ellis Island in 1919 called themselves "political prisoners of Ellis Island Room 203," and sent a letter to the headquarters of the Immigration Bureau in Washington asking for quicker deportation.[103]

The most prominent among the committed and outspoken anarchists were Emma Goldman and her partner Alexander Berkman. They belonged to a circle that Louis Post called "philosophical anarchists" (not members of any of the proscribed organizations singled out in 1919–1920). Goldman and Berkman's protests and writings about their situation gave the political deportations of 1919–1920 a high profile in the press and, at times, the aura of a personal crusade of J. Edgar Hoover against these two outspoken radicals.[104] Even though Goldman rejected the nationalist implications of seeking U.S. citizenship on principle, she had contested her deportation order at first on the grounds that she was still married to Jacob Kershner, a fellow immigrant and naturalized U.S. citizen.[105] Alexander Berkman was opposed to any claim of citizenship. He had refused to become a naturalized U.S. citizen and contested his deportation only to demonstrate the repressive nature of the United States as a capitalist state.

Berkman and Goldman exemplified the dilemma of all political anarchists in the struggle against deportation. On the one hand, they and other politically articulate deportees saw their forced border crossing as a clear attempt by the U.S. government to silence them, to suppress free speech, and to wipe out protest against aggressive nationalism. On the other hand, by denying the value of nation-based citizenship, the deportees disenfranchised themselves. Though Goldman was represented by able legal counsel at her deportation hearing, her continuous silence (meant to show her disdain toward the machinations of the state) was met with contempt by her adversary J. Edgar Hoover and was seen as nothing but assent to her own exile. In the end, even this most articulate of political deportees was hampered by her own radically alternative vision of citizenship in articulating her resistance to deportation.

On a wintry December afternoon in 1919, Berkman and Goldman, together with 182 much more anonymous immigrants, were deported on the *SS Buford* to Soviet Russia. Goldman seemed incredulous as she found herself on the boat. "I felt dizzy, visioning a transport of political prisoners doomed to Siberia. The Russia of the past rose before me and I saw the revolutionary martyrs being driven into exile. But no, it was New York, it was America, the Land of Liberty! Through the port hole I could see the great city receding into the skyline . . . It was my beloved city, the Metropolis of the New World!"[106]

Goldman was not alone in her bitterness and nervous anticipation of what was to come. Many of her unknown fellow revolutionaries awaited an uncertain fate as they landed in Finland and traveled on to revolutionary St. Petersburg. J. Edgar Hoover noted with satisfaction in a memorandum to Commissioner Caminetti that, according to his sources, most deportees who had arrived in Russia on the SS *Buford* "were made to work as soon as they got there . . . if they did not go to work as directed there was a fine institution in Russia, known as the Extraordinary Commission, and that this Commission would take measures to put them very quickly in a frame of mind which would dispose them to work." The Immigration Bureau collected information on some of the deportees which noted their prompt arrests by the Bolshevik authorities. Some were deported again to Siberia, and others perished in the maelstrom of postrevolutionary Russia.[107]

In the United States, the political deportations of the post–World War I era continued beyond the "delirium of 1919/1920," as Louis Post called it in his memoirs. As late as 1924, the Immigration Bureau deported 84 anarchists or communists. But overall the Bureau found relatively few radicals to deport in the 1920s. On average, fewer than 1 percent of all deportees were sent back based on their political beliefs between 1922 and 1925. While the Immigration Bureau (in cooperation with Hoover's newly founded Bureau of Investigation) continued its clandestine observation of leftist organizations and tried to control the entry of suspected radicals into the United States in cooperation with the State Department, this effort yielded little. Few immigrants were deported as anarchists.[108] As Assistant Secretary of Labor Robe Carl White noted to Congressman Hamilton Fish, many appeals courts in the 1920s no longer favored the 1919–1920 interpretation of the law that the federal government had used, namely, that affiliation with a communist organization rendered aliens deportable. Deportations had to be based on more than mere membership in a leftist organization.[109] Occasionally, immigrant

radicals would be identified and deported even under this more restricted approach, despite extended legal battles that at times reached
up to the Supreme Court.[110] By and large, deportation for political
reasons faded into the background after the early 1920s, though it
never vanished as a means to exclude immigrants from permanent
residence in the United States.[111]

"The Red Ark will loom big in American History" declared Berkman and Goldman melodramatically in a manifesto written before
their departure.[112] But in truth the departure of this vessel was soon
forgotten. The dominant legacy of the deportation cases of the Red
Scare period was the chill it put on all forms of radical politics, including unionization of workers in the subsequent decades. Throughout the 1920s, 1930s, and beyond, authorities investigated, arrested,
and sometimes deported immigrant labor leaders who were European immigrants, Mexicans, and Filipinos. Most of these actions
received little national notice. In the 1920s and 1930s, at the instiga-
tion of employers who wanted labor organizers deported, the Immigration Bureau kept files and investigated union activity among
immigrant workers in the West Virginia and Colorado mines and
among agricultural workers.[113] In the Southwest, raids and deportations usually took place when Mexican workers tried to join a union.
Ostensibly, the INS only took action to look for illegal immigrants,
but the connection to the unionization drives was not lost on the
participants.[114]

The early 1930s brought a revival of antisubversive legislation
with the passage of the Smith Act in 1940. Fanned by Martin Dies's
House Committee on Un-American Activities, which kept up the
warning cries of foreign subversion in the second half of the 1930s,
this substantial piece of legislation would shape the persecution of
suspected communists (both immigrant and native) in the postwar
era and beyond. It required all foreign-born noncitizens of the United
States to be fingerprinted and register with the federal government
(and to reregister if they moved). The law mandated the registration
of all communists (foreign or native-born) and prohibited certain
kinds of political activity. The Smith Act also rendered aliens deportable if they had antigovernment political beliefs, a much broader
category than the "anarchist" or "communist" formulations that had

been followed since 1920. The Smith Act strengthened the hand of the executive branch in deportation matters, giving the Attorney General explicit discretionary powers in matters of deportation.

A follow-up law, the Nationality Act of 1940, excluded all those covered under the Smith Act from naturalization. Coupled with the near absolute power of the Attorney General to exclude immigrants for any reason whatsoever and the lack of provisions for review of many deportation decisions, the 1940s and subsequent decades gave the federal government a wide range of powers to deport any non-citizen immigrants who were suspect because of their political beliefs, opinions, or affiliations.[115]

Considering the reach of the deportation law from the 1940s on, the actual number of deportations of political radicals was not high. Ellen Schrecker has counted 253 deportations of "alien subversives" between 1946 and 1966—a small annual number compared with the more than a million Mexicans apprehended during the height of Operation Wetback in 1954 alone.[116] Deportations for political reasons declined rapidly by the late 1950s; in the 1960s, only 15 men and women were deported as subversives or anarchists. The 1970s similarly saw only 18 such deportations (out of a total of over 231,000). The deteriorating political climate between the United States and Eastern European countries (from which many suspected immigrant radicals came) in the 1950s and 1960s made deportation to those countries nearly impossible. Instead, most of the deportations of radicals that actually took place in the cold war decades were to Western countries such as Great Britain or Canada.[117]

Yet, as Schrecker has pointed out, the modest number of deportations masked the large-scale effort at identifying and investigating subversives among immigrants and the chilling effect this had on working-class immigrants in general. Few organizations helped those who were in danger of getting deported for political reasons. Even the ACLU, an advocate for other groups of dissenters, endorsed purging of foreign radicals from the nation. The American Committee for the Protection of the Foreign Born was the only advocacy organizations that took on these political deportation cases. The combination of a lack of basic rights for prospective deportees, limited financial and organizational resources to fight accusations in court, and the lack of support from the press made life very difficult indeed for immigrant radicals in the late 1940s and the 1950s. These immigrants' claims for residency rested on the right to free speech and political freedoms, but the immigrant deportees found few defenders of their right to dissent during the McCarthy Era.[118]

Deportation law and practice has always been shaped by the same political principle that undergirded immigration law: to define national sovereignty by determining who is not suitable or worthy to remain in the United States. Establishing the parameters of deportation (and exclusion) was a fitful process, and executing the law proved even more problematic for immigration officials. In general, in the nineteenth century the removal of immigrants from the United States played a very limited role in shaping immigration policy and the administration of borders. It was not until the early twentieth century that deportation became a consistently used instrument in the arsenal of immigration enforcement. Though it established an important principle, the demographic and social impact of deportation remained limited to the Chinese and Japanese communities before World War I. Only when access to immigration was curtailed because of restriction laws and Border Patrol enforcement in the mid-1920s did deportation become a threatening reality to tens of thousands of would-be immigrants each year. This was first noticeable on the Mexican border, and the impact of deportations on the growing community of Mexican residents in the United States was substantial and shaped the social expectations and political orientation of both Mexican immigrants and white Americans in the United States from the 1920s on. Almost from the beginning, deportation policy was shaped by racial perception. White immigrants could be judged deportable if their individual behavior or life circumstances rendered them excludable. Mexican and Asian immigrants, on the other hand, remained suspect border crossers, and were susceptible to deportation no matter how they lived or what they did.

This is not to say that the threat of deportation did not also loom over many European immigrants. Fear of deportation, especially among single women and the poor, ran strong in the first decades of the twentieth century and may have shaped their thinking about institutions of support. Contact with public institutions such as the police, hospitals, juvenile bureaus, and even schools and (later) public employment programs might render immigrants vulnerable to deportation. In the end, the enforcement of deportations against poor and socially marginal immigrants reinforced ideas of individual and community self-reliance that kept individual immigrants at a distance from the civil state in the twentieth century.

The most distinct and ultimately successful effort at shaping the citizenry and the meaning of U.S. citizenship through deportation law was in the realm of political deportations. Although in absolute and relative numbers the deportations of anarchists and subversives were small except for a few years after World War I, the comprehensive nature of political deportation legislation, its expanding and contested reach, and its connection with the revocation of naturalizations rendered political deportation a powerful tool in many ways. Immigrants and citizens alike were, in Emma Goldman's words, "mentally fumigated, made politically 'reliable' and governmentally kosher, by eliminating the social critics and industrial protestant, by denaturalization and banishment,"[119] Political deportations limited the reach of radical workers' organizations in the 1920s and also further diminished the possibilities of the Communist Party to attract immigrants, especially during and after World War II. The few but highly visible cases of deportations that made it to the courts, from Emma Goldman on further, imprinted the limits of political activism and free speech on an immigrant working class trying to find a way to express its ambitions for political democracy.

Whether they saw the Statue of Liberty fading at the horizon from the porthole of an old Navy ship like Emma Goldman, or endured the reverse border crossing in a windowless padded cell like the stowaway Arthur Bowen or through the slits of a cattle car like countless anonymous Mexicans during the Depression, deportees have always stood for the failed promise of immigration to America. But the cases discussed in this chapter also show how immigrants could be quite successful at avoiding deportation, or at least at renegotiating their deportation and becoming successful immigrants after all. In the early years of deportation law, European immigrants, recognizing the vision of citizenship that lay behind the enforcement of immigration law for them, resorted to the personal plea, which emphasized character and economic independence. Asian immigrants, on the other hand, were forced to resort to procedural tactics involving lawyers and definitions of law, because they were not part of the imagined family of future citizens in the United States. Political deportees were in a more difficult position because some of them consciously articulated alternative visions of American citizenship and rejected compromise or even procedural arguments in their favor. But difficult (and unsuccessful) as their fight might be, most deportees saw themselves as part of the American fabric, relying on American freedoms and American ideas of civic identity. This was as true for Emma Goldman, who quoted Lincoln and Jefferson in her appeals to stave off deportation, as it was for the anonymous laborers who sympathized with the Russian revolution. In many ways, immigrants who were deported differed little from the others who stayed. When asked why he chose to live in the open and risk deportation as an illegal alien in a city where he had been picked up by immigration agents twice, Otto Heinmann declared simply, "I couldn't stay away from New York. I'm a hearty New Yorker . . . I love New York."[120]

CHAPTER 4

Americanization

In the mid-1930s, Fermin Souto, a Galician-born cigar maker who had lived in New York and Florida since the 1880s, told a Works Progress Administration (WPA) interviewer that he had a clear image of the United States and its inhabitants well before he set foot in the country.[1] He had read about the United States as a teenager when he devoured heroic stories about Lincoln and Washington. This motivated him to emigrate to the United States as a young man.[2] Like him, German emigrants of the early twentieth century had read plenty about life in America: among other sources, the stories of cowboys and noble Indians circulated widely through the popular fiction of Karl May, a German author who never visited North America. The America these immigrants faced after their arrival may not always have lived up to expectations nourished in faraway lands. Crossing the border into the United States as residents, and then as social and cultural citizens would be a winding road, marked by the immigrant's own sense of direction and the pressures of assimilation and Americanization.

Crossing the border into the United States and retaining the right to live in the country were necessary first steps for becoming "American," but for many immigrants this third border crossing did not fit neatly into the imagined sequence. Americanization, as the lengthy process of becoming acculturated to the United States was called for most of the twentieth century, could take place well before immigrants arrived at the border. It could also be absent afterward, at least in the eyes of Americans. Finally, becoming culturally and socially

150

American could happen quite independently of immigrants' legal or political status. Americanization was seen as necessary, but as a cultural process independent of legal status, it turned into contested territory for immigrant advocates and regulators alike.

Especially in the period before 1930, Americanization was dominated by state-directed programs and patriotic rhetoric. In the early years, immigrants were expected to be passive recipients of ideas about nation and citizenship and they were expected to reshape their lives according to such teachings. As we shall see, however, many immigrants became differentiated observers of the attempts to Americanize them, and ultimately they came up with their own, often highly individualistic ideas about becoming American. Some Americanized in an alternative fashion, in conscious resistance to public Americanization programs. Others reshaped the official rhetoric to fit their needs. Ultimately, Americanization was a border crossing constructed less by state power and the law than by the immigrants' desires and ideas about what America meant in their lives.

In the early twentieth century, Progressives in the United States held up the banner of formalized and codified Americanization with cheerful determination. "Every schoolboy knows what America is," wrote Peter Roberts, a leading figure in the Americanization movement in 1920.[3] By the time Roberts posed his thesis and published a book on the subject, Americanization had become a well-established national project, not just an individual, self-directed process. Yet disagreement and confusion over what constituted Americanization was almost universal. Roberts represented the formal, instruction-oriented part of the Americanization movement. Like many of his contemporaries, he understood Americanization as a set of classes in English, American history, and American customs that would lead immigrants through a gradual process of cultural assimilation and education. At its best, formal Americanization would not only teach literacy and an enlightened version of American history, but also explore ways to further Americans' understanding of their own nation's identity in light of immigrant experiences and insights.

But Americanization also took place wherever immigrants arrived, settled, and oriented themselves in an English-speaking world and an industrial economy. To immigrants, this process of adaptation was primary in Americanization. For them it was a development that often had begun before they entered the United States and continued for their entire lives. It could supplement the formal instruction offered by the Americanization movement.

For the most part, these two forms of Americanization, one public and the other more private, were uneasily poised between two different ideas of what it meant to be American: they exemplified taught versus practiced ideas of citizenship and integration. To many Americanizers, immigrants became American in problematic ways, associated with the wrong kind of Americans, and thus they avoided the true meaning and blessings of Americanization. To immigrants, the high-minded ideals of the Americanizers had very little to do with the day-to-day reality of their lives. They often rejected the dry and lifeless instruction offered under the rubric "Americanization" as meaningless for their experiences as future citizens.

Progressive Americanization

The Americanization movement's historic roots stretched far back into the nineteenth century, and the movement was closely connected to the struggle over what it meant to be an American that roiled the nation in the Gilded Age and Progressive Era. Defining the "American character" had been part of the discourse about the new nation ever since Crevecoeur posed his famous question, "What then is this American, this new man?" in 1787.[4] Observers came up with competing definitions over the next century. The historian Philip Gleason has noted that, for the early nineteenth century, a reliance on republican virtues, an orientation toward the future, and a fundamental openness to newcomers from different European backgrounds were perhaps the most significant features of the American character.[5] Others (notably Alexis de Tocqueville) also counted industriousness, independence, daring, disregard for formality, and a heightened respect for property as typically American.[6] How did one acquire these traits? Early observers emphasized that the lived experience of democracy with its presumption of equality and the demands of frontier or pioneer life made Americans out of Europeans.[7]

The list of American traits grew as the nation became more populated and differentiated in the nineteenth century. By the late nineteenth century, American had come to be identified with the racial designation "white" and to some extent also with Protestantism. These were characteristics one could not easily acquire, and increasingly they implied that new immigrants (a growing proportion of them non-Protestant, if not also non-white) could never be truly counted as Americans.[8] As a result of this sort of reasoning, the immigration restriction movement and the Americanization movement emerged in tandem during the late nineteenth century. Each addressed what it saw as the presence of too many un-American immigrants in the United States, and they offered overlapping solutions.

Both Americanizers and restrictionists had argued in favor of a uniform standard for the knowledge of English and the American constitution as a precondition for immigrants who wanted to become naturalized U.S. citizens. The naturalization law of 1906 formalized the connection between naturalization and Americanization to a certain degree: a knowledge of English and the U.S. constitution became a legal requirement for acquiring U.S. citizenship in addition to the longstanding racial qualifications—only whites and those of African descent were admitted. The minimum standards of constitutional and linguistic knowledge were not defined in the new naturalization law. Immigrant advocates interpreted the 1906 Naturalization Act's provisions as a mandate to make formal Americanization part of preparing for U.S. citizenship.[9]

Guided by the belief that American citizenship could be taught to almost any willing immigrant, Americanizers were Progressives in their core beliefs: they offered instruction to all comers, even to groups whom they considered racially inferior to European immigrants.[10] Americanization instruction took place in settlement houses where residents introduced immigrants to American culture, history, and literature.[11] Hull House in Chicago was typical for approaching Americanization in both formal and informal ways. It offered English lessons, classes in American history, political clubs, and reading groups that focused on American authors.[12] Yet social gatherings could be just as effective as structured learning. Hilda Satt, then a

14-year-old Jewish immigrant from Poland, remembered her 1896 encounter with Jane Addams's Hull House as an unexpected yet defining moment in her Americanization:

> I struggled with my conscience and finally decided to accompany my friend to the Hull House Christmas Party . . . It was the first time that I had sat in a room where there was a Christmas tree. In fact, there were two trees in a room on each side of the high brick fireplace. The trees looked as if they had just been brought in from a heavy snowfall. The glistening glass icicles and the asbestos snowflakes looked very real . . . People called to each other across the room. Then I noticed that I could not understand what they were saying. It dawned on me that the people in this room had come from other countries. Yet there was no tension. Everybody seemed to be having a good time . . . As I look back, I know that I became a staunch American at this party.[13]

Hilda returned to Hull House as an 18-year-old factory worker to socialize and participate in the many lectures, reading groups, theater performances, and writing classes.

The early Americanization efforts reflected Progressives' desire to create public yet supervised spaces for community self-improvement, open to all willing students and free from coercion. Such offerings could liberate immigrants from the confines and narrowness of their home culture. Hilda Satt remembered that "I felt myself being freed from a variety of century-old superstitions and inhibitions."[14] The alternative American offerings were also designed to keep at a distance the potentially demoralizing influences of commercial leisure culture in urban America, corrupt party politics, and the pressures of the workplace. Americanization classes were cultural and social offerings not only to entice immigrants across the border into social and cultural assimilation, but also into the proper neighborhood of responsible and self-aware citizenship.

Knowledge about one's traditional past was also necessary to nurture a sense of pride and self-knowledge. The "Labor Museum" of traditional immigrant artisan skills at Hull House as well as ethnic festivals and cultural events furthered this idea. The settlement house workers were confident that their American (and white Protestant) cultural norms would prevail and that European ideas and skills would merely survive as memories.[15]

By the early twentieth century, Americanization efforts had broadened beyond the settlement houses. Peter Roberts, a leader in the Young Men's Christian Association (YMCA) movement, started a series of English classes in anthracite coal miners' camps in Pennsylvania in the early years of the twentieth century. Prompted by Roberts' example, formalized English instruction for working-class men was offered by many local YMCAs by 1910. For women, the Young Women's Christian Association (YWCA) International Institutes, founded in 1912, had their own Americanization programs, which concentrated on women's lives and education.

Outside the YMCA and YWCA, the movement for adult education and literacy received a strong push from Progressives worried about immigrant illiteracy.[16] Concern with the vast needs of immigrant communities for education and the potentially corrupting influence of privately run "citizenship schools" in immigrant communities prompted many states and cities with large immigrant populations to build a full-fledged adult education system before World War I. These initiatives, mostly financed by state money, led to the establishment of evening high schools attended by working adults.[17] California was a pioneer initiator of immigrant education programs. It created a state agency for dealing with structural assimilation and Americanization of immigrants, the California Commission for Immigration and Housing. Many other states had followed by 1910. Among the voluntary associations, the North American Civic League for Immigrants coordinated and publicized Americanization efforts nationwide.[18]

Fifteen-year-old Louis Adamic, a recent immigrant from Slovenia who would become the most eloquent American writer about immigrants in the interwar years, enrolled in such a night school in Manhattan to learn English:

Our teacher was a thin, unhealthy looking, undersized native American perhaps of foreign parentage, who, I felt, was terribly ill at ease before this assemblage of thirty-odd Dagoes, Dutchmen, Jews, and Bohunks of all ages, many of them doubtless better educated in their native tongues than he was in English . . . At the beginning of each session he required us to rise, salute the American flag and pledge allegiance to the country for which it stood. Even the first evening, this seemed somewhat absurd to me.[19]

Adamic soon quit the school, in part because the 15-year-old daughter of his employer and landlord, "a girl of delicate charm," took up his attention. Instead of learning English in the stifling classroom of a night school, Adamic became self-taught with the help of billboards, then magazines, and finally popular books, which he read in public libraries. Formal instruction in English remained distant for Adamic, as it would for the majority of working-class immigrants before World War I.[20]

Americanization and World War I

It was during the World War I era that Americanization became an official, state-supported campaign to teach immigrants about American history, assimilate them into American society, and turn them into supporters of the American war effort. Naturalization was the goal of this part of the Americanization movement. Even before the official entry of the United States into the war, patriotic themes and the future of immigrants as American citizens became dominant in the discourse on immigrants and their fit into American society.

But amid the din of propaganda and call to political conformity, pluralist and humanist approaches and ideas persisted within the Americanization movement. Woodrow Wilson articulated the pluralist approach of many Americanizers. The occasion was the nation's first large-scale celebration of naturalizations, organized by the U.S. Naturalization Bureau in Philadelphia. In what turned out to be the opening speech for the World War I Americanization movement, the President welcomed about 20,000 newly naturalized U.S. citizens. He emphasized that becoming a U.S. citizen meant more than becoming an American in the legal sense—it also required the adoption of different national ideals and the wholehearted identification with an ideal of humanity that went beyond the borders of the United States. "You have just taken an oath of allegiance to the

United States . . . not of allegiance to those who temporarily represent this great government . . . You have taken an oath of allegiance to a great ideal, to a great body of principles, to a great hope of the human race." He added, "My urgent advice to you would be not only always to think first of America, but to think first of humanity." With their new citizenship and identity as Americans, immigrants should not separate themselves within the nation, though old identities need not be left behind either: "I certainly would not be one even to suggest that a man cease to love the home of his birth and the nation of his origin. These things are very sacred and ought not to be put out of our hearts."[21] Wilson's ideas reflected a humanitarian ideal of citizenship that went beyond national borders and was informed by mutual learning between immigrants and natives, a process which the Progressives had emphasized early on.[22]

During the war years, Wilson's humanitarian ideals were contradicted and often overruled by a much more coercive view of Americanization. Theodore Roosevelt, less inclined to inclusive sentiments and general humanism than Wilson, spoke for the more aggressive, nationalist side of Americanization during this period. In his 1915 essay, "Fear God and Take Your Own Part," he advocated national service for young men (a draft, in effect) as a means to a "thorough Americanization of ourselves." Immigrants might need additional prodding to join into such service. "The larger Americanism demands that we insist that every immigrant who comes here shall become an American citizen and nothing else. If he shows that he still remains at heart more loyal to another land, let him be promptly returned to that land . . . There is no room in this country for hyphenated Americanism." For Roosevelt, Americanism was inseparable from American citizenship, which in turn was an exclusive form of loyalty, irreconcilable with other allegiances.[23]

Roosevelt's rejection of any semblance of dual affiliation rather than Wilson's humanist patriotism dominated the Americanization campaign of 1916–1920.[24] Roosevelt's sentiments were echoed by other prominent reformers such as Frances Kellor, one of the most committed backers of state-directed Americanization. For Kellor, Americanization meant "the conscious effort to forge the people in this country into an American race that will stand together in time

of peace or of war. Every effort should be bent toward an Americanization which will mean . . . that we are one people in ideals, rights
and privileges."[25] Ignorance, distance from American institutions,
and an inability to connect and identify with the American cause
because of linguistic or sociocultural barriers were considered a
danger to the nation. In this context, Americanization consisted not
only of learning English and American values, it also meant naturalization and suppression of behaviors, cultural traits, and political
preferences considered un-American.[26]

Kellor was a particularly vigorous spokeswoman for the cause, but
by and large, all branches of the Progressive movement united behind rhetoric like hers during the war. Americanization became a
patriotic crusade that united a vast range of organizations and institutions of all political shades, including restrictionist groups such as
the Patriotic Order Sons of America, traditional conservatives such
as the Daughters of the American Revolution and the Baptist Home
Missionary Society, and immigrant advocates such as the settlement
houses and the YMCA.[27]

The YMCA and the adult school movement remained the prime
providers of Americanization classes during World War I and afterward, but the leading role in formal Americanization programs was
now reserved for federal and in some cases state agencies.[28] On the
federal level, the Bureau of Education and the Bureau of Naturalization became leaders in the effort during the war, often in competition
with each other over resources and publicity. Both agencies published
teaching materials, helped local school districts and voluntary agencies set up Americanization classes, and staged Americanization Day
celebrations to mark the naturalization of local citizens. On the state
and municipal level, Americanization heightened the profile of reformers in certain states as Progressives took charge of Americanization there.[29]

The Americanization crusade was intertwined with the war effort, and it reached its greatest intensity from 1919 to 1920. Voluntary organizations, state and municipal agencies, and the federal
government increased their ideological and financial investment in
Americanization as World War I wound down. Even after the armi-
stice, federal financing of Americanization classes and pressure on

immigrants to become U.S. citizens continued unabated, and funding spent for Americanization reached unprecedented heights during the immediate postwar years. Observers also noted a professionalization of the Americanizers during the years 1919–1920. Most of the materials published by state and local agencies were written and distributed during the postwar years as Americanization was transformed from a wartime propaganda tool into a permanent part of the educational landscape.[30]

The core activity of organized Americanization during the war remained the teaching of English and the rudiments of U.S. history. Ideally, classes in English (conversation and vocabulary) were to be supplemented by lectures and other types of presentations such as class projects to accompany the basic curriculum. Narrow skills building (in preparation for the naturalization exam, for example) would never suffice, argued Peter Roberts. Accordingly, Americanization teachers encouraged immigrants to write their memoirs, hold parades, and celebrate Americanization Day. Roberts and others urged immigrants to participate in American sports and games, organize clubs and stage plays, all in the name of assimilating young people into American culture.[31]

Probably the best-known spectacle of World War I Americanization was the "Melting Pot" reenactment performed by workers who attended the English School at the Ford Motor Company in Dearborn, Michigan. As the director of the school, Clinton DeWitt, described it to fellow Americanizers:

> Men stepped down from a boat scene representing the vessel in which they came over . . . down the gangway . . . into a pot which represented the Ford English School. Six teachers, three on either side, stir the pot with ten foot ladles, representing nine months of teaching in the school. Into the pot 52 nationalities with the foreign clothes and baggage go, and out of the pot, after vigorous stirring by the teachers, comes one nationality, viz. the American.[32]

The transformation enacted in this play had little in common with the emancipatory ideals of the original Progressive movement. Americanization as presented by the pupils of the Henry Ford School was sudden and complete. Immigrants were to endure Americanization,

not to forge it themselves. The idea of a largely passive immigrant
who was a vessel for teachings on America was also obvious from
the instruction materials used in the Americanization classes at the
Ford factory and elsewhere during this period.[33] An observer at Ford
reported that the first sentence the men were taught to speak (in
unison) was "Wake from sleep!" This was followed by "I open my
eyes," and "I find my watch."[34] The instruction booklets provided
from 1917 on by the federal Bureau of Naturalization showed that
rote learning of simple phrases and repetition of the simplest facts of
U.S. history held center stage in these manuals. In the materials for
men (who were a majority in almost all classes), work, time discipline, and obedience were behaviors that were taught as part of English lessons.[35]

In some schools, the lessons reflected a more emancipatory vision
of Americanization. Teachers in regular evening schools were urged
to teach their students public speaking and public demeanor. The
first lesson in California was thus about introducing oneself.[36] California authorities also urged teachers not only to emphasize "stories . . . honoring a national hero but choosing the hero from one of
the nationalities presented in the classroom," demonstrating that,
"these qualities in foreign heroes and statesmen are the same that our
own country most honors."[37] In Cleveland, the Superintendent of
Adult Instruction, Raymond Moley (a professor at Case Western
University), wrote a special text for Americanization classes. The
book began with a brief introduction on U.S. government and history
and quickly moved along to help the future citizens of Cleveland find
their way around the city and its history. Chapters contained practical lessons such as how to apply for a job or inquire at public offices.
Illustrations were included, showing the public buildings, iron and
ore mills, loading facilities on Lake Erie, and other parts of the city
where immigrants might work or live.[38]

Lessons on hygiene, care for the sick, proper cooking, and household
budgeting were part of the basic Americanization instruction for
women. Their first English lessons contained core words such as
"baby, bather, tub, water, mother, warm, stove, soap."[39] Another
manual issued by the same agency was more specific. Women were
to be instructed in the basics of hygiene, the home, and child care,

first and foremost. "Good citizens keep their houses clean, good citizens keep their yards clean," proclaimed the book, before it continued with the stories of Franklin, Washington, and Lincoln, almost as an afterthought. The setting into which these immigrant women were supposed to assimilate also varied very little: "In the mornings, women get breakfast. Their husbands go to work," proclaimed an early lesson.[40]

But the reality of the classes, reproduced and staged in photos in the *Report on the Instruction of Women Immigrants,* published by the California Commission of Immigration and Housing, was more varied. Americanization classes were held in a railroad car, in a labor camp for Mexicans, in the barrio, and in the home of Armenian women. Anglo women enrolled in a Spanish class at a "Labor Temple" to serve their constituents better. The California authorities also reported on immigrant women that, "in most cases they came for two hours, one hour of which was devoted to English and one to sewing." The Americanizers of Minneapolis reported that they did not teach formal classes at all for women but focused on home visits in which the social component was predominant and the formal instruction incidental. Women volunteers were taught how to befriend immigrant women, help them with mending and cooking, and, on occasion, instruct them informally in American behavior. "Sometimes book lessons are never attempted, for the mother may be too burdened with other cares, but she does enjoy the friendly contact and many indirect lessons are taught that way," explained Katherine Kohler, "Director of Americanization, Home-Work" for the public schools of Minneapolis. In any case, naturalization and preparation for legal U.S. citizenship was not necessary, because married immigrant women could not become U.S. citizens on their own before 1922.[41]

Not all Americanization took place in the context of supervised instruction. Immigrants, especially working-class immigrants, continued to shape their own Americanization in ways that did not necessarily conform to the ideals taught in textbooks and citizenship classes. Steve Radin, a Slovenian teenager who had arrived in New York as a stowaway before World War I, Americanized himself: "He went to the movies twice a week and read the *New York American,*" remembered his fellow countryman Louis Adamic. "He wore better clothes from season to season . . . Now and then after an especially thrilling movie he still thought of going West. Off and on he was still tempted to join the Army and the Navy." Radin did eventually end up in the West—as a bootlegger and Hollywood extra, after a stint in the army and as a prizefighter in New York's working-class districts. A taste for adventure, a desire for self-determination, and the ability to put up with considerable insecurity were traits that Adamic considered quintessentially American in Radin's life story. Adamic himself joined the U.S. Army in World War I; in the barracks, amid soldiers from a great variety of backgrounds, he learned about American ideals and the disappointing reality of soldiers' lives.[42]

James Barrett has pointed out that immigrant workers also tried to shape their own Americanization through membership in unions, churches, and political groups according to a more collective vision.[43] The "American standard of living" was a well-recognized idea for these immigrants, something to aspire to with the help of trade unions and apart from their pursuit of a naturalization certificate. Free speech and the right to organize were other fundamental parts of becoming and being American for workers. They were at the root of an upsurge in radical activism during World War I, which was often self-consciously "American"—though their critics branded the activists as foreign.[44] The official Americanization campaigns of the World War I era did not capture these experiences. In the years that followed, unions continued to self-consciously represent themselves as an Americanizing force though they turned much more conservative and aligned themselves ideologically, if not organizationally, with the mainstream Americanization movement of the 1920s

With nationalist fervor subsiding by 1920, the House of Representatives cut funding for Americanization through the federal Bureau of Education and the Bureau of Naturalization, and it eliminated support for the Foreign Language Information Service completely. Instead, once again, Congress turned its attention to a comprehensive immigration restriction law, which was passed in 1924. The federal budget cuts reduced the number and extent of federally supervised and funded Americanization activities nationwide. The Bureau of Naturalization still kept track of instruction and published and distributed teaching materials, but for all practical purposes the early 1920s marked the end of direct federal involvement and large-scale Americanization.[45]

State and local voluntary associations continued to carry on with their own Americanization programs despite the federal pullout. Indeed, many state legislatures created Americanization programs and bureaucracies in the early 1920s, often with the support of the American Legion and similar conservative and patriotic organizations. Voluntary organizations also tried to formalize a broad coalition interested in furthering Americanization. As a result, citizenship classes became a permanent part of the adult education landscape even without the federal government and the fervor of the wartime and immediate postwar years. Public school systems, settlement houses, and YMCAs continued to offer formal classes in English and U.S. history to help immigrants pass the naturalization exams.[46]

Direct involvement by the federal government increased again during the later years of the New Deal, when the Roosevelt administration paid the salaries of Americanization and naturalization class teachers through the WPA and similar programs. By the 1930s, special efforts were made to reach certain population groups who had remained outside earlier Americanization efforts. Among them were older immigrant women and poorer immigrants whose lack of naturalization papers kept them outside the emerging net of New Deal income supports. But despite this continuing campaign, the formal Americanization movement never again reached the political and ideological prominence it had attained during the era of World War I.[47]

Social Scientists and the Critique of Americanization

The retreat of the federal government from Americanization at the beginning of the 1920s proved to be a catalyst for an intellectual reassessment of the movement and its goals. Indeed, a high degree of self-reflection and theorizing became one of the salient characteristics of Americanization from then on. Some observers and participants, notably those who themselves were part of immigrant communities, had been critical of the Americanization campaign early

on. The sociologist Florian Znaniecki, for one, had recognized the
pitfalls of coercive Americanization as early as 1916.[48] Numerous
other observers had also disliked the coercive elements of Americanization during the war, which they saw as contrary to its true
spirit as a mutual and evolutionary process. Edward Hale Bierstadt,
a former employee of George Creel's federally financed Committee
on Public Information, (the most important U.S. propaganda agency
of World War I), wrote a highly critical assessment of mainstream
Americanization in 1919.[49] As a result of the intolerance it had fostered, believed Bierstadt, Americanization was badly discredited as
an idea and a movement. "The very word 'Americanization' is a
dangerous choice. It reminds the immigrant too strongly of 'Rus-
sianization' or 'Germanization.'"[50] His California colleague, Carol
Aronovici, himself an immigrant and the head of the California Commission on Immigration and Housing, concurred. In a 1919 assessment, he wrote,

> The spectacle of the rabid and ignorant Americanization efforts
> was disheartening. It did not represent America as the foreigner
> had pictured it in his dreams before landing upon these shores. It
> flavored more of Hungary where the magyarization of several mil-
> lions of people was attempted . . . of Russia of the Tsarish days with
> the persecution of the Jew and the denaturalization of Poles.[51]

Bierstadt's and Aronovici's critique was echoed by other Progressives, who argued that the chance to connect in a meaningful way
with immigrant communities had been squandered and that Americanization had become a mere propaganda tool, a repressive instrument to force immigrants into lives of political and social conformity.[52] As a result, a number of academics and writers, among
them Horace Kallen and Julius Drachsler, called for a return to the
community-based and culturally open roots of the Americanization
movement. Drachsler, author of a study about intermarriage among
second-generation immigrants, saw the need to continue Americanization programs under state guidance, but he also called for more
empowerment of immigrants as part of Americanization.[53]

Drachsler was joined by a group of academics in the newly emergent social sciences who supported a pluralist approach to organized

Americanization.[54] Financed in part by the Carnegie Foundation, these scholars published a series of books that became the foundation of social science research on American immigrant communities for decades to come.[55]

In fine-grained portraits, the studies buttressed the assessment that Americanization during the war and postwar years had been a failure by most measures, but that immigrants themselves were quite engaged in their own Americanization. Frank Thompson's *Schooling of the Immigrant* provided a critical assessment of Americanization classes taught to adult immigrants from 1916 to 1919.[56] Despite a lack of meaningful educational and organizational support, immigrants were quite motivated to naturalize, found John Gavit in his book *Americans by Choice.*[57] It just took time for the most recent generation of immigrants from eastern and southern Europe to catch up with those immigrants from western and northern Europe who had come earlier. Immigrants' high degree of motivation stood out for William Leiserson as well, who investigated Americanization among industrial workers.[58] Gavit, Thompson, and Leiserson all noticed how individual motivation often stood in contrast to the ineffective or coercive official programs for Americanization. The authors argued instead for a better-organized web of organizations that might represent the older Progressive principles of Americanization.

Sophonisba Breckinridge, in her monograph on families and Americanization, *New Homes for Old,* argued specifically in favor of involving a more tightly networked set of agencies such as the Immigrant Protective League of Chicago, the YWCA's International Institutes, and similar organizations that had emerged from the settlement house movement.[59] Leiserson also wanted to involve activist ethnic trade unions in the Americanization and assimilation of immigrants. For these authors, centralization and a certain degree of bureaucratization were rational responses to the individual and family-centered needs of immigrants and did not detract from the ideals of cooperation and mutuality that remained central to their conception of Americanization. Other studies came to similar conclusions by examining such topics as the immigrant press, immigrant neighborhoods, immigrant health, and immigrants in the justice system.[60]

The Americanization Studies series spawned more research, and a second batch of books was published in the late 1920s and 1930s. Among them were Sophonisba Breckinridge's *Marriage and the Civic Rights of Women*, Isaac Berkson's *Theories of Assimilation* (which dealt with assimilation and group cohesion of eastern European Jewish immigrants in the 1920s), and Caroline Ware's *Greenwich Village* (an ethnographic study of a mostly Italian immigrant community).[61] These and other books no longer focused on formal Americanization programs, but dealt with assimilation and group cohesion as measurable phenomena of social organization, especially among immigrants from southern and eastern Europe. The Americanization Studies depicted these communities at the point of permanent incorporation into U.S. society through work, schooling, and various forms of citizenship.[62]

The influence of academic research on immigrant incorporation in the interwar years was not limited to academic circles. Immigrant advocacy organizations also sought connections to social scientists, and they became active in disseminating information on ethnic communities and their social and political needs. A small, underfinanced, but articulate group of immigrant advocates began to collect and publish information on current immigration policy in the early 1920s and also acted on a national level as a proimmigrant lobby. The most important of these was the Foreign Language Information Service (FLIS). Its first director, Edward Bierstadt, played an important role as a mediator between the "American" public and immigrant communities through its monthly publication *The Interpreter*. The slim journal provided both a summary of the ethnic press for English speaking readers and a summary of immigration-related politics in Washington for immigrants. The FLIS suffered from a chronic lack of financial resources, but its staff members were among the most knowledgeable and critical experts on immigrant legislation and policy in the 1920s and 1930s.[63]

As the FLIS became the most important group uniting experts on immigrant policies and immigrant integration (an early think tank, in effect), the International Institutes of the YWCA were the primary group to work with immigrant communities in most major American cities during the postwar years. Members of the International

Institutes organized the teaching of English and citizenship classes and remained informed on the concerns of immigrants during the 1920s, the Depression decade, and beyond. Because of their decentralized nature, the International Institutes' national influence was never very large, but their longevity and the accumulated expertise of their members made them an important resource throughout this period as well.[64]

Both of these groups dealt only peripherally with non-white immigrants. Their central concern was Europeans who found themselves excluded from U.S. immigration and naturalization. In a climate of xenophobia and strong support for immigration restriction, the FLIS and the International Institutes were vital mediators between these white immigrant communities and Washington policy makers in the interwar decades.

Immigrants and Americanization in the 1920s and 1930s

The 1930s brought a new turn to Americanization in the public culture of the United States. Between greatly reduced immigration and the resurgent civic nationalism of the New Deal era, Americanization as a mandate for European immigrants faded in importance. During these decades, Americanizers still did not address the concerns of non-white immigrants, especially those of immigrants from Mexico and the Caribbean, who did continue to arrive in the United States in the 1920s and 1930s. Instead, Americans—including long-time immigrants—were urged to reshape their own citizenship and take their place in the nation as defined by the programs and priorities of the New Deal. Even though Americanization was no longer a priority for immigrants, American identity remained a core ideal of civic culture.[65]

For European immigrants who had arrived in previous decades, the 1930s brought on an increasingly self-reflective integration into American culture and society. As part of this process, immigrants became more articulate about their relationship to American society. In a series of interviews and oral histories collected by the WPA Writers' Project as part of its American Folk Life Project in the second half of the 1930s, immigrants from different European and non-European groups reflected on their own assimilation since arriving in the United States.[66] Testimonies by immigrants were also collected by the writer Louis Adamic and the social scientist Sophonisba Breckinridge as part of their large-scale projects on immigrant integration.[67]

In these collections, Americanization emerged as a dialogue between immigrants and the organizations that tried to represent them to the wider public. The testimonies show that the interwar years were not a period of gradual and inevitable assimilation for everyone. As in earlier decades, becoming American took many shapes, but in contrast to the prewar era, there was a widespread awareness of different routes taken and alternative possibilities and identities. The overwhelming number of immigrants still became American in some way, but their path to Americanization was not without ambivalence. From the reflections and stories of European immigrants (and in a few cases, of non-European immigrants as well), we see a range of possibilities for assimilation but also a range of "Americas," which these communities built for themselves.

Certain types of institutions and identities were almost universally important in Americanization for individuals and entire immigrant communities; others were important only in certain contexts. Among the elements that provided the building blocks of a unified perspective on Americanization and that held the promise of understanding one's own Americanization and place in America was above all the ethnic community. Ethnic identity always set the stage for Americanization, and by the 1920s, formal structures existed within each immigrant community to mediate Americanization as an informal process. Most often these were connected to an ethnic church or parish and to voluntary associations. The workplace, and to a lesser extent public and parochial schools, were other institutional framers of Americanization, though immigrants did not "own" them as they did the ethnic organizations. Other elements of American life prominent in the 1920s and 1930s, such as mass culture, political life, and consumer culture, were occasionally important in immigrants' narratives, but not central to their histories.

The role of religious and ethnic voluntary organizations as anchors and agents of Americanization was well recognized by reformers in the 1920s and 1930s. Some ethnic organizations encouraged their members to naturalize, and others would not even take non-naturalized immigrants as members.[68] "I am an American," stated a Portuguese American fisherman to his interviewer, adding by way of explanation, "I belong to the Portuguese American club."[69] Citizenship raised one's status in the ethnic community of the 1920s. Sociologist Sophonisba Breckinridge noted that the immigrant women who were most eager and successful in taking out citizenship papers were those connected to ethnic clubs. The WPA interviewers recorded that the women immigrants of Manchester, New Hampshire, were motivated to become citizens because this would make them eligible to become members of the Polish-American Club and participate in the annual parade, wearing special folkloric costumes. Here, the completed conversion to a new citizenship was expressed by wearing "old world" clothes in an American-style parade.[70] For Fermin Souto, the elderly cigar maker discussed at the beginning of this chapter, his citizenship certificate—one of the most precious things he owned—was kept at the Tampa Centro Español of which he had been secretary for decades.[71] For Mexicans in various Texas cities, the League of United Latin American Citizens—both a political pressure group and an ethnic voluntary association—provided a means for showing that members were both Mexican and American with an interest in good citizenship in both countries.[72] For the Germans in Philadelphia whose organizations had lost much of their ethnic identity by the 1920s, membership in a German American club could affirm their Americanness, as little German substance remained in these organizations.[73]

Many of those interviewed in the WPA program or by Breckinridge, as well as the communities described in the secondary literature of the era, were involved in the life of ethnic parishes or churches. The Reverend Elias Skipitares, a Greek Orthodox priest—largely self-educated, and ordained in the United States after life as a farmer, construction worker, and phrenologist in the American West—presented a vision of America as a country of material plenty but with a need to reconcile the needs of mind and body and to follow traditional church rules, at least among his countrymen. "The Graecians are a people of faith and devout" he told his WPA interviewer, and his parish secretary, William Felos, a storekeeper, agreed.[74] Both of these men saw no need to change their spirituality in any way; indeed, they saw a need to emphasize their traditional church ties in view of the obvious American deficiencies in this regard. The Italian stonemasons interviewed in Montpelier, Vermont, were not as articulate, but their involvement in the devotional life of their Catholic parish made their similar accent on organized religion clear as well. The interviewer noted how closely interwoven family and parish life were for these men, traditionally not a given for the Italians (as it had been for the Irish). The stonemasons themselves saw no contradiction in this: America was the greatest country (although Italy was more beautiful), but its realm was not a spiritual one—rather, it was a public and political sphere. In this sense, they had, of course, accepted a very American role for their church, one that would leave space for a secular patriotism whenever that seemed necessary.[75]

But in contrast to earlier decades, the religious organizations in many "new" immigrant communities during the 1920s and 1930s took a stand concerning questions of public life and politics. The Italians in Providence used ethnic parishes as their main outlet for organizing because the political machine was in the hands of the Irish and (Republican) native Protestants. From the parish-based organizations, they fought the battle against prohibition and for self-determination in liturgical, political, and educational matters. The Poles of Manchester went one step farther: together with other Polish Catholics (especially in the Chicago area), they seceded from the American Catholic church and formed the Polish National Catholic Church. For the Poles of Chicago the 1920s brought intense pressure to Americanize from the church hierarchy, a pressure the laity resisted; ethnic parishes were maintained, and the Polish National Church flourished although English became the language of most parishes.[76] Italian churches in New York tried to turn their precarious position around and "strove to place themselves in such a position that the process of Americanization would bring the Italian people to them rather than drive them away," as Caroline Ware has observed.[77]

Clergymen were usually important in these transformations, interpreting America to their flock and trying to demonstrate the value of

ethnic culture to outsiders. The Reverend Wilfred Ouelette, a French
Canadian priest in Maine, took pains to explain to the WPA interviewer that French Canadians in his community were not as French
as the Quebecois, nor were they assimilated into Yankee New England. As he saw it, his Acadian parishioners treasured their mixed
French-British-American heritage. This made them well-suited to
life in the borderlands. Their Arcadia was right there, and he was not
going to convert them one way or another; instead, he tried to help
them maintain their language and direct them in their history. "We
are loyal to the country in which we claim citizenship, but we are
also loyal to ourselves and our traditions." America allowed this and
was therefore a good place to be.[78] The Polish parish in Manchester
was headed by Father Bronislaw Krupski, and he, too, turned out to
be an advocate of Americanization. He was critical of the traditional-
ism in his flock and tried to replace it with a sense of American obligation and patriotism. In public life, priests and other religious workers kept their distance from the narrative of American citizenship,
though within their parishes they were openly engaged in negotiating American culture for themselves and their flock.[79]

"Americanization and citizenship are the usual resultants of all
school training," declared Frank Thompson, Boston's Superintendent of Public Schools, in 1920 with certainty.[80] Thompson was as
much expressing a hope as he was promoting a continued involvement of public schools in citizenship instruction. Public education
for children became widely recognized as a mechanism for Americanization for first- and second-generation immigrant children. The
pivotal role of public schools had long been recognized in densely
packed immigrant neighborhoods, but in the 1920s this became a
widespread part of the identity of public schools nationwide. Caroline Ware, a more critical voice on public institutions, agreed with
Thompson that the public schools in the neighborhood she studied
(New York's Greenwich Village) "were primarily concerned with the
problem of citizenship."[81] But she noted that this approach had pitfalls as well: for one thing, the Americanization of children without
simultaneous assimilation of their parents could weaken family solidarity and immigrant communities.[82] Louis Adamic also observed
that instruction in American culture alienated children from their

parents. He urged a return to more parental and community instruction, and a retreat from public institutions and what he considered their alienating effect on parent-child bonds.[83] In many cases, parents recognized the potential source for conflict between public institutions and community traditions and tried to mitigate it by keeping their children out of public schools and sending them to ethnic Catholic or other parochial schools. This modified Americanization did not follow the trajectory envisioned by Progressive Americanizers.[84]

In the adult education movement, citizenship and Americanization classes were still important in the late 1920s and 1930s. For the Polish and Jewish women interviewed by Sophonisba Breckinridge in Chicago in the middle and late 1920s, citizenship classes represented a first step into the public sphere, undertaken with great trepidation because many women preferred to be instructed by husbands or sons for their citizenship examination. Elizabeth Eastman reported that in the late 1920s immigrant women in western Pennsylvanian industrial towns did not have time to read or learn to speak English, and they could not attend English classes because of their heavy work and family schedules. "Americanization seems little more than a strange word and a vague ideal as yet far from attainment," she wrote in 1930.[85] Once in the class, however, which was often attended only by women, they became eager learners, though some never overcame their shyness or illiteracy.[86] In another close-up view, a WPA interviewer visited citizenship classes conducted among Polish women in a New Hampshire mill town. She found few of the women able to speak sufficient English to be interviewed, but all were eager to take out their citizenship papers independently of their husbands. The classes, though badly taught, offered companionship as much as an introduction to an America in which these women had lived for over twenty years with few outside contacts. The women met and studied to affirm their place in their ethnic community and to further their knowledge of the strange place beyond.[87] Immigrant men also testified to the importance of formal English and citizenship instruction. Roland Damiani, an Italian shoe worker in Beverly, Massachusetts, was proud of the Americanization classes conducted in his community. But while formal instruction might have had an empowering effect on immigrant women (as Breck-inridge and her fellow researchers clearly hoped), men were more likely to see it as an exercise of power by employers over workers' lives, as many of the Americanization classes designed for them were sponsored by their employers.[88]

The world of work was the public sphere that reached into every immigrant's home. It had been a battleground for Americanization since the late nineteenth century. For the men and women interviewed by the WPA, the workplace played an important role in their narratives of America and in their own Americanization and transformation—no great surprise during the period of mass unemployment.[89] Work could kill, or at least tire you out, but its redemptive qualities in America were also ever present. Compared with Europe, as immigrants remembered it, work was abundant in America, even during the lean 1930s. The immigrants interviewed by the WPA had had few problems finding work.

For many interviewees, the world of work, from the granite pits of Vermont to the cigar factories of Ybor City, functioned as a craft shop, a world where community and labor were united. For others, such as the many Greek restaurant owners interviewed, it was the small business anchored in the non-Greek community. In many cases, these men were farmers or laborers who had not re-created the world of Old Europe in their workplace but had entered a new world, transformed it, and re-interpreted it for themselves as part of their Americanization. Others sought redemption on the land or at sea as farmers, vintners, or fishermen—a specific kind of Americanization far away from urban or industrial environments.[90]

Trade unions had grown in Gilded Age America and the Progressive Era because of their promise of an Americanism that blended individual prosperity and collective solidarity. Employers denounced this as un-American, offering paternalism and the possibility of individual material success as alternatives. By the 1920s, with unions greatly weakened, corporate Americanism had become the dominant patriotic ideology in the workplace. This implied distance from leftist unions in general and from socialist political activism in particular. Employers continued to be ideological supporters of a classic Americanization that emphasized work discipline. They helped organize citizenship classes and persuaded their workers to enroll, lest they lose their jobs or a promotion. Especially in the conservative political climate of the 1920s, most unions provided little in the way of alternatives to corporate-dominated ideas of Americanization in the workplace.[91]

By the mid-1930s, some immigrant communities managed to wrest the narrative of Americanism away from employers to promote unionization. This was in keeping with the ideas of civic nationalism promoted by the Roosevelt Administration during the New Deal. As early as the 1920s, the Francophone textile workers of Woonsocket, Rhode Island, used the rhetoric of Americanism to promote their Textile Workers Union in terms acceptable to a conservative community.[92] As the pace of organizing picked up during the second half of the 1930s, joining a union once again became part of the process of becoming American for many immigrant workers. The packing house workers of the Armour plant in Chicago proclaimed their American ideals to promote the union cause to their largely immigrant clientele. In the Back of the Yards neighborhood where the WPA interviewed men and women from immigrant (Polish) families who worked as meatpackers in 1939, they found union sentiment at high tide. By the late 1930s, a sense of American citizenship was inseparable from a sense of belonging to both the union and the Polish community there. Helen Wocz, who had wanted to be a nun as a high school student but ended up as a meatpacker, was both a member of the CIO and a religious woman. Despite the admonitions of her parish priest to stay away from the union and not associate with atheists, she remained faithful to the labor movement. Like other Polish Americans interviewed, she no longer let the priest define her identity as a Polish American in the Chicago stockyards.[93]

Apart from the world of union activism, most testimonies about political citizenship were muted among immigrants, even in the middle and late 1930s. Democracy, the right to vote, and the rights of common citizens were often mentioned as ideals that, at least initially, seemed attractive about America and an important part of becoming a naturalized American citizen. In the 1930s, many of the immigrants interviewed by the WPA also were proud defenders of

Roosevelt and the civic nationalism that the New Deal had strengthened. But the connection between the abstract ideals and concrete
actions was rarely made. The Chicago women interviewed by Breckinridge often stressed the pride they felt because they could vote, but
it was not clear if the women actually voted or took any interest in
politics. Many of the men who told their stories to the WPA workers
had political opinions, but these more often showed their profound
alienation from day-to-day politics. Some were critical of Roosevelt,
others were supportive, and a few were quite knowledgeable on some
aspect of U.S. foreign policy, but whether this actually translated into
active participation in American political life was unclear. Legal
American citizenship was certainly not central to the way these men
experienced politics.[94]

"I suspect that with too many immigrants and their children,
"Americanism" is too much a matter of prosperity, of being able to
surround oneself with the symbols of material well-being and of being able to indulge in doings plainly indicative of your standing in
the community," wrote Louis Adamic in 1942, when the memory of
the Depression was fading.[95] The WPA interviews do not support
this assessment, but Adamic had picked up on something that ran
like a thread through noninstitutional Americanization in the years
between 1919 and the 1940s: the integration of immigrants into the
world of consumerism. Frances Kellor was among the first who used
the lure of the immigrant consumer market for the Americanization
movement. After World War I, she propagated the potential of immigrants as consumers to American businesses and organized adver-
tising campaigns by nonethnic merchants and manufacturers in
ethnic newspapers.[96] Others took up her call, urging the Americanization of the immigrants' hard-earned money through American
banks (in part as a way to prevent repatriation of the money to European economies). After all, immigrants were now taxpayers, so they
should also become earners of interest.[97]

Not all Progressives were so enthusiastic about supporting and encouraging immigrants as consumers. If left to fend for themselves
and without the guidance of teachers and helpers, some reformers
feared U.S. immigrants would fall prey to an unfortunate mix of
traditional thinking and false priorities. Jane Addams and a visiting

colleague from Bohemia observed early on that "the early immigrants had been so stirred by the opportunity to own real estate, and their energies had become so completely absorbed in money-making that all other interests had apparently dropped away."[98] Americanizers thus saw their mandate as teaching their foreign-born students to maintain their industrious sobriety even in the midst of the Roaring Twenties.[99]

It seems that most immigrants came with a home-grown thriftiness. Lizabeth Cohen has found that Chicago area immigrant families were reluctant to buy consumer goods on credit. A phonograph was the only truly popular item of the new mass culture that many households owned. Other household appliances and cars were rare. Shopping took place less in the new chain stores or downtown department stores than in the neighborhood-oriented discount stores that resembled indoor markets. Disposable income went more regularly toward entertainment such as the movies or the occasional visit to a dance hall. Few immigrants admitted to owning much property or participating in the world of finance. Only one WPA interviewee admitted to having invested in the stock market.[100] Less visible forms of wealth, such as membership in an immigrant insurance association, was more acceptable.

Once the Depression hit, money was even tighter, and holding on to one's possessions, especially a house, took up all of a family's financial resources. The immigrants themselves admitted that earning money was important, but they refused to see the fact that they could earn good money as being an Americanizing experience in itself. Although some acknowledged that America was a money-obsessed place, they did not want to convert to this value. "America is a land of easy money. There is more money in America and, strange to say, more suffering than in the old countries," thought Gus Geraris, a Greek immigrant. Ostentatious consumerism, seen by the Progressives as a regrettable but inevitable part of becoming American, would be reserved for the next generation of immigrants.[101]

Americanization and Race

Amid the reflections and analyses of immigrants on becoming American, the ideas and stories of non-whites were largely absent from the

WPA collections. The white cast of the immigrants in the narratives of the WPA reflected the predominant view of immigration and Americanization as a European American phenomenon. The WPA researchers who interviewed non-whites understood them as members of racial minorities, not as immigrants. Non-whites' distance from the "American" mainstream was more by racial otherness than their foreign birthplace.[102] Their Americanization occurred in the context of assimilating into the subculture of racial minorities, their potential for citizenship was truncated, and their naturalization as citizens of the United States was often impossible by law and custom.

Immigrant narratives from the Caribbean, China, and Mexico, collected by other scholars of the era, reflect frustration and bitterness over the assigned position of racial inferiority and truncated citizenship. They also reveal an intensive engagement with the United States as a society whose white majority was not welcoming.[103] At the same time, these stories also testify how non-European immigrant communities built their own America, albeit outside the field of vision of most white observers. This was a common fate, as people of color united different non-European immigrants in their journey toward becoming Americans during the 1930s and beyond, but their specific history and place in the United States also made for great variations in the shape and meaning of Americanization.

Among the non-white immigrants of the 1920s and 1930s, blacks were the most invisible. Sociologist Ira Reid 1939 observed that a black person from the Caribbean was an "immigrant who becomes a Negro upon arrival."[104] This could pose problems in many ways, even to those newcomers who clearly identified themselves as black. "It was not very comfortable for us because we had an accent, so the kids in school would make fun of us and call us monkey chasers. And we had to run the gamut of leaving school and getting home on time without getting into a fight," remembered Vera Clark Ifill, who arrived from Barbados in 1923.[105] Ifill felt acutely different from native African Americans, a separation emphasized for her by the growth of black nationalism, which was associated with West Indian immigration by her Harlem neighbors. The situation was even more problematic for those of mixed race, who had occupied a higher rung in the racial and social hierarchy of the Caribbean. Vernon Nicholls, whose Barbadian father was white, had to confront segregation only after his family moved to suburban New Jersey in the 1930s where the schools were segregated. By the standards of New Jersey schools, he was black, but he also did not fit readily into black America. "People used to [wonder] because you didn't speak Southern drawl," he remembered.[106]

In the eyes of white Americans, "successful" integration for black immigrants meant the stereotyped behavior prescribed for them: punctuality, sobriety, and subservience rather than the ability to earn a high income, entrepreneurial zest, or educational credentials.[107] Barbadian journalist Vernon Walker reflected later that no matter what the personal attributes or degree of Americanization, "the frustrating part of it was that we couldn't get the jobs that we were qualified to do, so we had to take other menial jobs." Regardless of their education, West Indian immigrants were most likely to work as maids, factory workers, or laborers, just like other African Americans. Unlike European immigrants, who might have faced similar mistrust and occupational segregation early on, West Indians had limited opportunities for advancement over many decades. Vera Ifill finished high school, but she became a seamstress for lack of better opportunities. Only many decades later did she become a professional as head of a Caribbean-American credit union. The sting of discrimination and occupational segregation was especially potent for those Caribbean blacks who had received much of their education back home.

Afro-Caribbean immigrants remained socially and politically segregated from native African Americans in the interwar years. Within their increasingly rich associational life, Americanization was not the focus. Instead, island concerns, a distance from U.S. politics, and an unwillingness to become U.S. citizens (which would render one even more defenseless against the sting of officially sanctioned segregation and discrimination) characterized the social life of Afro-Caribbeans. Early on, Caribbean Americans made an America for themselves that allowed for separation into ethnic social and cultural societies while adopting vigorous engagement in political groups that were focused on homeland political concerns. Engagement with U.S. urban politics would have to wait for a second generation, who came of age after World War II.[108]

Mexican immigrants were the largest non-white immigrant group in the interwar years and beyond. In the West and Southwest, these immigrants had been the target of a few Americanization efforts since the early twentieth century. But more often than not, Mexican immigrants were ignored by the Americanization movement, even in areas where Mexican immigrants were a large group such as California, Arizona, and Texas. Those Americanizers who did address Mexicans, framed their efforts in the context of the need to "elevate" the culture and social circumstances of an isolated, poor, and often native population through instruction in English, literacy, hygiene, and health—just as they did for other very poor immigrant groups in the early twentieth century such as urban Italians on the East Coast. But, in contrast to white immigrant groups, whose status began to improve after World War I, the extreme poverty, transience, and what white Americans considered the isolating nature of Mexican immigrant settlements continued throughout the interwar period and became more pronounced, making established approaches to Americanization ineffective.

Traditional settlement work, focusing on urban communities and building on the premise of upward mobility and racial permeability, did not address the problems faced by Mexican immigrants. Americanizers with their focus on community institutions (such as schools and YMCAs) and their reliance on reading and writing were ill equipped to address the specific cultural backgrounds of rural Mexican immigrants. Agricultural laborers and railroad workers, often men without their families, lived in camps, far from social infrastructures and with little opportunity to experience "mainstream America." With their lives confined to their isolated workplaces and their labor needed only on a seasonal basis in many cases, they could not have the goal of permanent settlement in the United States.[109]

By the 1930s, after more than two decades of sizable Mexican migration, Mexicans' readiness to become Americanized was therefore still subject to debate among immigrant advocacy groups such as the Foreign Language Information Service. "Are Mexicans Here to Stay?" asked Mexican American theologian Alberto Rembao in an editorial in 1930. He argued that in fact Mexicans were staying in the United States and that their children were becoming American.

But working against a conscious effort at assimilation was "the Mexicans' own frame of mind, his consciousness of not belonging here . . . This idea of not belonging here has been nurtured in the past by several causes of American origin" among which Rembao counted "injudicious attempts at Americanization." But, as he saw it, more problematic was the impossibility for Mexicans to be fully accepted as Americans because they were considered racially inferior.[110]

As European immigrant groups became indisputably "white" after World War I, Mexicans stood out more clearly as non-white immigrants. Observers agreed that discrimination against the dark-skinned Mexicans made U.S. society an inhospitable new home. Race was a border that became increasingly insurmountable for Mexicans, Rembao and others found.[111] Interviews conducted by the Mexican anthropologist Manuel Gamio confirmed this assessment: "The people here don't like us . . . They think that we aren't as good as they and as we are submissive, they do whatever they want to with our labor" was a typical response. Even Mexicans who were "light skinned" and could "pass" as Americans resented if they were not acknowledged as immigrants, because the alternative, to be a "colored person," was unappealing. "They mistake me very often for an American . . . and to tell the truth, that makes me very angry, for here and wherever I am, I am a Mexican and I won't change my citizenship," explained one immigrant to Gamio. Mexicans also felt ostracized by the Mexican Americans who were established in the United States. "Here the Mexicans, who have been born in this country and who are citizens, say that we come 'starving to death'; they don't like us at all," stated Juana de Hidalgo. For her, as for many other Mexicans, the solution to discrimination and second-class citizenship was to go back to Mexico.[112]

Mexicans' children, unlike their European counterparts, were often not a reason to put down roots but an incentive to return to Mexico. "My dream, and my husband's too, is to go back to our beloved Mexico, especially now that my children are growing up, for I want to give them a true Mexican education," thought one of Gamio's informants.[113] Her pride in Mexican schools may have been fanned by the fact that in Texas and California Mexican and Mexican American children were often confined to segregated and inferior schools, or were not expected to attend mainstream American schools. Some of California's Mexican schools were not even integrated into the U.S. public education system, but were run by Mexican expatriates and funded by the Mexican government until well after World War I. This meant that schools did not function as agents of Americanization as universally as they did for European immigrant children.[114] "I have four children now and even when they receive their education in El Paso they will be as Mexican as I am," one informant told Gamio. For this Mexican immigrant, the culture and language of El Paso were Mexican, not American. Even though he and his family had migrated across national borders, the social and cultural borders of what was understood to be American society were not crossed.[115]

Slowly, though, things began to change during the decade of the Great Depression. By the late 1920s, Mexican and Mexican American organizations in urban areas developed an alternative to mainstream Americanization: assimilation into a growing and diverse Mexican American social culture. Urban communities of Mexican immigrants found themselves courted and organized from both sides of the border: organizations that were primarily homeland-oriented promoted the continued contact of immigrants with Mexico, sometimes under the tutelage of the Mexican consul or prominent Mexican businessmen. The Mexican nationalism promoted by these organizations in urban areas proved to be an antidote to the isolation and fragmentation of Mexican Americans in the rural Southwest, at times even providing a type of resistance to the delegitimation and marginalization of Mexican immigrants in general. But especially in Texas, Mexican American voluntary organizations of the interwar era also began to espouse a more self-consciously assimilationist ideal of Americanism for their members. The businessmen and middle-class members of the League of United Latin American Citizens (LULAC, founded in 1929) pushed for the civil rights of their members and the full integration of Mexican Americans into U.S. politics. Many Mexican American organizations settled somewhere in between the homeland nationalism and the "purest Americanism" espoused by LULAC.[116]

Despite the sometimes emphatic assertion of Mexican nationalism and their distance from mainstream U.S. culture, most Mexican immigrants lived, worked, and became Mexican Americans in their day-to-day lives as wage earners, members of unions, entertainers, and consumers, often in a universe parallel to that of whites. By the 1940s, when a majority of Mexican Americans were in fact U.S. citizens (by birth or naturalization), this separation and segregation had not changed. The children of Mexican immigrants may have become American and often distant from their parents' traditional ways, but it was still a different America from that of their white peers. As with African Americans, Mexican Americans' civil rights and their opportunities in the labor market continued to be limited, and they wielded almost no political power. Americanization was never the answer to Mexican immigrants' search for opportunity and political rights in the United States.

If the racial divide meant that Mexican Americans became Americans without official "Americanization," Asian Americans suffered the opposite fate: they Americanized without ever becoming American citizens. Since the Nationality Act of 1870 had determined that only whites and those of African descent could become U.S. citizens by naturalization, Asian immigrants were classified as non-white and therefore "aliens ineligible for citizenship." This determination was rooted in the idea that East Asians, especially Chinese, belonged to a race that could never aspire to assimilate the meaning of American citizenship. As a consequence, Americanization was not considered suitable for this class of immigrants. Their presence in the United States was neither welcome nor acknowledged; they could never cross the border into citizenship.

In principle the position of Americanizers was clear toward Asian immigrants, but in practice the borders of racial exclusion in Americanization were soon exposed as permeable. Asian immigrants seized the social and economic opportunities of integration—however limited they were—and Americanized themselves, sometimes in ways that whites found deeply problematic. Filipino immigrants occupied a special position in the matrix of race and citizenship among Asian immigrants. As inhabitants of a U.S. overseas territory from 1898 to 1934, they were U.S. nationals, though not U.S. citizens. This meant that they were free to enter the United States with American passports, but they were still considered Asian and therefore ineligible for full citizenship. Americanization programs were not targeted at these recent immigrants, mostly young men who worked in agriculture on the West Coast, often as migrant laborers. In many ways, the lives of Filipino workers mirrored those of Mexican agricultural laborers, although Filipinos spoke English and had—as colonial subjects—already been Americanized before arrival in North America. (They had attended U.S. style schools, and had become enthusiastic consumers of U.S. popular culture, for example.) By the 1930s, Filipinos had come to shape a mainly urban subculture of leisure and sports, which mirrored white American working-class culture. This was to many white observers a deeply unsettling mirror of white America.[117]

In contrast to the fluid boundaries between American and alien that existed for Filipinos, the social and political isolation for the aging and shrinking Chinese American community after World War I was stark. A bachelor society, whose only younger members were paper sons of older male immigrants, Chinese America lacked that most important ingredient for Americanizers: families. Americanization of the home by teaching women, or children at school, or working men and women at multiethnic workplaces never reached the Chinese bachelor society. The strictly enforced segregation of the Chinese in urban areas also removed them, literally, from the horizons of immigrant reformers and advocates of assimilation during the interwar years. Chinese and Chinese American organizations did act as defenders of Chinese rights and as representatives of a more assimilated second generation of U.S.-born Chinese, but these groups (in contrast to the Mexican American or Caribbean groups, for example) did not act as bridges to social assimilation. Banned from most American organizations (such as mainstream unions), Chinese immigrants and Chinese Americans of the 1920s and 1930s may have come to look more American (Western clothing and short hair for men had become nearly universal), but in other ways the lives of the Chinese laborers, laundry men, and restaurant workers in American cities were only lightly touched by mainstream America.[118]

Chinese American families faced occupational and residential segregation and school discrimination into the second-generation. Chinese parents understood that the public school system did not welcome their children as future Americans, and in response some of them sent their children back home to receive schooling that they considered more appropriate. But as Ruth Chinn recalled in the late 1930s, Chinese boys from Seattle, sent back for their education to China, behaved "like Americans" and were therefore sent back to the United States. Though the United States would deny them a higher education, they had become too Americanized to be tolerated in China. Educated or not, Chinese youth, like other Asians, faced a severely restricted labor market and an uncertain future in which, even if they were native, citizenship and the right to residency were always doubted.[119]

Japanese and Korean immigrants, also classified as "Asiatic" by U.S. immigration authorities, faced similar struggles, but subtle differences emerged early on when it came to their purported ability to Americanize. The Gentlemen's Agreement of 1907, which limited Japanese immigration, had been negotiated between two sovereign governments and thus carried with it the implicit recognition that the Japanese were capable of regular and representative self-government, a notion taken seriously by Theodore Roosevelt and his confidant, Oscar Strauss, the Secretary of Labor and Commerce who oversaw the Bureau of Immigration. Other Progressives agreed about the capacity of the Japanese to succeed in and even assimilate into American society. In an extensive study of Japanese immigrants in northern California, Sidney Gulick, a Congregationalist minister and missionary who had lived in Japan for twenty years, argued that Japanese immigrant farmers had indeed "civilized" parts of California's Central Valley through their sophisticated farming practices, their stable home life, and their exemplary moral and civic ideals. As a result, Gulick argued, a more open immigration policy toward Asian, especially Japanese, immigration was necessary. But Gulick's recognition of the successful assimilation of Japanese immigrants found almost no echo before World War I. Americanization programs addressed the needs of Japanese immigrants only in the context of missionary activity. Because U.S. citizenship was out of reach for Japanese immigrants, who were excluded from naturalization because they were Asian, their Americanization was not pursued by American institutions.[120]

Despite the shadow of immigration restriction, the Japanese American community in the United States continued to grow after 1908 through the immigration of picture brides, hence the permanent establishment of Japanese American families on the West Coast and in Hawaii. In rural areas, where many of the first-generation Japanese lived before World War II, whites remained deeply hostile to their Japanese neighbors in the 1920s and 1930s and objected to the social and political integration of Japanese Americans throughout the interwar years. The memoirs of Mary Paik, a Korean immigrant (who was considered Japanese because her homeland was occupied by Japan), document a threadbare and isolated childhood in rural California within the very small community of early Korean immigrants. In order to attend high school at all, Paik had to become a boarder and maid to a white family in a town many miles away from her rural home. In other parts of California, Washington, and Oregon, however, Japanese American communities flourished, though largely outside the purview of American institutions.[121]

In more urban places, the social integration and Americanization of the Japanese were well under way by the 1930s. Writer Monica Sone described growing up in Seattle's harbor area among migrants and immigrants from many lands, quite unaware of how she was regarded as different by white America. Yuri Kochiyama remembered her childhood in San Pedro, in a largely white working-class neighborhood, as idyllic. She came from one of only two Japanese American families in her part of town, and her youth was dominated by volunteer work for organizations such as the Girl Scouts, the local church, and high school sports. "I was sheltered, lived comfortably and safely, religious, provincial, and apolitical in thought."[122]

By the 1930s, a growing number of Japanese communities had built Christian churches and Christian organizations. Japanese language schools for children and other Japanese cultural organizations were part of a rich associational life for West Coast Japanese. Some of these organizations, such as the Japanese-American Citizens League founded in 1929, were dominated by U.S. citizens of Japanese descent and had an assimilationist agenda. Others had a more nationalistic Japanese tone and were under the influence of Japanese officials and interests.[123]

The most public story of cultural assimilation among Japanese Americans was that of Takao Ozawa, who fought for the right to become a U.S. citizen on the basis of his (and his family's) complete Americanization. A Japanese-born Hawaiian whose case went all the way to the U.S. Supreme Court, Ozawa argued that he and his family were in fact American in every way: they spoke only English at home, they were Christians, and they lived their lives as part of mainstream institutions in Hawaii. Although in the end, the U.S. Supreme Court denied him the right to naturalization, Ozawa was merely the most visible member of a large and successful Japanese American community in Hawaii, which fought the discrimination against American- and Japanese-born members in schooling, employment, and other settings.[124]

Assimilation to American social and cultural norms became everyday practice for second-generation Japanese, who were U.S. citizens by birth. But structural segregation prevented this growing community (the majority of Japanese America by 1940) from recognition as being American. Access to higher education remained limited by quotas, the labor market was confined to ethnic businesses and agriculture even for highly educated second-generation Japanese, and housing discrimination remained the norm. If second-generation Japanese Americans were political citizens, their social citizenship was as limited as that of African Americans in the East and South, and resembled that of second-generation Mexicans as well. Japanese American internment became the final and cruelest expression of the paradigm of Americanization without citizenship for Japanese Americans. Hostility toward Japanese immigrants persisted, despite (or because of) the success of Japanese immigrants and their children in adapting to American economic and cultural norms.[125]

Americanization and the Second Generation in the 1940s and 1950s

As immigrants became increasingly reflective about their place in America and their future as Americans, official Americanization kept a low profile. Throughout the 1930s and 1940s, citizenship classes for immigrants who wanted to become naturalized U.S. citizens continued to be taught in adult education programs in many parts of the country. The Immigration and Naturalization Service continued to offer books for instruction in the rudiments of English and U.S. history. To complement the classes, more populist Americanization efforts, reminiscent of an earlier era, continued as well. St. Louis celebrated "I Am an American Day," for example, beginning in 1941, but the audience had dwindled for such efforts. "I Am an American Day" was finally cancelled in 1946 after five years of declining attendance. Citizenship classes similarly declined in number, and most immigrants who became U.S. citizens did not attend them. Men were naturalized with a minimum of formality in the 1940s because they had enlisted in the armed forces. Indeed, the lack of attention paid to making Americans out of immigrants during World War II stood in sharp contrast to the "Americanization fever" that had gripped the nation during World War I. There is evidence that this was deliberate on the part of officials, members of the education establishment, and immigrant advocates, who were fearful that a new outbreak of xenophobia and anti-immigrant hostility against Europeans would hurt the cause of the United States during wartime.[126]

But while Americanization ebbed as a political and pedagogical concern, Americanizers as well as immigrant advocates shifted their focus to a group considered to be sorely in need of knowledge about America and American citizenship: second-generation immigrants from Europe.[127] In his 1938 essay "Thirty Million New Americans," journalist Louis Adamic was concerned about the continuing problems faced by the "American" generation of eastern European and Mediterranean immigrants, the children of immigrants who had come in the early twentieth century. "All too many of them are oppressed by feelings of inferiority in relation to their fellow citizens of older stock, to the mainstream of American life, and the problem of life as a whole." Adamic saw this alienation as endangering not only the well-being of the second generation ("their personalities are faint, lopsided and out of focus") but also a threat to American democracy in the 1930s.[128] "These new Americans are ready for almost any sort of shallow, ignorant nationalist or fascist movement," he prophesized.[129] As a preventative measure, Adamic called on teachers, voluntary organizations, and others concerned with immigrants to devote themselves to teaching immigrants about their heritage "to create an "understanding of their own make up" and in turn to teach Americans about the contributions and specific histories of immigrant groups in the United States. This might take decades, Adamic conceded, and would be a vast undertaking with implications for social change, but nothing less would do to prevent a deterioration of American democratic culture.[130]

What Adamic did not mention in the 1938 version of his article was that a small group of progressive educators in New York City had already begun just such a campaign for the education of second-generation immigrants and "native stock" Americans on the importance and contributions of various immigrant groups and minorities. Rachel Dubois, a New Jersey Quaker and peace activist, had, since the mid-1920s, organized programs of public school assemblies and classes around what she called intercultural education. Dubois was not an academic or a writer, and she had originally approached the problem of the second generation as a high school teacher trying to grab the attention of her restless students.[131] But by the 1930s she had built a successful enterprise, the Service Bureau for Intercultural Education, which, by the time Adamic published his essay, was well known for its curriculum materials, assembly programs, and guest speakers. Dubois's ability to publicize her cause and to win friends among prominent immigrants and Americans alike (from Adamic himself to Pearl Buck) made her group into a movement and an important force in progressive education in the 1930.[132]

Dubois's programs focused on the idea that American culture was made out of a mosaic of contributions of immigrants and Americans of different "races." An understanding of American history and culture therefore also required an understanding of the separate histories and cultural traits of immigrants and minorities. Dubois refused to emphasize the transformative power of one America and stuck instead to the idea of flexibility and mutuality in her definition of American culture. In this she and Adamic agreed, but Dubois also met the resistance of other constituencies who were important for her as financial and political supporters.[133]

In 1939, the Office of Education hired Dubois to write and produce a series of educational radio shows (in cooperation with CBS) on the contribution of immigrants and domestic minorities to U.S. history. Called "Americans All, Immigrants All," this series—a pioneering event in the history of educational broadcasting—had a different goal from Dubois's original purpose: to educate American listeners about different immigrant cultures. The federal Office of Education saw the program as a way to build unity and cultural awareness for an American audience, not an immigrant audience. It was a training program in diversity for a nation that liked to see itself as white and homogenous. The topics of the twenty-six part series ranged from "Our English heritage" and "Our Spanish Heritage," to "The Negro," "Orientals," "Italians," and "The Near Eastern People." A brief history of each group before and after arrival in the United States was followed by a description of important contributions and famous representatives. A printed guide was meant to strengthen the adult education component of the series by emphasizing difficult words, structuring the narrative, and providing easily comparable data for each group. The instructional tone, the imagery used, and the qualities emphasized were quite reminiscent of the Americanization texts of an earlier generation: industriousness and persistence against the odds, individual achievement, and the strength of the nation were recurrent themes. The broadcasts showed what Adamic had argued for in his essay: the true strength of the nation lay in good part in the contributions of Americans from other countries. Americanization would therefore always entail the recognition that America was a nation continually under development through the arrivals of newcomers from elsewhere.[134]

The series was a resounding success, judging from the large number of letters and requests for reading materials received by CBS. But this turned out to be a problem for Dubois and the Committee for Intercultural Education. An analysis of the mail received at the time revealed that the responses came disproportionately from second-generation immigrant audiences and their teachers, not from the so-called native-stock American listeners. In fact, the broadcasts taught second-generation immigrants about their own heritage—a side effect that Dubois supported but the federal Office of Education did not. Federal funding to intercultural education was cut in the early 1940s, and Dubois's own organization was taken out of her hands.[135]

Intercultural education itself survived, however. Variations of it were adopted widely in American public schools during and after World War II. Its ideas were most widely used in public schools where the audience was composed of second-generation immigrant schoolchildren who were subject to political and social pressures in their day-to-day lives, such as Japanese Americans in Seattle and Latinos in San Diego.[136] Intercultural education was also enthusiastically promoted by the YWCA through its International Institutes and taken up by the Common Council for American Unity (successor to the Foreign Language Information Service). The Common Council devoted most of the pages of its journal (which was read by the native-stock Americans) to topics related to intercultural education. Dubois's forays may have seemed daring in the context of federal education efforts, but on the local level, in countless schools and within increasingly assimilated immigrant communities, they struck a chord. Long after its beginnings as an Americanization program for the second generation had been forgotten, intercultural education remained a permanent part of the landscape of American education.

Intercultural education, flourished in the cold war era beyond the United States as well. Internationally, cold war ideology mandated the spread of America as a cultural and political idea to other parts of the world. Eastern Europeans, for example, became targets of a long-distance Americanization attempt in the 1950s. Under the direction of the U.S. government, they became the focus of the "Letters from America" campaign, an attempt to spread the good news of a multicultural America to the native populations behind the Iron Curtain. Radio programs and postcards sent by immigrants and their children to their relatives were supposed to underline this exported message of America. Americanization became an export item during the postwar years in other ways, too. Rachel Dubois was sent in 1951 to teach cross-cultural understanding in Germany, now a country where refugees, displaced persons, and natives tried to build a new political and social order. Appreciation of difference and the advantages of an integrated multiethnic society were taught more safely abroad than at home at a time when American society was shaken by the demands of African American, Latino, and Asian citizens for full civil and political rights.[137]

Americanization began in the early twentieth century as the outgrowth of Progressive attempts at controlling immigration, assimilation, and naturalization for the large number of new immigrants arriving in the United States at that time. Conceived as a formal program of instruction for European newcomers who shared the reformers' vision of immigrants as future American citizens, Americanization soon met resistance from its intended audience, and it failed to include Asian, Mexican, and black immigrant groups altogether. Especially during World War I but also during the 1920s, official Americanization was thus a process filled with tensions over immigrants' place in American civic culture. A unified program of teaching citizenship and American culture never emerged, and the programs and lessons that were adopted reflected the immigrants' day-to-day reality only to a limited degree.

Unlike the other border crossings discussed in this book, Americanization occurred largely outside the framework of immigration and naturalization law. Despite efforts to link a minimum of Americanization to naturalization as a U.S. citizen, the connection between naturalization and Americanization was not tightly formalized and Americanization tests were never instituted for would-be citizens. In the end, Americanization was not a process in which the power lay with the government or its self-appointed representatives, the Americanizers. Public disapproval of certain un-American behaviors or legal exclusion of certain groups from citizenship could express the implicit state-sanctioned norms of what it meant to be American, but Americanization never became a mandated part of integration.

The limited success of formal Americanization left most immigrants to negotiate this process on their own, both as individuals and as members of their own ethnic communities. Immigrant-driven Americanization occurred in a wide variety of settings, from the workplaces and dance halls of urban America to the rural churches and voluntary associations of the Far West. It followed no clear trajectory and often occurred in ways that only partially reflected the wishes of Americanizers. It could be a subtle process, sometimes nearly invisible to outsiders, and deeply private. But much of it was public, taking place in a wide range of organizations whose immigrant members showed a dynamic and flexible understanding of how to mesh their need for cohesion and continuity as immigrant communities with the new demands of American culture and society.

Becoming American in behavior and spirit was the most flexible border crossing for immigrants in the twentieth century. It could be a lifelong process with few landmark events, or a very public journey highlighted by what most Americans considered the end point: naturalization as a U.S. citizen.

CHAPTER **5**

Becoming a Citizen

While World War I was claiming the lives of thousands in Europe, gratitude marked the celebrations of the Fourth of July, 1915. From Washington to Los Angeles, local committees of "leading citizens" made that year's national holiday into a celebration of American citizenship for newly minted Americans. The celebration in Washington, D.C., was particularly colorful. Before a backdrop of grazing sheep and children playing on the grounds of the Washington Monument and with the French ambassador in attendance, a Washington official proclaimed "only those who have chosen to become citizens of the United States, giving up but not forgetting their old homes, to risk their fortunes in a new land, can fully appreciate the peace and justice they find here."[1] Similar celebrations were held in many other parts of the country. The over two hundred new citizens of Kansas City sang patriotic hymns and were then treated to "motion pictures" with scenes from the early history of the United States.[2] Over twenty-five nationalities showed up in South Bend, Indiana, for the celebrations. New American citizens in Boston were treated to a speech by Justice Louis Brandeis at Faneuil Hall.[3]

Becoming a citizen of the United States has always represented a final step in the commitment of immigrants to their new home, a last border crossing in the public imagination. Small wonder then, that civic organizations and newspapers took up the idea of a public celebration of naturalization with gusto, and with presidents sometimes appearing in person to congratulate the new citizens. To this day, mass swearing-in ceremonies of the newly naturalized are held across the United States, especially on the Fourth of July, often with colorful pictures documenting a day of joy and solemnity. Expressed in these celebrations has always been the belief that naturalization is both the beginning of democratic participation for immigrants and an occasion for the American government to celebrate its welcome of a select group of immigrants into the national community.

The oath of citizenship and the abjuring of one's former government is in this view an inevitable outcome of properly lived lives for immigrants. But in reality, throughout American history naturalization has always been the result of a complex web of events, decisions, and negotiations for immigrants and the representatives of the American state. At the center stands the question of political citizenship: what does it signify, and what is it worth to immigrants on the one side and to the nation that awards it on the other?

The answers to this question have varied greatly for immigrants over the past two hundred years, depending on the immigrants' origins, their positions in U.S. society, and the politics of the times. For some immigrant groups, in the nineteenth and early twentieth centuries political citizenship was not meaningful or truly attainable, even after naturalization. For most others, this was a more nuanced decision, made voluntarily. After successfully negotiating earlier border crossings, immigrants became citizens in order to live in the United States. Like Americanization, naturalization was not a necessary step, and through most of the twentieth century, a large group—if not a majority—of immigrants never elected to cross this border.

To the U.S. government, awarding citizenship represented an opportunity to examine immigrants and to select the most deserving. How this selection was made, who would be invited and who excluded, was part of a lively and contentious debate over much of the nineteenth and twentieth centuries. On the one hand, the American state had a strong interest in making as many immigrants into citizens as possible during the nineteenth century, and in integrating newcomers into the fabric of a politically expansive world power during the twentieth century. The law and the politics of naturalization had to remain flexible. It would reflect the shifting expediencies of domestic and foreign policy during much of the past one hundred years. Through laws and administrative decisions, the agencies and representatives of government who dealt with naturalization had the power to heighten the value of political citizenship while lowering the status of noncitizen immigrants; at other times, the reverse took place, and immigrants were discouraged from or not supported in their quest for naturalization.

During the period under discussion in this book, gender and race were the primary determinants of access to naturalization and meaningful political citizenship. Black immigrants were excluded from naturalization until 1870 and were denied meaningful political participation (though not naturalization) afterward. Women, though not excluded from naturalization, could not achieve meaningful political citizenship until the 1920s. The naturalization of women was subservient to their partners if they were married until 1922. Most significantly, Asian immigrants were completely excluded from naturalization until 1952. Even in the few exceptional cases where citizenship was possible for these immigrants, meaningful political citizenship was out of reach. The naturalization exclusions mirrored immigration exclusions closely, though not perfectly. Additional points of conflict emerged in the twentieth century around an ever more finely grained web of race and economic status.

A significant difference between naturalization as a border crossing and the borders of immigration and deportation was that federal administration and control over naturalization came relatively late in the history of the United States. Even though the Constitution clearly empowered the federal government to oversee the naturalization of immigrants, the administration of naturalization was only unified under federal auspices in 1906. Despite this centralization, there continued to be flexibility in how the law was administered and interpreted on the part of the Bureau of Naturalization (later the Immigration and Naturalization Service) as well as the naturalization courts, which were ultimately responsible for determining who would become a citizen of the United States. More than in other border crossings, the independent judiciary played a key role in selecting citizens from a larger pool of immigrants. This selection process provided special challenges to immigrants and their advocates as well as to immigration authorities. It would be difficult to fashion a community response to judicial decisions among immigrant groups in the twentieth century. "Negotiating" with the Bureau of Naturalization and its representatives was difficult enough, but a response to the judicial system in naturalization matters required involvement in legislation and electoral politics. Naturalization and citizenship were touchstones for immigrant communities' increasingly systemic approach to reform in the late twentieth century.

Naturalization in the Nineteenth Century

Naturalization, the acquisition of U.S. citizenship by foreign-born men and women, was first spelled out in the Naturalization Act of 1802: applicants for naturalization as U.S. citizens had to be white and over 21 years of age. Only a modest set of requirements existed beyond that: immigrants had to have lived in the United Sates for at least five years and needed to have filed a declaration of intent to become a citizen of the United States two years before they sought naturalization. Both the declaration of intent and the naturalization petition had to be filed in a court of record, usually a district court. No central records were kept on the declarations, and immigrants could choose to abandon or pursue American citizenship after filing their declarations of intent. The naturalization itself was performed by a judge to whom the applicant for citizenship had to demonstrate that "he had behaved as a man of good moral character." The oath of naturalization contained a renunciation of allegiance or responsibilities to "every foreign prince, potentate, state or sovereignty" and was an oath of allegiance "to the United States and its constitutional principles." No examination of an immigrant's background, his economic or financial status, or his political beliefs was required. These basic citizenship procedures were kept in place throughout the nineteenth century.[4]

Because naturalization law specified only race and age, women were, at least in theory, qualified to request citizenship in their own right. But during the nineteenth century, they were almost never listed or counted among the petitioners for citizenship. After 1855, married women immigrants were always covered under the citizenship status of their husbands. They automatically became U.S. citizens if their husbands did; conversely, women who were citizens of the United States lost their citizenship upon marriage to a non-citizen. Married women immigrants could not become citizens on their own.[5]

Just as the citizenship of married women followed that of their husbands, so by extension minor children of immigrants became naturalized automatically when their fathers became citizens. Citizenship could not be conveyed to children through the naturalization of the mother. Beginning in 1824, young adults who had immigrated as children could petition for citizenship on their own without having filed a declaration of intent. This provision would later invite abuse, for before 1906 any immigrants could claim that they had entered the United States before the age of 18.[6]

The rather liberal provisions of American citizenship law were contested very little from 1802 until the middle of the nineteenth century. The main reason was that citizenship was worth relatively little to immigrants, but the value of making new citizens out of European immigrants was quite high for the U.S. government. Immigrants were needed and welcome but arrived in relatively modest numbers from western and central Europe during the first part of the nineteenth century. For the identity of the United States as a white nation, it was important to exclude free and enslaved blacks as well as American Indians from U.S. citizenship, while increasing the number of naturalized white immigrants. Citizens could vote and run for office, and as the political participation of white men increased toward the mid-nineteenth century, the franchise for immigrants through naturalization provided important momentum in the organization and reorganization of American regional and local politics.[7]

The value of citizenship for immigrants became most apparent in the cities of the eastern seaboard during the nineteenth century. Starting with the 1844 presidential election campaign of Henry Clay, the Democratic Party began to register large numbers of new voters by assisting in their naturalization just before election time. In the 1844 election the potential for fraud came to the attention of the courts, and an investigation resulted in the impeachment and removal of a state judge in Louisiana.[8] This investigation did little to hamper the increasing use of naturalization as an instrument of political empowerment. Between the mid-1840s and the late 1860s, recruiting immigrant supporters through naturalization became the favorite way for political bosses, development-hungry western politicians, and military leaders to further their goals. Immigrants emerged as an important, distinct political constituency during these decades, and all efforts to restrict the access of immigrants to U.S. citizenship in subsequent decades had to take this fact into consideration.[9]

But there were also voices that were critical of the lack of control exercised over who became a U.S. citizen in urban areas. Class and cultural characteristics separated many of the newcomers of the 1830s and 1840s from older generations of immigrants. The arrival of large numbers of very poor immigrants from Ireland during the 1840s and early 1850s served as a rallying point for what would become the most virulent anti-immigrant movement of the nineteenth century, the Know-Nothings. As the newcomers were blamed for increasing economic pressures on native workers and for the growing cost of poor relief, Know-Nothings pushed for immigration control and for limited access to naturalization of immigrants.[10] In effect, the Know-Nothings were the first political movement to favor raising the cost of citizenship for immigrants. To this end, they favored longer waiting periods before immigrants could become citizens and demanded other restrictions on naturalization, but their attempts to reintroduce longer waiting periods failed in Congress.[11] Only in the late 1850s did state legislatures in a number of states with heavy immigration from Ireland pass laws that reflected Know-Nothing demands: in Connecticut, naturalization became more difficult to attain, after new legislation stipulated that only federal judges could award it; in New York City, voter registration requirements became quite onerous for newcomers. The regional influence of the Know-Nothing movement was temporary, though an undercurrent of this movement remained an effective force throughout the late nineteenth century and showed in efforts to restrict the franchise for the poor or the highly mobile in many states.[12]

Besides the conflicting pressures that sought, on the one hand, to make citizenship easily attainable and, on the other, to limit the access to the franchise for immigrants, a third approach emerged in the mid-nineteenth century. As part of their attempts to lure European settlers to their frontier regions, a number of midwestern and western states passed laws that enfranchised white aliens: Michigan, Wisconsin, Indiana, Missouri, Minnesota, and even Arkansas allowed non-naturalized aliens to vote in local and state elections if they had taken out their "first papers" (filed a declaration of intent). Nebraska, Kansas, Texas, and Oregon had similar provisions. By disconnecting the franchise—the most important nineteenth-century attribute of citizenship—from naturalization, these states made naturalization less valuable. In addition to the franchise, the right to buy and own property, especially farmland, was sometimes connected to U.S. citizenship. But by the second half of the nineteenth century, immigrant men (and their families) who decided to homestead could avail themselves of free land under the 1862 Homestead Act, once they had filed their declaration of intent. These settlers were treated the same as U.S. citizens by local and state authorities.[13]

No wonder taking out U.S. citizenship had little allure for immigrants in many parts of the nineteenth-century United States: especially in rural areas—comprising the vast majority of counties in North America—citizenship was superfluous for full participation in the economic and public life of one's community. States and communities saw to it that their European immigrant residents were empowered by convention, cultural recognition, and legal arrangement. "The oath of naturalization never yet made a man an American citizen in heart. That is done by his coming here, by his casting his lot among us by his making this his home . . ." declared Senator Oliver Perry Morton of Indiana in 1870.[14]

In the Civil War decade and beyond, a new generation of immigrants grappled with the value and meaning of American citizenship for themselves and their communities. Some saw U.S. citizenship as a way to participate in a democratic republic, a nation which stood for constitutional values and protections that European governments had yet to embrace. Others had a much more pragmatic view of naturalization: they hoped for better access to jobs, and social and political connections. For the American state, naturalization continued to be instrumentalized in different ways by those who were empowered to award it. State and local judges and those who appointed them used U.S. citizenship as a reward for newcomers willing to serve the political and strategic interests of the state as voters and supporters.

During the Civil War years, immigrants were valuable to the state for an additional reason: they were a fresh source of recruits for the Union army. Male immigrants were subject to the draft, just like native U.S. citizens. But, since the union army relied mostly on volunteers, local politicians offered immediate U.S. citizenship to newly arrived immigrants if they enlisted. The cigar maker Albert Schorske, a German from Silesia, arrived with his family at New York's Castle Garden immigration station in 1861. There he was met by a Union army officer who offered instant U.S. citizenship to him if he enlisted right away. Schorske accepted the deal, enlisted, and served in one of four New York regiments made up entirely of German Americans. Schorske did not feel he was a victim of deceptive practices that cheapened American citizenship; he had strong pro-Union sympathies and had identified with the struggle against slavery long before he arrived in New York, as did many German immigrants.[15] After his return from the battlefield, he would become both an American patriot and a staunch supporter of German American socialists.[16] Easy naturalization may have been an incentive offered by army recruiters in their search for manpower, but it did not change Schorske's beliefs or his attachment to his new homeland. In practice and by law, U.S. citizenship became an easy prize to hand out by the Union (and Confederate) states. Any Union soldier could become a naturalized U.S. citizen after one year of service with no further requirements (such as a declaration of intent).[17]

In the long run, U.S. citizenship retained its value for urban immigrants mainly because of the franchise and—increasingly—the opportunity to gain access to better jobs with the municipal or state governments, which were limited to U.S. citizens. On the powerholders' side, the systematic use of naturalization as a means to increase one's electoral constituency made citizenship increasingly valuable to politicians during and after the Civil War. Thus, a symbiotic relationship emerged during the Gilded Age: for the politicians who recruited urban immigrants as voters through naturalization, awarding citizenship to voters was an instrument to increase the bosses' political power. To the immigrants, citizenship and its access to the politicians and, potentially, to patronage jobs represented the possibility of a better future, even if the franchise was not in itself meaningful.

In practice, naturalization worked almost entirely without the purview of the federal government in Gilded Age urban America. New York's Tammany Hall operated a "naturalization bureau" of its own—always open in the month before an election. This bureau helped immigrants become U.S. citizens by paying their naturalization fees, bringing them in front of sympathetic judges in whatever court would take them, providing paid witnesses, and instructing them in what to answer to the judges' questions should this be necessary (usually it was not). With the help of such measures, naturalizations usually shot up enormously in September and October of election years. The *New York Times* noted in 1864 that 20,000 to 25,000 naturalizations were performed in New York City in the days just before the election.[18] Sometimes as many as twenty prospective citizens were herded through the chambers of the naturalization judge in five minutes, the reporter estimated. Many of these clients of the Democratic Party (who would furnish a large chunk of the 110,000 or so votes cast in the city if they all went to the polls) maintained that they had arrived in the United States as minors and were thus exempt from presenting a Declaration of Intention. Others were Union soldiers or veterans who upon presenting discharge papers were exempted from the declaration of intent and only needed to "prove" their U.S. residence for the past three years. Ready witnesses were furnished to swear to the facts, if needed.[19] Because of such vigorous recruiting, the 60,000 new citizens added to the rolls in 1868 helped to defeat Republican presidential candidate Ulysses Grant in the state of New York. "No matter how great a Republican majority in the State of New York which lies outside the city, it will be overcome by a Democratic majority in the city of New York," complained Missouri Senator Charles Drake, blaming these results on "frauds practiced in the naturalization of aliens."[20]

The Naturalization Bill of 1870, which gave immigrants of African descent the right to become naturalized citizens, was the first significant change to naturalization law since 1802 and went into effect on July 14, 1870. It reflected the changes brought by the Fourteenth Amendment of the Constitution. Through its language of inclusion (applicants for citizenship had to be "white or of African descent") the Naturalization Act also excluded Asian immigrants from becoming U.S. citizens—a fact that Congress debated at length. The law was also passed with the intention "to purify naturalization," in the words of New York's Republican Senator Roscoe Conkling.[21]

Though the act sought to regularize naturalization procedures (and limit the potential for fraud), little changed when it came to making American citizens out of immigrants in most large urban centers. In fact, mass naturalizations under highly questionable circumstances became the rule, rather than the election-time exception.[22] Newspapers reported on numerous investigations of naturalization and election frauds in the U.S. cities of New York, St. Louis, Chicago, Richmond, Butte, Baltimore, and Cleveland. No longer were the mass naturalization campaigns directed mainly at Democratic voters, nor did they target just Irish immigrants. In Chicago, William Lorimer, Republican Party boss of Cook County in the last decades of the nineteenth century, listed his official job as "Chair of the Committee of Naturalization of Cook County" in the early 1890s. In late nineteenth-century New York, Italians became the target of Tammany Hall naturalization activities.[23] Attempts at reform never seemed to bear any fruit, despite the many investigations. Firm numbers were difficult to come by (the federal government kept no tally of naturalizations, nor did the states), and federal oversight did not exist. "To prove legally that there are many cases of fraud undoubtedly would be a difficult undertaking," wrote the *New York Times* with resignation in 1894. "To be morally certain of it after observing the process for a time is easy."[24]

For immigrants, the dominant role of urban machines in the naturalization process had ambiguous consequences. On the one hand, the help of the political machines' "bureaus of naturalization" made American citizenship accessible for tens of thousands of immigrants. On the other hand, the machines' role had grown so important that becoming a U.S. citizen on one's own in the late nineteenth century became quite difficult. Without facilitators and witnesses, figuring out the proper sequence of applications, fees, filings, and application dates could be a daunting enterprise. Newspapers reporting on the corruption surrounding naturalization in cities commented that upstanding working-class citizens who sought their citizenship papers but did not want to enlist Tammany Hall intermediaries were rudely treated or dismissed by court clerks without reaching their goal.[25] It is likely that tens of thousands of immigrants who had no affinity to existing political organizations were thus de facto excluded from crossing the border into American citizenship in the nineteenth century. "There are many thousands, here twenty to thirty years already, and still aren't citizens and don't want to be," wrote Christian Kirst, a Pittsburgh ironworker, to his family in Germany. "A citizen has no more rights than someone who isn't a citizen, except that he can vote for Congress and the President," he added resignedly.[26] While the corrupt mass naturalization had sprung from the demographic power immigrants had as voters in urban areas, this route to becoming a U.S. citizen was not necessarily an empowering act for individual immigrants whose lives were lived outside the orbit of machine politics.

In the last decade of the nineteenth and the first years of the twentieth century, both reformers and immigrants tried to change the political equilibrium that surrounded naturalization. To government reformers, especially Republicans in Congress and Progressives in urban areas, American citizenship was valued by immigrants for all the wrong reasons. As a result, reforms aimed at increasing the value of citizenship and making naturalization more difficult to gain. Western and midwestern states that had adopted the limited alien franchise in the mid-nineteenth century began to drop it. New York State passed a law that disenfranchised naturalized citizens for sixty to ninety days after their naturalization so that their votes could no longer tip forthcoming elections. Within the courts, some judges (often those who had run on "reform" tickets) went beyond the enforcement of procedural matters in naturalizations and began to thoroughly examine applicants for citizenship, sending home a considerable percentage of petitioners without a change in status for having failed to meet the necessary requirements. As a result of these efforts, the number of naturalizations declined in New York City and other urban areas in the 1890s. Newer immigrant groups

(Italians and eastern Europeans) especially felt the effects of more restricted access to naturalization during this decade.[27]

At the same time, other measures made American citizenship more valuable, especially for the immigrants from southern and eastern Europe who most needed access to jobs and political power brokers. In the midst of the depression of the 1890s, some municipalities drew a line between citizens and aliens by restricting public employment to those who were American citizens.[28] The Pendleton Act required U.S. citizenship of all federal employees, and "citizen only" membership policies were instituted at the same time in some labor unions.[29] In response to this increase in the value of citizenship (amid growing restrictions on naturalization), immigrants organized "naturalization rings" for the production and distribution of forged naturalization papers to be sold to fellow immigrants, often through the same networks used by contract laborers. Some papers were made or sold in the United States, others in Europe. Sometimes the genuine papers of naturalized Americans who had left the United States to return to Europe were put up for sale. Members of newer immigrant groups, such as the Italians, Lebanese, and Greeks, could avail themselves of forged naturalization papers provided by a "padrone" of their own community. Immigrants usually bought the papers in order to gain access to public jobs or to ease admission at the border; gaining the right to vote was usually not their objective. Without the protection of established political machines, such forgery rings were vulnerable in investigations by federal and state authorities, who broke up many of them. Forged papers were available only to a small minority of immigrants, and buying false papers did not become widespread in the nineteenth century.[30]

Naturalization Reform and the Law of 1906

Redrawing the border around naturalization and American citizenship became a central point on the agenda of Progressives in the late nineteenth and early twentieth centuries. The ostensible argument for tighter federal control of naturalization focused mainly on the "cheapening" of U.S. citizenship under the traditional system. Federal control was supposed to solve this problem by making access to naturalization more uniform and difficult.

With the election of Theodore Roosevelt to the presidency, the stage was set for federal action in naturalization. But this turned out to be more difficult than the Roosevelt administration anticipated. Congressmen, local politicians, and their constituents were reluctant to cede oversight of a border crossing that they considered an important instrument of political power. Their objections came to the fore-front in a series of debates over the naturalization reform bill held in the House of Representatives in March, May, and June 1906.[31] Congressmen were divided between those who saw the proposed reform law as a necessary way to protect naturalizations from fraud and those who wanted to keep access to naturalization as flexible and open as possible.[32] "Up to the present time the conditions of admission to our population and of admission to our citizenship have been practically identical. Under this proposal they are made wholly different," thundered Irish-born Bourke Cockran, one of the great orators of Congress and a representative from New York City.[33] Congressman Sylvester Smith from California was more specific. Commenting on the proposed reform bill he objected that "this procedure is entirely too complicated . . . The provisions of this bill would work a great hardship on many miners, stockmen, and ranchmen in my district." The strongest opposition to the proposed law came from representatives in both Republican and Democratic districts with large immigrant populations. Their objections focused on the requirement that petitioners for naturalization speak English.[34] "We do not want linguists but we do want laborers. I do not think we need men skillful in dialectics but we do need men efficient in wielding implements of production," was the way Cockran formulated it. "I have never known a man working with his hands who was dangerous to any community . . . the pests of society are all educated to some extent."[35] The vision of the good citizen conjured up by Cockran was, of course, a traditional image of the nineteenth century, often revived in debates about exclusion in the twentieth.[36]

The Naturalization Act of 1906 was passed by Congress without Senate debate in June of that year. In its final version, the bill retained a host of restrictive features that had been criticized by immigrant advocates. Among the most significant changes was the uniform requirement of a Declaration of Intention that all adult applicants for U.S. citizenship had to file two to seven years before their application for citizenship. Only children and married women were exempt. These "first papers" could only be filed if immigrants could prove that they had entered the country at least three years earlier and that they had resided in the United States continuously since then. Immigrants arriving in or after 1906 had to produce a Certificate of Arrival issued by the Bureau of Immigration (which kept a list of arriving passengers) in order to receive their first papers. Getting such a certificate turned out to be a significant problem for many immigrants—especially for those who had crossed U.S. land borders—because the official records were incomplete, faulty, or simply nonexistent.[37] If the petitioner could produce this document, he next filed the Declaration of Intention and waited for two years to file the petition with the federal naturalization examiner, who was supposed to make sure that the other basic requirements of the law were satisfied: that the petitioner knew some English and that he was accompanied by two U.S. citizen witnesses who knew him as a community resident. The examiner also tried to ensure that the questions on the naturalization form (country of origin, good moral character, family ties, and a life free of crime) were filled out truthfully. At that point, a candidate for naturalization paid the filing fee of $2.00. After this initial inspection, the examiner made a recommendation to the naturalization judge to accept or deny the petition for naturalization. If there was something in the application that did not satisfy the examiner, the applicant had to return with additional documents, verification, better knowledge of English, or more reliable witnesses.[38] It could take months of additional meetings, information gathering, witness preparation, and language learning before a petitioner crossed this hurdle. Many petitioners would become discouraged in the early stages of the process and abandon their petition before it has even registered with the Bureau.[39]

After a ninety day waiting period, during which the applicant's background was investigated by the Bureau of Naturalization, the petitioner was ordered to appear before a naturalization judge for the citizenship examination.[40] There was no fixed knowledge required, no set test. Judges determined an applicant's fitness for citizenship according to their own personal criteria, just as they had done before 1906.[41] In contrast to the immigrants who had to pass a literacy test after 1917, applicants for citizenship were supposed to demonstrate knowledge that was not codified and was not tied to formal instruction. If an immigration examiner or an immigration judge thought a petitioner was unprepared or not properly motivated ("not sufficiently attached to the principles of the Constitution"), he could turn him down for naturalization. Only at this final stage were the denials recorded. Between 3 and 11 percent of petitions were denied each year, depending on the region of the United States.[42]

On paper, the requirements of the new naturalization law were not a radical departure from the past. Rather, change came in the form of their more uniform enforcement—a welcome improvement for immigrants in many urban areas, whose access to U.S. citizenship was no longer governed by the vagaries of corrupt local machines. However, the rigidity with which the new rules were enforced made it difficult for immigrants to become U.S. citizens if their lives were mobile, if they returned to Europe frequently, or if they did not have much contact with U.S. citizens in their communities. The law favored those who remained in one place, could plan ahead, and could keep to the schedule required by the Bureau of Immigration.[43]

The 1906 law brought to an end the period of American naturalization in which federal citizenship was awarded by state and local institutions with little control by the federal government. It also marked the end of the individually negotiated route to citizenship that had characterized naturalization in the eighteenth and nineteenth centuries. In a development that presaged the redefinition of other border crossings for immigrants in the twentieth century, naturalization reform initiated more impersonal, uniform, and bureaucratic procedures on the way to becoming a citizen. Personal negotiations with officials, courts, or politicians mattered less as one crossed the final border into U.S. citizenship. At the same time, federalization shrank the space for individual immigrants to define and negotiate their own naturalization.

But for all its imposition of uniformity, the 1906 naturalization law was also a compromise. To the dismay of some reformers, the law dealt very little with the presumed intentions of immigrants who sought citizenship. Theodore Roosevelt's Commission on Naturalization Reform, for example, had condemned the motives of immigrants who wanted to become U.S. citizens solely because they wanted certain jobs, needed to qualify for union membership, or intended to travel to their homeland with an American passport. A second important piece of legislation, the Expatriation Act of 1907, addressed some of the perceived problems of dual citizenship, but otherwise the law skirted the question of motivation. It left the decision to seek U.S. citizenship entirely to individual immigrants, and the examiners did not probe into the motives of the applicants.[44]

The naturalization laws of 1906 and 1907 were administered by the newly created Federal Bureau of Naturalization, which instructed the examiners, applicants, and judges, collected the information, and checked the papers of petitioners. Field examiners of the Bureau could investigate naturalization petitions regionally, but their recommendations were not binding to the naturalization courts. Quite often, the courts would rule in favor of an applicant even though the Bureau of Naturalization and its examiners had favored denying the petition (863 times in 1915 alone). In many such cases, the Bureau would then alert the federal district attorney and recommend an investigation and cancellation, but this would not necessarily work in the Bureau's favor because the naturalization courts and the district attorneys were, of course, independent of the Bureau.[45]

The story of Frank Aaltonen, a Finnish immigrant in Michigan, illustrates how the different viewpoints and obstructionist tactics of agencies could prevent immigrants from attaining citizenship. When Aaltonen, a labor organizer active in socialist politics, applied around 1912, the naturalization examiner did not want to allow him to submit a petition. "He had received information that I was a 'red agitator' and a 'dangerous character,'" wrote Aaltonen in his memoirs in the late 1930s. After his petition had been denied twice, Aaltonen mobilized a friend, Richard Flanagan, who was a Michigan circuit judge. The judge told the naturalization examiner "that his patience was exhausted and that the only evidence the government had been able to produce is that Mr. Aaltonen is a man of very fine character." The judge swore in Aaltonen on the spot.[46]

The reorganization of naturalization under the new law did not eliminate the confusion or the contradictory interests of other agencies in regulating citizenship and naturalization. The U.S. State Department, the issuer of U.S. passports, continued to have an important say in matters of citizenship, as did the U.S. Attorney General. But within a few years of its establishment, the Bureau of Naturalization developed a clear focus. Like its sister agency, the Bureau of Immigration, the Bureau of Naturalization understood itself as part of a regulatory apparatus created to control and limit access to U.S. citizenship. It also had a mission of service to prospective citizens by educating them about American citizenship.

The Bureau's educational function, though important during the World War I and the postwar years, did not diminish its fundamentally restrictionist agenda. Unlike the Bureau of Immigration, which often operated differently in different regions and also saw itself as an agency to protect immigrants, the Bureau of Naturalization was an enforcement agency aligned with restrictionist forces. In a typical pronouncement, Naturalization Commissioner Richard Campbell praised the 1906 law and noted with satisfaction the appearance of "a greatly reduced number of naturalizations and, secondly, a high grade of the petitioners."[47] He and his successor, Raymond Crist, regularly commented on the selectivity of the naturalization law and lamented the Bureau's limited means to enforce a stricter screening of applicants. To these officials, the lower number of new citizens meant that the Bureau of Naturalization was proving its worth by screening out unsuitable petitioners. While the agency remained a minor player in the debates over immigration and citizenship, as an ideological force it remained firmly aligned with restrictionists throughout its existence from 1907 to 1932.

Immigrants and the Law of 1906

The Naturalization Law of 1906 had an immediate impact on immigrants everywhere in the United States. Millions of newcomers had arrived over the previous decade, yet only 8,000 immigrants filed for U.S. citizenship in the ten months after the law was passed. The next year saw 26,000 applicants for U.S. citizenship, still a very small number. Even though we do not have comparable data for the years before 1906, this was almost certainly a precipitous decline from previous decades. During the years 1888 and 1892, up to 15,000 naturalizations were completed in one New York court alone. Commissioner Campbell estimated that the number of completed naturalizations in the years before the passage of the law had been about 100,000 per year.[48]

The number of people who received their first papers was less affected by the law and climbed more steeply before and during World War I. Even so, only 65 percent of those who filed for first papers actually filed for citizenship within the prescribed number of years, as estimated the sociologist John Gavit in 1922.[49] Given the very large number of European immigrants who continued to enter the United States well into the 1920s, the rate of naturalization remained low (see Appendix 1, Figure 2). The census of 1920 showed that, as in 1910, the majority of foreign-born adults living in the United States were not U.S. citizens, a situation that would not change until 1930.[50]

Clearly, the law of 1906 had greatly raised the threshold for the immigrants who might consider naturalization. While the value of American citizenship did not change—no additional rights or privileges were connected to it after 1906—the "cost" of becoming a U.S. citizen had risen substantially. The longer preparation, increased time, higher fees, and greater uncertainty about the outcome dissuaded thousands of immigrants, especially poorer working-class immigrants, from seeking naturalization. Most immigrants continued to feel vulnerable when confronted by the naturalization examiners and their unpredictable demands, their suspiciousness, and their disorganization and inertia.

The Bureau of Naturalization published no data on the ethnic origins or previous nationality of new citizens until 1924. Even then age and length of residence of the newly naturalized were not revealed. Only the decennial U.S. census collected regular data that classified residents of the United States by citizenship status and ethnic origin.[51] Chicago sociologist John Gavit's study *Americans by Choice* analyzed in depth the impact of the new laws on naturalizations. Based on a large and representative sample of naturalization cases from fiscal year 1913–1914, Gavit investigated whether "new" immigrants took longer to become American citizens than the immigrants from northwestern Europe, and found no difference between the these two groups. On average, immigrants waited ten and a half years to apply for citizenship, with no clear distinction between "old" and "new" groups.[52] Gavit thought that it mattered more whether the immigrants came from a democratic or authoritarian society: those from democratic countries took their time, whereas those from oppressive regimes were more interested in a speedy passage to U.S. citizenship.[53]

Gavit did not probe into the motivations of immigrants who sought citizenship in the years before World War I, and immigrants did not leave a trail of witness reports in the files of the Bureau of Immigration. But we can assume that a powerful motivation for becoming a citizen was the immigrants' interest in gaining voting rights and access to jobs and certain professions. Though many states and territories had granted aliens the franchise in the late nineteenth century, the alien franchise was on the decline by 1906. Only Oregon, Kansas, Nebraska, South Dakota, Texas, Arkansas, and Indiana maintained it on the eve of World War I, and as a result, most of these states saw significantly fewer naturalizations.[54] As in the nineteenth century, American citizenship also opened the door to employment in the public sector and allowed immigrants to enter professions where licenses were required. States such as Wyoming, Arizona, Michigan, and New York prohibited aliens from practicing medicine and pharmacy, operating buses, or executing wills. Some states also tied land ownership to U.S. citizenship. Thus, both highly skilled and less skilled immigrants who wanted to get public sector jobs were motivated to petition for naturalization. Observers on Americanization Day may have believed they were seeing immigrants moved by the transcendent values of American citizenship, but the immigrants themselves were probably motivated by more pragmatic considerations, just as they had been in earlier decades.[55]

The World War I Era

The law of 1906 functioned well, in the eyes of its proponents, for it cut access to naturalization and reserved the rights and privileges of American citizenship to a "deserving" group. But the assumption that a more select cohort of naturalized immigrants might make for a better citizenry and, by extension, a better country, became untenable during wartime. For in wartime the United States, like any democracy, had to rely on the solidarity, labor power, and patriotism of all its inhabitants. As an immigrant country, the nation needed reassurance that its newcomers were willing to participate in the war effort. The American citizenship of immigrants served as the symbol of their wartime patriotism and support. To the nation, immigrants with citizenship increased in value during wartime. For immigrants, in turn, a more easily attained citizenship and its attendant rights became part of a bargain in exchange for patriotism and military service.

To address the political need for more citizen immigrants, the Bureau of Immigration and other federal agencies launched a large-scale campaign to identify noncitizen immigrants in a systematic way and to make naturalization part of its massive Americanization campaign. The agency was particularly interested in immigrants who had already taken out their first papers and would soon be eligible for naturalization. It forwarded the names of these petitioners to local school authorities and voluntary organizations that taught Americanization classes.[56] Thousands of additional names of longtime immigrants surfaced after mandatory alien enemy registration was introduced in November of 1917. "The registration . . . disclosed the most shocking state of affairs," commented John Gavit. "Men and women who have their children and grandchildren in the military forces of the United States were disclosed as being not only aliens but enemy aliens."[57] Many long established immigrants were able to erase the stigma of enemy alien status by becoming citizens after registering as enemy aliens. Congress passed special legislation that made this possible.

Noncitizen immigrants were also identified through registration for the military draft, which began in June 1917. The draft covered both citizens and aliens, and a considerable number of noncitizens, over 120,000, were in fact inducted into the armed forces.[58] The pressure to modify the existing system of naturalization was therefore almost immediate once the United States had entered World War I in April 1917. Under the law of May 1918, aliens who served in

the armed forces or the U.S. merchant marine could become naturalized U.S. citizens without submitting first papers, proof of long-
term residence, or background checks, nor did they need to prove
their knowledge of the English language and the U.S. constitution.
Immigrant soldiers who were ready to sacrifice their lives for their
new country would not be excluded from American citizenship just
because they might lack lesser qualifications.[59]

As a result of the military naturalization law, tens of thousands of
men became U.S. citizens within weeks. In fiscal year 1918, seven
months after the passage of the military naturalization law, almost
64,000 men became naturalized citizens while in uniform. Almost a
third of all naturalizations that year were of soldiers; the following
year, the total number of naturalizations doubled, with soldiers
making up more than half of all new citizens. The law was extended
until 1924 (it applied to veterans after an honorable discharge); in
all, over 288,000 men took advantage of it, almost a quarter of all
those naturalized during the years 1918 to 1924.[60]

These numbers forced the Bureau of Naturalization to change its
methods: it had to move away from its customary scrutiny of civilian
applicants to the new task of naturalizing new soldiers. Hundreds of
examiners moved to military camps in the spring of 1918 to make U.S.
citizens out of immigrants en masse before their units were moved
abroad. Even Asian immigrants were sometimes admitted to U.S. citizenship, though this was only grudgingly accepted by the Bureau.
Instead of control and denial, the Bureau's wartime mandate was to
reach out to almost everyone who did or could serve in the armed
forces. As Gavit observed, the effect of military naturalization was to
"nullify all the elaborate procedure and hypercritical precaution so
carefully constructed by the Naturalizations Service."[61]

Draftees who were not U.S. citizens could ask to be exempt from
military service under U.S. law. But such men were sanctioned by
the Bureau of Naturalization, which followed up on their cases and
told them that they were barred from future naturalization. This
proved to be no idle threat: over 31,000 applicants were denied naturalization in the 1920s by immigration judges because they had not
served in the U.S. military during the war. Such behavior showed
"insufficient attachment to the U.S. constitution" and was therefore

cause for denial. Wartime service thus became a precondition for naturalization of adult men, adding to the cost of American citizenship in a way that was not visible to many immigrants until later.[62]

Weighed against the vast resources devoted to Americanization and citizenship classes and the outreach effort that was military naturalization, the cumulative effect on naturalization was not large during World War I. Although the number of people who filed for first papers increased steeply between 1914 and 1919 (reaching a high point in 1917), naturalizations increased only in 1918 and 1919, almost entirely due to military naturalizations.[63] In other words, the Americanization and citizenship campaign of the war years had almost no effect on the rate of naturalization for civilians during the war years. For immigrants, the mixture of incentives and controls in government naturalization policies continued to send a contradictory message. The political and cultural pressure for aliens to turn themselves into citizens was high, and the cost seemed low—at least for those willing to serve in the military. The cost of remaining an alien loomed larger during wartime. Overall, even in wartime, the incentives for immigrants to become American citizens, except for men in the armed forces, were by themselves insufficient and the hurdles too high for most European immigrants, to prompt a visit to the Naturalization Bureau. Despite all out Americanization efforts and anti-alien sentiment running high, the number of new citizens remained modest, especially compared with the very large number of immigrants who had entered the country in the decade before World War I.

Quotas and Gender in the Interwar Years

The 1920s and 1930s brought an end to the era of minimally regulated immigration from Europe. As immigration was restricted under a system of racial quotas, naturalization also assumed a different position in the border crossing of immigrants. The Emergency Quota Act of 1921 was passed quickly in May of that year, and the sudden imposition of nationality quotas caught many immigrants by surprise.[64] Thousands were forced to return to Europe after they were not allowed to disembark at U.S. ports because the quota for their nationality had been filled by the time their ship arrived. This first quota law gave preference to immigration visas for family members of naturalized citizens, though such immigrants still had to await their spot in the line of quota applicants.

The provision immediately increased the incentive for immigrants to seek U.S. citizenship if they had family members in Europe who wanted to join them. Immigrant men who became citizens could bring their wives to the United States without delay because the wives were automatically covered under their husbands' naturalization until 1922. The quota law turned naturalization into a very valuable tool for immigrants, especially men, enabling them to reunite or build a family in the United States. For individual immigrants, U.S. citizenship became a primary means to further the immigration of kin rather than an end goal in itself. By becoming U.S. citizens immigrants supported the chain of migration for family and community in the decades to come.

But the Emergency Quota Act of 1921 and the more permanent quota of the Immigration Act of 1924 (Johnson-Reed Act) also affected the workings of another law, passed in 1922: the Cable Act. The Cable Act separated the citizenship of married women from that of their husbands. Immigrant women were no longer automatically awarded U.S. citizenship upon marriage to an American citizen or the naturalization of their husbands. Another consequence of the law was that women who were U.S. citizens no longer lost their citizenship upon marriage to a foreigner.[65] This reform of citizenship law was supported by both by advocates for women's suffrage and proponents of immigration restriction. Richard Campbell, the Commissioner of Naturalization at the time (and not a suffragist), had long argued for the abolition of derivative naturalization as part of naturalization reform: "There are about 2,000,000 women who will receive citizenship through the naturalization of their husbands within the next few years," he wrote in 1918, "the addition of such a large number of citizens who know nothing whatsoever about their responsibilities represents a grave problem . . ."[66] The Cable Act addressed Campbell's concerns: now all immigrant women, married or not, had to meet the same criteria for naturalization as adult men. Beginning in September 1922, women had to file a Declaration of

Intention, petition the Naturalization Court, and pass an examination before a judge, just like men. Immigrant women who had married a U.S. citizen husband abroad were also no longer admitted outside the quota (as they did not become American citizens upon marriage).[67] This effect of the Cable Act caught immigrants by surprise, especially in the fall of 1922 and in 1923. In many cases, naturalized immigrant husbands who returned to the United States after their wedding in Europe were admitted, but their newlywed wives were rejected because there was no immediate spot for them under the quota law. In some cases, immigrant husbands went to court and won the right to bring their wives in, regardless of the women's quota status. Under the political weight of these court decisions and amid much confusion, the Bureau of Immigration let in many women married to U.S. citizens under an unacknowledged parole status.[68]

The 1924 quota law cleared up some of the confusion connected to citizenship and the immigrant admission of family members, though it confirmed some hardships as well. This second quota law, which would remain in effect until 1965, formalized the preference for wives and children of U.S. citizens in immigrant admissions. After 1924, women whose husbands were both U.S. citizens and had lived in the United States continuously could enter outside the quota with their young children. Still, the requirement that women immigrants gain citizenship independently of men, while close to the heart of Progressives and early feminists, would lead to hardships and exclusions under the conditions faced by immigrants in the 1920s and beyond.[69]

The English immigrant Ettie Glaser was one of those women caught by surprise after the passage of the Cable Act. She arrived from England with her American husband shortly after their wedding in 1922. "When I married my husband the law had changed that year. And if you married an American, you automatically did not become a citizen. So I had to become one on my own," she remembered. Citizenship would elude her for another twenty years.[70] For some women, the necessity to naturalize independently of their husbands continued to be a source of confusion long after the Cable Act was passed. Mary Dunn, an Irish immigrant interviewed in

1986, was still not quite clear about the nature of her status when her husband gained U.S. citizenship in 1928. "And so after he got his citizenship papers I only had to wait ninety days to get mine," she remembered thinking. In 1941, Mary Dunn finally understood that no automatic naturalization would ever take place for her, and she filed for naturalization on her own.[71]

In fact, it is likely that Mary Dunn, like Ettie Glaser, became stateless after marriage to an American citizen: until 1948, British women who married a foreigner automatically lost their British citizenship (as was also the case for Canadian, German, and Japanese women). Like thousands of other wives of Americans, they remained without a nationality until they could naturalize on their own. In the case of Japanese and other Asian women who were ineligible for citizenship because of their race, they were condemned to statelessness for the foreseeable future. Under the circumstances of most immigrants in the interwar years, the value of independent citizenship for women remained ambiguous.[72]

Even after passage of the Cable Act, male immigrants benefited disproportionately from the family preferences bestowed by naturalization under the Immigration Acts of 1921 and 1924. The nationality quota of 1924 exempted the wives of citizens (and their minor children) from the quota entirely and gave quota preference to the wives of those who had filed their Declaration of Intention. As a result, over a quarter million immigrants filed their Declaration of Intention each year during the 1920s. Naturalizations fluctuated between 145,000 and 200,000 annually, and were primarily sought by men. They reached a high of over 250,000 in 1928 and 1929 (see Appendix 1, Figure 2). Men's willingness and ability to become political citizens was rewarded by permission to have family members join them under U.S. preference categories in America. Women citizens continued to be unable to sponsor their husbands outside the quota system.[73]

For male immigrants from small quota nations, naturalization became an important part of the strategy to reunite the families on the North American side of the Atlantic and to allow for a continued flow of immigrants from home. According to the Bureau of Naturalization, the largest groups of the newly naturalized in the 1920s were Italians, Poles, and eastern European Jews, precisely the ethnic and nationality groups who had been most numerous among immigrants during the previous decades and who were also hardest hit by the quota law. Together with other southern and eastern Europeans (especially Greeks and Czechs) they made up more than 50 percent of newly naturalized citizens in the 1920s.[74] In the long run, found the sociologist William Bernard, some "new" groups, notably eastern European Jews, exceeded the longtime Irish immigrants in their eagerness to become U.S. citizens.[75] *The Interpreter,* the monthly journal of the Foreign Language Information Service, remarked on this reversal not without irony in 1929: "By comparing the high percentages for southern and eastern Europe in the total number of recent naturalizations with the overall preponderance of arrivals from northern and western Europe in the immigration of the last few years, it would be easy to charge the 'Nordics' with indifference to American citizenship and to claim that the Slavs and the Italians show a greater aptitude and enthusiasm for American principles and government."[76]

If immigrants saw the increasing value of naturalization for themselves and their families, the strategic use of naturalization was greeted with displeasure by the Bureau of Naturalization. Commissioner Raymond Crist thought that becoming a citizen solely to reunite with wives and children represented a cheapening of naturalization. Crist also thought that it had become too easy to become an American citizen. "The standard of admission to citizenship should no longer be permitted to be substantially what it was in 1802" he argued in 1923, and asked for more stringent and uniform criteria for naturalization. Crist's supervisor, Secretary of Labor Davis, agreed. Criticizing immigrant men who sought U.S. citizenship in order to ease immigration by their wives and children he commented, "it is a matter of regret when American citizenship if sought for that reason alone."[77]

But to immigration advocates, this was hypocrisy. "Subjectively, citizenship has nearly always been sought for the sake of some benefit it confers and rarely because of the applicants' conviction as to the superiority of American institutions," wrote *The Interpreter* in 1929. The love of country and attachment to America might come later, the paper counseled, but would nonetheless be profound. "Primarily it is time, environment and some degree of success that will make America his home, remodel his habits and his behavior . . . and, finally develop the totality of reactions which are usually constructed as attachment to the country."[78]

The Bureau of Naturalization was unsuccessful in its efforts to make naturalization law more restrictive, but it and some naturalization courts found other ways to disqualify male applicants for citizenship: working-class men from southern and eastern Europe were sometimes denied their application by the examiners because their families did not live with them. Some naturalization examiners and judges argued that such men had abandoned their families in Europe and were therefore not of "good moral character." Of course, the petitioners had been unable to bring their loved ones to the United States because of quota restrictions and were seeking citizenship for just that reason. But without access to U.S. citizenship, bringing their wives and children to the United States would remain a distant dream for such applicants.[79]

For the remainder of the 1920s and beyond, the Bureau of Naturalization continued to skirmish with petitioners whom it deemed insufficiently qualified or motivated, while immigrants tried to make naturalization and U.S. citizenship one additional tool in their quest for security, permanence, and family unification. The Bureau of Naturalization won many small battles without winning the campaign for radical restriction. Despite the growing complexity of naturalization law, the Bureau of Naturalization gained neither in power nor expertise after the mid-1920s. As overseas immigration dropped precipitously, the size of the Bureau's client base—immigrants who were not (yet) citizens—also shrank. In 1932, the Bureau of Immigration and the Bureau of Naturalization were merged to form the Immigration and Naturalization Service (INS) within the Department of Labor. Thereafter, naturalization would always remain a secondary field of activity for immigration regulators.[80]

The merger of the Bureaus of Immigration and Naturalization did not receive much attention because it occurred at a time in U.S. history when both immigration and naturalization were at a low point. In 1930 the number of men who became naturalized citizens had begun to decline rapidly; it reached a low of 78,000 in 1933, thereafter slowly rising again for the remainder of the decade. Only during the special conditions of wartime in 1944 did the number of new citizens surpass the benchmark reached in 1928. The lower number of naturalizations in the 1930s was only partly due to the greatly slowed rate of immigration in the 1920s, which diminished the number of adult immigrants eligible for naturalization. A second reason was the diminished importance of naturalization itself for immigrant admission.[81] Beginning in 1929, U.S. consulates became very selective in granting immigration visas to ordinary immigrants, even those with U.S. citizen relatives. It became altogether impossible for women to sponsor family members (even their husbands), as women were always deemed unable to support relatives. Usually it was the financial resources of the sponsor alone that were considered important, and it made almost no difference if the sponsor was a U.S. citizen. Naturalization was no longer a useful tool to achieve family migration.[82]

Despite the declining number of naturalizations and the difficulties of linking citizenship to eased immigration for families, naturalizations continued to be useful during the Depression decade, although in different ways from before. Despite their inability to sponsor family members, an increasing number of immigrant women sought naturalization during the 1930s. After the passage of the Cable Act, women had at first made up a very small number of petitioners, but by 1941 more immigrant women than men became U.S. citizens.[83] The change in the proportion underlined the different uses of U.S. citizenship for men and women in the 1930s and beyond. For men, the two primary motivating factors of the past decades, to seek a political voice and to expedite the immigration of relatives, declined in importance. But in the 1930s, in hard times, American citizenship offered protective qualities that were especially important to poor women with families. In some states, women needed to be American citizens to qualify for so-called "mothers pensions" and for federal relief payments for abandoned women with children.[84] The Works Progress Administration (WPA) programs themselves did not require U.S. citizenship from applicants, but in practice accepting government support carried risk for noncitizens. Immigrant women and men who applied for relief faced a dilemma. If they tried to receive money under a federal program their names were forwarded automatically to the Immigration Service. The immigration officials then could and often did take steps to deport the applicants as public charges (or illegal immigrants), especially if the application for relief had taken place within five years of arrival in the United States. In 1931 alone, 731 applicants for relief were deported as illegal immigrants.[85] However, if immigrants decided to apply for citizenship first, before going on relief, they also risked deportation. The application and its examination of an immigrants' circumstances "outed" the applicant and made her or him vulnerable to unwanted attention from the authorities. Applicants not only risked being rejected for naturalization because of a "lack of moral character" as relief applicants, but they could also be deported as likely public charges, even if they never had applied for relief. Scrutiny of citizenship applicants by the federal government seems to have increased in the Depression decade, as the voluminous correspondence with immigrant advocacy groups suggests. In their letters, longtime residents of the United States described how their applications for naturalization were denied because they had not satisfied an ever-lengthening list of technical requirements, or because they had taken advantage of public support programs for the needy. Especially women felt acutely the humiliation of officials' attempts to impugn their honesty and character. In some cases, immigrants fought back and organized publicly for their cause, but in most cases they coped quietly.[86]

The increasing value of U.S. citizenship as a form of protection against deportation and participation in a nascent welfare system explains the rise in naturalizations from 1934 on (after a slump during the previous five years).[87] "Normally, it might be expected that a decline in immigration would be followed by a corresponding decline in naturalization," noted immigration commissioner Daniel MacCormack in his 1936 annual report to the Secretary of Labor. "But this has not been true of the past four years. There are many reasons why aliens hitherto indifferent to citizenship should now seek it, but the most cogent are economic pressure and fear of hostile legislation."[88] Whereas only 113,00 immigrants had become U.S.

citizens in 1934, after years of steady increase, more than twice that number had taken out citizenship papers by 1940. The community of immigrants who had not crossed the last border into citizenship would diminish greatly in the 1930s. The 1940 census showed that over 68 percent of immigrants living in the United States were naturalized U.S. citizens.[89]

Naturalization and Citizenship among Immigrants of Color

Amid a deeply racialized web of immigration and naturalization law, non-European immigrants faced very difficult hurdles in their struggle to become naturalized U.S. citizens. But despite the clear-cut exclusions of naturalization law that permitted only whites and those of African descent to become U.S. citizens until World War II, the history of this border crossing for immigrants of color was still quite varied, with important shifts taking place over time. Just as was the case in legal admission to the United States, the history of naturalization by non-white immigrants reflected the changing view of race and whiteness throughout the twentieth century. Courts were the major arbiters in the determination of race for citizenship purposes. Immigrants of color who pursued naturalization considered the value of U.S. citizenship to be high, despite the reality of limited social and economic citizenship rights for non-whites.

Given its primary importance as a qualification for citizenship, it is perhaps surprising that naturalization petition forms did not ask for applicants' race, though country of citizenship, skin color, eye color, hair color, and height were data that had to be provided. Instead, race was informally determined by an examiner and by the naturalization judge. Examiners could make a simple visual classification or a more "scientific" attribution of the applicant to a racial group such as "Caucasian" or "Asiatic." An examiner or judge could deny the petition simply on racial grounds. But few such decisions (so-called Section 2169 denials) were recorded annually in the 1920s, and even fewer afterward.

The examiner also could discourage applicants who appeared to be neither white nor black, without turning them down outright. Sefridi Alexander, a Muslim South Asian who had immigrated to

Washington State before World War I and become a wealthy rice grower in California, remembered vividly how he was denied naturalization during the era of World War I, though objections against his naturalization because of race were never articulated. The examiner had simply asked him impossibly detailed questions about the Constitution and U.S. history and then disqualified him for insufficient knowledge. The memory of this humiliation was still vivid, and the failure rankled over twenty years later. Alexander had yet to try again by the late 1930s.[90]

Other applicants from disfavored groups were sometimes successful because the net of racial exclusion was not woven tightly before the late 1920s. At times, the examiner approved the petitions of Asian immigrants, and the immigration judge, too, could find no evidence that the applicants from East or South Asia were not white and granted them citizenship.[91] Even after a special directive from the Commissioner of Naturalization to naturalization examiners required them to reject all applicants who were neither African nor white, the naturalization courts continued to make non-whites into U.S. citizens. The Bureau of Naturalization and later the INS continued to be divided over where to draw the line of racial exclusion from citizenship, and conflicting court decisions were no help.[92]

The case of S. R. Kokaturer, an immigrant from Bombay, shows how Asian immigrants could become U.S. citizens in some cases, while their friends and fellow immigrants were excluded. Kokaturer had arrived in Minnesota as a college student around 1910 and earned a degree in chemistry from the University of Minnesota. After working in the chemical industry during World War I, he applied for U.S. citizenship and received his naturalization certificate without problems. Married to a (white) Minnesotan, he noted in 1938 that he knew of other Indian immigrants of his generation who had become citizens. Most of them had lost their citizenship later in the wake of a Supreme Court decision (*Thind v. U.S.*) in the 1920s which determined that, all scientific and historical claims notwithstanding, men and women from India were not white because they did not look like Europeans. Kokaturer was lucky. He was among the South Asian immigrants who did not experience the retroactive loss of U.S. citizenship that many South Asian immigrants experienced as a result of this decision.[93] Only Turkish, Armenian, and Syrian immigrants were usually successful in getting approval for naturalization as whites. After years of activism and litigation, these former citizens of the Ottoman Empire were consistently able to secure their right to naturalization by the 1920s.[94]

Chinese, Japanese, and other East and Southeast Asian immigrants who were subject to Asian immigration exclusion were less successful in overcoming their exclusion from naturalization, although according to the 1910 census 1,788 Japanese and Chinese immigrants were naturalized U.S. citizens.[95] Chinese had the greatest difficulty convincing the U.S. authorities that they had any claim to naturalization, as they were explicitly excluded from naturalization under the Chinese Exclusion Act of 1882. Even Chinese immigrants with one European parent or those adopted by American citizens could not prevail in the courts and were excluded from naturalization and U.S. citizenship.[96]

The naturalization of Japanese immigrants was not expressly forbidden by a specific law before 1924, but such applicants usually ran afoul of the "non-white" provision of the naturalization law. A few Japanese immigrants, most notably Buntaro Kumagai and Takao Ozawa, contested the view that they were not white and pursued their cases all the way to the U.S. Supreme Court. Kumagai argued in 1908 that he had fulfilled all requirements for naturalization and should have access to citizenship as a veteran of the U.S. armed forces (he had fought in the Spanish-American War). But the federal district court in Washington State where his case was presented would hear none of it: "the use of the word 'white person' clearly indicates the intention of Congress to maintain a line of demarcation between races and to extend the privilege of naturalization only to those of that race which is predominant in this country" declared the judges.[97] Takao Ozawa, a resident of Hawai'i, argued that he was culturally indistinguishable from Americans in every way intended by the naturalization law. The Supreme Court in its 1922 decision did not deny Ozawa's claim to social or cultural Americanness, but still declared him racially ineligible for naturalization. Ozawa could not be white, said the court, because no American would perceive him as such. Therefore, he could not become a U.S. citizen through naturalization.[98] The *Ozawa* decision, a landmark case which would stand for the next thirty years, stifled any further attempts by East Asians to become U.S. citizens.[99]

After 1922 non-white petitioners for American citizenship could no longer claim that they had met the cultural and social ideals of assimilation and should therefore be eligible to become U.S. citizens regardless of a racial designation.[100] Only a small group of Japanese American veterans of World War I countered this argument successfully in the 1930s and were, retroactively, granted the right to the military naturalization that they had not received in 1918. In the first half of the twentieth century, the line separating whites from almost all Asian immigrants seemed stark in law and daily life, and the lack of opportunity to become a U.S. citizen underlined this separation.[101]

It was not until the end of World War II that the borders that limited naturalization to whites and people of African origin began to crumble before a new political reality: the need to forge global political alliances during the cold war. Naturalization rights (and immigration rights as well) could no longer be withheld outright from citizens of friendly nations who were at the core of American efforts to fight communism worldwide. The liberalization of naturalization and immigration law in the context of changing foreign policy priorities began with the repeal the Chinese Exclusion Act in December 1943. Thereafter, Chinese immigrants were eligible for naturalization as well as admissible as regular immigrants, although they were limited to a minuscule quota of 110 per year (Chinese wives of U.S. citizens could enter outside the quota).[102] The Chinese community was small in the United States, and it would only grow slightly under the tiny quota. No more than 840 Chinese immigrants were naturalized in 1945, the first year they were eligible under regular procedures. Seventy-one Chinese-born men became American citizens between 1943 and 1945 under the military naturalization law. But, in the long run, the 1943 act would pave the way for a sea change in Chinese immigration and a fundamental demographic shift for the Chinese community in the United States.[103]

The end of Asian exclusion accelerated in 1946, a year after the end of World War II. A few days before the formal independence of the Philippines, Filipinos were able to begin knitting their community on both sides of the Pacific together under U.S. immigration law. Since the passage of the Tydings-McDuffie Act in 1934, no new immigration and family reunification had been possible because the act declared Filipino aliens ineligible for citizenship and excluded them from immigration under the nationality quota law of 1924. But the wartime provisions that allowed for accelerated naturalization under military naturalization laws included Filipinos who served in the U.S. armed forces in the Philippines. Over 11,000 men were thus able to become U.S. citizens between 1943 and 1946, while they remained residents of the Philippine Islands. Only after the border into American citizenship was crossed could these Filipino Americans actually cross the physical border into the United States and immigrate—which nearly all of them did. The new group of veterans quickly grew to over 30,000 by 1949 and became the core of a renewed Filipino migration to post-war America.[104]

The passage of the so-called India Bill in 1946 gave Indians (and, after 1947, Pakistanis) the right to apply for immigration visas and become U.S. citizens as well, though again the quota was a symbolic one hundred a year.[105] Because the U.S. government recognized the right to U.S. citizenship as a valuable instrument to improve its international reputation among many (though not all) Asian countries, the racial hurdles to immigration and naturalization began to crumble. Immigrants had been criticized for instrumentalizing American citizenship for various purposes, but beginning in the mid-1940s, naturalization became a tool for the American state in the arsenal of cold war politics.

Not all immigrants from East Asia benefited from the postwar thaw of racial exclusion. Japanese immigrants were slow to gain admission as immigrants and the right to become citizens in postwar America. World War II had been a harsh time for Japanese immigrants and Japanese Americans in the United States. Even though a majority of Japanese Americans had been native born U.S. citizens in 1941, Executive Order 9066 had forced all residents of Japanese descent to evacuate their homes on the West Coast in February 1942 in order to relocate to internment camps deep in the interior West. What Mae Ngai has called the "nullification of American citizenship"

also meant that all mainland Japanese Americans had been dis-
charged from the U.S. armed forces in 1942. In 1944, Congress had
passed the denaturalization act, which made it possible to renounce
U.S. citizenship while living in the United States. Unsure of their
own future in the United States, over 5,000 Japanese Americans
(native U.S. citizens) had renounced their U.S. citizenship and declared themselves to be expatriated from the United States, even
though they had remained in the country. It was only with pro-
tracted litigation, that most of the renunciants had their U.S. citizenship restored after the war.[106] Not until the passage of the 1952
McCarran-Walter Act, which ended the racial restrictions on naturalization, could Japanese and other Asian immigrants apply for U.S.
citizenship.[107] The change in the law led almost 20,000 Japanese
immigrants to become U.S. citizens within four years of its passage,
most of them old-timers who had arrived in the United States long
ago.[108]

While "nullification of citizenship" occurred elsewhere in the
world before and after World War II, the story of Japanese Americans
was unique in U.S. citizenship history. The members of almost an
entire immigrant group were de facto incarcerated, regardless of
nationality, deprived of their U.S. citizenship and civil rights, and
pressured to declare themselves aliens in their own country. Despite
the experience of internment, expropriation, and continuing social
discrimination, this immigrant group quickly embraced the chance
to become naturalized citizens, defying the stereotype that citizenship had to "pay off" in order for immigrants to embrace it.

Japanese Americans had few family members follow them to the
United States after World War II, even after 1952. Most other immigrants from Asia, though, seized naturalization as a chance to unite
their families by bringing them to the North American side of the
Pacific. The nationality quotas for Asians continued to be tiny until
1965, too small to offer a realistic hope for bringing family members
under the quota for East Asians. But as naturalized U.S. citizens,
East and South Asian immigrants could sponsor spouses and younger
children outside the quota. No immigrant group made more use of
this mechanism than Chinese immigrants. Though their number remained small, with under 3,000 entering before the late 1950s,

naturalizations of Chinese rose gradually and, with a delayed effect, so did immigration from China. Over 7,000 Chinese immigrants entered the United States in 1947 and 1948. From 1955 to 1956, the number of naturalizations rose quite suddenly, doubling to almost 6,000 in this two-year period. The "shadow effect" where naturalizations reflected the number of immigrants five to seven years earlier continued to be strong for this nationality group until 1967. Chinese immigrants were not the only new Asian immigrants to become U.S. citizens quickly. Filipinos also naturalized in large numbers in the 1950s. As a result, the percentage of Asians among all naturalized Americans increased significantly from fewer than 7.2 percent in 1950 to 14 percent in 1964. Naturalization was clearly a stepping stone for Asian immigrants in making migration of kin possible.[109]

The exclusion of Asian-born immigrants from naturalization up to 1952 demarcated the line that naturalization law drew around white citizenship at its most rigid. In contrast, the position of Mexican immigrants and migrants in the naturalization process illustrated how legal theory and practice could be contradictory and how the social conventions of what made a citizen locally and regionally could be powerful in shaping the meaning of citizenship and naturalization for immigrants. Mexican Americans and Mexican immigrants were usually classified as "white" by the U.S. census and by the Bureau of Immigration. But at other times Mexican immigrants were labeled "colored" or indigenous by the INS. Indigeneity could disqualify Mexicans from naturalization before 1940, because Mexicans (or Canadians) who were classified as indigenous were not considered white and therefore not eligible for American citizenship.[110]

Most Mexicans, however, were not formally excluded from naturalization because of official racial designations. Rather, poverty, social segregation, and lack of documented immigration contributed to a very low naturalization rate for these immigrants. Mexican nationalism also contributed to the distance Mexican Americans felt toward the United States. In his extensive interviews with Mexican laborers during the 1920s, the Mexican anthropologist Manuel Gamio found that none of his interviewees were willing to consider becoming U.S. citizens. Wenceslao Orosco, a long-time resident of Los Angeles, was typical: "They have told Wenceslao that it would be a good thing to make himself into an American citizen so that he would find it easier to get into the Carpenters Union. But he says he would rather have his two eyes taken out than to change citizenship." What emerged from Gamio's interviews was not blind nationalism, but rather the assessment that the social, political, or economic rewards of American citizenship were elusive even after naturalization. "These people do not like us," Carlos Almazan told him, "they think we aren't as good as they." A U.S. passport did not represent a worthy exchange for Mexican citizenship under these circumstances even if it might bring the chance for better jobs.[111]

During the Depression decade, as the promise of jobs and a stable life north of the Rio Grande evaporated, poverty and isolation prevented even long-time Mexican residents from pursuing naturalization. To do so put them at risk for deportation because of poverty or dependency. In 1939, the WPA interviewed Juanita Hernandez Garcia, an elderly Mexican woman who had arrived in Texas in the 1880s. After sixty years of work as a cook, in her old age and widowhood she felt that, although she had become part of America as much as anybody else on the Texas range, citizenship had eluded her: "Me no citizen of the United States, no have same like citizen, no get pension, no have money," she said. "Me father, me family, me husband give life for this good country, me work all life here but no get nothing but good talk and $1.70 a week."[112]

The third barrier to naturalization for Mexicans was the difficulty of establishing a record of legal permanent residency, which had to be provided at the time of filing first papers. Despite their exemption from quotas, Mexican immigrants in the 1920s and beyond still had to fulfill the requirements of immigration law: they had to prove their literacy, health, and lack of dependency, and they had to pay processing fees. The majority of Mexicans entered without inspection, beginning in 1910, because they feared rejection under the law and because they were too poor to pay the entry fees. Therefore, they could not provide a Certificate of Arrival, rendering them unqualified for naturalization. As the director of St. Paul's International Institutes reflected in 1946, "Mexicans in the United States unable to prove legal entry have been afraid to come forward and make an application for citizenship. It is known that thousands of Mexicans waded the Rio Grande or slipped across the border in Arizona and New Mexico in 1925 and 1926 . . ."[113] Fewer than a dozen of his charges from the growing community of Mexicans in Minnesota had applied for citizenship in the mid-1940s.

Agricultural laborer programs, in place during and after World War I and from 1943 until 1962, also made it less likely that Mexican immigrants would apply for U.S. citizenship. During World War II, the majority of the more than 290,000 Mexican workers who entered the United States legally came in under these programs. But the so-called *braceros* did not legally qualify as immigrants, were not permitted to stay in the United States after their labor contracts had expired, and could not choose where to work or change employment after arrival.[114] Furthermore, time spent in the United States as contract workers did not count toward the residency requirement for naturalization. By the year 1950, when the bracero program was well established, only about 6,700 Mexicans per year entered the United States as immigrants, whereas over 26,000 came as temporary agricultural workers and 96,000 were legalized temporary workers who had been in the United States already. Temporary agricultural workers outnumbered regular immigrants from Mexico until the bracero program was phased out in 1962. No wonder the number of de facto Mexican immigrants who became citizens remained small: the cohort of official immigrants was tiny compared with the large number migrants who were classified as temporary workers.[115]

This exclusion of Mexicans from citizenship persisted for over half of the twentieth century. Fewer than 1,000 Mexicans became naturalized in the 1920s. No data were published during the Depression decade. Between 1941 and 1950, the number of naturalized U.S. citizens of Mexican origin rose to 43,600, a higher figure but still fewer than 2.5 percent of all naturalizations during this decade. Only in the 1950s did Mexicans become Americans in greater numbers, with over 5,000 Mexicans naturalized every year until the late 1970s when the number rose significantly. The naturalization rate of Mexicans remained anemic until after the passage of the 1986 Immigration Control and Reform Act.[116]

Black immigrants found themselves in a situation that was in certain ways similar to that of Mexicans. As people of "African descent," they were explicitly included in the circle of potential citizens after the passage of the 1870 Naturalization Act, yet the formal and informal racial segregation of American society tainted American citizenship for many black immigrants. Caribbean immigrants could see that African Americans experienced few meaningful citizenship rights, even in urban America; as a result, the lure of naturalization was not strong for them. Within the Caribbean communities of the East Coast, forswearing loyalty to the British Crown or the French Republic for the uncertain promise of naturalization as a U.S. citizen was even greeted with a certain amount of disdain, as sociologist Ira Reed observed. He noted two important factors which nonetheless could prompt Afro-Caribbean immigrants to become U.S. citizens: involvement in African American political life (especially in American cities of the northeast) and the possibility of civil service jobs. This apparently led some West Indian immigrants to pursue a clandestine dual nationality: they would declare themselves natives of the United States and indicate a birthplace in the southern United States that was known for its lack of recorded births of African Americans. Passing as a "native" without a birth certificate was possible for black immigrants and did not require them to give up their passport from the West Indies.[117]

In the 1920s and 1930s, the percentage of naturalized citizens among Caribbean immigrants was below 30 percent, and even though it increased over time, it remained far below the percentage of naturalized citizens among European immigrants.[118] The imposition of special, low quotas for immigrants from British Caribbean colonies under the McCarran-Walter Act of 1952 altered the situation: between 1952 and 1965, sponsorship by U.S. citizen relatives (or entry under temporary agricultural worker programs) often became the only legal way to enter the United States for newcomers from the West Indies. As a result, the number of Jamaicans, Haitians, and Barbadians who became U.S. citizens rose significantly in the latter half of the 1950s and the early 1960s.[119] Despite this pragmatic use of naturalization, large-scale adoption of U.S. citizenship among Caribbean immigrants only picked up once segregation began to fall away in the 1960s. By the 1990s, immigrants from Jamaica, Guyana, and Haiti were twice as likely to become naturalized citizens as Mexicans who had been in the United States for a similar number of years.[120]

Redrawing the Boundaries of Citizenship

The landscape of citizenship and border crossing became more complex in the United States during and after World War II for all arrivals, not just for immigrants of color. For it was during the war years that the U.S. federal government began to once again strengthen its control over naturalization and immigration affairs through administrative and legal means. The first measure to do so, which passed as an administrative reform, moved responsibility for the INS from the Department of Labor to the Department of Justice. This reflected a shift in thinking that had been long in the making. By the end of the 1930s, immigration was no longer seen as a way to primarily ensure labor supply and fuel economic growth. Immigrants, immigration, and naturalization were increasingly considered a matter of national identity, borders, and national security.

The Alien Registration Act of 1940, also known as the Smith Act, which was passed one week after the reorganization of the INS in June 1940, introduced mandatory registration at post offices of all aliens over the age of 14 with the Department of Justice. Registration included fingerprinting and was enforced until 1980. Within the first four months of passage, over 4.7 million noncitizen residents were registered—providing a glimpse of a much larger than expected immigrant population. The act also expanded the federal government's right to deport any noncitizen suspected of subversive activities, and it prohibited entry of suspected communists or communist sympathizers. This part of the act would later become a potent weapon to deport leftist dissidents or strip them of their American citizenship. The Naturalization Act of October 14, 1940, which followed the passage of the Smith Act by a few months, added to the exclusionary measures of the Smith Act by barring communists from naturalization. Taken together and in combination with the acts of 1943 and 1946 which opened naturalization to certain immigrants from Asia, these measures set the direction of immigration and naturalization policy in some important ways: the laws emphasized political conformity and control over immigrants rather than racial "fit." The stage was set to make immigration, naturalization, and deportation part of a national policy that emphasized political conformity in general and anticommunism in particular.[121]

The effect of these measures was muted by more visible developments of the war years. Right away, the Alien Registration Act and the changing domestic climate of wartime contributed to an increasing number of naturalizations. Ettie Glaser, the British immigrant mentioned earlier, was motivated by the new hazards for noncitizens. "When World War II came out and they said all people that were not naturalized would have to . . . either to become an American citizen or you have the probability of being sent back to wherever you came from . . . I went to school, took the test and became an American citizen."[122] Other old-time immigrants also remembered being afraid of deportation; some were threatened by officials with incarceration as enemy aliens.[123] The vast majority of the over 1.5 million immigrants who became U.S. citizens between 1941 and 1945 were, like Glaser, older female immigrants in their forties and fifties, who had come to the United States a long time ago. British, Canadian, Italian, German, and Polish immigrants were heavily represented among the newly naturalized. Tens of thousands had arrived from these countries decades ago, now their old homelands were at the vortex of World War II. While the public pressure to become a citizen never amounted to the high-pitch propaganda of World War I, clearly these old-timers were deciding that now, for both personal and political reasons, American citizenship was an offer that should not be refused.[124]

Immigrant men who enlisted in the army received eased access to naturalization during World War II. Beginning in 1942, many of the younger immigrants (from Germany or Italy, for example) escaped the stigma of being enemy aliens by taking out citizenship as soldiers. As in earlier periods of war, military recruiters were not picky when it came to making this offer to potential recruits. Illiteracy, limited English, or even a lack of documented entry were no hindrance to becoming a naturalized U.S. citizen. Joseph Novel, a Yugoslav seaman and waterfront worker who had originally jumped ship in the 1930s and then escaped deportation a number of times, was once again arrested for being an illegal immigrant and held at Ellis Island in 1942. This time "there was no immigration [officer]. The FBI was in charge," he later remembered. Threatened with incarceration in a federal penitentiary, Novel accepted the FBI agent's offer to enlist in the army instead, and he was sworn in on the spot. Naturalization followed a year later.[125] Like Novel, over 3,000 men became U.S. citizens under military naturalization programs in 1943 and almost 50,000 in 1944. Overall, however, military naturalizations amounted to only about 12 percent of all naturalizations in the war years.[126]

If men in the military were among the favored groups of new citizens during the war, cold war politics widened this circle. The European fiancées and wives of GIs also began to show up on the shores of the United States immediately after the European war was over. This was not a new phenomenon, some brides of American soldiers had been caught in the emerging quota system after World War I, but the war brides who married American servicemen overseas beginning in 1944 were far more numerous. The immigration of British and Australian women presented few legal hurdles (the British quota was ample), although logistical, cultural, and sometimes social and economic issues surfaced in their integration and assimilation.[127]

Women from former enemy alien nations were considered a bigger problem. The U.S. military did not favor such alliances because they were in defiance of nonfraternization rules put in place in Germany, Austria, and Japan. If a soldier asked for permission to marry a local woman, commanding officers usually withheld their consent, and often the men were immediately moved back to the United States in response.[128] Some couples married secretly in European countries in defiance of army regulations and confronted the U.S. authorities with thorny issues after the husband's return to the United States: marriages legally concluded abroad were valid in the United States and entitled the spouse to enter outside the quota.

Recognizing the political potency of GI brides being detained or rejected under immigration law, Congress passed the War Brides Act in December 1945, which loosened immigration requirements (such as the literacy provision) for war brides and made the immigration of brides from nonquota countries (such as Japan and Korea) possible.

The 1946 GI Fiancées Act extended most of these provisions to women who were not yet married. The largest groups of beneficiaries from these laws were—as intended—European women, especially British brides. But over 700 Chinese women benefited from the laws as well. Estimates put the number of Japanese women who married Americans in the decade following World War II at well over 10,000.[129]

Their future social, cultural, and legal citizenship varied among different groups of GI brides. In some cases, marriage to an American soldier cemented existing ethnic communities in the United States. In others, the immigrant women merged into a de-ethnicized white America or represented a pioneer generation of interracial marriages. Chinese wives usually were the brides of Chinese Americans who had served overseas. Some of them had been married for some time and could formally join their husbands thanks to the GI Brides Act. Marriage and family unification was a crucial step in the emerging growth of the Chinese American community in the United States after 1945.[130] European war brides sometimes married coethnics, as did many Italian and some German women, though the effect on shaping these ethnic communities was not pronounced. Japanese GI brides, on the other hand, almost never married Japanese American GIs. They usually came as the spouses of white men, and sometimes married African Americans. The same was true for Korean women who came after the Korean War. These women had very little connection to communities of coethnics in the United States. To varying degrees, they became socially and culturally assimilated into the families of their husbands.

Like all other (non-Asian) women who gained admission as wives of U.S. citizens, GI brides qualified for naturalization after three years of residence in the United States (instead of five), a provision still in place today. German women who married Americans before 1953 spent their first three years in the United States as stateless persons because German law stripped a woman of her German citizenship automatically upon marriage to a foreigner. These women were eager to become U.S. citizens just to regain some kind of citizenship. European women who retained their native citizenship after marriage (notably French, British, and Italians) took considerably longer to become U.S. citizens. The British women interviewed by Jenel Virden hesitated to become naturalized because they continued to "feel British" and did not consider naturalization an important part of their social and cultural identity.[131] Japanese GI brides could not become U.S. citizens because they were racially ineligible for American citizenship until after the passage of the 1952 McCarran-Walter Act. From then on Japanese GI brides would make up a considerable percentage of the large number of Japanese immigrant naturalizations throughout the decade.[132]

Once American immigration law welcomed GI brides, their integration into American civic life proceeded quietly, in keeping with the 1950s ideal of domestic tranquility that underscored cold war patriotism. In a return to the early twentieth-century ideals of domesticity, which had assigned immigrant women a role as mothers and nurturers of future American citizens, war brides during the 1950s seldom became engaged American citizens in their own right.

European refugees from communist countries were a much larger group of postwar immigrants than the GI brides, and their emblematic position was important for cold war immigration and naturalization policy. With the tight nationality quota system of 1924 still in place, Europeans who had lost their homes in eastern and central Europe ("displaced persons") or had found themselves unwelcome after their nation became part of the Soviet orbit ("refugees") often found the door to the United States locked. Stateless or homeless people had virtually no chance of gaining a U.S. immigration visa right after the war. In most cases, these men and women could get neither an exit visa from their country of residence nor a quota spot and immigrant visa from the United States. On the American side, regular immigration law had no special provisions for refugees or for persons displaced and made homeless by the war. Gradually, a combination of voluntary agencies and interest groups such as the "Citizens' Committee on Displaced Persons," the Hebrew Immigrant Aid Society (HIAS), and liberal forces in U.S. Congress with support from the Truman administration worked to provide for special admissions for refugees and displaced persons through the 1948 Displaced Persons Act and a succession of special exemption acts. Between 1946 and 1960, over 700,000 men and women were admitted under these provisions, the vast majority of them from European countries. Most of these immigrants admitted under special provisions came from countries with very low nationality quotas under the 1924 quota law. The Communist takeover of their homelands, however, had changed their status from members of undesirable "races" and nationality groups to persons displaced by Nazi rule and refugees from communism.[133]

As applicants for American citizenship, many of the immigrants, refugees, and displaced persons of the late 1940s and the 1950s took their assigned seats at differing speeds. Immigrants who represented the "classic" countries of immigration, such as the United Kingdom, Germany, and Ireland, arrived in relatively large numbers from the late 1940s to the mid-1960s. These immigrants tended to become citizens after a long waiting period, and many were never naturalized at all. A comparison of the number of immigrants from these countries between 1948 and 1958 with the naturalizations of nationals from the same countries between 1954 and 1964 shows that three times as many immigrants were counted in the earlier period as naturalizations that occurred in the later years. The second cohort of immigrants, eastern and southeastern Europeans, (mostly admitted as displaced persons between 1948 and 1954) became citizens quickly, leading to a rapid rise of naturalizations especially between 1954 and 1956. Poles, Romanians, and Lithuanians naturalized at particularly high rates. But as few family members followed them after the mid-1950s, the number of newly naturalized U.S. citizens from eastern Europe declined as rapidly as the number of immigrants had increased earlier.

Together, these two developments, reluctance to become citizens among quota immigrants and the drop off in immigration of the "special provision immigrants," led to a sinking number of naturalizations beginning in 1958, and with the exception of the early 1960s, continuing until 1969. Only 98,700 immigrants became U.S. citizens in 1969 (see Appendix 1, Figure 2). By 1970, the census reported that only a little more than 60 percent of foreign-born residents were U.S. citizens.[134]

The 1965 Immigration Act abolished the nationality quota system that had governed immigrant admission since 1921. Instead, immigrants were admitted according to a preference system that gave the highest priority to those with relatives already in the United States. The family preference was most likely to benefit European immigrants, whose coethnics were relatively numerous among recent immigrants. A second group, those with special or needed skills, also received priority admission.[135] Spouses and younger children of U.S. citizens remained exempt from the quota. The system was designed to lift the obvious racialized nationality restrictions that had been in force for over sixty years, but it continued the preference for European immigrants, though in a less visible way.[136]

As it turned out though, relatively few Europeans were ready to emigrate in the 1960s and 1970s, and the bridge that naturalization provided to quicker immigrant sponsorship was used sparingly by immigrants from Europe. Few siblings of German or Italian immigrants, for example, wanted to leave their increasingly prosperous homelands to join their brothers or sisters in the United States during the 1970s and beyond.

Asian and Caribbean immigrants, on the other hand, used the advantage of naturalization frequently for the sponsorship of family members as immigrants after 1965. For immigrants from the Philippines and China, the line for regular immigration visas soon became lengthy after 1965, even with family sponsors in the United States. A wait for a visa to immigrate could stretch over a decade for applicants from these countries. Naturalization of a close relative was the only way to shorten the wait. Citizenship of pioneer immigrants opened the door for extensive migration chains from Korea, the Philippines, Taiwan, and Hong Kong. Indeed, the high priority Asian immigrants put on naturalization meant that a large percentage of the new American citizens were Asians from the early 1970s on. This in turn fueled the growth of sponsored immigrants from East Asia. Long excluded from American citizenship by law, Asian immigrants by the 1970s were seizing the opportunity that the law now presented to them, just as European immigrants had done in the 1920s.[137]

The abolition of the quota law had a very different effect on Mexican immigrants. Mexico, like other North and South American countries, was now included in the worldwide immigration limits and the maximum of 20,000 per country per year established in 1978. This could mean a lengthy wait for an immigration visa for Mexicans. Naturalization offered the same advantages to reunite with family on the northern side of the border to Mexicans as for other immigrant groups: a shorter wait or no wait at all. Nonetheless, naturalization rates for Mexicans remained anemic during the first decade of the new law, with the annual number of new U.S. citizens from Mexico hovering around 6,000 in most years. The alternative to a long wait for many Mexicans in the 1960s and 1970s turned out to be undocumented migration by family members. This appeared to be nearly costless in the first two decades after passage of the 1965 act, since enforcement of immigration law at the southern border remained irregular and penalties for undocumented migration (other than deportation) were non-existent. It was not until the 1986 Simson Mazzoli Act (which established increasing sanctions against undocumented workers) that Mexican immigrants, too, began to use naturalization in greater numbers to affirm their permanent status in the United States and to maintain a chain of migration. By the mid-1990s, Mexicans had become the largest group of immigrants to seek U.S. citizenship.[138] Among the last groups to seek out American citizenship for its practical benefits, Mexican immigrants in the twentieth century were more attached to ideas of cultural nationalism and a homeland political identity than many European immigrant groups that came before. Becoming American for Mexicans was a grave step, not a bureaucratic procedure. But for many American observers tardy naturalization symbolized a lack of loyalty to the new home, more than anything else. Even as American citizens, Mexican immigrants in the twenty-first century continue to struggle with the limited social and cultural citizenship accorded to them in many areas of life.[139]

Throughout the twentieth century and beyond, the American public has always viewed naturalization as the logical end point of the immigrant's journey. The journey could be circuitous, and the moment of the last border crossing could be postponed by happenstance or historic circumstance. For Ettie Glaser, who had expected to become a U.S. citizen upon her marriage in the 1920s, the moment did not arrive until 1942, when she finally took the oath of citizenship. In her old age, she remembered that when the judge declared her a citizen of the United States "everybody . . . cried and they laughed and they clapped hands and they were so happy that they were [citizens] . . . I felt I belonged to America."[140]

Many other elderly men and women interviewed about their immigration and naturalization in the 1970s and 1980s shared Glaser's happiness and gratitude about becoming citizens as they reminisced about their own border crossings. Few liked to dwell on the pragmatic considerations and the pressures that might have prompted them to seek citizenship when they did. This may have been because at first glance, naturalization, as defined by law, offered immigrants so little room for negotiation. But over the twentieth century, the law did change as did the circumstances under which it was administered and how it was applied. Requirements and inducements closely reflected shifts in immigration law, which in turn was shaped by domestic and international political considerations. Racial and gender restrictions kept many immigrants from seeking naturalization, especially in the first half of the twentieth century. Economic qualifications played a role during the interwar years. Even when the U.S. government could not mandate naturalization directly, it could use various means to induce immigrants to take up the offer of U.S. citizenship. This became a particularly important factor during wartime. During World War I and to a lesser extent in World War II, the national politics created a climate where becoming a citizen seemed a necessary demonstration of one's patriotism. Immigrants resisted such pressure as best they could.

More pragmatic considerations influenced their choices: for young men, military service made it easy and cheap to become a U.S. citizen, for example. Others became U.S. citizens in the 1920s and from the 1950s onward because naturalization helped with the sponsorship of relatives under the immigration law. In the 1930s, thousands of longtime immigrants were prompted to seek U.S. citizenship to partake in the benefits of New Deal programs. Such choices signified that, as in other border crossings, immigrants had carved out a zone of negotiation when it came to naturalization. In the end, immigrants negotiated naturalization on their own terms, often in ways that made sense to them as individuals in the context of their quite specific life situations. The law would always try to make naturalization a uniform procedure and an act of fundamental political allegiance, but immigrants made it a meaningful border crossing in simple or complex ways that no government could anticipate or prescribe.

Epilogue

Crossing Borders in the
Late Twentieth Century

On October 3, 1965, President Lyndon B. Johnson signed the Immigration and Nationality Bill of 1965, ending over four decades of racialized nationality quotas in U.S. immigration law. At the signing, which was picturesquely recorded next to a flagpole at the bottom of the Statue of Liberty, Johnson's remarks were brief, and he summarized the intention of the new immigration law plainly: "This bill says simply that from this day forth those wishing to immigrate to America shall be admitted on the basis of their skills and their close relationship to those already here . . . Those who can contribute most to this country—to its growth, to its strength, to its spirit—will be the first that are admitted to this land."[1]

The new law, also known as the Hart-Celler Act, freed U.S. immigration policy from the weight of racialized immigration quotas. Family ties and occupational qualifications, not nationality or "race," were the fundamental criteria on which all immigrant admissions were to be based from then on. But while the law of 1965 did away with many of the old restrictions, the new system was at least as rigid and comprehensive as the one it replaced. Unlike the 1924 law, which had exempted the Western Hemisphere, the Hart-Celler Act covered all nations worldwide. The law also imposed so-called hemispheric quotas (on the Western and Eastern Hemispheres), and after 1978 instituted a worldwide yearly maximum of 280,000 quota immigrants. No more than 20,000 immigrants a year could enter the United States from any one nation. Within a few years, it had become obvious that the primary effect of the law was not to liberalize immigrant admission in general but to make immigration more diverse: new immigrants came from a much larger variety of countries than ever before. The days when most new immigrants came from Europe quickly faded, as Asians and people from the Americas arrived in greater numbers.[2]

The Act did not change the nature of border crossings for immigrants in any fundamental way. Qualifying for an immigrant visa still meant a lengthy wait abroad for a visa spot assigned by the U.S. consulate. Dual screening, by consular officers who issued the visa and U.S. immigration officials who examined immigrants at the border entry, remained as before. The largely invisible supervision of foreign residents in the United States also continued: immigrants still had to register with the Immigration and Naturalization Service (INS) once they lived in the United States, and their political activity as aliens in the United States was restricted as before. Deportation remained an important and drastic sanction against resident aliens who had not followed the rules. The Hart-Celler Act also did not affect naturalization law.

Immigrants understood that the new law represented a reaffirmation of the U.S. government's power over its borders and border crossings. For some, the law brought new opportunities, for others new limitations. Depending on many factors—one's country of origin, economic circumstances, family status, or political environment—border crossings would have to be reorganized or only slightly modified in the last decades of the twentieth century. In the long run, the 1965 law would be only the beginning of a series of legal and policy changes that affected all border crossings in the late twentieth century: leaving home, border admission, deportation, as well as social and political citizenship.

Leaving home to make it to the United States continued to be a vexing problem for tens of thousands during the 1960s and beyond, as oppressive regimes, wars, and the Iron Curtain kept the populations of China, some Southeast Asian countries, Russia, and most of Eastern Europe inside their nation's borders. For those who managed to leave, often clandestinely, the U.S. government offered little respite. The 1965 immigration act made no provisions for the admission of politically "deserving" immigrants, those who had fled oppression or political persecution. Refugees and the displaced continued to be dependent on special congressional acts and exemptions to be admitted as immigrants if they wanted to skip ahead of the line of visa applicants. In the wake of the Vietnam era, streams of immigrants entered under special refugee categories from Southeast Asia, but there were also Jewish immigrants from the Soviet Union and, in early 1980, over 100,000 "boat people" from Cuba. Refugee status depended on the political climate in the United States or on Congressional power plays rather than on the desperate need of the persecuted.

The Refugee Act of 1980 remedied this problem to a considerable extent by separating refugees from regular immigrants. Under the Act, refugees had to be processed by the United Nations in refugee camps abroad before the State Department could decide on their admission to the United States. Hence, the most difficult border crossing for these immigrants lay abroad, often very distant from the legal, political, and social systems of the United States. Refugees needed to show few of the attributes of economic independence and physical health typically and traditionally demanded of immigrants. As a rule, they could be sponsored by American community organizations (not just relatives), and they were eligible for some financial support by the federal government after their arrival in the United States. A year after arrival, refugees automatically qualified for permanent residence in the United States.[3]

Once persecuted people had qualified as refugees, they were considered a "deserving" class of immigrants, which eased their entry into the United States and often their integration as well. Former refugees became U.S. citizens more quickly than other immigrants—and they would turn into reliable allies of the American political system. Only sporadically, when new immigrant groups appeared in places that had seen few newcomers before, was their entry and settlement in the United States seen as a problem. Few politicians wanted to change refugee policy toward the end of the twentieth century.

While refugees garnered much political attention in the post–Vietnam era, a more long-standing problem emerged at the nation's entry points. For the federal government, the regulation of immigration and border crossings under the 1965 law proved unsatisfactory. For the first time, the law had brought immigrants from the Americas under the purview of immigration restrictions. Mexicans, for example, had to wait in line for an immigrant visa with everyone else. The 20,000 per year country ceiling presented a special problem for Mexicans, especially if they had no close relatives in the United States who could sponsor them outside the quota. For many, undocumented border crossings or entry as a visitor then staying on proved to be the alternative, faster way to come to the United States rather than waiting for many years to get a visa.[4]

Assigning numbers to the undocumented border crossings and to illegal immigration was difficult, but the immigration debate of the 1980s and beyond was increasingly characterized by the realization that the physical border crossing into the United States took place virtually without any state control at the southern border. Amid a resurgent conservative movement in the United States in the 1980s, calls for stricter border controls became louder, focusing on the Southwest. To anti-immigration lawmakers, the border of the United States had become too porous.[5]

After lengthy public debate over the effects of undocumented migration and the need for stricter border control, Congress passed the Immigration Reform and Control Act (IRCA, also known as the Simpson-Mazzoli Act) in November 1986. The new law did not tamper with the preference system established by the 1965 law, but it did reorganize border crossings of immigrants in three significant ways in an attempt to reestablish the power of the federal government over the immigration process. The Act financed a border fortification system and increased the number of border personnel, especially at the U.S.-Mexico border. For the first time, crossing into the United States by land would involve navigating a heavily guarded portion of American territory. Circumventing border patrols now demanded physical risk and financial sacrifice—to pay experienced smugglers and to obtain false documents, for example. As the law intended, entering the United States by land became much more costly after 1986.

The net of immigration control was drawn more tightly by IRCA to exclude the undocumented within the United States as well. A All workers in the United States now were required to prove their legal status (that is, their work authorization) to their employers, who were in turn threatened with fines for not enforcing this provision. In the 1980s and 1990s, the need to identify oneself as "legal" in situations beyond employment (such as when opening a bank account) also increased for immigrants more rapidly than for other Americans. For the undocumented immigrants who were already on U.S. territory, the Act of 1986 thus fortified the second border against them: the border that would lead to economic and social integration.[6]

But in an acknowledgment of the decades of illegal immigration, IRCA also made it easier for many long-time undocumented immigrants to cross the border from undocumented worker to legal immigrant status without leaving U.S. territory. Under the provisions of the law, undocumented workers could qualify for a permanent residency visa ("green card") if they could prove continuous residence and a life free of crime for at least five years prior to 1986. This so-called amnesty provision made legalization as a permanent resident alien possible for 2.7 million men and women, 75 percent of them Mexicans. A large number of the newly legalized proceeded to sponsor relatives for legal immigration and acquire U.S. citizenship in the 1990s and beyond.[7] For immigrants from the Western Hemisphere especially, IRCA provided a special opportunity to overcome the restrictions put in place by the 1965 immigration law. It helped Mexican American communities in particular to come out of the shadow of illegality and led to a resurgence in political participation, unionization, and social activism in some parts of the United States.[8]

Amid the ups and downs of immigration reform from the 1960s to the 1990s, deportations became an ever more important weapon to force unwanted immigrants to leave the United States. Between 1965 and 1970, the number of deportations more than tripled, with over 90 percent of them taking place across the U.S.-Mexico border. Deportations increased further in the subsequent decade and a half, reaching a total of 1.6 million in 1985 alone. But as an instrument of permanent control, deportations did little to change the flow across the borders. As hundreds of thousands of clandestine border crossers were picked up and sent back in the Southwest, the churn of illegal immigration continued nearly unabated. The amnesty provisions of the 1886 law did lessen the undocumented migration across the southern border temporarily in the late 1980s, but by the mid-1990s the number of deportations had reached its old heights.[9]

The limited effect of the changes of the 1960s and 1980s on immigrant flow and border control had become obvious by the 1990s. Fanned by growing restrictionism and anti-immigrant sentiments, immigration reform turned to changing the citizenship and naturalization requirements for Americans and for immigrants in particular in order to restrict their border crossing into full legal, social, and political citizenship. In two much debated signature laws, Congress limited the rights of immigrants (documented and undocumented) by cutting their access to many social benefits. The Illegal Immigration Reform and Personal Responsibility Act, and the Personal Responsibility and Work Opportunity Act, both passed within months of each other in 1996, limited eligibility for public aid, food stamps, Supplemental Security Income, and Medicaid to U.S. citizens. Together, these laws redefined the meaning of citizenship not just for immigrants but for all residents of the United States.[10]

While immigrant advocacy groups raised their voice during the debate of the 1996 laws, immigrants were largely silent. But ultimately they would not be passive bystanders. Beginning in the early 1990s, their numbers grew exponentially in part as a result of the amnesty provisions of IRCA. The Immigration Service counted well over 4 million new legal immigrants in the years 1988–1991. By 1996, this group began to file for citizenship in large numbers. Between 1996 and 1998, over 3.5 million immigrants applied for naturalization, and 2 million were sworn in as U.S. citizens. As the twentieth century ended, the number of naturalizations remained high. By the year 2008, over 12 percent of all residents of the United States were foreign born, the same percentage as a hundred years earlier. But this time, the majority had crossed one more border and had become naturalized citizens, and any future debates on immigration and citizenship would have to take their voices and votes into account.[11]

From the Progressive Era to the end of the twentieth century and beyond, immigration policy has always provided the United States with a stage to define its identity as a nation. The rules of borders and border crossings have shown this identity as well. Through numerous changes in policy and law, the immigration, deportation, and naturalization rules have mirrored far more than labor market considerations, racial prejudice, or international alliances. Taken as a whole, few other arenas have reflected national identity more comprehensively than immigration and naturalization law and practice.

Immigrants have been well aware of the centrality of immigration and citizenship policy, and have known that defining the borders of the United States is a central enterprise for the nation. There might have been times when the borderlands seemed empty, barely touched by the presence of government. At other times, emigration and immigration stations were so overrun with newcomers that government representatives seemed overwhelmed. But the newcomers were not fooled; they knew that under whatever circumstances they arrived, crossing the border meant an all-important encounter with the nation and its official representatives, the guardians of the border. The border administrators and the zealous politicians who watched over them signaled to all immigrants that only some were welcome, that the welcome was conditional, and that the United States was deeply committed to shaping the nation through border control.

From the late nineteenth century, immigrants have been well aware that the stakes are high as they have tried to enter the United States, and they have known that power of selection seemed to rest with the U.S. government alone. For many, this knowledge was an incentive for much preparation: knowing and learning about the United States in advance, staying aware of the shifting laws and diverse practices employed by government officials at every stage, and marshaling support among family and community. In this manner, immigrants could hope to create a counterweight to the political and legal power of the U.S. authorities encountered at border crossings. Indeed, in the flexible border zone, the meeting of government representatives and migrants usually opened a zone of negotiations rather than a series of confrontations. Sometimes the negotiations appeared in the open; at other times they were more covert, as immigrants tried to avoid certain routes and choose others.

With all the persistence and support they could muster, migrants have organized their avenues of exit to ensure their smooth passage from home to North America. This might involve circuitous routes; it might involve direct contact with U.S. officials or avoidance of such contact by using transit through third countries. At the border station itself, immigrants, realizing that immigration officials were above all interested in the newcomers' physical and economic fitness for life in the new land, made a careful and sometimes selective self-presentation. They laid out their story and their claim to a future in the United States with a good knowledge of the law and the practices of border admissions. Given the heavily racialized criteria for admission, chances for successful negotiation could be very low, as the Chinese and Mexican immigrants knew full well. In these cases, presentation as an "American" or a temporary border migrant was the only opening for admission. At other times, the attributes of class, health, and morality were anticipated by the newcomers and shaped their self-presentation. Altogether, as the low percentage of rejections demonstrates, immigrants were highly successful in negotiating this border crossing.

Subsequent border crossings have presented their own challenges and opened different zones of negotiation for immigrants. Avoiding deportation meant enlisting the help of family and community, though increasingly in the twentieth century the mobilization of legal experts was also required. This was costly; as a rule, poor, working-class immigrants did not have the opportunity to renegotiate their stay in the United States through the judicial system. But in some precedent-setting cases immigrants fought in court for their right to stay, changing the law and shaping the identity of the United States as a country offering refuge to some and excluding many others.

Americanization and naturalization have opened different zones of negotiation. These are areas immigrants have not been forced to enter, and many choose never to become naturalized U.S. citizens. Americanization in particular is a process of near infinite variety, and immigrants themselves have defined it more than any government sponsored activity ever would. Making cultural and social integration into something the law or the government could shape in a positive, lasting way turned out to be nearly impossible.

Crossing into U.S. citizenship has been governed by a rigid set of requirements for immigrants. However, as in the case of deportations, the struggle for the right to gain citizenship by a few on behalf of the many has yielded important results that would shape the nation for many decades. The rigidity of racial exclusions from citizenship, which increased during the first decades of the twentieth century, only fell in the 1950s and 1960s. Ultimately, the elimination of overt racial preferences in immigration and naturalization law was not the result of judicial cases but of immigrants seizing the opportunities of naturalization and making the United States truly a nation of citizens from many lands. At the same time, delineating borders and determining who belongs on which side has remained a national task. As immigrants have arrived, settled, and become citizens of the United States, they have helped change where the nation's borders are, continuing the work and the negotiations of those who came before them.

APPENDIXES

NOTES

INDEX

Appendix 1: Figures

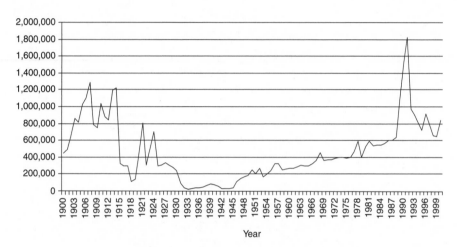

Figure 1. U.S. immigration, 1900–2000

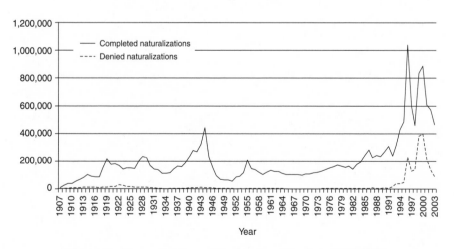

Figure 2. Naturalizations completed and denied, 1907–2003

Appendix 2: Deportation Categories, 1917

The following list of deportation categories is taken from the *Annual Report of the Commissioner General of Immigration* for 1917.

Deportable within three years of entry:

• Entered without inspection

Deportable within five years of entry:

• Members of excluded classes at time of entry

Imbeciles, feeble minded, epileptics, insane, constitutional psychopathic inferiority, suffering from loathsome or dangerous diseases, chronic alcoholism, professional beggars, likely to become a public charge, unaccompanied and under 16 of age, contract laborers, criminals, assisted aliens, prostitutes and women coming for immoral purpose, procurers of prostitutes, those who attempted to bring prostitutes, entered within one year of deportation, geographically excluded classes (Asians) under passport provision of section 3, unable to read and over 16 years of age.

• Public charges from conditions existing prior to entry

Insanity, other mental conditions, loathsome and dangerous diseases (TB), other physical conditions, pregnancy.

• In the United States in violation of Chinese Exclusion Laws

Deportable without time limit:

- Prostitutes
- Aliens who assist prostitutes
- Immigrants supported by the proceeds from prostitution
- Aliens previously deported as prostitutes or in connection with prostitution
- Convicted and imprisoned for a violation of section 4.
- Anarchists after entry
- Criminals after entry (sentenced for one year or more or multiple sentences)
- Criminals prior to entry

Notes

Introduction

1. Dorothee Schneider, "Symbolic Citizenship and Immigration in the Congressional Debates of 1996," *Citizenship Studies* 4 (2000): 255–273; and "'I Know All about Emma Lazarus': Nationalism and Its Contradictions in Congressional Rhetoric of Immigration Restriction," *Cultural Anthropology* 13 (1998): 82–99.
2. Amanda Levinson, "Immigrants and Welfare Use," Migration Information Source, August 2002, www.migrationinformation.org (accessed 9/1/10); on the effects of restrictive welfare legislation on naturalization, see Lisa Magana, *Straddling the Border: Immigration Policy and the INS* (Austin: University of Texas Press, 2003), pp. 52–76.
3. Rogers M. Smith, *Civic Ideals: Conflicting Visions of Citizenship in U.S. History* (New Haven, Conn.: Yale University Press, 1997); Michael Walzer, *Spheres of Justice: A Defense of Pluralism and Equality* (New York: Basic Books, 1983); T. Alexander Aleinikoff, *Semblances of Sovereignty: The Constitution, the State, and American Citizenship* (Cambridge, Mass.: Harvard University Press, 2002).
4. Lizabeth Cohen, *Making a New Deal: Industrial Workers in Chicago, 1919–1939* (Cambridge, U.K.: Cambridge University Press, 1990); Gary Gerstle, *American Crucible: Race and Nation in the Twentieth Century* (Princeton, N.J.: Princeton University Press, 2001).
5. David Gutierrez, *Walls and Mirrors: Mexican Americans, Mexican Immigrants, and the Politics of Ethnicity* (Berkeley: University of California Press, 1995); George Sanchez, *Becoming Mexican American: Ethnicity, Culture, and Identity in Chicano Los Angeles, 1900–1945* (New York: Oxford University Press, 1993). Lucy Salyer, *Laws Harsh as Tigers: Chinese Immigrants and the Shaping of Modern Immigration Law* (Chapel Hill: University of North Carolina Press, 1995); Erika Lee, *At America's Gates: Chinese Immigration during the Exclusion Era, 1882–1943* (Chapel Hill: University of North Carolina Press, 2003).

6. Martha Gardner, *The Qualities of a Citizen: Women, Immigration, and Citizenship, 1870–1965* (Princeton, N.J.: Princeton University Press, 2005); Candice Lewis Bredbenner, *A Nationality of Her Own: Women, Marriage, and the Law of Citizenship* (Berkeley: University of California Press, 1998); Irene Bloemraad, *Becoming a Citizen: Incorporating Immigrants and Refugees in the United States and Canada* (Berkeley: University of California Press, 2006); Aristide Zolberg, *A Nation by Design: Immigration Policy and the Fashioning of America* (New York and Cambridge, Mass.: Russell Sage Foundation and Harvard University Press, 2006); Mae M. Ngai, *Impossible Subjects: Illegal Aliens and the Making of America* (Princeton, N.J.: Princeton University Press, 2004).

7. Among the most significant works relating transnational migration to U.S. immigration historically has been that of Donna Gabaccia, especially her book *Italy's Many Diasporas* (Seattle: University of Washington Press, 2000), and Donna Gabaccia and Fraser Otanelli, eds., *Italian Workers of the World* (Urbana: University of Illinois Press 2001). For Asians, see Adam McKeown, *Melancholy Order: Asian Migration and the Globalization of Borders* (New York: Columbia University Press, 2008); and for eastern Europeans, see Tobias Brinkmann, "Traveling with Ballin: The Impact of American Immigration Policies on Jewish Transmigration within Central Europe, 1880–1914," *International Review of Social History* 53 (2008): 459–484.

8. Some scholars have provided important insights into the social effects of immigration law on community formation. Among those whose works informed my research were Nancy Abelmann and John Lie, *Blue Dreams: Korean Americans and the Los Angeles Riots* (Cambridge, Mass.: Harvard University Press, 1995); Philip Kasinitz, *Caribbean New York: Black Immigrants and the Politics of Race* (Ithaca, N.Y.: Cornell University Press, 1992); Russell Kazal, *Becoming Old Stock: The Paradox of German-American Identity* (Princeton, N.J.: Princeton University Press, 1994); Peter Kwong, *Chinatown, N.Y.: Labor and Politics, 1930–1950* (New York: Monthly Review Press, 1979); and Valerie Matsumoto, *Farming the Home Place: a Japanese American Community in California, 1919–1982* (Ithaca, N.Y.: Cornell University Press, 1993).

9. Mark Wyman, *Round-trip to America: The Immigrants Return to Europe, 1880–1930* (Ithaca, N.Y.: Cornell University Press, 1993).

1. Leaving Home

1. Leslie Page Moch, *Moving Europeans: Migration in Western Europe since 1650* (Bloomington: Indiana University Press, 1992), pp. 147–153; Marcus Lee Hansen, *The Atlantic Migration, 1607–1860: A History of the Continuing Settlement of the United States,* ed. Arthur M. Schlesinger (Cambridge, Mass.: Harvard University Press, 1940), pp. 79–84; Mack Walker, *Germany and the Emigration, 1816–1885* (Cambridge, Mass.: Harvard University Press, 1964), pp. 3–41.

2. Alexander Murdoch, *British Emigration, 1603–1917* (Houndsmills/Basingstoke, U.K.: Palgrave, 2004), pp. 11–17; David Feldman and M. Page Baldwin, "Emigration and the British State, ca. 1815–1925," in *Citizenship and Those Who Leave: The Politics of Emigration and Expatriation*, ed. Nancy L. Green and François Weil (Urbana: University of Illinois Press, 2007), pp. 135–155, esp. 136–146; Dudley Baines, *Emigration from Europe, 1815–1930* (Cambridge, U.K.: Cambridge University Press, 1991), pp. 46–48.

3. François Weil, "The French State and Transoceanic Migration," in *Citizenship and Those Who Leave*, pp. 114–134; Camille Maire, *En route pour l'Amérique: L'odyssée des émigrants en France au XIXe siècle* (Nancy: Presses Universitaires de Nancy, 1992), pp. 19–24, 33–41.

4. Walker, *Germany and the Emigration*, pp. 86–87; John Torpey, *The Invention of the Passport: Surveillance, Citizenship, and the State* (New York: Cambridge University Press, 2000), pp. 62–66, 71–88.

5. Ibid., pp. 75–76; Andreas Fahrmeir, "From Economics to Ethnicity and Back: Reflections on Emigration Control in Germany, 1800–2000," in *Citizenship and Those Who Leave*, pp. 179–181.

6. Edwin Guillet, *The Great Migration: The Atlantic Migration by Sailing Ship since 1770* (Toronto, New York: Thomas Nelson and Sons, 1937); Hansen, *Atlantic Migration*, pp. 69–70, 82–83, 97–98, 170, 234–236, 303–204.

7. Johann Pritzlaff to his mother and brother, June 28, 1839, *News from the Land of Freedom: German Immigrants Write Home*, ed. Walter D. Kamphoefner, Wolfgang Helbich, and Ulrike Sommer (Ithaca, N.Y.: Cornell University Press, 1988), pp. 303–305.

8. Olof Olson, "A letter from One Generation to Another," in *Clipper Ship and Covered Wagon: Essays from the Swedish Pioneer Historical Quarterly*, ed. H. Arnold Barton (New York: Arno Press, 1979), p. 242.

9. Carl Berthold to his siblings, March 23, 1852, in *News from the Land of Freedom*, p. 323.

10. Maire, *En Route pour l'Amerique*, pp. 79–86.

11. Eric Richards, *Britannia's Children: Emigration from England, Scotland, Wales, and Ireland since 1660* (New York: Hambledon and London, 2004), esp. pp. 117–162; Feldman and Baldwin, "Emigration and the British State," pp. 135–155; Guillet, *Great Migration*, pp. 20–33.

12. Walker, *Germany and the Emigration*, pp. 87–94; Michael Just, "Schiffahrtsgesellschaften und Amerika-Auswanderung im 19. und frühen 20 Jahrhundert," in *Auswanderung und Schiffahrtsinteressen: Little Germanies in New York, deutschamerikanische Gesellschaften*, ed. Michael Just, Agnes Bretting, and Hartmut Bickelmann (Stuttgart: Steiner Verlag, 1992), pp. 11–18, 39–45.

13. Kerby A. Miller, *Emigrants and Exiles: Ireland and the Irish Exodus to North America* (New York: Oxford University Press, 1985), pp. 252–265.

14. Guillet, *Great Migration*.

15. Anna Maria Klinger to her parents, in *News from the Land of Freedom*, p. 537.

16. Jacob Harms Dunnink to the Harms Dunnink family, in *Dutch American Voices: Letters from the United States,* ed. Herbert Brinks (Ithaca, N.Y.: Cornell University Press, 1995), p. 30.

17. Angela Heck to her relatives, July 1, 1854, in *News from the Land of Freedom,* pp. 371–372.

18. Guillet, *Great Migration,* pp. 233–248; Maire, *En Route pour l'Amerique,* pp. 95–114; Just, "Schiffahrtsgesellschaften," pp. 26–27, 32–38.

19. Aristide Zolberg, *A Nation by Design: Immigration Policy and the Fashioning of America* (New York and Cambridge: Russell Sage Foundation and Harvard University Press, 2006), pp. 185–198.

20. Aristide Zolberg, "The Exit Revolution," in *Citizenship and Those Who Leave,* pp. 33–60.

21. Gunther Barth, *Bitter Strength: A History of the Chinese in the United States, 1850–1870* (Cambridge, Mass.: Harvard University Press, 1964), pp. 22–26.

22. Adam McKeown, "Global Migration, 1846–1940," *World History* 15, no. 2 (June 2004): 169–175; Sing-Wu Wang, *The Organization of Chinese Emigration: With Special Reference to Chinese Emigration to Australia* (San Francisco: Chinese Materials Center, 1978), pp. 17–24, 95; Mary Coolidge, *Chinese Immigration* (New York: Henry Holt, 1909), pp. 18–21; Carine Pina-Guerassimoff and Eric Guerassimoff, "The 'The Overseas Chinese': The State and Emigration from the 1890s to the 1990s," in *Citizenship and Those Who Leave,* pp. 245–247.

23. McKeown, "Global Migration," p. 175.

24. Barth, *Bitter Strength,* pp. 20–31; Wang, *Organization of Chinese Emigration,* pp. 13–17.

25. U.S. Congress, *An Act to Prohibit the "Coolie Trade" by American Citizens in American Vessels,* 37th Cong., 2d sess., February 19, 1862, Chap. 27; 12 Stat. 340. An Act Supplementary to the Acts in Relation to Immigration, (Page Law) Sect. 141, 18 Stat. 477, 1873-March 1875; Goerge H. Peffer, *They Don't Bring their Women Here: Chinese Female Immigration before Exclusion* (Urbana: University of Illinois Press, 1999), pp. 36–37, 44–45.

26. Erika Lee, *At America's Gates: Chinese Immigration during the Exclusion Era, 1882–1943* (Chapel Hill: University of North Carolina Press, 2003), pp. 200–201; Lucy Salyer, *Laws Harsh as Tigers: Chinese Immigrants and the Shaping of Modern Chinese Immigration Law* (Chapel Hill: University of North Carolina Press, 1995), pp. 19–22.

27. William Fook Yee, interview by Janet Levine, 18 July 1994, Ellis Island Oral History Project, Series EI, no. 503.

28. Sometimes the U.S. consulate and the steamship company disagreed on this, an embarrassment for the consul. See *Records of the Immigration and Naturalization Service,* Series A, subject correspondence files [microform] (Bethesda, Md.: University Publications of America, 1992), pt. 1, reel 1, 0140 (RG 9, file 51881/85).

29. Him Mark Lai, Jenny Lim, and Judy Yung, eds., *Island: Poetry and History of Chinese Immigrants on Angel Island, 1910–1940* (Seattle: University of Washington Press, 1991), p. 45–49.

30. Ibid., pp. 47–48.

31. Ibid.; Tung Pok Chin, *Paper Son: One Man's Story* (Philadelphia: Temple University Press, 2000), p. 11.

32. Barth, *Bitter Strength,* pp. 51–69; Wang, *Organization of Chinese Emigration,* pp. 89–112.

33. Chin, *Paper Son,* p. 12.

34. Lai, Lim, and Yung, *Island,* pp. 46–47.

35. Barth, *Bitter Strength,* pp. 69–70; On Japanese ownership of these ships and steamships in the 1880s, see Robert Barde and Wesley Uenten, "Pacific Steerage: Japanese Ships and Asian Mass Migration," *Pacific Historical Review* 73, no. 4 (2004): 653–660.

36. Barth, *Bitter Strength,* pp. 71–74; Coolidge, *Chinese Immigration,* p. 17.

37. Barde and Uenten, "Pacific Steerage."

38. Eiichiro Azuma, *Between Two Empires: Race History, and Transnationalism in Japanese America* (New York: Oxford University Press, 2005), p. 29.

39. Alan Takeo Moriyama, *Imingaisha: Japanese Emigration Companies and Hawaii, 1894–1908* (Honolulu: University Press of Hawaii, 1985), pp. 74–88; Eiichiro Azuma, "Interstitial Lives: Race, Community, and History among Japanese Immigrants Caught between Japan and the United States, 1885–1941" (Ph.D. diss., University of California–Los Angeles, 2000), pp. 72–78.

40. Ibid., pp. 69–72.

41. Azuma, *Between Two Empires,* pp. 29–30; and "Interstitial Lives," pp. 71–80.

42. Oscar Strauss, *Under Four Administrations, From Cleveland to Taft* (Boston: Houghton Mifflin, 1922), p. 218.

43. Azuma, *Between Two Empires,* pp. 17–22; Moryiama, *Imingaisha,* pp. 34–42; Roger Daniels, *Asian America: Chinese and Japanese in the United States since 1850* (Seattle: University of Washington Press, 1988), pp. 102–106, 120–133; Investigation of Inspector Marcus Braun, *Records of the Immigration and Naturalization Service,* Series A, subject correspondence files (Bethesda, Md.: University Publications of America, 1992) pt. 1. Reel 4, 0462.

44. Moriyama, *Imingaisha,* pp. 39–40; Roger Daniels, *Coming to America: A History of Immigration and Ethnicity in American Life* (New York: Harper, 2002), p. 255; Azuma, *Between Two Empires,* pp. 53–55.

45. Daniels, *Coming to America,* p. 186; U.S. Immigration Commission, *Reports of the Immigration Commission,* vol. 4: *Emigration Conditions in Europe* (Washington, D.C.: U.S. Government Printing Office, 1911), pp. 42–43; Dirk Hoerder, *Cultures in Contact: World Migration in the Second Millenium* (Durham, N.C.: Duke University Press, 2002), pp. 355–356.

46. Thomas Archdeacon, *Becoming American: An Ethnic History* (New York: Free Press, 1983), pp. 118–119; U.S. Commissioner General of Immigration, *Annual Report of the Commissioner General of Immigration to the Secretary of Commerce and Labor: For the Fiscal Year Ending June 1905* [hereafter cited as *Annual Report* with year of publication] (Washington, D.C.: U.S.

Government Printing Office, 1905), pp. 129–130; *Annual Report, 1906,* pp. 50–56.

47. Immigration and Naturalization Service [INS], subject correspondence files, National Archives, RG 85, entry 9, file 51411/51, pp. 9, 12, 22–23, 34, also pp. 41–43 (Powderly report); file 51411/52, p. 3 (Semsey/Dobler report).

48. Zolberg, *A Nation by Design,* pp. 199–238; John Higham, *Strangers in the Land: Patterns of American Nativism, 1860–1925* (New York: Atheneum, 1963), pp. 68–105, 158–193.

49. U.S. Immigration Commission, *Emigration Conditions in Europe,* pp. 70–71.

50. RG 85 entry 9, file 51411/51 (Powderly report). Powderly's report and the reports cited later were conducted parallel to the investigation of the members of the U.S. Immigration Commission in 1907. The Commission's focused on governments and transportation companies. Few commission members spoke to actual emigrants and the final report, published as volume 4 of the *Reports of the U.S. Immigration Commission,* bespeaks the distance to actual emigrants and their perspective; see U.S. Immigration Commission, "Emigration Conditions in Europe," (Washington D.C. 1911), see also Robert F. Zeidel, *Immigrants, Progressives and Exclusion Politics: the Dillingham Commission 1900–1927* (DeKalb: Northern Illinois University Press, 2006), pp. 51–68.

51. On Semsey see, Vasvary Collection newsletter, vol. 2004, no. 1, Stephen Beszedits, "Charles Semsey: Hungarian Patriot, Union Soldier, and Ellis Island Official," www.skszeged.hu/szolgaltatas/vasvary/newsletter/04jun/beszedits.html.

52. As early as 1901, the New York Commissioner, who had investigated labor migration and assisted immigration in Europe, was urging further studies by other officials of the service abroad; see *Annual Report, 1902,* p. 58. The other reports were published as part of the *Annual Report, 1904,* pp. 50–52 (Marcus Braun report on the Near East); *Annual Report, 1905* (unnamed inspector); *Annual Report, 1906,* pp. 50–56 (Fishberg report); and *Annual Report, 1914,* Appendix IV (Kate Waller Barrett report). The originals of many comprehensive reports are part of the subject correspondence files of the INS at the National Archives, RG 85, entry 9, file nos. 51411/54 (Eppler report), 51411/51 (Powderly report), 51411/1 (Seraphic report on Europe and Mexico), 51831/55 (Watchorn investigation), 51411/53 (first Trenor report), 51411/53 (Cowan report), 51411/53 (Semsey/Dobler report), 51652/13 (second Trenor report), 51352/1 (third Trenor report), 51841/129 (George Stone investigation), 52320/47 (Marcus Braun report on Hungary, 1903), 52011/folders 1 and 2 a–c (Marcus Braun report on Hungary 1907–08), 52066/1 (John Gruenberg report on contract labor), and 52714/1–3 (Inspector J. D. Whelpley abroad). See also, Zeidel, *Immigrants, Progressives,* pp. 51–68.

53. U.S. Immigration Commission, *Emigration Conditions in Europe.*

54. U.S. Immigration Commission, *Reports of the Immigration Commission,* vol. 37: *Steerage Conditions* (Washington, D.C.: U.S. Government Printing Office, 1911), pp. 1–29; Zeidel, *Immigrants, Progressives,* pp. 73–74.

55. INS, subject correspondence files, National Archives, RG 85 entry 9, file 51411/26, pp. 50, 57.

56. Ibid., file 51411/52, p. 7.

57. Ibid., file 51411/51, p. 54–59; quotation from p. 59.

58. Ibid., file 51411/54, p. 24 (Eppler report).

59. *Annual Report, 1914,* p. 373.

60. INS, subject correspondence files, National Archives, RG 85, entry 9, file 51652/13, p. 9 (second Trenor report).

61. Ibid., file 51411/53, p. 3.

62. Anna Hinitz, interview by Margo Nash, 6 October 1974, Ellis Island Oral History Project, Series NPS, no. 076.

63. INS, subject correspondence files, National Archives, RG 85, entry 9, file 51652/13, pp. 8–9.

64. Kalman Borko, interview by Nancy Dallett, 18 December 1985, Ellis Island Oral History Project, Series KEKK, no. 112.

65. INS, subject correspondence files, National Archives, RG 85, entry 9, file 51411/52, p. 16, quote, pp. 8–9.

66. Blanca Sánchez Alonso, "The Other Europeans: Immigration into Latin America and the International Labour Market (1870–1930)," *Revista de Historia Económica (Second Series)* 25 (2007): 395–426. U.S. Immigration Commission, *Emigration Conditions in Europe,* p. 35.

67. Rose Breci, interview by Willa Apple, 21 October 1985, Ellis Island Oral History Project, Series KECK, no. 051; Mauro C. Rio, interview by Edward Applebome, 11 October 1985, Ellis Island Oral History Project, Series AKRF, no. 49.

68. In Great Britain, authorities regulated and limited immigration from eastern and southern Europe under a special alien and immigration law passed in 1905. The law was supposed to have a secondary effect on the United States, discouraging eastern Europeans from using Great Britain as a way station, but U.S. investigators saw no such effect. See James Walvin, *Passage to Britain: Immigration in British History and Politics* (London: Puffin, 1984), pp. 62–67. See also comments by U.S. inspectors in *Annual Report, 1904,* p. 129; INS, subject correspondence files, National Archives, RG 85, entry 9, file 52483/1–18 and file 51411/51, pp. 17–18 (Powderly report).

69. U.S. Immigration Commission, *Emigration Conditions in Europe,* pp. 265–336; INS, subject correspondence files, National Archives, RG 85, entry 9, file 51411/56, pp. 2–30 (Cowan report).

70. Frank Shelibovsky, interview by Margo Nash, 28 March 1974, Ellis Island Oral History Project, Series NPS, no. 057.

71. U.S. Immigration Commission, *Emigration Conditions in Europe,* pp. 265–336; Hinitz, interview.

72. Morris U. Schappes, interview by Margo Nash, 23 January 1975, Ellis Island Oral History Project, Series NPS, no. 081.

73. INS, subject correspondence files, National Archives, RG 85, entry 9, file 51411/56 (Cowan report), pp. 2–30; see also file 51411/54, p. 29 (Eppler report).

74. U.S. Immigration Commission, *Emigration Conditions in Europe*, pp. 241, 251, 265.

75. Irving Howe, *The World of Our Fathers: The Journey of East European Jews to America and the Life They Found and Made* (New York: Harcourt, Brace, Jovanovich, 1975), pp. 28, 36–39; see also INS, subject correspondence files, National Archives, RG 85, entry 9, file 51411/56, p. 31 (Cohen report).

76. Polly Adler, *A House Is Not a Home* (New York: Rinehart, 1953), p. 11.

77. Rose Cohen, *Out of the Shadow: A Russian Jewish Girlhood on the Lower East Side*, introduction by Thomas Dublin (Ithaca, N.Y.: Cornell University Press, 1995), pp. 51–52.

78. Dr. Samuel Nelson, interview by Nancy Dallett, 16 January 1985, Ellis Island Oral History Project, Series KECK, no. 002.

79. *Annual Report, 1905*, p. 53 (Fishberg report).

80. Andreas Fahrmeir, *Citizens and Aliens: Foreigners and the Law in Britain and the German States* (New York: Berghahn Books, 2000); René del Fabbro, "Italienische Wanderarbeiter im Deutschen Kaiserreich," *Fremde in Deutschland, Deutsche in der Fremde: Schlaglichter von der frühen Neuzeit bis in die Gegenwart*, ed. Uwe Meinders and Christoph Reinders-Duselder (Cloppenburg, Germany: Museumsdorf, 1999), pp. 193–199; Klaus Bade, "German Emigration to the United States and Continental Immigration to Germany in the Late Nineteenth and Early Twentieth Centuries," *Central European History* 13, no. 4 (Dec. 1980): 348–378; on transit migration, see Michael Just, *Ost- und südosteuropäische Amerikawanderung 1881–1914: Transitprobleme in Deutschland und Aufnahme in den Vereinigten Staaten* (Stuttgart: Steiner Verlag, 1988), pp. 97–98.

81. INS, subject correspondence files, National Archives, RG 85, entry 9, file 51411/51, p. 23 (Powderly report).

82. *Annual Report, 1905*, p. 56; Just, *Ost- und südosteuropäische*, pp. 97–105.

83. Just, *Ost- und südosteuropäische*, pp. 105–107.

84. Ibid., pp. 105–107, 110.

85. Ibid., pp. 108–112.

86. INS, subject correspondence files, National Archives, RG 85, entry 9, file 51411/51, pp. 22–35 (Powderly report); file 51411/52, 3a.–4 (Semsey/ Dobler report); U.S. Immigration Commission, *Emigration Conditions in Europe*, pp. 96–102.

87. Ibid., file 51411/54, p. 29. German Social Democrats and labor activists criticized the conditions to which eastern European emigrants were submitted and the dangerous practices that prevailed from a public health standpoint after a series of articles appeared in the Socialist daily *Vorwärts*

by a reporter who had traveled the route disguised as a Russian emigrant. Just, *Ost- und südosteuropäische,* pp. 113–115.

88. Adler, *House Is Not a Home,* p. 12.

89. INS, subject correspondence files, National Archives, RG 85, entry 9, file 51411/51, p. 48 (Powderly report).

90. Ibid., file 51411/52, pp. 6–7.

91. Ibid., file 51652/13, p. 7.

92. Zeidel, *Immigrants, Progressives,* pp. 59–60.

93. Archdeacon, *Becoming American,* p. 139; Baines, *Emigration from Europe,* pp. 35–38.

94. INS, subject correspondence files, National Archives, RG 85, entry 9, file 51411/51, pp. 52–53 (Powderly report).

95. U.S. Immigration Commission, *Emigration Conditions in Europe,* pp. 92, 110–124; INS, subject correspondence files, National Archives, RG 85, entry 9, file 51411/53.

96. INS, subject correspondence files, National Archives, RG 85, entry 9, file 52011/B, F (Braun report); 51630/44, B–F. See also Gunther Peck, *Reinventing Free Labor: Padrones and Immigrant Workers in the North American West, 1880–1930* (Cambridge, U.K.: Cambridge University Press, 2000), p. 93.

97. INS, subject correspondence files, National Archives, RG 85, entry 9, file 51411/52, p. 8.

98. Ibid., pp. 11–15.

99. Leopold Caro, "Auswanderung und Auswanderungspolitik in Österreich," *Schriften des Vereins für Socialpolitik* 131 (Leipzig, 1909), p. 62., cited in Agnes Bretting, *Funktion und Bedeutung der Auswanderungsagenturen in Deutschland im 19. Jahrhundert* (Stuttgart: Franz Steiner Verlag, 1991), pp. 87–88.

100. INS, subject correspondence files, National Archives, RG 85, entry 9, file 51698/7 a–d.

101. Ibid., pp. 11, 92, 124.

102. Ibid., file 51411/53 (Trenor report), p. 7; see also U.S. Immigration Commission, *Emigration Conditions in Europe,* p. 111.

103. Hoerder, *Cultures in Contact,* pp. 364–365.

104. Daniels, *Coming to America,* p. 188; Archdeacon, *Becoming American,* p. 139.

105. Theodore Saloutos, *The Greeks in the United States* (Cambridge, Mass.: Harvard University Press, 1964), pp. 29–33.

106. See Chapter 5, note 98.

107. INS, subject correspondence files, National Archives, RG 85, entry 9, file 51960/1, esp. pp. 4–10 (third Trenor report); U.S. Immigration Commission, *Emigration Conditions in Europe,* pp. 292–415.

108. INS, subject correspondence files, National Archives, RG 85, entry 9, file 51460/44B, file 51463/B (Braun report), file 51423/1 (Seraphic report), and file 51652/13, pp. 20–31. Greek observations also were reprinted in *Annual Report, 1909,* p. 129. See also Grace Abbott, "A Study of the Greeks

in Chicago," *American Journal of Sociology* 15 (1909): 379–393; Peck, *Reinventing Free Labor*, pp. 98–100; Seraphic followed the migration of "Syrians" from Greece to Marseilles and from there to Mexico and finally across the U.S. border. INS, subject correspondence files, National Archives, RG 85, entry 9, file 51411/1.

109. Ibid., file 51411/51, p. 56.

110. Ibid., file 51652/13, pp. 13–15 (second Trenor report); file 51411/51, p. 64.

111. Rocco Morelli, interview by Willa Apple, 16 September 1985, Ellis Island Oral History Project, Series AKRF, no. 31.

112. INS, subject correspondence files, National Archives, RG 85, entry 9, file 51411/51, p. 64 (Powderly report). Powderly also thought that some emigration agents reproduced letters or made up "decoy" letters to drum up enthusiasm for emigration and business for themselves.

113. INS, subject correspondence files, National Archives, RG 85, entry 9, file 51411/52, p. 4 (first Trenor report).

114. Ibid., file 51411/53, p. 4.

115. Abbott, "Greeks in Chicago," pp. 384–390.

116. Maria Alexaki, interview by Nancy Dallett, 27 November 1985, Ellis Island Oral History Project, Series KECK, no. 087; James Apanomith, interview by Janet Levine, 17 June 1992, Ellis Island Oral History Project, Series EI, no. 173.

117. Helen Nitti, interview by Debby Dane, 19 November 1985, Ellis Island Oral History Project, Series KECK, no. 078.

118. Ercole Sori, "Emigration Agents in the History of European and Italian Emigration," *AEMI Journal* 1 (2003): 1–4.

119. INS, subject correspondence files, National Archives, RG 85, entry 9, file 51411/51, p. 59 (Powderly report).

120. Breci, interview.

121. Dona Gabbaccia, *Italy's Many Diasporas* (Seattle: University of Washington Press, 2000), pp. 62–66; Peck, *Reinventing Free Labor*, pp. 18–22.

122. INS, subject correspondence files, National Archives, RG 85, entry 9, file 51411/53 (first Trenor report); 51411/51, pp. 56–75 (Powderly report); file 51652/13 (second Trenor report); *Annual Report, 1914*, pp. 268–269 (Barett report); Donna R. Gabaccia, "Emigration and Italian Nation Building", paper for Citoyennetés et Emigrations, XIXe–Xxe siecles," Paris, École des Hautes Études en Sciences Sociales (Dec. 2001).

123. Saloutos, *Greeks in the United States*, p. 33.

124. Peck, *Reinventing Free Labor*, pp. 118–120.

125. Persephone Lianides Milos, interview by Janet Levine, 9 August 1993, Ellis Island Oral History Project, Series EI, no. 367.

126. Anna Spanos Sofranos, interview by Janet Levine, 29 August 1991, Ellis Island Oral History Project, Series EI, no. 081.

127. Maria Spanos, interview by Janet Levine, 22 November 1994, Ellis Island Oral History Project, Series EI, no. 572.

128. Constantine Moschos, interview by Janet Levine, 11 August 1993, Ellis Island Oral History Project, Series EI, no. 379.

129. Panagiotis Chletsos, interview by Nancy Dallett, 26 November 1985, Ellis Island Oral History Project, Series KECK, no. 085.

130. Saloutos, *Greeks in the United States*, pp. 32–34, 38; U.S. Immigration Commission, *Emigration Conditions in Europe*, pp. 397–199; Thomas Burgess, *Greeks in America: An Account of Their Coming, Progress, Customs, Living, and Aspirations* (Boston: Sherman French, 1915), pp. 47–48.

131. INS, subject correspondence files, National Archives, RG 85, entry 9, file 51411/53, pp. 16–19 (first Trenor report).

132. *Annual Report, 1905*, pp. 50–54; when the cooperative arrangement was first put in place in Naples in 1899, the U.S. government ordered (and paid for) the inspections as part of the quarantine measures put in place. The system simply continued in southern Italy after the original quarantine measures had been lifted and was then paid for by the steamship companies. U.S. Immigration Commission, *Emigration Conditions in Europe*, pp. 77, 113–126, 210–220.

133. INS, subject correspondence files, National Archives, RG 85, entry 9, file 51652/13, pp. 20–30.

134. Saloutos, *Greeks in the United States*, p. 34.

135. Rae Levin, interview by Margo Nash, 15 November 1973, Ellis Island Oral History Project, Series NPS, no. 030.

136. Rebecca Gold, interview by Margo Nash, Ellis Island Oral History Project, Series NPS, no. 014 (orig. 13).

137. Peter Gatrell, *A Whole Empire Walking: Refugees in Russia during World War I* (Bloomington: Indiana University Press, 1999).

138. Vera Kaplan, interview by Margo Nash, 23 October 1973, Ellis Island Oral History Project, Series NPS, no. 026 (orig. 34).

139. Rose Krawetz, interview by Nancy Dallett, 6 August 1985, Ellis Island Oral History Project, Series KECK, no. 013.

140. Irving Markman, interview by Margo Nash, October 3, 1973, Ellis Island Oral History Project, Series NPS, no. 016.

141. David Tulin, interview by Margo Nash, 16 November 1973, Ellis Island Oral History Project, Series NPS, no. 032.

142. Harry Aprahamian, interview by Margo Nash, 10 September 1974, Ellis Island Oral History Project, Series NPS, no. 074 (orig. 37); Mary Assadourian, interview by Paul E. Sigrist, Jr., 16 September 1993, Ellis Island Oral History Project, Series EI, no. 390; The Ellis Island Oral History Project recorded interviews with 78 elderly Armenians who left for the United States after 1919 under often harrowing circumstances and taking circuitous routes.

143. Roger Daniels, *Guarding the Golden Door: American Immigration Policy and Immigrants since 1882* (New York: Hill and Wang, 2004) p. 46; Michael LeMay and Elliott Robert Barkan, eds., *U.S. Immigration and Naturalization Laws and Issues: A Documentary History* (Westport, Conn.: Greenwood Press, 1999), pp. 113–114.

144. Daniels, *Guarding the Golden Door*, pp. 46–58; Baines, *Emigration from Europe*, pp. 67–69.

145. *New York Times*, June 7, 1921, p. 3; June 28, 1921, p. 1; July 14, 1921, p. 10; July 21, 1921, p. 18.

146. *New York Times*, December 4, 1922, p. 11.

147. Markman, interview.

148. Helen Hartunian Chakmakian, Rose Hartunian Antrasian, and Lydia Hartunian Minassian, interview by Paul E. Sigrist, Jr., 15 April 1992, Ellis Island Oral History Project, Series EI, no. 135. The family was neither Turkish nor Syrian, but Armenian—a nationality the U.S. did not recognize under the quota law.

149. Otto Heinemann, interview by Margo Nash, 31 January 1974, Ellis Island Oral History Project, Series NPS, no. 046; Ngai, *Impossible Subjects: Illegal Aliens and the Making of Modern America* (Princeton, N.J.: Princeton University Press, 2004), esp. pp. 56–90.

150. Daniels, *Guarding the Golden Door*, pp. 61–63.

151. Ngai, *Impossible Subjects*, pp. 66–67; Heinemann, interview.

152. Daniels, *Guarding the Golden Door*, pp. 71–82; see also David Wyman, *Paper Walls: America and the Refugee Crisis* (Amherst: University of Massachusetts Press, 1968).

2. Landing in America

1. Mary Antin, *From Plotzk to Boston*, foreword by Israel Zangwill (Boston: W.B. Clarke, 1899), p. 78.

2. Alexander Brown, interview by Nancy Dallett, 19 August 1985, Ellis Island Oral History Project, Series KECK, no. 020.

3. See, for example, photos on the The Statue of Liberty-Ellis Island Foundation, Inc., Web site at www.ellisisland.org/photoalbums/ellis_island_then.asp.

4. James Alner Toby, *The National Government and Public Health* (Chicago: University of Chicago Press, 1926), pp. 90–92.

5. Allen M. Kraut, *Silent Travelers: Germs, Genes, and the Immigrant Menace* (New York: Basic Books, 1994), pp. 35–36.

6. Edwin Guillet, *The Great Migration: The Atlantic Migration by Sailing Ship since 1770* (Toronto, New York: Thomas Nelson and Sons, 1937), pp. 145–154, 181–182; Frederic M. Miller, "Immigration through the Port of Philadelphia," in *Forgotten Doors: The Other Ports of Entry to the United States*, ed. M. Mark Stolarik (Philadelphia: Balch Institute Press, 1988), pp. 37–54; Olof Olson, "A Letter from One Generation to Another," in *Clipper Ship and Covered Wagon: Essays from the Swedish Pioneer Historical Quarterly*, ed. Hildor Arnold Barton (New York: Arno Press, 1979), p. 244.

7. A Supreme Court decision in 1837, *City of New York v. Milne*, sanctioned this type of immigrant regulation by the state; William S. Bernard, "Immigration, History of US Policy," in *Harvard Encyclopedia of American*

Ethnic Groups, ed. Stephan Thernstrom (Cambridge, Mass.: Harvard University Press, 1980), p. 488; on federal tax, see Michael LeMay and Elliott Robert Barkan, eds., *U.S. Immigration and Naturalization Laws and Issues: A Documentary History* (Westport, Conn.: Greenwood Press, 1999), pp. 55–56.

8. Friedrich Knapp, *Immigration and the Commissioners of Emigration of the State of New York* (New York: Douglas Taylor, 1870), pp. 105–124.

9. "Marine Intelligencer," *New York Times,* December 23, 1866.

10. Miller, "Port of Philadelphia."

11. Dean R. Esslinger "Immigration through the Port of Baltimore," in *Forgotten Doors,* pp. 69–72.

12. On the character of the nineteenth century land border, see *Report of the Boundary Commission upon the Survey and Re-marking of the Boundary between the United States and Mexico West of the Rio Grande, 1891 to 1896* (Washington, D.C.: U.S. Government Printing Office, 1898).

13. LeMay and Barkan, *U.S. Immigration,* pp. 55–56.

14. *Congressional Globe,* 41st Cong., 2d sess., July 4, 1870, p. 5152; Kitty Calavita, *U.S. Immmigration Law and the Control of Labor: 1820–1924* (London and Orlando, Fla.: Academic Press, 1984), p. 72.

15. The Foran Act and its enforcement remained controversial enough to necessitate an amendment in 1887, extending the enforcement authority of the Secretary of the Treasury and triggering the first set of congressional hearings on immigration in 1889. U.S. Congress, House of Representatives, *Report of the Select Committee of the House of Representatives to Inquire into the Alleged Violation of Laws Prohibiting the Importation of Contract Laborers, Paupers, Convicts and Other Classes,* 50th Cong., 2d sess. (Washington, D.C.: U.S. Government Printing Office, 1889) [hereafter cited as *Contract Labor Hearings, 1889*]; LeMay and Barkan, *U.S. Immigration,* pp. 55–56; Rogers Smith, *Civic Ideals: Conflicting Visions of Citizenship in U.S. History* (New Haven, Conn.: Yale University Press, 1997), p. 359; Edward P. Hutchison, *Legislative History of American Immigration Policy: 1798–1965* (Philadelphia: University of Pennsylvania Press, 1981), pp. 79–81.

16. Testimony of Charles Tinko, Commissioner of Immigration of the State of New York, *Contract Labor Hearings, 1889,* pp. 255–269; U.S. Department of the Treasury, "Report on Immigration," in *Annual Report of the Secretary of the Treasury, 1891* [hereafter cited as *Treasury Annual Report* with year of publication] (Washington, D.C.: 1891), p. 859.

17. This and the following information taken from *Congressional Record,* U.S. Congress, House of Representatives, 50th Cong., 2d sess., January 19, 1889, pp. 997–999; as well as *Contract Labor Hearings, 1889,* pp. 433–447.

18. "Report on Immigration by the Chief of the Miscellaneous Division Secretary's Office," in *Treasury Annual Report, 1890,* pp. 790–791.

19. *Treasury Annual Report, 1889,* pp. 790–793; Thomas Archdeacon, *Becoming American: An Ethnic History* (New York: Free Press, 1983); Sharon D. Masanz, *The History of the Immigration and Naturalization Service: A Report*

Prepared at the Request of Senator Edward M. Kennedy, Chairman, Committee of the Judiciary, United State Senate, for the Use of the Select Commission on Immigration and Refugee Policy, 96th Cong., 2d sess. (Washington, D.C.: U.S. Government Printing Office, 1980), p. 9.

20. LeMay and Barkan, *U.S. Immigration,* pp. 66–70; *Congressional Record,* February 16, 1891, pp. 2740–2741.

21. The right of the federal government to assume such powers was unsuccessfully challenged in *Nishimura Eiku v. United States.* See LeMay and Barkan, *U.S. Immigration,* pp. 70–71; Secretary of Labor's Committee on Administrative Procedure, "The Immigration and Naturalization Service," typescript (Washington, D.C.: Immigration and Naturalization Service, 1938), pp. 3–4; Masanz, *History of the INS,* p. 11.

22. Goldie Tuvin Stern, *My Caravan of Years: An Autobiography* (New York: Bloch, 1945), p. 252.

23. Erika Lee, *At America's Gates: Chinese Immigration during the Exclusion Era, 1882–1943* (Chapel Hill: University of North Carolina Press, 2003), pp. 41–42, 47–58; George Anthony Peffer, *They Don't Bring Their Women Here: Chinese Female Emigration before Exclusion* (Urbana: University of Illinois Press, 1999), pp. 57–72; Estelle Lau, *Paper Families: Identity, Immigration Administration, and Chinese Exclusion* (Raleigh, N.C.: Duke University Press, 2007), p. 36.

24. Roger Daniels, *Guarding the Golden Door: American Immigration Policy and Immigrants since 1882* (New York: Hill and Wang, 2004), pp. 48–58; LeMay and Barkan, *U.S. Immigration,* pp. 133–135, 148–151; Daniel Tichenor, *Dividing Lines: The Politics of Immigration Control in America* (Princeton, N.J.: Princeton University Press, 2002), pp. 144–146.

25. Lucy Salyer, *Laws Harsh as Tigers: Chinese Immigrants and the Shaping of Modern Immigration Law* (Chapel Hill: University of North Carolina Press, 1995), pp. 57–59; Lee, *At America's Gates;* U.S. Commissioner General of Immigration, *Annual Report of the Commissioner General of Immigration to the Secretary of Commerce and Labor: For the Fiscal Year Ending June 1914* [hereafter cited as *Annual Report* with year of publication] (Washington, D.C.: U.S. Government Printing Office, 1914), p. 106. This report lists 23 classes of excludable immigrants; Thomas A. Aleinikoff, David A. Martin, and Hiroshi Motomura, *Immigration and Citizenship: Process and Policy,* 4th ed. (St. Paul, Minn.: Westlaw, 1996), pp. 179–213; Salyer, *Laws Harsh as Tigers,* pp. 69–93.

26. Tichenor, *Dividing Lines,* pp. 69–75, 98–108, 117–120; U.S. Immigration and Naturalization Service [INS], subject correspondence files, National Archives, RG 85, entry 9, file 51777/164; Charles C. Howe, *The Confessions of a Reformer* (1925; repr., Kent, Ohio: Kent State University Press, 1988), pp. 152–165.

27. John Higham, *Strangers in the Land: Patterns of American Nativism: 1860–1925* (New York: Athenaeum, 1964), pp. 149–157; U.S. Industrial Commission, *Reports* (now searchable in digital form under: www.archive.org/search

.php?query=%22United%20States.%20Immigration%20Commission
%20(1907–1910)%22%20AND%20mediatype%3Atexts); U.S. Immigration Commission (1907–1910), *Reports of the Immigration Commission,* vols.
1–42 (Washington, D.C.: U.S. Government Printing Office, 1911), also
published as documents of the 61st Cong., 2d and 3d sess. The Dillingham
Commission itself consisted of Republicans known for their restrictionist
leanings and southern Democrats. See Lawrence Fuchs, "Immigration
Reform in 1911 and 1981: The Role of Select Commissions," *Journal of
American Ethnic History* 3, no. 2 (1983): 58–60. See also John Higham, *Send
These to Me: Immigrants in Urban America* (Baltimore: Johns Hopkins
University Press, 1984), pp. 45–47; Tichenor, *Dividing Lines,* pp. 117–121;
Robert F. Zeidel, *Immigrants, Progressives, and Exclusion Politics: The Dilling-
ham Commission, 1900–1927* (DeKalb: Northern Illinois University Press,
2005).

28. INS, subject correspondence files, National Archives, RG 85, entry 9, file,
    52729/9 ("Classification of Races," 1910).

29. On uses of racial classification and "blood" designation, see INS, subject
    correspondence files, National Archives, RG 85, entry 9, file 54281/36B
    ("Salvador Lyncet"); Victor Stafford, *Immigration Problems: Personal Experi-
    ences of an Official* (New York: Dodd, Mead, 1925), pp. 4–15.

30. Bertha Boody, *A Psychological Study of Immigrant Children at Ellis Island* (1926;
    repr., New York: Arno Press, 1970).

31. Amy Fairchild, *Science at the Borders: Immigrant Medical Inspection and the
    Shaping of the Modern Industrial Labor Force* (Baltimore: Johns Hopkins
    University Press, 2003), pp. 98–102; a similar reluctance prevailed in the
    use of the most advanced methods to diagnose other diseases (for example,
    the use of laboratory specimens) by the Immigration Bureau, though its
    central office in Washington maintained files on classifications and
    diagnoses of some illnesses in order to make uniform diagnosis easier and
    measure the shortcomings of "defective" persons who could be rejected.
    INS, subject correspondence files, National Archives, RG 85, entry 9, file
    52495/65 ("Admission of Physically Defective") and file 52600/30
    (tuberculosis).

32. INS subject correspondence files, National Archives, RG 85, entry 9, file
    52424/13 ("Japanese Picture Brides"), file 51520/21 ("Japanese Picture
    Brides in Hawaii"), 51938/13 ("Yoshida Kinu"), 52241/33 ("Kisi Obata"),
    52483/1–18 ("White Slave Traffic 1909, reports filed by US city"), and
    52484/25 (prostitution).

33. INS, subject correspondence files, National Archives, RG 85, entry 9, file
    51423/1 (Seraphic report); see also Chapter 1 of this book (pp. 30–33).

34. Good examples of the increasingly scientific display and dissemination of
    knowledge were the *Annual Report, 1902* and *1914.*

35. On the two-faced nature of these reports, see Fuchs, "Immigration Reform
    in 1911 and 1981," pp. 58–89; Oscar Handlin, *Race and Nationality in
    American Life* (Boston: Little, Brown, 1957), pp. 92–138.

36. INS, subject correspondence files, National Archives, RG 85, entry 9, file 53173/12 ("Jewish Immigrants"); Lee, *At America's Gates,* pp. 123–131.

37. INS, subject correspondence files, National Archives, RG 85, entry 9, file 51424/1,2; Mary Shapiro, *Gateway to Liberty: The Story of the Statue of Liberty and Ellis Island* (New York: Random House), pp. 133–135, 138–139; Thomas Pitkin, *Keepers of the Gate: A History of Ellis Island* (New York: New York Univerity Press, 1975), pp. 29, 31–32, 36–34.

38. INS, subject correspondence files, National Archives, RG 85, entry 9, files 51424/2 and 51424/1; Pitkin, *Keepers of the Gate,* pp. 29, 31–32, 36–45; Shapiro, *Gateway to Liberty,* pp. 135–136, 140–156, 172–193.

39. Secretary of Labor's Committee on Administrative Procedure, "The Immigration and Naturalization Service," typescript (Washington, D.C.: Immigration and Naturalization Service, 1938), p. 3; Masanz, *History of the INS.*

40. The only exceptions were habeas corpus proceedings, where immigrants could challenge the fact that they were held without charges brought against them. These were used especially in Chinese exclusion cases. Salyer, *Laws Harsh as Tigers,* pp. 69–117.

41. Robert Watchorn to Oscar Strauss, April 24, 1908, in INS, subject correspondence files, National Archives, RG 85, entry 9, file 51831/55, also file 51411/46 (Wm. Bennett report); *Annual Report, 1912* and *1914.*

42. *Annual Report, 1920,* p. 327.

43. See correspondence between Prescott Hall and Commissioner General F. P. Sergeant, and Robert Watchorn to Oscar Strauss April 24, 1908, in INS, subject correspondence files, National Archives, RG 85, entry 9, file 51762/21.

44. *Annual Report, 1900,* pp. 43; *1904,* pp. 79–80; *1908,* pp. 144–146; *1909,* pp. 5–6; INS, subject correspondence files, National Archives, RG 85, entry 9, file 53371/74.

45. Commissioner General Caminetti was clearly aware of this dilemma; in 1919, he tried to promote both a comprehensive exclusion law that would have enhanced the power of the Immigration Bureau. "Memorandum Explaining Proposed New Immigration Law," *Annual Report, 1919,* Exhibit A, pp. 65–80.

46. Louis Adamic, *Laughing in the Jungle: The Autobiography of an Immigrant in America* (New York: Harper Brothers, 1932), p. 41; *Annual Report, 1903,* following pp. 96 and 114; see also Augustus F. Sherman, *Ellis Island Portraits: 1905–1920,* introduction by Peter Mesenhöller (New York: Aperture, 2005), p. 5.

47. Stafford, *Immigrant Problems,* pp. 112–115, 117–119; INS, subject correspondence files, National Archives, RG 85, entry 9, file 51774/90 ("Alien Escapees") and file 51424/1; Samuel Nelson, interview, in *Voices from Ellis Island.* For the account of an escape from Ellis Island detention, see Arthur Bohn, interview by Eugenia Tetserkis, 18 September 1978, Ellis Island Oral History Project, Series NPS, no. 112.

48. Ivan Chermayeff, Fred Wasserman, and Mary J. Shapiro, *Ellis Island: An Illustrated History of the Immigrant Experience* (New York: Macmillan, 1991), pp. 164–180.

49. Fairchild, *Science at the Borders*, pp. 124–126.

50. Sherman, *Ellis Island Portraits*.

51. Eiichiro Azuma, *Between Two Empires: Race, History, and Transnationalism in Japanese America* (New York: Oxford University Press, 2005), p. 56.

52. INS, subject correspondence files, National Archives, RG 85, entry 9, files 51831/28 and 52423/47.

53. INS, subject correspondence files, National Archives, RG 85, entry 9, file 55480/745 ("Vera Cathcart").

54. The best general survey of the immigration ports of the East Coast can be gleaned from the reports filed by the local heads of immigration stations, reprinted in the *Annual Report*. See, for example, *Annual Report, 1914,* pp. 221–258.

55. INS, subject correspondence files, National Archives, RG 85, entry 9, files 51389/6, A–B, and file 51389/8; also *Annual Report, 1907,* pp. 66–67.

56. On Florida cases, see INS, subject correspondence files, National Archives, RG 85, entry 9, file 52423/37; on corruption, see file 51831/28; *Annual Report, 1900,* p. 44.

57. Shapiro points to the special relationship between Secretary of Labor Strauss and New York Commissioner William Watchorn, both New Yorkers, Republicans, and of immigrant background; Shapiro, *Gateway to Liberty,* pp. 191–192.

58. Ibid., pp. 133–135, 138–139; INS, subject correspondence files, National Archives, RG 85, entry 9, files 51424/2 and 51424/1; Pitkin, *Keepers of the Gate,* pp. 29, 31–32, 36–45.

59. Shapiro, *Gateway to Liberty,* pp. 135–136, 140–156, 172–193.

60. Edward Corsi, *In the Shadow of Liberty: The Chronicle of Ellis Island* (New York: Macmillan, 1935), pp. 72–73, 76–79.

61. Passengers with those diseases were put in a special quarantine hospital on Hoffman's Island before being sent back; Corsi, *In the Shadow of Liberty,* p. 121; Fairchild, *Science at the Borders,* pp. 121–131.

62. Clara Larsen, interview by Nancy Dallett, 17 January 1986, Ellis Island Oral History Project, Series KECK, no. 003.

63. INS, subject correspondence files, National Archives, RG 85, entry 9, file 53531/41. See also Fairchild, *Science at the Borders,* pp. 129–130.

64. Estelle Schwartz Belford, interview by Paul E. Sigrist, Jr., 14 May 1991, Ellis Island Oral History Project, Series EI, no. 047.

65. Kraut, *Silent Travelers,* pp. 54–77; Fairchild, *Science at the Borders,* pp. 119–159. The catalogue of diseases for which people were excluded was characterized by illnesses that were easily recognized in brief visual inspections: visible infections of the eye or skin, skeletal malformations,

and obvious mental illness or developmental delays. Other illnesses that would render men and women unable to work, such as tuberculosis or heart disease, usually went undetected.

66. Fairchild, *Science at the Borders,* pp. 38–40; *Annual Report, 1907,* p. 14, and *1914,* p. 29; Shapiro, *Gateway to Liberty,* pp. 159–164.

67. Minnie Nydick Edelman, interview by Janet Levine, 2 March 1994, Ellis Island Oral History Project, Series EI, no. 448.

68. Appeals sometimes resulted in admission if the petitioner was found to be a U.S. citizen because of marriage, for example. See INS, subject correspondence files, RG 85, entry 9, file 52531/198A ("Thakla Nicola"), file 52545/91 ("Wong See").

69. Ibid., file 51465/7 ("Rosa Semiana").

70. Ibid., file 52809/12, 12a.

71. Passports were not required from non-Chinese immigrants until July 1917, when this requirement was introduced as a temporary war measure to protect against the infiltration of enemy aliens. The requirement became permanent after a passport law was passed by Congress a year later. *Annual Report, 1918,* pp. 10–11. Prior to the passport law, some U.S. officials, notably the Police Commissioner of New York, argued for the introduction of "certificates of character" issued to immigrants by their country of origin. In the end, nothing came of the idea, which was directed against Italian immigrants for the most part. INS, subject correspondence files, RG 85, entry 9, file 52423/37 a–c.

72. Shapiro, *Gateway to Liberty,* pp. 156–157, 164–165, 170; Corsi, *In the Shadow of Liberty,* pp. 73–76; *Annual Report, 1902,* p. 9, *1907,* p. 49.

73. Adamic, *Laughing in the Jungle,* p. 41.

74. Ivan Chermayeff, Fred Wasserman, and Mary Shapiro, *Ellis Island: The Illustrated History of the Immigrant Experience* (New York: Macmillan 1991), pp. 132–133, 142. Very few immigrants were excluded as prostitutes. In 1907, only 18 women were debarred for this reason out of a total of 1.2 million immigrants admitted to the United States. By 1914, the number had risen somewhat to about 0.02 percent of the total arrivals. This masks the fact that many women were debarred for other reasons, but the suspicion of prostitution was still present; *Annual Report, 1908,* and *1914,* p. 106.

75. INS, subject correspondence files, National Archives, RG 85, entry 9, file 53173/12 ("Jewish Immigrants").

76. Corsi, *In the Shadow of Liberty,* pp. 86–87.

77. Shapiro, *Gateway to Liberty,* p. 168; Corsi, *In the Shadow of Liberty,* pp. 75–76, 122–123. See also the case of Concetta Sortine, who arrived to join her husband in the United States but had a child from another relationship. This rendered her excludable, a decision made at Ellis Island but seen as precedent setting by officials. INS, subject correspondence files, RG 85, entry 9, file 52388/24.

78. Corsi, *In the Shadow of Liberty,* pp. 80–81; INS, subject correspondence files, National Archives, RG 85, entry 9, files 5250/13, 51698/7, and 55235/188.

79. INS, subject correspondence files, National Archives, RG 85, entry 9, files 52809/12,12A; 51424/1,2; 53371/74; and 53173/12.

80. Pitkin, *Keepers of the Gate,* pp. 44–45; Shapiro, *Gateway to Liberty,* pp. 170–174; "Societies to Plead for Immigrants," *New York Times,* Jan. 4, 1903, p. 6.

81. Pitkin, *Keepers of the Gate,* pp. 48–49, 59; Shapiro, *Gateway to Liberty,* pp. 199–201. The investigation resulted in a complete vindication of the immigration officials.

82. William Williams to Charles Nagel, April 5, 1911, in INS, subject correspondence files, National Archives, RG 85, entry 9, file 53108/78.

83. On Williams's career at Ellis Island, see Pitkin, *Keepers of the Gate,* pp. 48–64; William Williams to Commissioner General Keefe, September 14, 1909, and Charles Ormsby McHarg to William Williams, September 15, 1909, minutes September 27, 1909, in INS, subject correspondence files, National Archives, RG 85, entry 9, file 52600/13A, 53108/78; Shapiro, *Gateway to Liberty,* pp. 205–212.

84. Marian Smith, "The Immigration and Naturalization Service (INS) at the U.S-Canadian Border, 1893–1993: An Overview of Issues and Topics," *Michigan Historical Review* 26, no. 2 (Fall 2000), p. 127. The best overview is still Marcus Lee Hansen, *The Mingling of the Canadian and American Peoples,* vol. 1 (New Haven, Conn.: Yale University Press, 1940), and Edgar McInnis, *The Unguarded Frontier: A History of American Canadian Relations* (New York: Doubleday, 1942). For a newer assessment of borderlands studies from the northern perspective of the United States, see Robert Lecker, ed., *Borderlands: Essays in Canadian American Relations* (Toronto: ECW Press, 1991), and Lauren McKinsey and Victor Konrad, *Borderlands Reflections: The United States and Canada* (Orono: University of Maine, 1989); see also Bruno Ramirez and Yves Otis, *Crossing the 49th Parallel: Migration from Canada to the United States, 1900–1930* (Ithaca, N.Y.: Cornell University Press, 2001), p. 34.

85. Hansen, *Mingling,* p. ix.

86. Ramirez and Otis, *Crossing the 49th Parallel,* pp. 1–33, 39–45; Marian Smith, "By Way of Canada: U.S. Records of Immigration across the U.S.-Canadian Border, 1895–1954 (St. Albans Lists)," *Prologue* 32, no. 3 (Fall 2000), p. 192.

87. Leon E. Truesdell, *The Canadian Born in the United States: An Analysis of the Statistics of the Canadian Element in the Population of the United States, 1850 to 1940* (New Haven, Conn.: Yale University Press, 1943), pp. 2–3; R. H. Coats and M. C. Maclean, *The American Born in Canada: A Statistical Interpretation* (Toronto: Ryerson Press, 1943), p. 15; *Annual Report, 1902;* see also Alan Sears, "Immigration Controls as Social Policy: The Case of Canadian Medical Inspection, 1900–1920," *Studies in Political Economy* 33 (Autumn 1990): 90–112.

88. The railroad lines were willing to enter into such an arrangement because it minimized their financial risk for transporting back rejected immigrants. Railroad lines were responsible for the cost of transporting rejected immigrants back to their country of origin, just like ship lines on the Atlantic and Pacific Coasts. Smith, "(INS) at the U.S. Canadian Border," pp. 128–130; Fairchild, *Science at the Borders*, pp. 144–150; Sears, "Immigration Controls," esp. pp. 94–99.

89. The Immigration Bureau's controlling and sorting mechanisms for Canadian migrants had a fine administrative mesh: depending on how much time migrants had previously spent in Canada, they were called class B (less than a year), class C (more than a year), or class D (long-term resident aliens of Canada). Some immigrants in these classifications needed to pay a head tax, others were exempt; some could be deported to Canada, others to Europe; some were admitted as temporary, others as permanent immigrants. INS, subject correspondence files, National Archives, RG 85, entry 9, file 52903/43C; Smith, "By Way of Canada," pp. 197–198.

90. *Annual Report, 1913*, p. 168; *1914*, p. 191; *1915*, pp. 222–223; *1916*, p. 220; and *1917*, p. 313; Smith, "By Way of Canada," p. 193; Smith, "(INS) at the U.S-Canadian Border," p. 129; Immigrant aid organizations seem to have been absent from the border stations in Canada. Local Jewish communities did help transit migrants occasionally in Montreal and Toronto. Stephen Scheinberg, "From Self-Help to Community Advocacy: The Emergence of Community Activism," in *From Immigration to Integration: The Canadian Jewish Experience* (Toronto: Institute for International Affairs, B'nai Brith Canada, 2000), www.bnaibrith.ca/institute/millennium/millennium04.html (accessed 09/02/10).

91. *Annual Report, 1913*, p. 177; see also Smith, "(INS) at the U.S-Canadian Border," pp. 142–147.

92. Smith, "By Way of Canada," p. 195; Smith, "(INS) at the U.S-Canadian Border," p. 130.

93. INS, subject correspondence files, National Archives, RG 85, file 52925/83; see also files 53086/58 and 52841/5; 55880/500 (Nov. 5, 1937); file 55754/736 ("Alien Nurses," 1931–40).

94. The refusal cases represented those immigrants who had not paid head taxes and had not shown up for special hearings to have their cases cleared. *Annual Report, 1914*, pp. 167–168; see also *Annual Report 1902*, p. 3.

95. *Annual Report, 1916*, p. 222.

96. INS, subject correspondence files, National Archives, RG 85, entry 9, file 53360/71 a–b ("Inspection and Admission of Aliens"); also Smith, "(INS) at the U.S-Canadian Border."

97. The U.S. and the Mexican government spent considerable resources on remeasuring and re-marking the border in 1890. See Oscar Martinez, *Troublesome Border* (Tucson: University of Arizona Press, 1988), pp. 16–27;

Leon Metz, *Border: The US Mexico Line* (El Paso, Tex.: Mangan Books, 1989). It should be pointed out here that compared with the conflict around European or even South American borders, the U.S. Mexican border was tranquil territory after 1850.

98. *Report of the Boundary Commission between the United States and Mexico.*

99. Martinez, *Troublesome Border,* pp. 5–6; Jay Stowell, *The Near Side of the Mexican Question* (New York: George Doran, 1921), pp. 13–15.

100. Martinez, *Troublesome Border,* pp. 2–3, 8–20; for an interesting set of reflections on this theme, and partially contradictory conclusions, see Lawrence A. Herzog, *Changing Boundaries in the Americas: New Perspectives on the U.S.-Mexican, Central American, and South American Borders* (San Diego: Center for U.S.-Mexican Studies), pp. 3–12, 38–41.

101. Metz, *Border,* pp. 367–369.

102. *Annual Report, 1907,* p. 99; compare with *Annual Report, 1903,* p. 112; INS, subject correspondence files, National Archives, RG 85, entry 9, file 51748/1A-B. 52370/1-1A; 52541/44.

103. INS, subject correspondence files, National Archives, RG 85, entry 9, file 51646/1C (Eagle Pass Station); 52541/44 (Richard Taylor report); file 51831/21, 21A; file 52730/75 E–H (Tucson investigation); and file 51701/2–3 (Texas).

104. *Annual Report, 1908,* pp. 144–146.

105. *Annual Report, 1913,* p. 250.

106. INS, subject correspondence files, National Archives, RG 85, entry 9, files 51463/41, 41 A–C, file 52175/1; *Annual Report, 1907,* pp. 109, 130–131, 141–143.

107. INS, subject correspondence files, National Archives, RG 85, entry 9, file 51423/1. Seraphic's report was one of three larger investigations. The others were by Special Inspector Marcus Braun in the same year (focusing on Japanese immigration), file 51463/B (Braun report on the Mexican border), and a 1909 report on Chinese illegal immigration by Richard Taylor (file 52541/44).

108. Fairchild, *Science at the Borders,* pp. 150–159; Mae Ngai, *Impossible Subjects: Illegal Aliens and the Making of Modern America* (Princeton, N.J.: Princeton University Press, 2004), p. 68; Alexandra Minna Stern, "Buildings, Boundaries, and Blood: Medicalization and Nation Building on the U.S.-Mexican Border," *Hispanic American Historical Review* 79, no. 1 (1999): 41–89.

109. INS, subject correspondence files, National Archives, RG 85, entry 9, file 54281/36B ("Children under 16 without Parents, Mexicans: Guadalupe and Manuel Munoz, 4/2/18").

110. Fairchild, *Science at the Borders,* pp. 156–158.

111. INS, subject correspondence files, National Archives, RG 85, entry 9, file 54281/36B ("Salvador Lyncet, Nogales, 2/28/1917").

112. Ibid., file 54281/36B ("Children under 16 without Parents, Mexicans: Carmen Moctezuma, Laredo, 2/15/1918"), filmed in *Records of the*

Immigration and Naturalization Service, Series A, subject correspondence files [microform] (Bethesda, Md.: University Publications of America, 1992), Series A, pt. 2, reel 9. See also Martha Gardner, *The Qualities of a Citizen: Women, Immigration, and Citizenship, 1870–1965* (Princeton, N.J.: Princeton University Press, 2005), pp. 88–89.

113. INS, subject correspondence files, National Archives, RG 85, entry 9, file 52423/21 (memorandum, March 16, 1909). *Annual Report, 1908,* p. 145, records only 43 appeals to over 2,000 exclusion decisions, and all but six were rejected. See also *Annual Report, 1912,* p. 41, and *1913,* pp. 250–251; for appeals, see INS, subject correspondence files, National Archives, RG 85, entry 9, files 52730/77; 52503/1–11, 11A; 53303/2; and successful appeals recorded in file 54281/36, 36A–Q.

114. Gunther Peck, *Re-inventing Free Labor: Padrones and Immigrant workers in the North American West, 1880–1930* (New York: Cambridge University Press, 2000), pp. 102–103; Mark Reisler, *By the Sweat of Their Brow: Mexican Immigrant Labor in the United States, 1900–1940* (Westport, Conn.: Greenwood Press, 1976), pp. 29–39.

115. In the same year, 29,818 Mexicans entered after passing the literacy test and paying the head tax. In addition, inspectors at the Texas border universally noticed an increase in what they called "illegitimate immigration" beginning in 1918. Metz, *Border,* pp. 374–375. *Annual Report, 1920,* p. 24.

116. *Annual Report, 1911,* p. 163. Martinez, *Troublesome Border,* pp. 46–48.

117. *Annual Report, 1915,* Appendix III, pp. 177–231; INS, subject correspondence files, National Archives, RG 85, entry 9, files 51701/2A and 51701/3B.

118. INS, subject correspondence files, National Archives, RG 85, entry 9, file 51686/17A,B.

119. *Annual Report, 1907, 1913, 1920,* Table I.

120. Most of these resources did not go to services to immigrants, but toward intensive and detailed examinations and background research on Asian arrivals. *Annual Report, 1915,* Appendix III, pp. 177–231.

121. Lee, *At America's Gates,* pp. 49–63.

122. On the conditions in Asian countries, see report by a State Department official: "William M. Rice on Japanese Emigration," in INS, subject correspondence files, National Archives, RG 85, entry 9, file 52705/1.

123. Lee, *At America's Gates,* pp. 52–53; Mark Him Lai, Genny Lim, Judy Yung, eds., *Island: Poetry and History of Chinese Immigrants on Angel Island 1910–1940* (Seattle: University of Washington Press, 1988), p. 16.

124. Lai, Lim, and Yung, *Island,* pp. 13–20; Lee, *At America's Gates,* pp. 63–64, 123–130; Azuma, *Between Two Empires,* pp. 38–46.

125. Gunther Barth, *Bitter Strength: A History of the Chinese in the United States, 1850–1870* (Cambridge, Mass.: Harvard University Press, 1964), pp. 74–75.

126. On the early inspections, see Bob Barde, *Immigration at the Golden Gate: Passenger Ships, Exclusion, and Angel Island* (Westport: Preager, 2008), pp. 53–57.

127. Quoted after Judy Yung, *Unbound Feet: A Social History of Chinese Women in San Francisco* (Berkeley: University of California Press, 1995), p. 63.

128. Lee, *At America's Gates*, pp. 59–63; *Annual Report, 1911*, p. 165. The conditions in San Francisco were deplored in almost every *Annual Report* to the Immigration Bureau. See also Lai, Lim, and Yung, *Island*, p. 13; Barde, *Immigration at the Golden Gate*, pp. 57–77.

129. Victor G. Nee and Brett de Bary Nee, *Longtime Californ': A Documentary Study of an American Chinatown* (Boston: Houghton Mifflin, 1972), p. 73; Lee, *At America's Gates*, pp. 123–124.

130. The cost of isolation also affected the Bureau, which began to complain about the inadequately built structures in 1922 and incurred a high cost for administering this remote facility. Lai, Lim, and Yung, *Island*, pp. 13–14.

131. Fairchild, *Science at the Borders*, pp. 132–139. Barde, *Immigration at the Golden Gate*, pp. 10–52, provides a survey of the procedures at Angel Island.

132. Judy Yung, Gordon H. Chang, and Him Mark Lai, eds., *Chinese American Voices: From the Gold Rush to the Present* (Los Angeles: University of California Press, 2006), p. 120.

133. Barde and Bobonis have calculated a median of 2.5 days for Asian passengers. By contrast, the overwhelming majority of Ellis Island arrivals were detained less than a day. Robert Barde and Gustavo Bobonis, "Detention at Ellis Island: First Empirical Evidence," *Social Science History* 30, no. 1 (Spring 2006): 106–132; Yung, *Unbound Feet*, p. 67.

134. Fairchild, *Science at the Borders*, pp. 132–138.

135. Lai, Lim, and Yung, *Island*, p. 108. See also Yung, *Unbound Feet*, pp. 64–65.

136. Fairchild, *Science at the Border*, pp. 180–184, 199; Lai, Lim, and Yung, *Island*, p. 15.

137. Lai, Lim, and Yung, *Island*, p. 117.

138. Ibid., p. 116.

139. INS, subject correspondence files, National Archives, RG 85, entry 9, file 52961/2; Lee, *At America's Gates*, pp. 196–198, 213–216.

140. Ibid., pp. 90–92.

141. INS, subject correspondence files, National Archives, RG 85, entry 9, files 53560/221 and 225, A–C ("Hom Che Gow case") available in *Records of the Immigration and Naturalization Service*, Series A, subject correspondence files [microform] (Bethesda, Md.: University Publications of America, 1992), vol. 1 reel 26; Lee, *At America's Gates*, pp. 89–92; INS, subject correspondence files, National Archives, RG 85, entry 9, file 51952/4.

142. Yung, Chang, and Lai, *Chinese American Voices*, p. 159.

143. *Annual Report, 1913*, pp. 239–240; *1914*, p. 318.

144. "Margarita Lake to Commissioner General of Immigration," in INS, subject correspondence files, National Archives, RG 85, entry 9, file 52424/13.

145. Lee, *At America's Gates*, p. 135; Azuma, *Between Two Empires*, pp. 52–56.

146. INS, subject correspondence files, National Archives, RG 85, entry 9, files 52241/22 and 51938/13; Lee, *At America's Gates,* p. 199.

147. Lee, *At America's Gates,* pp. 123–131.

148. *Annual Report, 1902,* p. 71.

149. Attorneys were never allowed to interview their clients directly while they were detained at Ellis Island either, but they could ask for a copy of the Board of Special Inquiry report. INS, subject correspondence file, National Archives, RG 85, entry 9, files 52320/11 and 52363/14.

150. Lee, *At America's Gates,* pp. 131–134.

151. Ibid., pp. 137–138.

152. Lai, Lim, and Yung, *Island,* p. 109.

153. Lee, *At America's Gates,* pp. 14, 138–141.

154. INS, subject correspondence files, National Archives, RG 85, entry 9, file 51952/4.

155. On the history of Chinese litigation in immigration cases in the nineteenth century, see Salyer, *Laws Harsh as Tigers,* pp. 33–116, 169–177; and Lee, *At America's Gates,* pp. 131–132.

3. Forced Departures

1. Doukenie Babayanie Bacos, interview by Paul E. Sigrist Jr., 23 May 1991, Ellis Island Oral History Project, Series EI, no. 049.

2. Sophia Krietzberg, interview by Dana Gumb, 6 December 1985, Ellis Island Oral History Project, Series AKRF, no. 98.

3. Clement Bouve, *A Treatise on the Laws Governing the Exclusion and Expulsion of Aliens in the United States* (Washington, D.C.: J. Byrne, 1912), pp. 74–75.

4. Asian prostitutes had already been excluded under the 1875 Page Law—the first exclusion law passed by Congress. See the appendix of this book for a detailed list of deportation categories in effect at the end of this first period of deportation law (1917).

5. Michael LeMay and Elliott Robert Barkan, eds., *U.S. Immigration and Naturalization Laws and Issues: A Documentary History* (Westport, Conn.: Greenwood Press, 1999), pp. 108–112.

6. Prior to 1917, only Chinese and Japanese immigrants, prostitutes, and those connected to prostitution were deportable without this time limit.

7. U.S. Immigration and Naturalization Service [INS], subject correspondence files, National Archives, RG 85 entry 9, file 54871/genl. ("Alien Public Charges").

8. For a broader-based argument to limit and refine exclusion and deportation by an immigrant advocate, see Max Kohler, "Immigration and the Jews of America," *American Hebrew,* January 27, 1911, and February 3, 1911. The essay prompted a critical response from the Immigration Bureau; see Memorandum by the Commissioner General (Daniel Keefe) to the Secretary (of Labor) February 16, 1911, in INS, subject correspondence files, National Archives, RG 85, entry 9, file 53173/12.

9. U.S. Commissioner General of Immigration, *Annual Report of the Commissioner General of Immigration to the Secretary of Commerce and Labor: For the Fiscal Year Ending June 1914* [hereafter cited as *Annual Report* with year of publication] (Washington, D.C.: U.S. Government Printing Office, 1915), pp. 106, 155.

10. John Higham, *Strangers in the Land: Patterns of American Nativism, 1860–1925* (New York: Atheneum, 1963), pp. 209–211. LeMay and Barkan, *U.S. Immigration,* pp. 120–121; LeMay and Barkan, *U.S. Immigration,* pp. 120–121.

11. *Annual Report, 1920,* pp. 150, 267, 274, 278.

12. INS, subject correspondence files, National Archives, RG 85, entry 9, file 52600/2 ("Deportations U.S. Canadian border"). See also the file on deportations at the Mexican border, in *Records of the Immigration and Naturalization Service,* Series A, subject correspondence files [microform] (Bethesda, Md.: University Publications of America, 1992), pt. 2, reel 17, 0264–0416 (Mexican immigration, 1906–1930).

13. Joseph Novel, interview by Harvey Dixon, 26 September 1980, Ellis Island Oral History Project, Series NPS, no. 124.

14. Louise Vobril and Joseph Vobril, interview by Anna Kuthan, 31 January 1974, Ellis Island Oral History Project, Series NPS, no. 045.

15. Otto Heinmann, interview by Margo Nash, 31 January 1974, Ellis Island Oral History Project, Series NPS, no. 046.

16. *Annual Report, 1930,* p. 35.

17. U.S. Secretary of Labor, *Reports of the Department of Labor, 1931: Report of the Secretary of Labor and Reports of Bureaus* (Washington, D.C.: U.S. Government Printing Office, 1932), p. 58; Mae Ngai, *Impossible Subjects: Illegal Aliens and the Making of Modern America* (Princeton, N.J.: Princeton University Press, 2004), pp. 60, 64–70.

18. *Annual Report, 1931,* pp. 60–61.

19. On voluntary departures, see *Annual Report, 1931,* p. 36; *1932,* p. 28.

20. INS, subject correspondence files, National Archives, RG 85, entry 9, 55739/930 ("Indigents," 1931–1940); entry 26, file 23/25502 ("Enrique Olivares"); *Annual Report, 1930,* p. 22; *1931,* p. 26; *1932,* p. 28.

21. Quoted in Marion Schibsby, *An Immigration Summary: Outstanding Facts about the Admission, Exclusion, and Deportation of Aliens by the United States* (New York: Common Council for American Unity, 1947), p. 18.

22. In this comprehensive measure to trace all aliens in the United States, registration uncovered thousands of illegal immigrants. To ensure cooperation in the registration of aliens, the Attorney General had the authority to suspend deportations. Mae Ngai, "The Strange Career of the Illegal Alien: Immigration Restriction and Deportation Policy in the United States, 1921–1965," *Law and History Review* 21, no. 1 (Spring 2003): 69–107, esp. pp. 104–105; Schibsby, *Immigration Summary,* p. 17.

23. A good survey table on this is to be found in U.S. Department of Justice, *Annual Report for the Immigration and Naturalization Service for the Fiscal Year*

Ending June 30, 1955 [hereafter cited as *INS Annual Report* with year of publication] (Washington, D.C.: U.S. Government Printing Office, 1955), pp. 106–107.

24. Ngai, *Impossible Subjects,* pp. 152–158.

25. I have grouped the following categories of exclusion into the "social exclusion" category (terminology used by the Immigration Bureau): imbeciles, feeble minded, epileptics, insane, suffering from loathsome or dangerous diseases, professional beggars, public charges, likely to become a public charge, professional beggars, paupers, unaccompanied and under 16 years of age, prostitutes, procurers of prostitutes, other mental conditions, criminals. See Appendix 2 for classifications.

26. *Annual Report, 1916,* pp. 86–91; Bouve, *Exclusion and Expulsion;* Jane Perry Clark, *The Deportation of Aliens from the United States to Europe* (New York: Columbia University Press, 1931), pp. 50–51.

27. On expulsion of young and elderly men and women, see INS, subject correspondence files, National Archives, RG 85, entry 9, file 51465/1–10. On women, see Clark, *Deportation of Aliens,* pp. 43–44, 49–54; INS, subject correspondence files, National Archives, RG 85, entry 9, file 53173/12; Deirdre Moloney, "Women and Morality in U.S. Deportation Policy" (paper presented at the European Social Science History Conference, Berlin, March 2004); Zosa Szajkowski, "Deportation of Jewish Immigrants and Returnees before World War I," *American Jewish Historical Quarterly* 67, no. 4 (June 1978): 294–295.

28. INS, subject correspondence files, National Archives, RG 85, entry 9, file 52903/43.

29. Ibid., file 52503/13 ("Maria Raciti").

30. File 53529/38A ("Christina Bycroft").

31. Ibid., file 51777/265 ("Anna Williams," 1908) and files 51777/265, 52484/25, 51777/149; Candice Bedbrennner, *A Nationality of Her Own: Women, Marriage, and the Law of Citizenship* (Berkeley: University of California Press, 1997), pp. 31–33, cites a similar case from the files of the Dillingham Commission.

32. In 1915/16, the number was under 400. The figures were even paltrier for earlier years (121 in 1914, and 25 in 1906/07). An investigation of prostitution in major U.S. cities undertaken in 1909 revealed that many prostitutes in American urban areas were indeed immigrants, but—aware of the statue of limitations in force—maintained that they had entered the United States more than five years earlier. Thus, they were liable only under criminal law, and their cases rarely pursued by the police. INS, subject correspondence files, National Archives, RG 85, entry 9, files 51461/1, 52484/3, 51777/164, and 52483/1–18 ("White Slave Traffic").

33. Clark, *Deportation of Aliens,* esp. pp. 71–158; William C. Van Vleck, *The Administrative Control of Aliens: A Study in Administrative Law and Procedure* (New York: Commonwealth Fund, 1932). See also INS, subject correspondence files, National Archives, RG 85, entry 9, files 54871/genl. ("Deportation of alien public charges, 1920–1930") and 53173/12.

34. For exceptions, see INS, subject correspondence files, National Archives, RG 85, entry 9, files 51389/6, A–B ("South Carolina Immigration," 1907), and 51389/8 ("Georgia Immigration," 1907).
35. *Annual Report, 1931,* p. 256; Clark, *Deportation of Aliens,* pp. 151–214.
36. Clark, *Deportation of Aliens,* pp. 43–44, 49–54; INS, subject correspondence files, National Archives, RG 85, entry 9, file 53173/12 ("Jewish Immigrants"), *New York Times,* April 23, 1911, p. 3; Szajkowski, "Deportation of Jewish Immigrants," pp. 294–295.
37. Ibid. and file 53186/2,2A ("Jewish Immigrant Societies and the Press"); the data in the Immigration Commissioner's *Annual Report* show that the number of debarment decisions appealed rose between 1904 and 1914 in proportion to the rising number of debarments. The percentage of successful appeals fell in this period from over 50 percent in 1907 to less than about 35 percent in 1914. A growing majority of successful appeals (between 60 percent and nearly 90 percent) were filed in New York.
38. T. Alexander Aleinikoff, David Martin, and Hiroshi Motomura, *Immigration and Citizenship: Process and Policy,* 4th ed. (St. Paul, Minn.: Westlaw, 1996), pp. 68–79; Will Irwin, "Communists and Deportation," *The Interpreter* 9, no. 8 (1930): 115–117.
39. Lucy Salyer, *Laws Harsh as Tigers: Chinese Immigrants and the Shaping of Modern Immigration* Law (Chapel Hill: University of North Carolina Press, 1996), pp. 157–162; Wischnitzer, *Visas to Freedom: The History of HIAS* (Cleveland: World Pub., 1956).
40. Salyer, *Laws Harsh as Tigers,* pp. 38–39, 100–102.
41. The enforcement of Chinese Exclusion was handled by a Chinese Inspector who worked under the Commissioner General of Immigration. Statistical records were kept separately for Chinese and Japanese immigrants until 1930. On the connection between Chinese Inspectors and the border patrol, see Kathleen Lytle, "Entangling Borders and Bodies: Racial Profiling and the History of the U.S. Border Patrol, 1924–1955" (Ph.D. diss., University of California–Los Angeles, 2002), pp. 25–27.
42. Salyer, *Laws Harsh as Tigers,* pp. 46–47, 57, 90–91; INS, subject correspondence files, National Archives, RG 85, entry 9, file 52132/2.
43. *Records of the Immigration and Naturalization Service,* Series A, subject correspondence files [microform] (Bethesda, Md.: University Publications of America, 1992), pt. 1, reel 17, 0909 (presumably RG 85, entry 9, file 52500/56, "Chinese Exclusion").
44. Salyer, *Laws Harsh as Tigers,* pp. 58–63, 86–91, 148–151.
45. During the same period 7,700 non-Chinese (mostly Europeans) were also deported, although about sixty times as many immigrants came from Europe and the Americas during that time as arrived from China. *Annual Report, 1907,* p. 92.
46. The INS counted over 2,100 Chinese deportations in 1932; however, this exceptionally high figure was caused by a change in Mexican law that did not allow for Chinese caught at the Mexican border to be deported back to Mexico. Those Chinese arrested for illegal entry at the southern border had

to be deported directly to China from then on unless they could prove Mexican citizenship. The Immigration Commissioner suspected that some of the border crossers entered the United States openly in order to be arrested and sent back to China at government expense during the Depression. The Immigration Service called them "free trippers." *Annual Report, 1929,* p. 17; *1931,* p. 53; *1932,* pp. 38, 166.

47. The number of Japanese deported was small and declined from about 5 percent of those admitted in 1908 to fewer than 0.3 percent in 1913, the same proportion as for European immigrants in that year. A good survey of Japanese deportations as compared with deportations of European and other immigrants is provided in *Annual Report, 1927,* p. 232.

48. INS, subject correspondence files, National Archives, RG 85, entry 9, file 53531/48 ("Victoria Immigration Society").

49. Lytle, "Entangling Borders and Bodies," pp. 25–27.

50. U.S. immigration officials used the designation "peons" to describe the lower-class social profile of the majority of Mexican immigrants in the early decades of the twentieth century. INS, subject correspondence files, National Archives, RG 85, entry 9, files 51748/IIB, 51831/21, 52541/44, 52903/43, 53108/71, and 54152/79a–c.

51. Lytle, "Entangling Borders and Bodies," pp. 43–45.

52. *Records of the Immigration and Naturalization Service,* Series A, pt. 2., reel 17, 0264–0416 (Mexican immigration, 1906–1930).

53. Lytle, "Entangling Borders and Bodies," pp. 52–57.

54. INS, subject correspondence files, National Archives, RG 85, entry 9, file 52730/77; see also file 52503/11.

55. *Annual Report, 1907, 1914, 1915,* and *1928.* Between one-fifth and one-third of all deportations of Mexicans were for prostitution.

56. Ngai, "Strange Career," pp. 37–46.

57. On police function at the Mexican border by the Border Patrol, see *Annual Report, 1917,* pp. xxiv, 227–231; Ngai, *Impossible Subjects,* pp. 67–81; George Sanchez, *Becoming Mexican-American: Ethnicity, Culture, and Identity in Chicano Los Angeles, 1900–1945* (New York: Oxford University Press, 1993), pp. 58–62.

58. *Annual Report, 1932,* pp. 28–29; *Reports of the Department of Labor, 1933,* p. 53.

59. Sanchez, *Becoming Mexican-American,* pp. 38–39.

60. Dennis Valdez, *Al Norte: Agricultural Workers in the Great Lakes Region, 1917–1979* (Austin: University of Texas Press, 1991), pp. 31–33; Abraham Hoffman, *Unwanted Mexican Americans in the Great Depression* (Tucson: University of Arizona Press, 1954), pp. 118–119.

61. Hoffmann, *Unwanted Mexicans,* pp. 37, 118–127; Sanchez, *Becoming Mexican American,* pp. 209–225; Francisco Balderrama, *Decade of Betrayal: Mexican Repatriation in the 1930s* (Albuquerque: University of New Mexico Press, 1995), pp. 49–125; Camillle Guerin-Gonzalez, *Mexican Workers and American Dreams: Immigration, Repatriation, and California Farm Labor, 1900–1939* (New Brunswick, N.J.: Rutgers University Press, 1994), pp. 77–109; Valdez, *Al Norte,* pp. 30–33.

62. INS, subject correspondence files, National Archives, RG 85, entry 9, file 54933/351 C–I; Balderrama, *Decade of Betrayal,* tells the story of the repatriated Mexicans, see esp. pp. 157–192. See also Guerin-Gonzalez, *Mexican Workers,* pp. 97–110.

63. Hoffmann, *Unwanted Mexicans,* p. 151; *Reports of the Department of Labor, 1936,* p. 97.

64. *Reports of the Department of Labor, 1936,* p. 97.

65. U.S. Congress, House of Representatives, *Report of the Select Committee of the House of Representatives to Inquire into Alleged Violations of Laws Prohibiting the Importation of Contract Laborers, Paupers, Convicts and other Classes,* 50th Cong., 2d sess. (Washington D.C.: U.S. Government Printing Office, 1889).

66. LeMay and Barkan, *U.S. Immigration,* pp. 90–92.

67. William Preston, *Aliens and Dissenters: Federal Suppression of Radicals, 1903–1933* (Urbana: University of Illinois Press, 1994), pp. 63–73; Henry Hazard, Naturalization Examiner, Washington, D.C., to John Speed Smith, Naturalization Examiner, Seattle, June 28, 1913, in INS, subject correspondence files, National Archives, RG 85, entry 9, file 53531/192A.

68. INS, subject correspondence files, National Archives, RG 85, entry 9, files 51924/30 and 51924/192.

69. George Cullen to the Commissioner General in Washington, March, 31, 1908, in INS, subject correspondence files, National Archives, RG 85, entry 9, file 51924/30.

70. Wilhelm Lutz to Graham Rice, May 28, 1908, in INS, subject correspondence files, National Archives, RG 85, entry 9, file 51924/192.

71. June 6, 1908, May 22, 1908, and May 28, 1908, in INS, subject correspondence files, National Archives, RG 85, entry 9, file 51924/30 ("Anarchists").

72. Preston, *Aliens and Dissenters,* pp. 56–62; see also Melvyn Dubofsky, *We Shall Be All: A History of the IWW* (New York: Quadrangle Books, 1969), pp. 174–184.

73. J. T. Sullivan. Acting Chief of Police, Spokane, to A. F. Richardson, Immigration Inspector, Spokane, Nov. 20, 1909, in INS, subject correspondence files, National Archives, RG 85, entry 9, file 52548/197.

74. A. F. Richardson to Commissioner Ellis de Bruler, Seattle, Nov. 22, 1909, in INS, subject correspondence files, National Archives, RG 85, entry 9, file 51924/192.

75. Ibid., file 54809/genl. ("Cases Paroled from Ellis Island").

76. Ibid., file 53531/192A; Preston, *Aliens and Dissenters,* p. 33.

77. Preston, *Aliens and Dissenters,* pp. 82–83. In addition, by 1914 the concern over domestic radicals was eclipsed by the focus on German and other potential enemy socialists and others opposed to the European war.

78. LeMay and Barkan, *U.S. Immigration,* pp. 120–121; Louis F. Post, *The Deportation Delirium of Nineteen-Twenty: A Personal Narrative of an Historic Official Experience* (1923; repr. New York: Da Capo, 1970), pp. 62–67.

79. Higham, *Strangers in the Land,* pp. 209–211.

80. Higham, *Strangers in the Land,* pp. 209–211; Preston, *Aliens and Dissenters,* pp. 63–64, 185–186. On cases of such denials in Washington State, see Henry B. Hazard to John S. Smith, June 28, 1913, in INS, subject correspondence files, National Archives, RG 85, entry 9, file 53531/192, also file 54235/36. Nathaniel Hong, "The Origins of Legislation to Exclude and Deport Aliens for Their Political Beliefs, and Its Initial Review by the Courts," *Journal of Ethnic Studies* 18, no. 2 (1990): 22–25.

81. Preston, *Aliens and Dissenters,* pp. 164–168; INS, subject correspondence files, National Archives, RG 85, entry 9, file 53531/192.

82. Preston, *Aliens and Dissenters,* p. 165, quoting from RG 85, entry 9, file 54379/76. I could not locate this file at the National Archives; however, see Thomas Fisher to Henry M. White, August 24, 1918, in INS, subject correspondence files, National Archives, RG 85, entry 9, file 54235/36.

83. Preston, *Aliens and Dissenters,* p. 206; INS, subject correspondence files, National Archives, RG 85, entry 9, file 54809/genl.

84. INS, subject correspondence files, National Archives, RG 85, entry 9, file 53990/142A ("Alien Enemies"); Higham, *Strangers in the Land,* pp. 194–217; Frederick Luebke, *Bonds of Loyalty: German-Americans and World War I* (DeKalb: Northern Illinois University Press, 1974); Peter Conolly Smith, *Translating America: An Immigrant Press Visualizes American Popular Culture, 1895–1918* (Washington, D.C.: Smithsonian Press, 2004), pp. 243–270.

85. Hoover's boss, Attorney General Palmer, remained in the background of this particular campaign. Richard Gid Powers, *Secrecy and Power: The Life of J. Edgar Hoover* (New York: Free Press, 1987), pp. 65–80.

86. On mass arrests of radicals in late 1918 and 1919, see Powers, *Secrecy and Power,* pp. 74–80.

87. Jan. 12, 1920, in INS, subject correspondence files, National Archives, RG 85, entry 9, file 54809/genl.

88. Apparently Hoover also used agents provocateurs to infiltrate radical groups and provoke immigrant members to behave in ways that prompted their arrest and deportation. INS, subject correspondence files, National Archives, RG 85, entry 9, file 54809 (esp. August 24, 1920); see also Constantine M. Panunzio, *The Deportation Cases of 1919–1920* (New York: Federal Council of the Church of Christ in America, 1921), pp. 30–34; Post, *Deportation Delirium,* pp. 82–83.

89. Panunzio, *Deportation Cases,* pp. 13–16; Post, *Deportation Delirium,* pp. 52–53.

90. INS, subject correspondence files, National Archives, RG 85, entry 9, file 54235/36, 54809/genl.; Post, *Deportation Delirium,* pp. 14, 85–86, 214–217; W. Anthony Gengarelly, "Secretary William B. Wilson and the Red Scare, 1919–1920," *Pennsylvania Magazine of History* 47, no. 4 (Oct. 1980): 311–317.

91. In the spring of 1920, Labor Secretary Wilson took an extended leave from his duties, possibly because the political pressures on him had taken a toll on his health. His right-hand man, John Abercrombie, the solicitor of the Department, was also on leave at the time. This cleared the way for the Assistant Secretary of Labor, Louis F. Post, to take over Wilson's duties temporarily. Post proceeded to cancel over a thousand deportation warrants during this time. Congressional Republicans immediately prepared to impeach Post, but failed to muster the votes to convict him. Post, *Deportation Delirium*, pp. 175, 223–277; Robert K. Murray, *Red Scare: A Study in National Hysteria, 1919–1920* (Minneapolis: University of Minnesota Press, 1955), pp. 249–250.

92. Panunzio, *Deportation Cases*, p. 16; Post, *Deportation Delirium*, pp. 22–23, 84–85; INS, subject correspondence files, National Archives, RG 85, entry 9, file 54809/genl.

93. Post, *Deportation Delirium*, pp. 1–27, 166–188; Gengarelly, "William B. Wilson and the Red Scare," pp. 324–327.

94. Post, *Deportation Delirium*, pp. 192–202.

95. *New York Times*, February 10, 1919, p. 3.

96. Panunzio, *Deportation Cases*, pp. 74–79.

97. Post, *Deportation Delirium*, p. 217.

98. Panunzio, *Deportation Cases*, p. 75.

99. Post, *Deportation Delirium*, p. 209.

100. Panunzio, *Deportation Cases*, p. 73.

101. Ibid., p. 209.

102. Feb. 24, March 20, and March 31, 1920, in INS, subject correspondence files, National Archives, RG 85, entry 9, file 54809/genl.

103. Feb. 24, March 20, March 31, and May 20, 1920, in INS, subject correspondence files, National Archives, RG 85, entry 9, file 54809/genl.

104. Alice Wexler, *Emma Goldman in Exile* (Boston: Beacon Press, 1989), pp. 13–18; Emma Goldman, *Living My Life*, vol. 2 (New York: Alfred A. Knopf, 1931), pp. 703–725; Powers, *Secrecy and Power*, pp. 80–89.

105. Goldman had married Kershner in 1887 but separated from him permanently after less than a year. She never divorced. Kershner had become a U.S. citizen in 1884, and therefore Goldman automatically became a U.S. citizen upon marriage according to the law then in force. The U.S. government, motivated by Goldman's activities as an anarchist speaker in the early twentieth century, conducted an investigation and stripped Kershner of his U.S. citizenship in 1908. Goldman's claim to U.S. citizenship rested on the assertion that the government's denaturalization of Kershner was fraudulent. Richard Drinnon, *Rebel in Paradise: A Biography of Emma Goldman* (Chicago: University of Chicago Press, 1961), pp. 15–16, 112–120, 218–220.

106. Goldman, *Living My Life*, p. 717.

107. J. Edgar Hoover to Anthony Caminetti, Sept. 8, 1920, in INS, subject correspondence files, National Archives, RG 85, entry 9, file 54809/genl. File 55055/414 ("Finnish Communists") deals with the fate of deported U.S. immigrants in Finland and Russia.

108. For attempts at deportation in the 1920s, see INS, subject correspondence files, National Archives, RG 85, entry 9, files 55119/112, /119, /132, /133, /151, /160, /172, /173; 55135/1, /1A, /3, /4; 55197/304.

109. Robe Carl White to Hamilton Fish, April 11, 1930, in INS, subject correspondence files, National Archives, RG 85, entry 9, file 54809/genl. (part III). Also see Howard Bevis, "The Deportation of Aliens," *University of Pennsylvania Law Review* 68, no. 2 (January 1920): 97–119.

110. Sidney Kansas, *U.S. Immigration: Exclusion and Deportation and Citizenship of the United States of America*, 2nd ed. (Albany and New York: Matthew Bender, 1941), pp. 155–160.

111. Panunzio, *Deportation Cases*; Aleinikoff, Martin, and Motomura, *Immigration and Citizenship*, pp. 697–712; National Commission on Law Observance and Enforcement, *Report on the Enforcement of the Deportation Laws of the United States* (Washington D.C.: U.S. Government Printing Office, 1931), pp. 132–150; Ngai, "Strange Career," pp. 90–100; Irwin, "Communists and Deportation," pp. 115–118.

112. Alexander Berkman and Emma Goldman, *Deportation—Its Meaning and Menace: Last Message to the People of America* (New York: Ellis Island, December 1919), pp. 3, 19.

113. On unsuccessful attempts to deport in the 1920s, see INS, subject correspondence files, National Archives, RG 85, entry 9, files 55119/172–173, 55600/416, 54809/genl., box 313.

114. D. H. Dinwoodie, "Deportation: The Immigration Service and the Chicano Labor Movement in the 1930s," *New Mexico Historical Review* 52, no. 3 (1977), pp. 193–197, 201–203.

115. Postwar legislation that furthered the Smith and the Nationality Acts were the 1950 Internal Security Act, which barred communists and those who supported "a totalitarian dictatorship" from immigrating, and the McCarran Walter Act of 1952, which made immigrants deportable when there was "reasonable ground to believe that they should engage in subversive activities." The same law made it possible for naturalized U.S. citizens who engaged in activities that fell under the Smith Act (i.e., they belonged to organizations considered communist) to be denaturalized within five years of their original naturalization. Aleinikoff, Martin, and Motomura, *Immigration and Citizenship*, pp. 52–54, 699–712; Marion Bennett, *American Immigration Policies* (Washington, D.C.: Public Affairs Press, [1963]), pp. 133–193.

116. Ellen Schrecker, "Immigration and Internal Security: Political Deportations during the McCarthy Era," *Science and Society* 60, no. 4 (1996), p. 416; Ngai, *Impossible Subjects*, pp. 155–156.

117. Schrecker, "Immigration and Internal Security," p. 401.

118. Ibid. pp. 404, 409.

119. Berkman and Goldman, *Deportation,* p. 19.

120. Otto Heinemann, interview by Margo Nash, 31 January 1974, Ellis Island Oral History Project, Series NPS no. 046.

4. Americanization

1. Parts of this chapter have been published in different form in "American Immigrants Look at Their Americanization," in Leo Lucassen, David Feldman, and Jochen Oltmer, eds., *Paths of Integration: Migrants in Western Europe, 1880–2004* (Amsterdam: Amsterdam University Press, 2006).

2. "Life History of Mr. Fermin Souto," American Life Histories, Manuscripts from the Federal Writers Project, 1936–1940, memory.loc.gov/ammem/wpaintro/wpahome.html.

3. Peter Roberts, *The Problem of Americanization* (New York: MacMillan, 1920), p. 1.

4. J. Hector St. John Crevecoeur, *Letters from an American Farmer* (New York: Fox, Duffield, 1904), p. 54.

5. Philip Gleason, "American Identity and Americanization," in William Petersen, Michael Novak, and Philip Gleason, eds., *Concepts of Ethnicity* (Cambridge, Mass.: Harvard University Press 1980), pp. 58–65.

6. Alexis de Tocqueville, *Democracy in America,* trans., ed., and introduction, Harvey C. Mansfield and Delba Winthrop (Chicago: University of Chicago Press, 2000).

7. Gleason, "American Identity," p. 65; John Higham, *Strangers in the Land: Patterns of American Nativism, 1860–1925* (New Brunswick: Rutgers University Press, 1963), pp. 19–21.

8. Higham, *Strangers in the Land,* pp. 87–105; Desmond King, *Making Americans: Immigration, Race, and the Origins of the Diverse Democracy* (Cambridge: Harvard University Press, 2000), pp. 19–21; Mathew Frye Jacobson, *Whiteness of a Different Color: European Immigrants and the Alchemy of Race* (Cambridge: Harvard University Press, 1998), esp. pp. 39–90.

9. The judgment about an applicant's sufficient knowledge of English and the U.S. government was made personally by the naturalization judge.

10. Frank Van Nuys, *Americanizing the West: Race, Immigrants, and Citizenship, 1890–1930* (Lawrence: University Press of Kansas, 2002), pp. 27–30, 32.

11. Mina Carson, *Settlement Folk: Social Thought and the American Settlement Movement, 1885–1930* (Chicago: University of Chicago Press, 1990); Jane Addams, *Twenty Years at Hull House* (New York: MacMillan, 1910), pp. 230–258.

12. Addams, *Twenty Years at Hull House,* pp. 342–370.

13. Hilda Satt Polacheck, *I Came a Stranger: The Story of a Hull House Girl,* ed. Dena J. Polachek-Epstein (Urbana: University of Illinois Press, 1991), pp. 51–52.

14. Ibid., p. 52.

15. Carson, *Settlement Folk*, pp. 104–109.

16. Dietrich Herrmann, *"Be an American!": Amerikanisierungsbewegung und Theorien zur Einwandererintegration* (Frankfurt: Campus Verlag, 1996), pp. 52–54, 70–71, 215–220; Van Nuys, *Americanizing the West*, pp. 33–34, 36–37.

17. John McClymer, "The Americanization Movement and the Education of the Foreign-Born Adult, 1914–1925," in *American Education and the European Immigrant, 1840–1940,* ed. Bernard Weiss (Urbana: University of Illinois Press, 1982), pp. 98–99.

18. Nan Nuys, *Americanizing the West*, pp. 33–34, 37; "Americanization vs. 'Americanization,'" *The Interpreter* 2, no. 4 (April 1923): 3–5.

19. Louis Adamic, *Laughing in the Jungle: The Autobiography of an Immigrant in America* (New York: Harper Brothers, 1932), p. 73.

20. Ibid., pp. 74–79.

21. Woodrow Wilson, "The Meaning of Citizenship," in Winthrop Talbot, ed., *Americanization: Principles of Americanism, Essentials of Americanization, Technic of Race-Assimilation* (New York: H. W. Wilson, 1920), pp. 78–80.

22. Herrmann, *"Be an American!"* pp. 78–79.

23. Theodore Roosevelt, "Fear God and Take Your Own Part," in Talbot, *Americanization*, p. 39.

24. Herrmann, *"Be an American!"* pp. 117–123.

25. Frances Kellor, "Americanization," *Immigrants in America Review* 1, no. 1 (March 1915): 15.

26. Herrmann, *"Be an American!"* pp. 96–198, 100–102; McClymer, "Americanization Movement"; Frederick Luebke, *Bonds of Loyalty: German Americans and World War I* (Lincoln: University of Nebraska Press, 1974); Edward George Hartman, *The Movement to Americanize the Immigrant* (New York: Columbia University Press, 1948), pp. 155, 158–159, 182.

27. Van Nuys, *Americanizing the West*, pp. 46–52; Herrmann, *"Be an American!"* pp. 109–117, 127–131; Hartman, *Movement to Americanize*, pp. 188–197.

28. Herrmann, *"Be an American!"* pp. 53–55; Van Nuys, *Americanizing the West*, pp. 59–61; King, *Making Americans*, pp. 87–92.

29. King, *Making Americans*, pp. 95–98; Herrmann, *"Be an American!"* pp. 71, 93–100, 105–106, 133–174; Van Nuys, *Americanizing the West*, pp. 38–40, 64–65, 148–63; Hartman, *Movement to Americanize*, pp. 153–160, 174–184.

30. Herrmann, *"Be an American!"* pp. 179–225; Hartman, *Movement to Americanize*, pp. 216–222.

31. Roberts, *Problem of Americanization*, pp. 131–177; Herrmann, *"Be an American!"* pp. 84–93; Hartman, *Movement to Americanize*, pp. 108–124, 130–131.

32. Clinton DeWitt, "Industrial Teachers," U.S. Department of the Interior, Bureau of Education, *Proceedings of the Americanization Conference* (Washington, D.C., U.S. Government Printing Office, 1919), p. 116, quoted in Steve Meyer, "Adapting the Immigrant to the Line: Americanization in

the Ford Factory, 1914–1921," *Journal of Social History* 14, no. 1 (Fall 1980): 77.

33. Roberts, *Problem of Americanization,* pp. 68–71; McClymer "Americanization Movement," pp. 104–108.

34. California Commission on Immigration and Housing, *A Discussion of Methods of Teaching English to Foreigners* (Sacramento, 1917), pp. 37–38.

35. Herrmann, *"Be an American!"* pp. 104–105; McClymer, "Americanization Movement," pp. 108–111.

36. California Commission, *Discussion of Methods,* p. 9.

37. State Commission on Immigration and Housing of California, *Heroes of Freedom* (Sacramento, 1920).

38. Raymond Moley, *Lessons on American Citizenship for Men and Women Preparing for Naturalization* (Cleveland: Board of Education, 1918).

39. California Commission, *Discussion of Methods,* p. 13.

40. California Immigration and Housing Commission, *Americanization of Foreign-born Women* (Sacramento, 1917).

41. Ibid. Part 2; Minneapolis Council of Americanization, *Papers and Resolutions Passed at the Second Minnesota State Americanization Conference,* May 1920, p. 16.

42. Adamic, *Laughing in the Jungle,* pp. 49–59, 120–180, 308–319, quote from p. 55.

43. James Barrett and David Roediger, "The Irish and the 'Americanization' of the 'New Immigrants' in the Streets and Churches of the Urban United States," *Journal of American Ethnic History* 24, no. 4 (2005): 3–33.

44. James Barrett, "Americanization from the Bottom Up: Immigration and the Remaking of the Working Class in America, 1880–1930," *Journal of American History* 79, no. 3 (December 1992): 996–1020.

45. Herrmann, *"Be an American!"* pp. 222–225; Hartman, *Movement to Americanize,* pp. 209–210; Higham, *Strangers in the Land,* pp. 300–330; Records of the U.S. Immigration and Naturalization Service, National Archives, RG 85, entry 30; "Education and Americanization," 1914–1936; entry 33, "Citizenship Education Programs," 1935–1954; entry 34, "Citizenship Training Texts"; U.S. Secretary of Labor, "Bureau of Naturalization," in *Reports of the Department of Labor, 1932: Report of the Secretary of Labor and Reports of Bureaus* (Washington, D.C.: U.S. Government Printing Office, 1933), p. 105; *1933,* p. 84; *1935,* p. 92.

46. The National American Council, a coalition of patriotic societies and social service agencies, was founded in 1921 but never mounted any national campaigns and dissolved quietly by 1923. See Herrmann, *"Be an American!"* pp. 240–241; King, *Making Americans,* pp. 107–110, 113–115.

47. *Reports of the Department of Labor, 1934,* p. 31; Foreign Language Information Service Files, box 58, file 10, "Naturalization Difficulties"; and file 13, box 10, "Educational Requirements for Naturalization," Immigration History Research Center, University of Minnesota, Minneapolis.

48. Florian Znaniecki, "Social Attitudes of the Peasant and the Problem of His Americanization," *Immigrant in America Review* 2, no. 2 (1916): 38.

49. Edward H. Bierstadt, *Aspects of Americanization* (Cincinnati: Stewart Kidd, 1922), pp. 93–123.

50. Ibid., p. 50.

51. Carol Aronovici, "Americanization," in "Present-Day Immigration with Special Reference to the Japanese," ed. Clyde L. King, special issue, *Annals of the American Academy of Political and Social Science* 93 (Jan. 1921): 134–138, esp. p. 134; Hartman, *Movement to Americanize*, pp. 254–263.

52. Hartmann, *Movement to Americanize*, pp. 255–260; Znaniecki, "Social Attitudes"; Bierstadt, *Aspects of Americanization*, pp. 93–136.

53. Julius Drachsler, "The Immigrant and the Realities of Assimilation," *The Interpreter* 3, no. 9 (Sept. 1924): 3–10; quote is from p. 7. See also Drachsler's book, *Democracy and Assimilation, the Blending of Immigrant Heritages in America* (New York: Macmillan, 1920).

54. Gary Gerstle, "Liberty, Coercion and the Making of Americans," *Journal of American History* 84 (1997): 524–558; Russell Kazal, "Reinventing Assimilation: The Rise, Fall, and Reappraisal of a Concept in American Ethnic History," *American Historical Review* 100 (1995): 437–471.

55. Herrmann, *"Be an American!"* pp. 200–202, 297–301.

56. Frank V. Thompson, *Schooling of the Immigrant* (New York: Harper, 1920).

57. John P. Gavit, *Americans by Choice* (New York: Harper, 1922).

58. William M. Leiserson, *Adjusting Immigrant and Industry* (New York: Harper, 1924).

59. Sophonisba Breckinridge, *New Homes for Old* (New York: Harper, 1921): pp. 219–277.

60. Besides the studies by Gavit and Thompson already cited, Harper published the following books as part of its Americanization series: Kate Holladay Claghorn, *The Immigrant's Day in Court* (1923); John Daniels, *America via the Neighborhood* (1920); Michael M. Davis, *Immigrant Health and the Community* (1921); Robert Park, *The Immigrant Press and Its Control* (1922), and *Old World Traits Transplanted* (1921); and Peter Speek, *A Stake in the Land* (1921).

61. Sophonisba Breckinridge, *Marriage and the Civic Rights of Women: Separate Domicile and Independent Citizenship* (Chicago: University of Chicago Press, 1931); Leiserson, *Adjusting Immigrant and Industry;* Caroline Ware, *Greenwich Village: 1920–1930* (Boston: Houghton Mifflin, 1935).

62. Only one book, Manuel Gamio's *The Mexican Immigrant: His Life Story* (Chicago: University of Chicago Press, 1931), dealt with non-white immigrants. As a Mexican-trained archeologist who also studied under Franz Boas at Columbia University, Gamio was marginal among social scientists in the United States (he returned to Mexico), and his study did not put Americanization at the center of the inquiry.

63. *The Interpreter,* vols. 1–9 (1922–1930), was published monthly by the Foreign Language Information Service. On the history of the FLIS, see

Daniel Weinberg, "The Foreign Language Information Service and the Foreign Born, 1918–1939" (Ph.D. diss., University of Minnesota, 1973); also Herrmann, *"Be an American!"* pp. 223–225. For the 1940s, see the FLIS journal *Common Ground,* esp. vol. 1 (1940–1941) and vol. 2 (1941–1942).

64. Hermann, *"Be an American!"* pp. 217–223.

65. Gary Gerstle, *American Crucible: Race and Nation in the Twentieth Century* (Princeton, N.J.: Princeton University Press, 2001), pp. 128–186.

66. The oral histories were part of the Works Progress Administration (WPA) American Folklife Project, now collected and digitized by the Library of Congress: *American Life Histories: Manuscripts from the Federal Writers Project, 1936–1940,* memory.loc.gov/ammem/wpaintro/wpahome.html.

67. Breckinridge, *Marriage and the Civic Rights;* letters by immigrants to Louis Adamic are collected as part of the Louis Adamic Papers, Seely Mudd Library, Princeton University, Princeton, New Jersey. Adamic published some of the letters verbatim (though without quotation marks or clear attribution) as part of his books; I have found unattributed quotes in *From Many Lands* (New York: Harper & Brothers, 1940) and *Grandsons: A Story of American Lives* (New York and London: Harper & Brothers, 1945).

68. "Polish of Manchester," interviews by Julia M. Sample, 1938–39, *American Life Histories;* Breckinridge, *Marriage and the Civic Rights,* pp. 69–77.

69. "Portuguese Fisherman [Manuel]," interview by Alice D. Kelly, 14 December 1938, *American Life Histories.*

70. "Polish of Manchester," interviews by Julia M. Sample, 1938–39; "Here We Can Be Glad #7 [Katherine]," interview by Julia M. Sample, 2 March 1939, *American Life Histories.*

71. "Life History of Mr. Fermin Souto," interviewer unknown, n.d., *American Life Histories.*

72. David Gutierrez, *Walls and Mirrors: Mexican Americans, Mexican Immigrants, and the Politics of Ethnicity* (Berkeley: University of California Press, 1995), pp. 74–92.

73. Russell Kazal, *Becoming Old Stock: The Paradox of German-American Identity* (Princeton, N.J.: Princeton University Press, 2004), pp. 223–245.

74. "Rev. Elias Skipitares," interview by Rose Shepherd, 22 August and 16 October 1939, *American Life Histories.* "William Felos," interview by Rose Shepherd, 18 August 1939, *American Life Histories.*

75. "Giacomo Coletti," interview by Mary Tomasi, 1938–39, *American Life Histories.*

76. Lizabeth Cohen, *Making a New Deal: Industrial Workers in Chicago: 1919–1939* (New York: Cambridge University Press, 1990), pp. 83–87.

77. Ware, *Greenwich Village,* p. 316.

78. "Personal History of Rev. Wilfred Ouelette," interviewer unknown, 1938–39, *American Life Histories.*

79. "Polish of Manchester," interviews by Julia M. Sample, 1938–39, *American Life Histories.*

80. Thompson, *Schooling of the Immigrant,* p. 16.

81. Ware, *Greenwich Village*, p. 318.

82. Ibid., pp. 169–171, 319–320.

83. Louis Adamic, *My America, 1928–1938* (New York: Harper & Brothers, 1938), pp. 210–232.

84. Ware, *Greenwich Village*, pp. 132, 325–344.

85. Elizabeth Eastman, "Two Thousand Immigrant Women and Their Jobs," *The Interpreter* 9, no. 1 (April 1930): 62.

86. Breckinridge, *Marriage and the Civic Rights*, pp. 71–74, 76, 79–80.

87. "Polish of Manchester," interviews by Julia M. Sample, 1938–39, *American Life Histories.*

88. "Italian Shoe Machine Worker #7 [Roland Damiani]," interview by Merton R. Lovett, 13 April 1939, and "Italian Shoe Machine Worker #4 [Roland Damiani]," interview by Merton R. Lovett, 24 March 1939, *American Life Histories.*

89. "Giacomo Coletti," interview by Mary Tomasi, 1938–39, *American Life Histories.*

89. Ibid.

90. "The Schmidts," interview by Adyleen G. Merrick, 13 January 1939; "Portuguese Fisherman [Manuel]," interview by Alice D. Kelly, 14 December 1938; "Judge J. Faudie," interview by Effie Cowan, n.d.; "Virginia Suffolk," interview by Barbara Berry Darsey, 14 February 1939; "Giacomo Coletti," interview by Mary Tomasi, 1938–39; "The Tool Grinder," interview by John Lynch, n.d.; *American Life Histories.*

91. Foster Rea Dulles, *Labor in America,* 4th ed. (Arlington Heights, Ill.: Harlan Davidson, 1984), p. 238; Gary Gerstle, *Working Class Americanism: the Politics of Labor in a Textile City, 1914–1960* (New York: Cambridge University Press, 1989), pp. 1–14; Leiserson, *Adjusting Immigrant and Industry,* pp. 65–79.

92. Gerstle, *Working Class Americanism,* pp. 53–60.

93. "Packinghouse Workers," interview by Betty Burke, 15 June 1939; "Mary Siporin," interview by Betty Burke, 19 April 1939; "Mrs. Betty Pionkowski," interview by Betty Burke, 5 April 1939; *American Life Histories.* See also Dorothee Schneider, "Polish Peasants into Americans: U.S. Citizenship and Americanization among Polish Immigrants in the Inter-War Era," *Polish Sociological Review* 2/158 (2007): 159–172.

94. "Mr. Mankowski," interview by Robert Wilder, 12 June 1939, *American Life Histories.*

95. Louis Adamic article published in *Woman's Day,* 1942, no. 12, p. 21, in Louis Adamic Papers, box 91, folder 5, Mudd Library, Princeton University, Princeton, New Jersey.

96. Frances Kellor, "Citizenship," *Immigrants in America Review* 1, no. 1 (Spring 1916): 67–75.

97. Cohen, *Making a New Deal,* pp. 64–83; Kellor, "Citizenship."

98. Addams, *Twenty Years at Hull House,* p. 234.

99. Ibid., p. 232; Carson, *Settlement Folk,* pp. 112–114.

100. "George Mehales," interview by R. V. Williams, December 1938; "Greek Restaurants [Gus Constantin Geraris]," interview by W. O. Saunders, n.d.; *American Life Histories*.

101. "Greek Restaurants [Gus Constantin Geraris]," interview by W. O. Saunders, n.d.; "Interview with Vito Cacciola," interviews by Merton R. Lovett, 29 November 1938–16 May 1939; *American Life Histories*; "Polish of Manchester," interviews by Julia M. Sample, 1938–39, *American Life Histories*; Cohen, *Making a New Deal*, pp. 104–120.

102. Vera Clark Ifill, interview by Andrew Phillips, 23 May 1989, Ellis Island Oral History Project, Series EI, no. 552; Vernon O. Nicolls, interview by Paul E. Sigrist, Jr., 29 September 1994, Ellis Island Oral History Project, Series DP, no. 028; "A Riviera 'Conch,' [Wilbur Edward Roberts]," interview by Veronica D. Huss, 14 November 1936, *American Life Histories*.

103. On Caribbean immigrants, see notes 121 and 122. On Mexican oral histories, see Gamio, *Mexican Immigrant*. For Chinese immigrants, see Tung Pok Chin and Winifred C. Chin, *Paper Son: One Man's Story* (Philadelphia: Temple University Press, 2000); Victor G. Nee and Brett de Bary Nee, *Longtime Californ': A Documentary History of an American Chinatown* (Boston: Houghton Mifflin, 1972); and Judy Yung, Gordon H. Chang, and Him Mark Lai, eds., *Chinese American Voices: From the Gold Rush to the Present* (Berkeley: University of California Press, 2006).

104. Ira Reid, *The Negro Immigrant: His Background Characteristics and Social Adjustment, 1899–1937* (1939; repr., New York: AMS Press, 1969), pp. 32, 35.

105. Vera Clark Ifill, interview by Andrew Phillips, 23 May 1989, Ellis Island Oral History Project, Series DP, no. 028.

106. Vernon O. Nicolls, interview by Paul E. Sigrist, Jr., 29 September 1994, Ellis Island Oral History Project, Series EI, no. 552.

107. INS, subject correspondence files, National Archives, RG 85, entry 9, file 53531/48.

108. King, *Making Americans*, pp. 152–163; Reid, *Negro Immigrant*, pp. 32–41, 160–164; Irma Watkins Owens, *Blood Relations: Caribbean Immigrants and the Harlem Community, 1900–1930* (Bloomington: Indiana University Press, 1996), pp. 82–85. Most pertinent on the subject of Afro-Caribbean self-organization is Philip Kasinitz, *Caribbean New York: Black Immigrants and the Politics of Race* (Ithaca, N.Y.: Cornell University Press, 1992), pp. 3–11. See also Mary Waters, *Black Identities: West Indian Immigrant Dreams and American Identities* (Cambridge, Mass.: Harvard University Press, 1999), esp. pp. 65–89.

109. Van Nuys, *Americanizing the West*, pp. 26–30, 32, 102–104, 123–129, 180–182; Sanchez, *Becoming Mexican American*, pp. 99–107; Mario Garcia, "Americanization and the Mexican Immigrant, 1880–1930," *Journal of Ethnic Studies* 6, no. 2 (1978): 19–34.

110. Alberto Rembao, "Are Mexicans Here to Stay?" *The Interpreter* 9, no. 1 (1930): 7–11.

111. "The Mexican in the United States" (unsigned), *The Interpreter* 5, no. 3 (March 1926): 4–7; Rembao, "Are Mexicans Here to Stay?"

112. Gamio, *Mexican Immigrant*, pp. 91, 181, 162.

113. Ibid.

114. Ernesto Galarza, *Barrio Boy* (Notre Dame, IN: University of Notre Dame Press, 1971), pp. 257–266; Sanchez, *Becoming Mexican American*, pp. 105, 116–119.

115. Gamio, *Mexican Immigrant*, p. 181.

116. Sanchez, *Becoming Mexican American*, pp. 108–109, 113–119, 123–125, 167–170, 173–190, 215–217, 227–252; Gutierrez, *Walls and Mirrors*, pp. 74–116.

117. Linda Espana-Maram, *Creating Masculinity in Los Angeles' Little Manila: Working Class Filipinos and Popular Culture, 1920s–1950s* (New York: Columbia University Press, 2006); Ngai, *Impossible Subjects*, pp. 96–126.

118. Harry H. L. Kitano and Roger Daniels, *Asian Americans: Emerging Minorities,* 3rd ed. (Upper Saddle River, N.J.: Prentice Hall, 2001), pp. 25–31; Quingsong Zhan, "The Origins of the Chinese Americanization Movement: Wong Chin Foo and the Chinese Equal Rights League," in *Claiming America: Constructing Chinese American Identities during the Exclusion Era*, ed. Sucheng Chan and K. Scott Wong (Philadelphia, Temple University Press, 1998), pp. 41–63; also Sue Fawn Chung, "Fighting for Their American Rights: A History of the Chinese American Citizens Alliance," in *Constructing Chinese American Identities*, pp. 95–126; Nee, *Longtime Californ'*, pp. 13–122; Renquiu Yu, *To Save China to Save Ourselves: The Chinese Hand Laundry Alliance in New York* (Philadelphia: Temple University Press, 1992), pp. 8–31, 77–100.

119. "Chinese and Japanese Folk Stuff [Ruth Chinn]," interview by Stafford Lewis, 21 December 1938, *American Life Histories.*

120. Sidney Gulick, *The American Japanese Problem: A Study of the Racial Relations of the East and the West* (New York: Charles Scribner, 1914).

121. Valerie Matsumoto, *Farming the Home Place: A Japanese American Community in California, 1919–1982* (Ithaca, N.Y.: Cornell University Press, 1993), pp. 25–86; Mary Paik, *Quiet Odyssey: A Pioneer Korean Woman in America,* ed. Sucheng Chan (Seattle: University of Washington Press, 1990), pp. 45–48, 54–57.

122. Monica Sone, *Nisei Daughter* (Boston: Little, Brown, 1953), pp. 3–19; Yuri Kochiyama, *Passing It On: A Memoir* (Los Angeles: UCLA Asian American Studies Center Press, 2002), p. 9.

123. Brian Masaru Hayashi, *For the Sake of Our Japanese Brethren: Assimilation, Nationalism, and Protestantism among the Japanese of Los Angeles, 1895–1942* (Palo Alto, Calif.: Stanford University Press, 1994), pp. 108–137.

124. On the Ozawa case, see Taro Iwata, "Race and Citizenship as American Geopolitics: Japanese and Native Hawaiians in Hawai'i, 1900–1941" (Ph.D. diss., University of Oregon, 2003), pp. 16–22; the Japanese community in Honolulu did not support Ozawa's quest for U.S. citizenship.

125. Azuma, *Between Two Empires;* Matsumoto, *Farming the Home Place,*
pp. 25–86; Bill Hosokawa, *Nisei: The Quiet Americans,* rev. ed. (Boulder:
University Press of Colorado, 2002), pp. 151–169; Eileen Tamura,
*Americanization, Acculturation, and Ethnic Identity: The Nisei Generation in
Hawaii* (Urbana: University of Illinois Press, 1994), pp. 45–88; David
Yoo, "Testing Assumptions: IQ, Japanese Americans, and the Model
Minority Myth in the 1920s and 1930s," in *Re-mapping Asian American
History,* ed. Sucheng Chan (Walnut Creek, Calif.: AltaMira Press, 2003),
pp. 72–81. A detailed analysis of the interaction between Japanese
Americans and American whites in the internment era which empha-
sizes the distance of the two groups is Brian Masaru Hayashi, *Demo-
cratizing the Enemy: The Japanese American Internment* (Princeton, N.J.:
Princeton University Press, 2004).

126. New York State Education Department, Bureau of Adult Education,
Education for Citizenship (Albany, 1953); Yaroslaw Cych, "I am an American," *Common Ground* 2, no. 1 (Fall 1941): 117. See *Common Ground,*
pp. 1940–1942 passim. Nicholas Montalvo, *A History of the Intercultural
Education Movement, 1924–1941* (New York: Garland, 1982), pp. 271–286.

127. This had been the topic of writers in the 1920s already. See, for example,
Sara Hrbkova, "Young Jan and Ole and Their Parents," *The Interpreter* 4,
no. 3 (1925): 9–11.

128. Louis Adamic, "Thirty Million New Americans," *My America* (New York,
1938), p. 213.

129. Ibid., p. 214.

130. Adamic, "Thirty Million New Americans," pp. 211–230, quotes are from
pp. 211, 213, 214, 215–230.

131. Diana Selig, *Americans All: The Cultural Gifts Movement* (Cambridge, Mass.:
Harvard University Press, 2008), pp. 68–112; Rachel Davis Dubois, *All
This and Something More: Pioneering in Intercultural Education* (Bryn Mawr,
Penn.: Dorrance, 1984), pp. 51–61.

132. Dubois, *All This and Something More,* pp. 61–91; Montalvo, *History of the
Intercultural Education,* pp. 109–123.

133. Montalvo, *History of the Intercultural Education,* pp. 160–162, 170–187;
Dubois, *All This,* 76–77; Selig, *Americans All,* pp. 139–140, 237, 245–246.

134. Montalvo, *History of the Intercultural Education,* pp. 149–170; Federal Radio
Education Committee and U.S. Office of Education, *Americans All,
Immigrants All: A Handbook for Listeners* (Washington, D.C., U.S. Govern-
ment Printing Office, 1939).

135. Selig, *Americans All,* pp. 249–255; Montalvo, *History of the Intercultural
Education,* pp. 222–250.

136. See, for example, the essays in *Americans All: Studies in Intercultural
Education,* Department of Supervisors and Directors of Instruction of the
National Education Association (Washington, D.C.: National Education
Association, 1942); Yoon K. Pak, "Teaching for Intercultural Understand-
ing: A Teacher's Perspective in the 1940s," in *Social Education in the*

Twentieth Century: Curriculum and Context for Citizenship, ed. Joseph Watras, Margaret Smith Crocco, and Christine Woyshner (New York: Peter Lang, 2004); Yoon Pak, *"Wherever I Go I Will Always Be a Loyal American": Schooling Seattle's Japanese American Schoolchildren during World War I* (New York: Routledge/Falmer, 2002); Yoon Pak, "'If There Is a Better Intercultural Plan in Any School System in America, I Do Not Know Where It Is': The San Diego City Schools' Intercultural Education Program, 1946–1949," *Urban Education* 37, no. 5 (2002): 588–609.

137. "Letters from America," Series 8, Record Group 2, Common Council for American Unity, Immigration History Research Center Archives, University of Minnesota, Minneapolis; see also, "First Person America" (Record Group 3, Series 9) and "Letters from America" (Series 10) in the same collection. Ewa Morawska, "Immigrants, Transnationalism, and Ethnicization," in *E pluribus unum?: Contemporary and Historical Perspectives on Immigrant Political Incorporation,* ed. Gary Gerstle and John Mollenkopf (New York: Russell Sage Foundation, 2001), pp. 189–190; Dubois, *All This,* pp. 135–154.

5. Becoming a Citizen

1. *Washington Post,* July 6, 1915, p. 10.
2. *New York Times,* July 5, 1915, p. 15
3. *Indianapolis Star,* July 5, 1915, p. 1. See also "True Americanism: Address of Louis D. Brandeis at Faneuil Hall, July 5, 1915," University of Louisville, Louis B. Brandeis School of Law, www.law.louisville.edu/library/collections/brandeis/node/224 (accessed 9/3/10).
4. E. P. Hutchison, *Legislative History of American Immigration Policy: 1798–1965* (Philadelphia: University of Pennsylvania Press, 1981), pp. 23–24, 28–29; Michael LeMay and Eliott Robert Barkan, eds., *U.S. Immigration and Naturalization Laws and Issues: A Documentary History* (Westport, Conn.: Greenwood Press, 1999), pp. 17–18.
5. James H. Kettner, *The Development of American Citizenship, 1608–1870* (Chapel Hill: University of North Carolina Press, 1978), p. 236n61; Virginia Sapiro, "Women, Citizenship, and Nationality: Immigration and Naturalization Policies in the United States," *Politics and Society* 13, no. 1 (1984): 1–24. On women and citizenship in the nineteenth century, see Nancy Cott, "Marriage and Women's Citizenship in the United States, 1830–1934," *American Historical Review* 103, no. 5: 1440–1474; Linda Kerber, *No Constitutional Right to Be Ladies: Women and the Obligations of Citizenship* (New York: Hill and Wang, 1998); Candace Lewis Bredbenner, *A Nationality of Her Own: Women, Marriage, and the Law of Citizenship* (Berkeley: University of California Press, 1998).
6. LeMay and Barkan, *U.S. Immigration,* p. 22; Kettner, *Development of American Citizenship,* pp. 236, 246n; Hutchison, *Legislative History,* p. 23.
7. In the 1820s, Congress tried a number of times to ease naturalization requirements. Hutchison, *Legislative History,* pp. 23–24, 27–29.

8. *Report on the Commission on Naturalization,* House Doc. 45, 59th Cong., 1st sess. p. 21, also cited in U.S. Department of Labor, "Historical Sketch of Naturalization," (Washington, D.C., typescript, [1926]), National Archives, RG 85, entry 26, file 23/3583.

9. For short overviews of the Democratic and Republican parties and their relationship to immigrants, see Joel Silbey, *A Respectable Minority: The Democratic Party in the Civil War Era, 1860–68* (New York: W. W. Norton, 1977), pp. 14–16; Eric Foner, *Free Soil, Free Labor, Free Men: The Ideology of the Republican Party before the Civil War* (New York: Oxford University Press, 1970), pp. 232–237.

10. Alexander Keyssar, *Out of Work: A Century of Unemployment in Massachusetts* (New York: Cambridge University Press, 1989), pp. 19–20, 89–91; Edith Abbott, *Historical Aspects of the Immigration Problem: Select Documents* (1926; repr., New York: Arno Press, 1969), pp. 539–687.

11. Over forty petitions reached the House of Representatives in the 1843/44 legislative session, almost all of them demanding stricter naturalization laws for these newcomers; a later debate in Congress in 1855/56 similarly yielded no results. Hutchinson, *Legislative History,* pp. 165–183.

12. Keyssar, *The Right to Vote,* pp. 85–86, 134–136; Lawrence McCaffrey, *The Irish Diaspora in America* (Bloomington: Indiana University Press, 1976), p. 96; Thomas H. O'Connor, *The Boston Irish: A Political History* (Boston: Northeastern University Press, 1996), pp. 80–81.

13. Leon Aylsworth, "The Passing of Alien Suffrage," *American Political Science Review* 35 (1931): 114–116; Report of the Commission on Naturalization, pp. 16–17; Kirk Porter, *A History of Suffrage in the United States* (Chicago: University of Chicago Press, 1918), pp. 112–115; Keyssar, *The Right to Vote,* pp. 136–138. See also Hattie Plum Williams and Anne Diefendahl, "The Road to Citizenship: A Study of Naturalization in a Nebraska County," *Nebraska History* 68, no. 4 (1987): 166–182.

14. *Congressional Globe,* 41st Cong., 2d sess., July 2, 1870, p. 5115.

15. Bruce Carlan Levine, *The Spirit of 1848: German Immigrants, Labor Conflict, and the Coming of the Civil War* (Urbana: University of Illinois Press, 1992) and by the same author "Free Labor, Free Soil, and Freimänner: German Chicago in the Civil War Era," in *German Workers in Industrial Chicago, 1850–1910: A Comparative Perspective,* ed. Hartmut Keil and John Jentz (DeKalb: Northern Illinois University Press, 1984), pp. 163–182.

16. Communication with grandson Carl Schorske, Oct. 11, 2000. Schorske returned unharmed from service in the eighth New York regiment.

17. Ella Lonn, *Foreigners in the Union Army and Navy* (Baton Rouge: Louisiana State University Press, 1952); Wilhelm Kaufmann, *Die Deutschen im Amerikanischen Bürgerkriege* (München/Berlin: R. Oldenbourg, 1911). While immigrants put their lives on the line for the Union effort in disproportionate numbers, their ideas about individual freedom and the rights of

citizens also led them to resist the draft in some areas of the Union. See Iver Bernstein, *The New York City Draft Riots: Their Significance for American Society and Politics in the Age of the Civil War* (New York: Oxford University Press, 1990); Frank L. Klement, "Copperheads as Soldiers during the Civil War," *Catholic Historical Review* 80 (1994): 36–57; Donald DeBats and Paul Bourke, *Washington County: Politics and Community in Ante-Bellum America* (Baltimore: Johns Hopkins University Press, 1995).

18. Gustavus Myers, *The History of Tammany Hall* (New York: Boni and Liveright, 1917), pp. 128–130; Abbott, *Historical Aspects of the Immigration Problem,* pp. 575, 644, 648–560; *New York Times,* Oct. 26, 1864, p. 4.

19. *New York Times,* Oct. 26, 1864, p. 4; Oct. 24, 1866, p. 4.

20. *Congressional Globe,* 41st Cong., 2d sess., June 25, 1870, p. 4836; see also July 2, 1870, pp. 5120–5121.

21. Andrew Gyory, *Closing the Gate: Race, Politics and the Chinese Exclusion Act* (Chapel Hill: University of North Carolina Press, 1998), pp. 51–55; *Congressional Globe,* 41st Cong., 2d sess., July 8, 1870; Conkling quote from *Congressional Globe,* 41st Cong., 2d sess., July 2, 1870, p. 5121. The law also prescribed an oath, a hearing, witnesses, and other basic mechanics of the procedure. In addition, it made the swearing of false oaths or procurement of false witnesses punishable by law.

22. On lack of effect, see *New York Tribune,* Oct. 7, 1876, p. 3; Oct. 21, 1876, p. 3; *New York Times,* Oct. 8, 1894, p. 4. According to the *Times,* most years saw no more than 5,000 to 8,000 naturalizations, a figure that grew to double that number in the early 1890s. Given the rapid increase in immigrants during the 1870s and 1880s, this is a modest number.

23. *New York Tribune,* Dec. 8, 1897, p. 3; also May 21, 1891, p. 2; Oct. 21, 1893, p. 3; Oct. 23, 1893, p. 1; Oct. 24, 1893, p. 1; Oct. 27, 1893, p. 3; Joel A. Tarr, "William Lorimer of Illinois, A Study in Boss Politics" (Ph.D. diss., University of Michigan, 1963), pp. 22–23, 39; *Chicago Tribune,* July 10 and Aug. 3, 1892; Bessie L. Pierce, *A History of Chicago,* vol. 2 (New York: A.A. Knopf, 1937), pp. 25–28, 799; vol. 3, appendix; *New York Tribune,* Oct. 30, 1887, p. 1.

24. *New York Times,* Oct. 24, 1894, p. 4

25. *New York Tribune,* Oct. 18, 1892, p. 1

26. Christian Kirst to his brothers and sisters, January 1, 1884, in *News from the Land of Freedom: German Immigrants Write Home,* ed. Walter Kamphoefner, Wolfgang Helbich, and Ulrike Sommer (Ithaca: Cornell University Press, 1991), p. 482.

27. *New York Tribune,* Oct. 24, 1891, p. 1; Feb. 9, 1894, p. 3; Sept. 25, 1894, p. 12; Oct. 30, 1895, p. 3.

28. *New York Tribune,* March 25, 1894, p. 10; May 17, 1894, p. 3; Oct. 8, 1894, p. 4; Sept. 25, 1894, p. 12.

29. William Leiserson, *Adjusting Immigrants and Industry* (New York: Harper, 1924), pp. 403–413.

30. For example: *New York Tribune,* Oct. 21, 1893, p. 3; Oct. 24, 1893, p. 6; Oct. 26, 1893, p. 3; Oct. 27, 1893, p. 3; Oct. 4, 1894, p. 3; Oct. 8, 1894, p. 4; Oct. 28, 1894, p. 4; see also March 25, 1894, p. 10; May 17, 1894, p. 3; Oct. 30, 1895, p. 10; Feb. 2, 1896, p. 10; March 30, 1896, p. 4.

31. U.S. Congress, House of Representatives, 59th Cong., 2d sess., 1906: *Congressional Record* (CR), pp. 3640–3654, 7033–7057, 7761–7778. The proposal contained virtually all the committee's recommendations except the abolition of the declaration of intention.

32. U.S. Congress, House of Representatives, 59th Cong., 2d sess., 1906. See, for example, remarks by Republicans Barthold (St. Louis, Missouri), *CR,* pp. 3648–3649; and Halvor Steenerson (rural Minnesota), as well as Democrats Goldfogle (New York), *CR,* pp. 3649, 7042–7043, and McNary (Massachusetts), *CR,* pp. 3640–3641.

33. Ibid., p. 7770.

34. Ibid., p. 7042. See also remarks by Rep. Mann (R-Illinois) who otherwise supported restrictionist legislation (*CR,* p. 7051), and by Smith (*CR,* p. 7042), Powers, and Steeneerson (*CR,* pp. 3642–3643).

35. Ibid., p. 7774.

36. Ibid., pp. 3648–3649 (Barthold); p. 7770 (Wharton).

37. The correspondence files of the Bureau of Immigration for decades after 1906 are full of sometimes desperate petitioners who could not get a record certifying their original arrival and thus remained vulnerable to exclusion and deportation. By the 1920s, the problem had reached such proportions that Congress passed the so-called Registry Act in 1929, which allowed European and Canadian immigrants (though not Mexicans) who lacked legal entry documents to register their earlier entry retroactively so that they could qualify for legal residency or naturalization. Mae Ngai, *Impossible Subjects: Illegal Aliens and the Making of Modern America* (Princeton, N.J.: Princeton University Press, 2004), p. 82.

38. LeMay and Barkan, *U.S. Immigration,* pp. 93–97. The basic elements of the law are still in force. An English literacy requirement was added as part of the Internal Security Act of 1950. See also David S. North, "The Long Grey Welcome: A Study of the American Naturalization Program," *International Migration Review* 21, no. 2 (1987): 311–326.

39. U.S. Bureau of Naturalization, *Annual Report of the Commissioner of Naturalization to the Secretary of Commerce and Labor* [hereafter cited as *Naturalization Report* with year of publication] (Washington, D.C.: U.S. Government Printing Office, 1906–1932), with "denials" recorded annually. Almost half of the denials occurred "for want of prosecution"—that is, immigrants had given up on pursuing citizenship after filing their petition. John P. Gavit, *Americans by Choice* (New York: Harper, 1922), p. 232.

40. U.S. Department of Labor, "Historical Sketch of Naturalization in the United States," (Washington, D.C., typescript, 1926), in National Archives,

RG 85, entry 23, file 23/3583, 13–15; Frances Kellor, "Citizenship," *Immigrants in America Review* 1, no. 1 (Spring 1916): 67–75; Gavit, *Americans by Choice*, pp. 80–82.

41. Grace Abbott, *The Immigrant and the Community* (New York: Century, 1917), pp. 250–251.
42. *Naturalization Report, 1927*, p. 36; *Naturalization Report 1931*, p. 18. Only in 1940 did Congress pass an amended naturalization law, which exempted those physically unable to speak from the language requirement; Arnold Leibowitz, "The Official Character of Language in the United States: Literacy Requirements for Immigration, Citizenship, and Entrance into American Life," *Aztlan* 15, no. 1 (1984): 32–35, 47; Gavit, *Americans by Choice*, pp. 332–333.
43. On mobility and the question of citizenship, see Gavit, *Americans by Choice*, pp. 247–248.
44. Gavit, *Americans by Choice*, pp. 12–14. The act limited the protection of U.S. authorities for naturalized holders of U.S. passports to six months and eliminated such protection for the countries of origin of the naturalized citizens. See also LeMay and Barkan, *U.S. Immigration*, pp. 99–100; Thomas Alexander Aleinikoff, David A. Martin, and Hiroshi Motomura, *Immigration and Citizenship: Process and Policy*, 5th ed. (St. Paul, Minn.: Thomson/ West, 2003), pp. 107, 113–124; Rogers M. Smith, *Civic Ideals: Conflicting Visions of Citizenship in U.S. History* (New Haven, Conn.: Yale University Press, 1997), pp. 456–457.
45. Over 100 such cases occurred in 1915 alone; see *Naturalization Report, 1915*, pp. 4–5.
46. "Frank Aaltonen," Louis Adamic Papers, box 52, folder 1, Manuscript Division, Princeton University Library, Princeton, New Jersey.
47. *Naturalization Report, 1907;* for nineteenth century data, see *New York Tribune*, Aug. 7, 1895, p. 1
48. *New York Tribune*, August 7, 1895, p. 1; *Naturalization Report, 1907*, p. 12.
49. Gavit, *Americans by Choice*, pp. 221–222.
50. The actual number of newly naturalized immigrants was likely higher because until 1922 the Bureau of Naturalization did not enumerate married women or minor children, who were naturalized when their husbands or fathers became citizens. In 1915, the Commissioner of Naturalization estimated that about 75 percent of petitioners were married and that including their wives and children into the count of new citizens would raise the number fourfold. *Naturalization Report, 1915*, pp. 3–4; Gavit, *Americans by Choice*, p. 247.
51. On the census and naturalization, see Campbell J. Gibson and Emily Lennon, "Historical Census Statistics on the Foreign Born Population of the United States, 1850–1990," Population Division Working Paper (Washington, D.C.: U.S. Bureau of the Census, February 1999), www. census.gov/population/www/documentation/twps0029/twps0029.html.

52. Gavit, *Americans by Choice*, pp. 240–241; Gavit only studied naturalization candidates, not all immigrants. For a broader view with essentially similar results, see Avery M. Guest, "The Old-New Distinction in Naturalization: 1900," *International Migration Review* 14, no. 4 (Winter 1980): 492–510.

53. Gavit, *Americans by Choice*, pp. 241–243.

54. Leon Aylsworth, "The Passing of Alien Suffrage," *The American Political Science Review* 35, no. 1 (1931): 114–116.

55. Reed Ueda, "Historical Patterns of Immigrant Status and Incorporation," in *E Pluribus Unum?: Contemporary and Historical Perspectives on Immigrant Political Incorporation*, ed. Gary Gerstle and John Moellenkopf (New York: Russell Sage Foundation, 2001), p. 307; Frederick Cleveland, *American Citizenship as Distinguished from Alien Status* (New York: Ronald Press, 1927); John Higham, *Strangers in the Land: Patterns of American Nativism, 1860–1925* (New Brunswick, N.J.: Rutgers University Press, 1955), pp. 300–301.

56. Darell Hevenor Smith, *The Bureau of Naturalization, Its History, Activities, and Organization* (Baltimore: Johns Hopkins University Press, 1926), pp. 11–12, 14.

57. Gavit, *Americans by Choice*, pp. 260–261.

58. Under the Selective Service Act, immigrants were covered but could claim exemption if they were not U.S. citizens. In all, over 1.2 million noncitizen immigrants registered. Most of the alien draftees waived their right to an exemption. Gavit, *Americans by Choice*, pp. 256–260. See also Lucy Salyer, "Baptism by Fire: Race, Military Service, and U.S. Citizenship Policy, 1918–1935," *Journal of American History* 91, no. 3 (December 2004).

59. Salyer, "Baptism by Fire," pp. 12–13; Gavit, *Americans by Choice*, pp. 261–265.

60. *Naturalization Report, 1918;* Peter Roberts, *The Problem of Americanization* (New York: Macmillan, 1920), pp. 119–120; Gavit, *Americans by Choice*, pp. 255–294.

61. Gavit, *Americans by Choice*, pp. 262, 268; Salyer, "Baptism by Fire," pp. 21–25, 28.

62. Salyer, "Baptism by Fire," pp. 14, 39.

63. *Naturalization Report, 1918.*

64. The law was passed by Congress on May 19, 1921, and went into effect in early June. See U.S. Congress, 67th Cong., H.R. 4075, Public Law 67–5; 42 Stat. 5. See also Chapter 1, pp. 57–58.

65. For a comprehensive description of the Cable Act, see Bredbenner, *Nationality of Her Own*, pp. 80–150.

66. Campbell wanted a minimal language and knowledge tests for women immigrants but would not go as far as denying married women the right to become citizens under their husband's naturalization. *Naturalization Report, 1918.*

67. Bredbenner, *Nationality of Her Own*, pp. 113–115.

68. Martha Gardner, *The Qualities of a Citizen: Women, Immigration, and Citizenship, 1870–1965* (Princeton, N.J.: Princeton University Press, 2005), pp. 124–130; U.S. Immigration and Naturalization Service [INS], subject correspondence files, National Archives, RG 85, entry 9, file 59903/83.

69. Gardner, *Qualities of a Citizen*, pp. 132–148; Bredbenner, *A Nationality of Her Own*, pp. 159–163.

70. Ettie Glaser, interview by Dana Gumb, 24 January 1986, Ellis Island Oral History Project, Series KECK, no. 129.

71. Mary Dunn, interview by Dana Gumb, 23 January 1986, Ellis Island Oral History Project, Series KECK, no. 127.

72. Bredbenner, *Nationality of Her Own*, pp. 101–102, 157–158, 171. White immigrant women who married Asian men remained ineligible for naturalization even after passage of the Cable Act. These women became "racially ineligible" for U.S. citizenship by virtue of their marriage to an Asian; Gardner, *Qualities of a Citizen*, pp. 140–148.

73. *Naturalization Report, 1922–1930*; A. Warner Parker, "The Quota Provisions of the Immigration Act of 1924," *American Journal of International Law* 18, no. 4 (Oct. 1924): 739.

74. *Naturalization Report, 1922–1930.*

75. William S. Bernard, "Cultural Determinants of Naturalization," *American Sociological Review* 1, no. 6 (Dec. 1936): 946–947.

76. "Why Men Become Naturalized," *The Interpreter*, Dec. 1929, 156–157.

77. *Naturalization Report, 1923*, p. 4. See also Gardner, *Qualities of a Citizen*, p. 195.

78. "Why Men Become Naturalized," p. 158.

79. "Relief for Separated Families" *The Interpreter* 8, no. 4 (April 1928): 3–6.

80. Hevenor Smith, *Bureau of Naturalization*, pp. 5–11.

81. *Naturalization Report, 1930.*

82. For an exception to this general rule, see Bredbenner, *Nationality of Her Own*, pp. 174–182, 167n27; Gardner, *Qualities of a Citizen*, pp. 178–180.

83. U.S. Bureau of the Census, "Aliens Naturalized, by Sex and Area of Former Allegiance: 1907 to 1970," in *Historical Statistics of the United States, Colonial Time to 1970*, Bicentennial Edition, Part 2 (Washington, D.C.: U.S. Government Printing Office), p. 168. *Naturalization Report, 1922–1930*; Bredbenner, *Nationality of Her Own*, p. 158; Donna Gabaccia, *From the Other Side: Women, Gender, and Immigrant Life in the U.S., 1820–1990* (Bloomington: Indiana University Press, 1994), p. 114; Sophonisba Breckinridge, *Marriage and the Civic Rights of Women* (Chicago: University of Chicago Press, 1928), pp. 101, 106, 111. Women retained their dominance in naturalizations for much of the rest of the twentieth century. The exceptions were the years 1946 and 1947, which were affected by special naturalization provisions for GIs.

84. Even during the more prosperous 1920s, many poor, working-class women became U.S. citizens to become eligible for "mothers pensions"

and other support programs. Breckinridge, *Marriage and the Civic Rights*, pp. 65–67.

85. Gardner, *Qualities of a Citizen*, pp. 180–181.

86. National Council on Naturalization and Citizenship, "Selecting New Citizens: A Study of Persons Naturalized in Philadelphia during One Year" (New York, typescript, 1931); Gardner, *Qualities of a Citizen*, pp. 180–183, 188–190, 194–198; Bredbenner, *Nationality of Her Own*, pp. 160–162, 185; INS, subject correspondence files, National Archives, RG 85, entry 28, files 23/25397, 23/25398, 23/25403, 23/26690; Foreign Language Information Service Files, box 58, file 10, "Naturalization Difficulties" (1930s), Immigration History Research Center Archives, University of Minnesota, Minneapolis.

87. U.S. Secretary of Labor, "Report of the Commissioner of Naturalization," in *Reports of the Department of Labor, 1933: Report of the Secretary of Labor and Reports of Bureaus* (Washington, D.C.: U.S. Government Printing Office, 1934), 1933ff.

88. *Reports of the Department of Labor, 1936*, p. 101.

89. Gibson and Lennon, "Historical Census Statistics."

90. "Sam Alexander," January 24, 1939, folder 6, box 58 (Hindus), Louis Adamic Papers, Mudd Library, Princeton University, Princeton, New Jersey.

91. Oscar S. Strauss, *Under Four Administrations, From Cleveland to Taft* (Boston: Houghton Mifflin, 1922), p. 221.

92. For the impact of conflicting classifications, see Marian L. Smith, "Race, Nationality, and Reality: INS Administration of Racial Provisions in U.S. Immigration and Nationality Law since 1898," *Prologue* 34, no. 2 (Summer 2002), www.archives.gov/publications/prologue/2002/summer/immigration-law-1.html.

93. "R. S. Kokaturer," folder 6, box 58 (Hindus), Louis Adamic Papers, Mudd Library, Princeton University, Princeton, New Jersey; John R. Wunder, "South Asians, Civil Rights, and the Pacific Northwest: The 1907 Bellingham Anti-Indian Riot and Subsequent Citizenship and Deportation Struggles," *Western Legal History* 4, no. 1 (Winter/Spring 1991): 65–66; Smith, "Race, Nationality, and Reality."

94. Consistent advocacy and intervention with Bureau of Naturalization officials seemed to have been effective in removing Syrians and Turks from the list of those automatically denied a petition by naturalization examiners; Smith, "Race Nationality, and Reality," part 2, p. 1.; see also Reed Ueda, "Naturalization and Citizenship," *Harvard Encyclopedia of American Ethnic Groups* (Cambridge, Mass.: Harvard University Press, 1980); Ian Haney Lopez, *White by Law: The Legal Construction of Race* (New York: New York University Press, 1996), pp. 61–77.

95. Oscar Strauss, the Secretary of Labor under Theodore Roosevelt, supported the naturalization of Japanese because he believed "that it was doubtful whether the Japanese could be classified as Mongolians." Strauss,

Under Four Administrations, p. 221; Smith, "Race, Nationality, and Reality," part 2; Ngai, *Impossible Subjects,* p. 41.

96. Haney Lopez, *White by Law,* pp. 59–60; Erika Lee, *At America's Gates: Chinese Immigration during the Exclusion Era, 1882–1943* (Chapel Hill: University of North Carolina Press, 2003), pp. 106–109; see also note 103 below.

97. "In re Buntaro Kumagai," *American Journal of International Law* 3, no. 2 (April 1909): 491–492. See also Julie Novkov, "Rights, Race, and Manhood: The Spanish American War and Soldiers' Quests for First Class American Citizenship," 2009, works.bepress.com/julie_novkov/6, pp. 11–12.

98. On *Ozawa,* see Taro Iwata, "Race and citizenship as American geopolitics: Japanese and Native Hawaiians in Hawai'i, 1900–1941" (Ph.D. diss., University of Oregon, Eugene, 2003), esp. pp. 12–57; see also Ngai, *Impossible Subjects,* pp. 42–46.

99. Claims to citizenship by a Burmese, some partially Chinese, and half-Japanese immigrants were also rejected. For immigrants with only one East Asian parent, appellate courts usually opted to apply the rule that even partial ancestry disqualified anyone from being classified as "white." Haney Lopez, *White by Law,* pp. 56–61.

100. Ibid., pp. 86–92.

101. Salyer, "Baptism by Fire," pp. 30–36.

102. Roger Daniels, *Guarding the Golden Door: American Immigration Policy and Immigrants since 1882* (New York: Hill and Wang, 2004), pp. 89–93.

103. Xiaojian Zhao, *Remaking Chinese America: Immigration, Family, and Community, 1940–1965* (New Brunswick, N.J.: Rutgers University Press, 2002), pp. 48–93. See also LeMay and Barkan, *U.S. Immigration,* pp. 196–197; U.S. Department of Justice, *Annual Report of the Immigration and Naturalization Service for the Fiscal Year ended June 30, 1945* [hereafter cited as *INS Annual Report* with year of publication] (Washington, D.C.: U.S. Government Printing Office, 1945), pp. 103–105.

104. *INS Annual Report, 1946,* pp. 111, 149; Reimers, *Still the Golden Door,* pp. 27–29.

105. Daniels, *Guarding the Golden Door,* pp. 95–97; Reimers, *Still the Golden Door,* pp. 16–17.

106. Ngai, *Impossible Subjects,* pp. 187–191.

107. "Act of June 27, 1952: The Immigration and Nationality Act," in LeMay and Barkan, *U.S. Immigration,* pp. 220–225; U.S. President's Commission on Immigration and Naturalization, *Whom We Shall Welcome: Report of the President's Commission on Immigration and Naturalization* (Washington, D.C.: U.S. Government Printing Office, 1952), p. 251; Milton Konvitz, *Civil Rights in Immigration* (Ithaca, N.Y.: Cornell University Press, 1953), pp. 109–131; Daniels, *Guarding the Golden Door,* pp. 113–114; Daniel Tichenor, *Dividing Lines: the Politics of Immigration Control in America* (Princeton, N.J.: Princeton University Press, 2002), pp. 189–191.

108. *INS Annual Report, 1960,* p. 79.

109. My data are based on the *INS Annual Report, 1947–1967.* On the general strategy, see Eliott Barkan, "Whom Shall We Integrate? A Comparative Analysis of the Immigration and Naturalization Trends of Asians before and after the 1965 Immigration Act (1951–1978)," *Journal of American Ethnic History* 3, no. 1 (Fall 1983): 29–56; on newer data, see Guillermina Jasso and Mark Rosenzweig, "Family Reunification and the Immigration Multiplier: U.S. Immigration Law, Origin Country Conditions, and the Reproduction of Immigrants," *Demography* 23, no. 3 (August 1986): 291–311.

110. The Nationality Act of 1940 eliminated the exclusion of indigenous people of the Americas from naturalization. Gardner, *Qualities of a Citizen,* pp. 150–151; Smith, "Race, Nationality, and Reality," part 2, p. 2.

111. Manuel Gamio, *The Mexican Immigrant: His Life Story* (Chicago: University of Chicago Press, 1931), pp. 53, 91, 125–126, 132, 138.

112. "Juanita Hermandes Garcia," interview by Ruby Mosley, n.d., Works Progress Administration (WPA) American Folklife Project, *American Life Histories: Manuscripts from the Federal Writers Project, 1936–1940,* Library of Congress, memory.loc.gov/ammem/wpaintro/wpahome.html; see also testimonies of Mexican agricultural laborers collected by the California Division of Immigration and Housing in the late 1930s, cited in Gutierrez, *Walls and Mirrors,* pp. 89, 237n44.

113. Governor's Interracial Commission [Minnesota], *The Mexican in Minnesota: A Report to Governor C. Elmer Anderson of Minnesota* (1953; repr., San Francisco: R&E Research, 1972), pp. 74–75.

114. Ngai, *Impossible Subjects,* pp. 138–147.

115. See, for example, *INS Annual Report, 1950,* pp. 32–33.

116. *INS Annual Report* and the *Statistical Yearbook of the INS* detail this development. See, for example, *INS Annual Report, 1950,* pp. 78–79 for a survey of Mexican naturalization in the 1950s, and *1995 Statistical Yearbook,* p. 145 for a survey of the 1980s and early 1990s

117. Ira De Augustine Reid, *The Negro Immigrant: His Background, Characteristics, and Social Adjustment, 1899–1937* (1939; repr., New York: AMS Press, 1969), pp. 160–164.

118. Reid, *Negro Immigrant,* pp. 163–169.

119. Aristide Zolberg, *A Nation by Design: Immigration Policy and the Fashioning of America* (New York and Cambridge: Russell Sage Foundation and Harvard University Press, 2006), pp. 311–317; Ngai, *Impossible Subjects,* p. 238; Daniels, *Guarding the Golden Door,* pp. 116–120. Immigration from the British Caribbean to the United States declined between 1953 and 1965.

120. U.S. Immigration and Naturalization Service, *Statistical Yearbook of the Immigration and Naturalization Service, 1995* (Washington, D.C.: U.S. Government Printing Office, 1996), pp. 137–138.

121. See Chapter 4. The act gave the Attorney General the discretionary power to suspend deportations if this threatened the lives or livelihoods

of the deported. Tichenor, *Dividing Lines*, p. 165; Ngai, *Impossible Subjects*, pp. 87–88; Daniels *Guarding the Golden Door*, pp. 83–84, 182–184; Barkan, "Whom Shall We Integrate?" p. 235.

122. Ettie Glaser, interview by Dana Gumb, 24 January 1986, Ellis Island Oral History Project, Series KECK, no. 129.

123. Marianthe Chletsos, interview by Nancy Dallett, 26 November 1985, Ellis Island Oral History Project, Series KECK, no. 086.

124. *INS Annual Report, 1945*, p. 96.

125. Joseph Novel, interview by Harvey Dixon, 26 September 1980, Ellis Island Oral History Project, Series NPS, no. 124.

126. *INS Annual Report, 1946*, pp. 21–22, 95.

127. Jenel Virden, *Good-bye Picadilly: British War Brides in North America* (Urbana: University of Illinois Press, 1996), pp. 49–62; Elfrieda Shukert and Barbara Scibetta, *War Brides of World War II* (New York: Penguin Press, 1989), pp. 7–94.

128. Petra Goedde, "From Villains to Victims: Fraternization and the Feminization of Germany, 1945–47," *Diplomatic History* 23, no. 1 (Winter 1999): 1–20.

129. *War Brides Act of 1945 (An act to expedite the admission to the United States of alien spouses and alien minor children of citizen members of the United States armed forces)*, 79th Cong. (December 28, 1945), H.R. 4857, Public Law 79–271, 59 Stat. 659. For Asian War Brides see Gerald Schnepp and Agnes Masako Yui, "Cultural and Social Adjustment of Japanese War Brides," *American Journal of Sociology* 61, no. 1 (July 1955): 48–50; see also Gardner, *Qualities of a Citizen*, pp. 224–235.

130. Daniels, *Guarding the Golden Door*, p. 94.

131. Virden, *Good-bye Piccadilly*, pp. 140–141.

132. Over 60 percent of Japanese naturalizations were by women under the age of 40 during the late 1950s and early 1960s; see for example, *INS Annual Report, 1958*, p. 82 and *INS Annual Report, 1959*, p. 81.

133. Gil Loescher and John A. Scanlan, *Calculated Kindness: Refugees and America's Half Open Door 1945 to the Present* (New York: Free Press, 1986), pp. 1–60; Daniels, *Guarding the Golden Door*, pp. 98–112, 124–128, 190–194; Zolberg, *Nation by Design*, pp. 304, 306–308, also p. 327 on a late special program to benefit Italians, passed in 1962.

134. Gibson and Lennon, "Historical Census Statistics"; Dorothee Schneider, "Assimilation and Transnationalism as Considerations in Naturalization of Immigrants after World War II" (paper presented at the 2005 annual meeting of the Social Science History Association, Portland, Oregon, 2005).

135. Daniels, *Guarding the Golden Door*, p. 134.

136. LeMay and Barkan, *U.S. Immigration*, pp. 257–261; Zolberg, *Nation by Design*, pp. 328–336; Daniels, *Guarding the Golden Door*, pp. 129–136.

137. Philip Q. Yang, "Citizenship Acquisition of Post-1965 Asian Immigrants," *Population and Environment* 23, no. 4 (March 2002): 377–404. The 1978 cohort study of the Immigration and Naturalization Service (published in

the *Annual Report* up to 1999) points to a more differentiated picture. As Asian immigration became more diverse, large differences emerged among different Asian groups. Those differences point to the importance of social and economic status in the United States for different immigrant groups.

138. INS, *Statistical Yearbook*, 1995, pp. 144–145.

139. Dorothee Schneider, "'I Know All about Emma Lazarus': Nationalism and Its Contradictions in Congressional Rhetoric of Immigration Restriction," *Cultural Anthropology* 13 (1998): 82–99.

140. Ettie Glaser, interview by Dana Gumb, 24 January 1986, Ellis Island Oral History Project, Series KECK, no. 129.

Epilogue

1. "Remarks at the Signing of the Immigration Bill, Liberty Island, New York, October 3, 1965," in *Public Papers of the Presidents of the United States: Lyndon B. Johnson, 1965,* vol. 2 (Washington, D.C.: Government Printing Office, 1966), pp. 1037–1040. Also available at www.lbjlib.utexas.edu/Johnson/archives.hom/speeches.hom/651003.asp (accessed 09/03/10).

2. James G. Gimpel and James R. Edwards, Jr., *The Congressional Politics of Immigration Reform* (Boston: Allyn and Bacon, 1999), pp. 99–109; Roger Daniels, *Guarding the Golden Door: American Immigration Policy and Immigrants since 1882* (New York: Hill and Wang, 2004), pp. 127–144; Daniel J. Tichenor, *Dividing Lines: The Politics of Immigration Control in America* (Princeton, N.J.: Princeton University Press, 2002), pp. 211–218.

3. The refugee act left the issue of political asylum seekers (those already in the United States seeking protection because they are politically persecuted in their homelands) unresolved. Aristide Zolberg, *A Nation by Design: Immigration Policy and the Fashioning of America* (New York and Cambridge: Russell Sage Foundation and Harvard University Press, 2006), pp. 244–250; Daniels, *Guarding the Golden Door,* pp. 202–208.

4. Daniels, *Guarding the Golden Door,* pp. 224–225; for deportation and voluntary repatriation figures, see U.S. Department of Justice, *Statistical Yearbook of the Immigration and Naturalization Service, 1995* (Washington, D.C.: U.S. Government Printing Office, 1997), pp. 161–164.

5. Tichenor, *Dividing Lines,* pp. 224–241; Gimpel and Edwards, *Congressional Politics,* pp. 133–136.

6. Daniels, *Guarding the Golden Door,* pp. 224–231.

7. Nancy Rytina, "IRCA Legalization Effects: Lawful Permanent Residence and Naturalization through 2001," U.S. Immigration and Naturalization Service, Office of Policy and Planning, Statistics Division [2002], www.dhs.gov/xlibrary/assets/statistics/publications/irca0114int.pdf (accessed 09/03/10). The newly legalized showed up as new immigrants in the statistics of the INS, leading, on paper, to a large increase in immigration between 1988 and 1992; see Appendix 1, Figure 1 at the end of this book.

8. Lisa Magana, *Straddling the Border: Immigration Policy and the INS* (Austin: University of Texas Press, 2003), pp. 42–46, 52–54.

9. U.S. Department of Homeland Security, *2009 Yearbook of Immigration Statistics*, (Washington, D.C.: Office of Immigration Statistics, 2010), p. 95, table 36.

10. Gimpel and Edwards, *Congressional Politics,* pp. 202–296.

11. *2009 Yearbook*, p. 51, table 20.

Index